GW00675492

THE McKENNEY-HALL PORTRAIT GALLERY OF

AMERICAN

INDIANS

Red Jacket

THE McKENNEY-HALL PORTRAIT GALLERY OF
AMERICAN INDIANS

BY JAMES D. HORAN

BRAMHALL HOUSE · NEW YORK

This 1986 edition is published by Bramhall House,
distributed by Crown Publishers, Inc., by arrangement with
Crown Publishers, Inc., 225 Park Avenue South,
New York, New York 10003

Manufactured in Italy

Library of Congress Cataloging in Publication Data

Horan, James David, 1914–
The McKenney-Hall portrait gallery of American
Indians.

Originally published: New York : Crown Publishers,
1972.
Bibliography: p.
Includes index.
1. Indians of North America—Biography.
2. Indians of North America—Portraits.   3. McKenney,
Thomas Loraine, 1785–1859.   I. McKenney, Thomas
Loraine, 1785–1859.   II. Hall, James, 1793–1868.
III. Title.
[E89.H67   1986]   970.004'97 [B]   85-30873
ISBN 0-517-60527-9
Designed by George Hornby
h g f e d c b a

For Gertrude: *Favorite Paleface*

Contents

Acknowledgments

————— ◆•◀▶•◆ —————

The search for the heart and character of Thomas Loraine Mc-Kenney must, of course, begin in official Washington with its seemingly endless volumes of letters, journals, manuscripts, then spread out to libraries, museums, state and local historical institutions whose archives might contain material on either McKenney or his contemporaries.

My interest in McKenney and his Indian gallery began in the early 1950s; I devoted a chapter to him and used some of the superb prints from his portfolio in my book *The Great American West* published in 1956. However, my ultimate goal was a full-length biography of the colonel, accompanied by portraits from his gallery and individual biographies of the chiefs and warriors.

To help me prepare this book a number of friends and complete strangers were most generous with their facilities and their time. I would like to thank the staff of the New-York Historical Society; Dr. James Heslin, Director; Miss Sue Adele Gillies, Reference Librarian; Robert Slevin, Newspaper Librarian; John A. Lovari, Reference Assistant; Robert N. Mohovich, Reference Assistant; Thomas J. Dunnings, Jr., Assistant Curator of Manuscripts; Wilson G. Duprey, Curator of Maps and Prints; Jan B. Hudgens, Assistant, Maps and Prints; Miss Mildred Goosman, Curator, Western Collections, Joslyn Art Museum, Omaha, Nebraska; Mrs. Shirley Hickman, Assistant in Manuscripts, Henry E. Huntington Library and Art Gallery, San Marino, California; The Library of Congress, Bernard A. Bernier, Jr., Head, Reference Section, Serial Division; Paul G. Sifton, Specialist, Early American History, Manuscript Division; Ray P. Basler, Chief, Reference Department, Manuscript Division; Virginia D. Daiker, Head, Reference Section, Prints & Photographs Division; Smithsonian Institution, James Steed, Assistant Archivist; National Archives, Richard S. Maxwell, Assistant Director, Social and Economic Records Division; Richard Crawford; Burton Historical Collections, Detroit Public Library, Mrs. Bernice C. Sprenger, Chief; Mrs. Alice C. Dalligan, First Assistant; William L. Clements Library, The University of Michigan, John C. Dann, Manuscript Librarian; Newberry Library, Chicago, Diana Haskell, Assistant Librarian for Special Collections; The Houghton Library, Harvard University, Cambridge, Mass., Suzanne Nicole Howard, Manuscript Division; W. H. Bond, Librarian, The State Historical Society of Wisconsin, Paul Vanderbilt, Curator, Division of Archives and Manuscripts; The Metropolitan Museum of Art, John Buchanan, Archivist; John K. Howat, Curator, American Paintings and Sculpture; Chicago Historical Society, Lucy F. West, Manuscript Division; American Philosophical Society, Murphy D. Smith, Assistant Librarian.

Also, the Redwood Library and Athenaeum, Newport, R.I., Donald T. Gibbs, Librarian; Buffalo and Erie County Historical Society, Mrs. Clyde E. Helfter, Curator of Iconography; Somerset County Historical Society, Curator, Ruth D. Brittingham; The Public Library of Newark, William J. Dane, Supervising Art and Music Librarian, Art and Music Department; The Newark Museum, Mrs. Robert Solomon, Curator of Painting and Sculpture; Rutgers University Library, Donald A. Sinclair, Curator, Special Collections; Amon Carter Museum of Western Art, Mrs. Frances M. Gupton, Registrar; Archives of American Art, Garnett McCoy, Deputy Director-Archivist; The State Historical Society of Wisconsin, Dr. Josephine L. Harper, Reference Curator; West Point Museum, Richard E. Kuehne, Director; Library of the Boston Athenaeum, Jack Jackson, Assistant, Art Department; Institute of Early American History and Culture, Williamsburg, Va., Stephen G. Kurtz, Director; Valentine Museum, Richmond, Mrs. Stuart Gibson, Librarian; Pennsylvania Academy of Fine Arts, Marily A. Fiegel, Assistant to the Registrar; University of Michigan Library, Harriet C. Jameson, Head, Department of Rare Books and Special Collections; Maryland Historical Society, Mrs. Mary K. Meyer, Reference Librarian; The University of Texas Art Museum, Donald G. Goodall, Director; The R. W. Norton Art Gallery, Shreveport, La., Jerry M. Bloomer, Secretary-Registrar.

The McKenney-Hall prints used in this book are from the portfolios in the James D. Horan Civil War and Western Americana Collection. Others used are: Three Henry Inman Indian portraits in the collection of the Peabody Museum, Harvard University, by whose courtesy they are reproduced.

A personal note of appreciation must be given to Gertrude, who shared the days and hours of institutional quiet in reading and selecting McKenney's long, long letters, then typing a manuscript of 150,000 words and making valuable and critical observations.

Foreword

AN AUTHOR'S REPORT ON COLONEL McKENNEY, INDIAN PORTRAITS, AND BIOGRAPHIES

———————◆‧◄►‧◆‧◆———————

SOME MEN said it happened overnight. That's the way it seemed. First there were the wild lands, millions of buffalo, endless varieties of game, clear sparkling streams and lakes, and vast distances, the only sound the high keening wind of the Great Plains. Then in a man's lifetime, the American West of the buffalo, Indian, mountain men, stagecoach, explorer, keelboat, fur trapper, forty-niners, outlaws, and cattle barons was gone.

From 1866 when the brilliant Timothy O'Sullivan brought his Civil War camera, courage, and genius to the frontier, photographers captured the passing of an era on their glass plates. But before Daguerre, the artists of the early nineteenth century had made the American Indian the best-known primitive people of the world.

The tribes they painted came from a West that knew only the occasional trapper and the intrepid Lewis and Clark; they represented a land as remote to the nation's leaders and the people of the eastern cities as our most distant stars.

The rarest collection of portraits of these warriors, chiefs, orators, and women hung in the office of Thomas Loraine McKenney, Superintendent of the Indian Trade Bureau abolished by Congress in 1822 and later head of the Bureau of Indian Affairs created in 1824 by Secretary of War John C. Calhoun and established within the War Department. The portraits are included in this book.

Colonel McKenney spent a great deal of time and money researching the life and culture of the American Indian for the text of his famous portfolio, published in the 1830s. The three volumes contained superb lithographic reproductions of the paintings accompanied by a text written by James Hall, a literary pioneer of the Midwest.

A great deal of their text is archaic and at times simply nothing more than nineteenth-century rhetoric, but there are nuggets to be found, especially when McKenney records what he heard or witnessed or when he recalls the myths and legends he gathered from the old chiefs, agents, Indian commissioners, and frontier officers. He was there. For sixteen years he was associated with the founders of the Republic and with them faced the task, seemingly insurmountable at times, of what to do and how to care for the Indian nations of the United States.

I have used McKenney's eye-witness and firsthand material for my individual Indian biographies but I have also augmented them with what I found in early pamphlets, government reports, memoirs, treaties, records of councils, historical quarterlies, journals, and frontier newspapers.

I was interested not only in ethnological information but also in the anecdote, the story, the interview, or speech which could make these Indians flesh and blood.

Gradually they appeared to be more human than the stereotyped Indians of our overglamorized post–Civil War period. They had dimensions, senses, affections, passions. One hundred fifty years later their problems are strangely recognizable. Who cannot sympathize with the chief driven to distraction by his several quarreling wives, who sought the refuge of a hotel bar? Or the penny-conscious Winnebago who swept the remnants of his dinner into a buckskin bag along with the silver and chinaware because the Great Father paid for it "and why leave it for the dogs?" There is also the Choctaw who admitted he had promised not to sell his gift horse for whiskey but was puzzled that the agent was angry because he had bet and lost it on a ball game. These Indians who came to Washington to see the Great Father had their own generation gap: some young braves decided it was wiser to fight the white man than talk to him. When the older chiefs were unsuccessful in persuading their youth that violence was not always the answer, they buried their sons.

For present-day Americans the biographies of the Seminole have an eerie echo. The chiefs and warriors in McKenney's gallery fought a savage guerrilla war for years in the swamps of Florida Territory, outlasted and outfought the best of four American generals, the cream of the Dragoons, and millions of dollars spent by Washington. When a war-weary public incessantly demanded that it be ended, one general captured Osceola under a flag of truce. The wily, patriotic chieftain died in his cell of a broken heart and the general was denounced by the same public that had originally praised him. Atrocities in war were commonplace to McKenney. His friend Red Jacket, whose "Washington medal" he always tried to buy, could have told him of Cherry Valley in the Revolution and the butchery at Wyoming, the Pennsylvania frontier post.

Inevitably there is some repetition because each biography is self-contained: chiefs, warriors, and orators may have attended the same council, belonged to the same band or tribe, or been members of the same delegation that visited Washington and the Great Father, or had their portraits painted by the same artist.

Some biographies are longer than others. They vary with their importance to history and the events of their day. There are the famous chiefs such as Joseph Brant, Red Jacket, Cornplanter, Black Hawk, Keokuk, Osceola, Sequoyah. Others were included because McKenney found them colorful, unusual, or even notorious in their time, such as Tshusick, the beautiful Chippewa confidence woman who came out of a wintry night to steal, most literally, the purse and admiration of official Washington, including President John Quincy Adams, his First Lady, the General-in-Chief of the Army, a good part of Congress, and the son of the famous Irish-French patriot Wolfe Tone. Or the chief who was celebrated not only for his exploits in war and in wilderness diplomacy but for his notorious homosexual son. This is a case in point where we find only a brief reference by the prim McKenney but discover more about this gay Indian warrior from the narrative of John Tanner, who for years had been an Indian prisoner. It is an indignant Tanner who reveals how the brave, who dressed as a woman, whistled after him in the forest to the amusement of the other Indian warriors. This was a hundred thirty years ago.

Many of the portraits are a direct link to the very beginnings of our nation. We have Indians who participated in Penn's infamous "Walking Treaty," helped to wipe out Braddock's command, fought with Simon Girty in the border wars and led the warriors of the Six Nations against Washington's Continentals during the American Revolution. McKenney himself bridges Jefferson's administration to the very brink of the Civil War.

I believe an important contributor to McKenney's gallery was James Otto Lewis, the Detroit and frontier artist who accompanied McKenney to the great Indian councils in the northwest in 1826–1827.

One wonders why some specialists have abruptly dismissed Lewis as a buffoon, capable only of grotesque caricatures. Admittedly, Lewis did not have the classic skill of Charles Bird King, but a study of his portfolio will reveal that many of his watercolor sketches must have been at least competent studies of the chiefs and warriors who attended those historic councils. He did paint about eighty-five Indian portraits and scenes of which forty-five or more were copied in Washington by King and his pupil George Cooke and A. Ford, a local artist. Lewis's *Aboriginal Port-Folio* appeared in 1835; the color is crudely washed on by hand but some of the portraits give a feeling of the subject, the time, and place.

There is one harsh, bitter note. It is evident from McKenney's correspondence covering his sixteen years in office and from the Indian biographies that, even in those early years, not only land-hungry settlers but also state and government leaders were defrauding and betraying Indian nations to an appalling extent. McKenney was a humanitarian and one of their champions. As he once predicted, the tribes would soon vanish and their culture be forgotten; he insisted his gallery was meant for future generations of Americans who might be "curious" how these great men of the plains or the forest looked and dressed.

They came to McKenney's office from the vastness beyond the frontier and he escorted them to a succession of Great Fathers who listened, promised, and did nothing.

In this book you will find the portraits and the biographies of a people from the time when the West was lost.

JAMES D. HORAN

BOOK ONE

Thomas Loraine McKenney: Shadow Catcher of the Indians

Faithfully Yours

Thos. L. McKenney

CHAPTER I:

McKenney's Great Dream

I.

JESSE BROWN was justifiably proud of his Indian Queen, the most popular of Washington's hotels and inns of the 1820s. Stagecoaches and carriages were always lined up along Pennsylvania Avenue waiting to discharge their travel-worn passengers all anxious to occupy one of the Queen's sixty "well proportioned and well furnished rooms."

There was never any rush. Each guest had to be greeted personally by Brown who not only saw to their luggage but escorted them to the front door under the sign of a fanciful and beautiful Pocahontas.

Mealtimes found Brown in the sumptuous dining room carving the roasts and piling high the plates. Beautiful crystal decanters of whiskey graced the sideboards, secretaries, and tables while servants glided about with little silver trays of cigars, toddies, cocktails, and "whiskey straights"—all on the house.[1]

Brown's pride was his room service system. A series of cords connected to tiny bells hung behind the bar; a single yank of the cord would send a servant flying up to the room.

There were other fine hotels along Pennsylvania Avenue, Pendleton's House run by Basil Williamson or Tennison's, but in addition to its fine room service Brown's hotel had another and more colorful attraction—its Indian guests.

Delegations from almost every tribe in the nation who came to Washington to see their Great Father were usually lodged at the Indian Queen. Pendleton's had the most luxurious gambling quarters in the capital but what inn could boast of statuesque, copper-skinned guests who walked with the dignity of ancient kings, clad in buffalo robes decorated with dyed porcupine quills? Or who paraded down Pennsylvania Avenue wearing headdresses of buffalo horns?

Then again the Indians were never deadbeats who left behind a battered leather trunk with a few worn socks in lieu of paying the bill. Brown knew the Indian Department might trim his padded bills but a government check was always delivered. He would be the first to admit the bar bills of the Indians were staggering; one ten-man dele-gation consumed $2,149.50 worth of beer, gin, whiskey, and cocktails while breakage was considerable.[2]

Brown acknowledged his redskin guests could be troublesome, especially when they had finished a great deal of whiskey. Then the warriors might take their rooms apart, smashing mirrors which they feared and detested, hurling fragile chairs about, beating their wives, or running up and down corridors whooping and dancing. Female guests were known to faint when evilly painted braves waved their tomahawks and demanded a kiss.

Not all the ladies fainted. After a group of boisterous Winnebago had made their way along Pennsylvania Avenue grabbing and kissing female strollers, socialite Margaret Bayard Smith stalked into the War Department and demanded protection for the women of Washington against the "ferocious Winnebagos." Mrs. Smith later recalled: "You have no idea what a general dread they inspired."[3]

The abrupt confrontation with the white man's world produced sad, tragic, and sometimes hilarious moments of comedy for the Indian visitors who only weeks before had been living in a primeval forest or on the vast plains of the unknown western lands across the Mississippi—"land beyond the Sabbath," as one missionary called it.

Indians walked off cliffs in the darkness, were stricken by the diseases of civilization like smallpox and measles, were run down by carriages or clobbered each other with war clubs in a drunken fury.

All these were minor compared to the unfortunate Iowa chief who brought his several wives to Washington. Just before leaving his forest home he had added a young and pretty bride who was detested by the others.

The journey by keelboat, steamship, and stagecoach was a shambles with the women fighting and clawing at each other. When the delegation finally arrived in Washington, the harassed chief sought the traditional refuge of the bar. He consumed an awesome amount, then made his way to his second floor suite.

A short time later servants heard screaming and the sounds of smashing furniture. The innkeeper summoned the Indian agent who ran upstairs and battered down the

21

door. The chief sought to escape an embarrassing confrontation with the agent and walked out the window. There was one problem: he had lived all his life in a tepee and had forgotten he was on the second floor. As the agent entered the room the chief abruptly vanished. He was found in the courtyard alternately cursing his wives, now shocked into silence, and moaning with the pain of a broken arm.[4]

The Indians usually stayed in Washington for a week or two. During this time they were treated like celebrities from a far-off planet, deluged with gifts from leather trunks to bright yellow shoes, and then returned to their lands to try vainly to describe to councils of skeptical fellow tribesmen the fantastic wonders of the white man's world.

2.

BRINGING INDIANS to the nation's capital began when representatives of the vanquished but still powerful Iroquois Confederacy were entertained in Philadelphia. Washington's theory was that this could be an inexpensive diplomatic maneuver to avoid costly frontier wars.[5] Whiskey, glowing promises, bribes, cheap presents, behind-the-scenes maneuvers to split delegations and to court those most receptive to the wishes of the federal government, parades and tours, easily influenced and awed the American primitives. What painted chief from the western plains would not be filled with profound respect and even fear of the white man after a visit to his cannon foundries and military installations?

The man most responsible for bringing the Indian delegations to Washington in the early years of the nineteenth century is one of the most important yet little-known figures in the history of the frontier and the American Indian.

He is Thomas Loraine McKenney, Superintendent of Indian Affairs under Presidents Madison, Monroe, Adams, and Jackson. For sixteen years, as he liked to boast, he controlled the destinies of more Indian nations on the American continent than any one man. He was tall, with a hawklike nose, piercing blue eyes, and a shock of grizzled white hair that seemed to belong to a man with a wet finger in an electric socket. Henry Rowe Schoolcraft, the celebrated early-nineteenth-century explorer, ethnologist, and Indian agent at Sault Ste. Marie, found him to be a man "characterized by great amenity of manners, as well as ready business tact." There were some who didn't share Schoolcraft's opinion: Robert Stuart, John Jacob Astor's agent in the Northwest, viewed McKenney as "a good hearted, feather headed old man."

He was an early champion of the Indians and to protect their rights he fought Senate giants like Thomas Hart Benton, the flamboyant Sam Houston, powerful politicians such as Duff Green, owner and publisher of *The Washington Telegraph* and a member of Jackson's so-called "kitchen cabinet"; he included among his enemies John Jacob Astor, one of the world's richest men who made loans to presidents and commanded a good section of Congress. McKenney made the charge to James Madison that Astor had spent at least two million dollars to defeat him and his Indian policies.[6]

He was a tireless, precise man, a faithful government servant who gave a full measure of loyalty to the four Presidents he served, even to Jackson whom he despised. He was no desk administrator. At President Adams's request he traveled more than seven thousand miles in canoe and on horseback along a dangerous frontier, settling treaties with the western and southern tribes. He was rewarded with a congressional investigation of his travel expenses.

He was part of America's earliest and wildest frontier, a rural society of combined innocence, virtue, and unbelievable cruelty. But it was real, a happy antidote to the over-romanticized West of the post–Civil War years, a West of unreal cowboys, moronic gunmen, and plastic Indians. McKenney's world had a tragic message—this is where the infamous, shocking betrayal of the American Indian took place. This was the beginning of our century of dishonor. This is where the West was lost.

Throughout his sixteen years as head of the government's Indian bureaus, the tribes existed under the shadow of Washington's domination and menace. McKenney played a solid role, many times ineffectual, as their champion. In his time there were two kinds of people, two philosophies of life, two contending cultures, always on a collision course: practical, greedy, compromising politicians, backed by land-hungry whites, and the embittered Indian nations and their harassed leaders. McKenney was usually in the middle of their constant battles, large and small.

He was a controversial figure in Washington, a prime target for partisan congressional committees who unsuccessfully fine-combed his bills and finances in an attempt to embarrass his White House friends and sponsors.

From his correspondence he seemed to be in constant financial difficulty; it is a tribute to his honesty that he refused to be corrupt in a day when bribery was commonplace, especially in the governmental control of the Indian nations. However, McKenney could be a political opportunist. He was serving under Adams, yet in letters to men of affairs and influence he boomed the popular Calhoun for the presidency. In a final confrontation during Jackson's administration he met the world of ruthless power politics head on. His moral strength could not stand the weight of the truth: he wasn't needed anymore and he desperately wanted to remain in the post that had given him so much power and prestige. He surrendered to the stern rule of practical politics—to survive one must be flexible. He formed a committee of naïve clergy and laymen to support Jackson's plan to remove the Cherokee from their homeland to the west. He tried to court his executioners but failed. McKenney foolishly believed the promises of Jackson and his followers that this wholesale uprooting would be done peacefully.

In his last years he was reduced to begging loans from old friends like Jared Sparks, president of Harvard, and extolling the virtues of his Philadelphia boardinghouse in his letters, perhaps for free board.

McKenney's memorial is not in the system of schools he helped the missionaries establish and maintain among the Choctaw, Chickasaw, Cherokee, Creek, and Seminole —the southern Indian nations known as the Five Civilized Tribes—nor in the important treaties he concluded on the southern and western frontiers, but rather in the portrait gallery of famous American Indians which he established soon after he took office. It was the heart of what he lovingly called his "Archives," a collection of things "relating to our aborigines preserved there for the inspection of the curious and for the information of future generations and long after the Indians will have been no more...."[7]

The majority of the paintings were by Charles Bird King, a Washington artist who had won a reputation for his portraits of Calhoun, Monroe, John Quincy Adams, and Henry Clay. Ironically, although he would become famous because of his Indian studies, King never saw an Indian village, a tepee, the prairies, the majestic distances of the Great Plains, or heard the unforgettable screech of a war whoop. All the portraits were either copied from original watercolor sketches done by James Otto Lewis, a young frontier artist, or painted from life when McKenney brought the chiefs and warriors to King's studio. Here he painted portraits of famous Indian leaders of more than a score of tribes.[8]

McKenney began dreaming of an Indian Archive soon after he took office in 1816 but it wasn't until the winter of 1821–1822 when a large delegation of Pawnee, Sauk, Fox, Menominee, Miami, Sioux, and Chippewa Indians came to see President Monroe that McKenney commissioned King to paint their portraits, the first for his gallery.

The delegation was colorful. The Pawnee chief wore a feathered headdress that flowed to his waist, while the faces of his braves were painted red from eyebrows to cheekbones. John Quincy Adams, then Secretary of State, who attended the meeting with Monroe, marveled in his diary at the "gravity and painful earnestness" of the chiefs as they addressed the Great Father and noted that "part of them [were] all but naked . . . one had his whole face colored with yellow ochre."[9]

On New Year's Day the chiefs and warriors performed a war dance on the White House lawn witnessed by an estimated six thousand spectators. Congress had adjourned for the day and every store and business house was closed.[10]

King painted twenty-five portraits of the chiefs and warriors in that delegation. The bill he sent McKenney charged the government twenty dollars for busts and twenty-seven dollars for full-length figures.

King continued to paint Indian visitors and the gallery grew larger until 1828, when a congressional committee investigating government expenditures charged McKenney with spending $3,100 "painting portraits of these wretches," as one congressman put it. McKenney, a veteran of Washington's political wars, rode out the storm and continued to give King commissions to paint portraits of Indian visitors.

After his dismissal by President Jackson in 1830, Mc-

Kenney launched his project to publish a series of Elephant Portfolios containing lithographs in color accompanied by an extensive text. He was to experience a great deal of frustration, unbelievable obstacles, and financial hardship before Volume I of the first Folio Edition was issued by Edward C. Biddle in 1836.

Biddle, a Philadelphia printer, reissued Volume I the following year. Volume II appeared in Philadelphia in 1838 from a different publisher, and Volume III in 1844.

The volumes entitled *The Indian Tribes of North America with Biographical Sketches and Anecdotes of the Principal Chiefs* first appeared in London in 1837 where Catlin's Gallery was attracting wide attention.

The text was written by James Hall based on material supplied by McKenney who had spent considerable time, energy, and money researching the staggering subject of the Indian tribes of the American continent.

It was a curious partnership. Hall appears to have been a complex, flamboyant frontiersman and a literary pioneer of the Ohio Valley. He was a competent backwoods prosecutor of early western outlaws, newspaper editor, and publisher, collector of folklore, founder of one of the first "literary" magazines in Illinois, biographer, author of frontier histories and at least one romantic novel, probably the earliest of western fiction. He was also personally courageous; to obtain material for a book, he took a dangerous keelboat trip down the Missouri.

As the years passed, McKenney survived near-poverty and bitter battles with a succession of printers before his portfolio was published. It was a staggering, expensive project even one hundred thirty years ago. One report in the 1830s estimated the cost at $100,000.

The three-volume set is now one of the most valued items of Americana, usually found only in rare book rooms of big city libraries and museums. They offer the finest example of early American lithography on stone. It is exciting news when a complete set reaches the auction block.[11]

It is fortunate that McKenney forced his dream to become a reality. In 1865, the gallery of original portraits, then housed in the Smithsonian Institution, was destroyed by fire.

McKenney's portfolios are truly a landmark in American culture as one historian has described them.[12] The value of this magnificent work is chiefly in its faithful recording of the features and dress of celebrated American Indians who lived and died long before the age of photography.

The tribes of the post–Civil War frontier were captured on wet plates by O'Sullivan, Gardner, Jackson, Hillers, and the other great photographers of their time. In McKenney's day only the artist's brush and talent preserved on canvas the great chiefs and warriors, some of whose lives appeared to be as brief as a flash of light on steel.

My Great Father, I have travelled a great distance to see you. I have seen you and my heart rejoices . . . I have seen your people, your homes, your vessels on the big lake and a great many other things beyond my comprehension, which appear to have been placed into your hands by the Great Spirit.[13]

Thus began the moving speech to President Monroe by a Pawnee chief who came to Washington in 1822. It was moving and prophetic. Matched with the chief's brilliantly colored lithograph in McKenney's portfolio, one can not only see him but hear his strong voice ringing out in the crowded room of the White House where the logs crackled in the fireplace, as Monroe, Adams, Calhoun, Webster, and all the other men of living American history, listened intently to the copper-skinned man bitterly crying out in the white man's wilderness.

CHAPTER II:

The Early Years

I.

THE YEAR was 1785, two years after the Treaty of Paris had ended the American Revolution. The place, Somerset County, Maryland. Thomas Loraine McKenney was born on March 21 in the McKenney homestead, a beautiful plantation called Hopewell.

In a rare, autographical letter written long after he had left the Indian service, McKenney said of his parents: "My father was born in Maryland—his father in Ireland and my great grandfather, as I reason to believe, in Scotland. My mother was born in Annapolis and her mother in London." A grandniece, discussing McKenney's father, William, and his mother, Anne Barbour, once said of them: "They were sturdy and consistent Quakers."[1]

McKenney grew up in a time of momentous changes within the infant Republic; state legislatures passed measures introducing new social and economic trends which shaped the lives and destinies of the American people. He was two years old at the time of the Philadelphia Convention. Many of the famous Americans who signed the Constitution would become his friends and political mentors.

We know almost nothing of McKenney's formative years. A terse, poignant paragraph in one of his books reveals that his mother died when he was ten. It must have been an indelible experience; forty years later in an uncharted wilderness he wept when he heard a bluebird's song—"that bird of pensive note"—and recalled how he had heard it the morning his mother lay dying. Time, he vowed, would never erase that scene.

He was the oldest of five boys, his brothers were William, Samuel, Edward, and Edwin. McKenney seldom mentioned them in his letters or journals but apparently they were close enough to rush to his aid with testimony and affidavits when a politically motivated congressional committee was investigating his administration.[2]

His father remarried and had other children; McKenney it appears, was devoted to his stepmother and his much younger four half brothers and sisters.

He first studied to be a physician but, as he wrote years later, "my delicate appearance led my father to change his

purpose...he feared the consequences of the exposure to a country practice."

McKenney turned from medicine to business and became an apprentice in his father's "counting house." His proud boast was," I was bred a merchant." At nineteen he took over the family business, then the largest on Maryland's eastern shore and his father retired to the family farm. At twenty-two McKenney married Aditha Gleaves; two years later his father died at forty-seven.

The "considerable" estate dwindled after creditors had been satisfied. McKenney recalled, "I found there would be not much more left after sett'ling the mercantile concern, than would support by stepmother and her four young children. I remembered my father's dying words, 'My son, take care of your mother and her little children.' I drew up a paper and procured the signatures of my Brothers and Sisters to it, giving the Farm to our stepmother and her children, with the stock, etc."

McKenney was twenty-four when he first visited Washington and decided to settle in Georgetown. About 1808, he opened "two large establishments," dealing in dry goods, one in Georgetown, the other in Washington.

Georgetown was a charming place to live with its beautiful old brick mansions set in deep gardens filled with flowering trees. In the winters its curbs were lined with the carriages of planters from Maryland's Eastern Shore, the many paned windows glowed with soft candlelight, and a passerby could hear the faint music of harpsichords and violins. Two miles beyond was the racetrack, and in the late fall even Congress adjourned at an early hour to enable the legislators sufficient time to walk to the track, arm in arm with their wives and sweethearts, "decorated as if for a ball." Perhaps, more important for McKenney, the Bureau of Indian Trade had been transferred from Philadelphia to Georgetown. The office was at 3810 M Street NW.

He soon became a familiar figure in Georgetown: tall, distinguished, hawknosed, a friendly but reserved man who many predicted was on his way to become one of the capital's leading businessmen.[3]

The elections of 1810 brought new and powerful voices to Congress—John C. Calhoun of South Carolina and Henry Clay of Kentucky. In the following year James Monroe was appointed Madison's Secretary of State. They all became friends of McKenney and helped to change him from an ambitious young Washington businessman into a combined career government servant and a shrewd politician whose shadow was to linger over the frontier for generations to come.

It had taken this off-year congressional election to change Washington. McKenney saw the new men of Congress riding up Pennsylvania Avenue. They were more his age—lawyers, planters, farmers, sons of Indian fighters. There was an air of the frontier about them; they walked with the easy lope of the trail and ignored the courtly manners, the velvet pantaloons, and gold-buckled shoes of the aging statesmen who had founded the Republic.

The question of what to do with the Indian tribes in the West, soon to become a part of McKenney's life, frequently was the subject of impassioned speeches by Calhoun whose grandmother had been scalped by the Cherokee, Felix Grundy of Tennessee who had lost three brothers in Indian battles, and Clay, the imperious young Kentuckian who had been elected Speaker of the House.

In the northwest, Tecumseh, one of the most extraordinary Indians in our history, and his brother, called the Prophet, had formed an Indian Confederation to resist the steady advance of white settlers. In 1811 Washington eagerly read the news of Tippecanoe. While both sides had suffered about equal losses, the Americans destroyed Tecumseh's village. When British arms were found, the war hawks demanded an invasion of Canada with Clay telling Congress: "The conquest of Canada is within your power."

For three tense years Madison tried to find a peaceful solution to the continuing problems of British interference with American trade and their arming of the Indian tribes on the frontier. He experimented with Jefferson's economic boycott but was finally maneuvered into war by the combination of Napoleon's tactics and the pressure of the land-hungry war hawks in Congress.

On June 1, 1812, Madison delivered his war message to Congress. Unfortunately the American Minister had left his post in London and the Madison administration had no way of knowing that a new British government had yielded to the demands of merchants and manufacturers. It was too late—the war neither the United States nor Great Britain wanted had begun.

CHAPTER III:

McKenney and the War of 1812

I.

Mc KENNEY, the Quaker, was determined to go to war. He left his dry-goods shops in charge of his clerks and enlisted. Appointed adjutant of the Legion of Light Infantry, District of Columbia, he served under General J. Thompson stationed at Piscataway in the summer of 1813 when the British ships controlled the Potomac.

Rather than request supplies, especially medical, through the creaking bureaucracy of the War Department, Thompson made McKenney his liaison officer with Secretary of War Armstrong who had his headquarters in Fort Washington on the river.[1]

McKenney then became aide to General John P. Van Ness, briefly the army's commander. When Van Ness resigned following a dispute with Armstrong and was replaced by General Winder, McKenney became an aide without a general.

After the news swept down the river that a powerful force of Wellington's veterans had landed, McKenney followed the Georgetown Volunteer Riflemen under Captain J. L. Stull on foot to Old Battalion Fields, the main army encampment, eight miles east of the capital. He sold his two shops, bought his own uniform, and enlisted as a private in Stull's company.

General Walter Smith, second in command to Winder, took over the motley army at "Old Fields," as it was called, and during the sultry August days of 1814 tried to make a fighting force of the poorly equipped mob of two thousand militiamen, volunteers, and a few professional soldiers.

McKenney had a strict code of honor and when Smith offered him the comparable comfortable post of aide-de-camp McKenney first went to Stull who urged him to accept it. McKenney took Smith's offer and once again found himself liaison officer between the army and Secretary of War Armstrong.

One of his duties was to report to Armstrong the numerical strength of newly arrived companies and their need for equipment and rations, which he distributed. Although scouts brought in daily reports of the growing British strength, Armstrong scoffed at the idea that the enemy would try to capture Washington. McKenney discovered that the more adamantly the Secretary of War believed in his theory, the harder it became for McKenney to obtain supplies.

In August 1814, after a British force had moved up the Patuxent, Smith ordered McKenney to reconnoiter the enemy lines. McKenney not only found evidence that the British were preparing to move out on Washington but also returned with two British deserters.

He brought them into Smith's tent to find the general with President Madison, Secretary of War Armstrong, and their staffs. McKenney reported the British were breaking camp and starting their advance on the capital.

"They have no such intention," Armstrong stiffly replied. "They are only foraging and if any attack is meditated by them it will be on Annapolis."

Smith later recalled Armstrong's "great apathy and inertness in regard to the defences of the District and his frequent discourtesy toward those who pressed him on the subject."

Madison then questioned McKenney's deserters but the

privates insisted "they didn't know the name of their commander or the numbers of their regiments." When Madison asked if Washington was the British target, one smiled and said: "We think it is, sir."

Madison ordered McKenney to make another tour of the British lines. Then the President and his aides returned to Washington. As he approached the enemy's positions, McKenney found Secretary of State Monroe studying the lines with a glass and joined him. Both men watched the British halt and bivouac. Then Monroe set out for Bladensburg and McKenney returned to Old Battalion Fields to report to Smith that the British had halted about a mile down the Marlborough Road, on the outskirts of a woods that separated the two armies.

2.

IN THEIR breastworks on the outskirts of Bladensburg the Americans first heard the skirl of bagpipes and the tapping of the drums before the British troops appeared. For a short time it was Lexington and Concord all over again. Green-clad American riflemen hidden on both sides of the road took a heavy toll but the men who had smashed the best troops Napoleon could offer continued to advance until they carried the breastworks and the guns. It became a rout, with the defeated, shattered American army streaming back toward unprotected Washington.

After their easy victory at Bladensburg, the British took the city and burned the Capitol and the White House.

In the capital, society woman Mrs. Margaret Bayard Smith, who protested years later about McKenney's wild Indians prowling the streets, watched Winder's troops "pale with fright, retreating by, hour after hour," while over the measured booming of the cannons she could hear the anguished cries of her Negro cook that "Mr. Madison had done sold the country to the British."

3.

ALEXANDRIA HAD been sacked, spies claimed new landings could be expected, and Winder's officers were on the verge of mutiny. It was no secret that the incompetence of Secretary of War Armstrong had led to their humiliating defeat. When they heard that Armstrong was on his way to their camp, the officers held a meeting in Georgetown's Union Tavern.

When General Winder appeared, a spokesman pointed to a row of swords on a table and said:

"Here are our swords. We will not employ them if General Armstrong is to command us in his capacity as Secretary of War but we will obey the orders of any other member of the Cabinet."

Word of the officers' action spread through the camps and artillerymen "threw down their spades avowing a like resolve."

General Smith summoned McKenney and ordered him to find President Madison.

"Say to the President," Smith ordered "that under the orders of any other member of the Cabinet, what must be done will be done."

McKenney found the President "riding down F Street reorganizing the government" and gave him Smith's message. Madison told McKenney: "Say to General Smith, the contingency [namely that of any further orders being given by General Armstrong] shall not happen."

A short time after McKenney reported back to Smith, the presidential order removing Armstrong was read and cheered in the camp; Monroe was appointed the new Secretary of War.

In September a Special Session of the Thirteenth Congress assembled in the ruins. The Federalists lost their dream to move the nation's capital to another city and the work of rebuilding Washington began. Congress meanwhile was assigned a dilapidated clapboard building which had served as a post office, tavern, inn, and theatre. The members of Congress who could not find seats made their speeches from a window seat.

The war dragged on until January 1815 when news of a major victory won in the swamps of New Orleans by a ragtag band of riflemen under Andrew Jackson spread across the country. Cities exploded. Figures danced about bonfires, crowds of men and women, arms locked together, reeled up and down dark streets, horse pistols were fired, cannon boomed. The war was over and no one seemed to care that the end had come fifteen days after the formal peace treaty had been signed at Ghent.

After the burning of Washington, McKenney had taken part in the defense of Baltimore. Perhaps he read the dispatch in the *National Intelligencer* of how the red-haired general had set up his sharpshooters in the swamps to cut down the British regulars as they marched toward his lines.

Andrew Jackson. One day he and Colonel McKenney would meet toe to toe.

4.

AN INGLORIOUS peace brought demands for a scapegoat. Former Secretary of War Armstrong was selected after whispers had him committing treason because of relatives among the British officers at Bladensburg. When a newspaper reported he had shrugged off the burning of the capital with the comment: "The city would make a good sheep walk as before and was never fit for anything else." Effigies dangling from gallows with the sign "Armstrong the Traitor" were burned throughout Washington.

Armstrong's defenders insisted the general had been ousted from his office by a "Georgetown mob committee" headed by Colonel McKenney and joined by Alexander Conte Hanson, editor of the *Georgetown Federal Republican*, and Washington Bowie, a prominent Federalist. The trio supposedly had met with President Madison as representatives of the citizens of the District of Columbia to demand Armstrong be replaced by their friend James Monroe.

The story that made the rounds of official Washington had McKenney, Hanson, and Bowie calling at the White House but "when their names were announced, the President declined communicating with more than one of these unwelcome visitors, and designated Mr. McKenney as the least obnoxious of the three. With him he was closeted for upwards of an hour..."

The story may have been a political tale manufactured by Armstrong's defenders but it was to haunt McKenney, Madison, and Monroe for years—Monroe to his deathbed.

The indignant denials of Hanson and Bowie and McKenney's explanations were never accepted by Armstrong's son or his father's supporters. As McKenney wrote almost forty years later:

It was too ridiculous to believe that the simple citizens of Washington could select as their representatives to the President of the United States, two of his most detested enemies. And also that the President was lulled by this committee into a state of imbecility as to have no will of his own and that his great wisdom and untarnished virtue could be neutralized by this magic-working committee . . .

President James Monroe

John Jacob Astor
Founder of the early fur trading companies.

CHAPTER IV:

Superintendent of Indian Trade

MᴄKENNEY ALWAYS insisted that "unsolicited by myself, and, as far as I know, by anyone for me," President Madison appointed him Superintendent of Indian Trade in 1816.[1] This may have been true but certainly Madison, an astute politician, would never have selected an unknown for this responsible post. One can assume that McKenney's background as a Washington and Georgetown businessman influenced the President. After the War of 1812, McKenney had entered into a partnership with Joseph C. Hall who owned a dry goods store on Pennsylvania Avenue. The contract was for five years but it appears to have been a struggling firm; McKenney's first year's profits totaled only $1,000. The store may have brought him closer to Madison, however. He later claimed "Mr. Madison passed nearly the whole of his dealings through me." McKenney's performance as General Smith's aide-de-camp in the crucial hours of the so-called "Georgetown Mutiny" had also clearly impressed both Monroe and Madison.

McKenney was appointed on April 2 but he informed Madison he would not take office until he had completely severed his relationship with the Hall firm "because my oath of office forbade me to participate directly or indirectly in any trade or barter except on public account."

It was a time when corruption and political expediency were commonplace in Indian trading. McKenney was determined not only to protect his own honor, "my pearl of great price," but also to make sure no hint of scandal ever tarnished his friendship with Madison whom he had come to regard as one of the finest statesmen in the Republic.

He sold out his partnership to the Halls for $2,000 with the explanation: "The necessity of my oath of office made it necessary to relinquish all of my mercantile business." Edward Hall suggested that the firm could now deal with the Indian Department but, as he recalled, McKenney indignantly replied that he "make no stipulations on this subject . . . I cannot hold out any inducements of the sorts."

The embarrassed Hall pointed out he had not meant to ask McKenney to "barter his honor" but the new superintendent stiffly replied that "it was a matter that had to

be dropped." When Hall persisted, McKenney "begged that no more be said about the matter."[2]

On April 12, 1816, McKenney was sworn in as the nation's second Superintendent of Indian Trade. The ceremonies took place in his Georgetown office with Secretary of War William H. Crawford and Secretary of the Navy William Jones on hand to represent the President.

The solemnity of the occasion prompted McKenney to write his own prayer:

> Almighty God! This day I have sworn faithfully and honestly to discharge the duties as Superintendent of Indian Trade. But as man in his best estate is weak and helpless, always able to err, and continually subject to casualties which always involve his good name and honest interests I do most humbly beseech Thee to grant me in all my labours the assistance of the Holy Spirit, through Jesus Christ our Lord, Amen.[3]

Now with eyes open, always conscious of his personal honor and reputation, McKenney walked into a government post lined with bear traps.

MᴄKENNEY TOOK over a vast, controversial and complex government institution which had been established in the earliest days of the Republic. After the Revolution, Indian nations were both fearful and hostile. To secure a lasting peace Washington supported the government's "factory" system. A government factory was simply a post where Indians traded furs for necessities. Washington had always insisted that trade must be conducted honestly and with a steady flow of reliable goods at reasonable prices. In 1794 Congress had accepted his recommendations for trading houses; after a year's trial the Indian Trade Bureau received final approval, April 18, 1796. The act allowed the President to appoint the factors and to set their salaries.

When McKenney took office there were four basic reasons for the factory system: diplomatic, to weaken foreign influence, Spanish or British, over the tribes; economic, to force out British traders; military, to keep peace on the frontier and control the Indian nations through dependency; humanitarian, to supply the Indians the goods they needed and to prevent whiskey from debauching them.

From Washington's day to the War of 1812 the American factory system had worked well; with the coming of hostilities it had slipped badly. The British had burned large stores of supplies along the border; only shabby, unsalable goods now filled the warehouses.

McKenney first made an inventory of the unwanted goods, then ordered them "sold without regard to cost even at a loss." He restocked the factories with prized Mackinac blankets, strouding, rifles, powder, trade knives, traps, and numerous articles his factors had informed him were badly needed by the tribes.[4]

McKenney also refused to wield a new broom and retained all career employees. He recalled:

"When I succeeded to its [Indian Bureau's] management it no more occurred to me to turn them out than it did to cut their throats."[5]

A few months after he had taken office McKenney, with the assistance of his chief clerk, Jere W. Bronaugh, established a new bookkeeping method. Accounts were to be done in triplicate, separately for salary, for subsistence, and for items purchased from the factory. When vouchers for funds had been received from his office, agents and sub-agents were immediately to send back a receipt listing the amount and its purpose.

A circular signed by McKenney and detailing his new method was sent to all factories.[6]

McKenney also protected himself from political chicanery by submitting a duplicate set of his quarterly vouchers to the Secretary of War, a second set was locked in his private safe, and a third sent to the Government Auditing Department.

Two months after he had taken office, McKenney was writing to his factors ordering them to submit periodic reports detailing "the wants of the Indians." He pointed out to Jacob B. Varnum, who operated the large Chicago factory:

> . . . blankets and strouds and similar articles are mainly important. But as our Border neighbors are quickening in their advance to civilization and growing fond of agricultural life, I have to request that you ascertain what particular implements of husbandry would be more acceptable, and also I have to request to keep me informed of their general wants, having an eye upon that assortment at the Factory the keeping of which is so essential to its prosperity.[7]

3.

By the winter of 1816, McKenney was deep in the Bureau's staggering paper work. It appears he read every line written by his factors and personally examined their accounts. While he had made it clear to his Washington staff the haphazard organization of the Indian Trade Bureau was now a thing of the past McKenney found it difficult to force his factors to follow their new instructions.

Varnum in Chicago was a perennial problem. At Christ-mastime, 1816, McKenney was wearily advising the factor that although he had sent in his accounts, he had again failed to sign his salary voucher. But he was also quick with praise and encouragement when Varnum protested at the inferior goods still in his warehouse. McKenney agreed they were of poor quality, "a resort in time of war but you shall have *good goods.*" He also told Varnum that if the poor quality goods could not be sold he was free to give them away as presents to the tribes.

"It is easier to give away bad goods than to sell them..."[8]

A problem that continued to plague McKenney was the army's suspicion and contempt for Indian traders. He was constantly receiving complaints from factors that post commanders grudgingly allotted them small spaces to conduct their business and assigned them inferior living quarters.

An angry protest from Varnum in Chicago brought a swift reply from McKenney that he was "pained" to learn of the factor's difficulty with the army. The Indian Superintendent sadly pointed out:

> The want of a cooperating spirit in the officers of the army is presented too generally. . . . If the cause were not a common cause and did not relate to our common country this indifference might be acccounted for. But under the circumstances of the case it is hard to ascertain the principle or the grounds of it, which revolts at aiding you. It is nothing to recommend itself to anybody unless it be to those who take pleasure in thwarting the designs of the General Government, one of which is to benefit the Indians, and one of the many adopted to do is through the medium of trade.

A circular distributed among the Indian factories reveals McKenney had started his research among the Indian tribes as early as the summer of 1817 when he requested factors to send on to him Indian artifacts and "natural curiosities which they [the Indians] in their roaming might pick up."

He asked for "bows, arrows, articles of ornaments and such, skins, variously and peculiarly dressed."

Factors were permitted to buy artifacts by an exchange of goods valued at a hundred dollars, "which you can charge to me as Superintendent of the Indian Trade, and the articles received for it will remain as appendages to the Indian Department to which curiosities would be interesting ornaments—always worth in this country their original cost, whilst with you, from the frequency with which they are viewed, they are matters of no importance except to their owners."[9]

After a year and a half in office McKenney's letters reveal how intensely devoted he had become to his bureau. He tried new procedures in merchandising, shifting goods from overloaded warehouses to other agencies "with a view to augment the sales and serve the Indians"; he also insisted that all factors maintain a daily journal which had to accompany their monthly returns. One can see how deeply he was immersed in the daily operations of the bureau in his sharply critical letter to Varnum, taking his favorite factor to task for failing to send in his monthly journal. Almost as an afterthought he added a hastily written postscript:

"I console with you on the loss of Mrs. Varnum . . ."

During this period McKenney was also concerned with

personal financial problems. As he wrote to Isaac Thomas, chairman of the House Committee on Indian Affairs in the winter of 1816, he was finding it impossible to support his family on his government salary; it was just too expensive to live in Washington. He pointed out to Thomas, yearly rents had soared to $500, butter was fifty cents a pound and a cord of wood was as high as ten dollars.

"What can a man do when he has to pay these prices, when he is limited and tied down by the sacred obligation of an oath—on $2,000 a year?" he asked Thomas.

Yet while McKenney was appearing as an impoverished government employee he was closing a deal to buy Weston, a mansion on the heights of Georgetown; the price was $15,000. He paid it with a loan from the government Bank of Columbia.

This appears to be the beginning of McKenney's lifelong struggle to pay off loans, debts, and creditors. Some were like leeches, others he voluntarily accepted through an elaborate sense of honor. For example, he and his brother William shared a loan of several thousand dollars when William's Georgetown house burned to the ground. McKenney quickly informed his penniless brother he was not to worry, he had notified their creditors he would assume the total financial responsibility.[10]

4.

COLONEL McKENNEY'S problems on the northwestern frontier during his superintendency were varied, complex, and politically delicate. His many recommendations were ignored by Congress. For six years he was faced with finding a solution to ending whiskey smuggling, seeking out corrupt Indian agents, and countering the swift mobility of experienced foreign traders who were the chief competitors of the federal government's factory system. But none was comparable to John Jacob Astor's far-reaching political influence that not only affected the career of McKenney's Green Bay factor but also the destiny of the American fur trade and the men who worked it.

Astor was one of the richest men in America. Ship tycoon, owner of a large part of New York City's real estate, he was both friend and creditor of many influential statesmen in Washington, including the President of the United States.

Astor's strong influence over the nation's leaders grew out of his dealings with the government during the War of 1812 when he shrewdly established a powerful political base in Washington.

When the government needed money, Secretary of War Albert Gallatin asked four of the nation's richest men to subscribe to ten million of the sixteen million dollar issue of government stock. Astor took two million and persuaded two others to buy the rest. Washington would always remain in his debt and Astor was never reluctant to collect debts owed.

During the period when his American Fur Company was seeking to obtain a monopoly over the western fur trade, Astor was particularly close to James Monroe and

demanded and received special favors from the Virginia President. The reason may have been in their financial dealings: during the war the New York financier loaned Monroe five thousand dollars. In the winter of 1821 Astor wrote to the White House and strongly suggested—after discussing some bills before Congress which could affect his company's position in the fur trade—the President might sell his property and repay the money he had loaned him.

In 1828, three years after he had left Washington, Monroe revealed in a letter to former President Madison that he had been forced to sell his slaves to settle the Astor loan. During the period of this loan, Monroe was Secretary of State, Secretary of War, and President.[11] Astor is also said to have given Michigan Territorial Governor Lewis Cass a $35,000 bribe but Kenneth Porter, Astor's biographer, carefully searched the books of the American Fur Company in the Canadian Archives and failed to find such an entry. However, Cass's treatment of the American Fur Company can only be described as unusually friendly in contrast to his many public statements denouncing the selling of whiskey to the Indians. And as Colonel McKenney had pointed out, it was common knowledge on the northwestern frontier that Astor's traders were constant violators of the federal statutes forbidding the sale of alcohol to the tribes.

The business philosophy of Ramsay Crooks, Astor's manager at Michilimackinac was this: If you needed whiskey to get the furs from the Indians, forget the moral issue and the law—sell it to them.

There is no documentary evidence that Astor ever paid Cass a bribe. The Michigan governor was a sophisticated, ambitious politician and the explanation for his cooperation with Astor's company may have been this: he was aware of the New York City tycoon's friendship with Monroe, Gallatin, Crawford, and the others who held high places in the government. If a personal friend of these powerful men wanted a favor and it would not hurt the national interest or stain his personal honor, Cass would grant it.

But McKenney refused to compromise with Astor or Missouri's Senator Thomas Hart Benton, whom the Indian Superintendent would one day describe as the "legitimate voice of the American Fur Company."

Less than a year after he took office McKenney had his first experience with Astor's power—not in a personal confrontation in Washington but by way of distant Green Bay, the Bureau of Indian Trade's most far-off factory. It had been established in the land of the Winnebago in 1816 along with a military installation, at the suggestion of Governor Cass. He had proposed to Secretary of War William H. Crawford a series of combined factories and forts at Chicago, Prairie du Chien, and Green Bay to counteract the British influence on the northern frontier. In the past the Indian nations had come to Drummond's Island to receive their presents and to trade. Their major routes were up the Illinois River, through Chicago, Prairie du Chien, and then on to Green Bay. By placing factories and posts along these points, Cass suggested, the Indians would be halted at three stops before they reached the large British fort. Crawford accepted the plan and the installations were established. Major Matthew Irwin, Sr., an Irish immigrant who had a colorful career during the Revolution was appointed Chicago's first factor in 1810.

When the War of 1812 broke out President Madison appointed him Commissary General. In 1816 at about the time of McKenney's appointment as Superintendent of Indian Trade, Irwin was made factor at Green Bay.[12]

From their correspondence Irwin, Jacob Varnum, who succeeded him in Chicago, and Colonel McKenney had common interests; they were hard-nosed businessmen, they hated John Jacob Astor, his American Fur Company, and whiskey peddlers in that order and sincerely liked the Indians.

In March 1817, at McKenney's request, Irwin outlined the reasons why the Green Bay factory had done so little trading with the Indians in the year since it had been established. He listed them as: admission of British traders who had been long associated with the northern tribes and "who placed themselves in the most advantageous places for business within fifty, seventy and a hundred miles of the United States post; threats made to the Indians that the Americans would prosecute them for siding with the British during the war; smuggling whiskey into the frontier for sale to the Indians and the intensive campaign being conducted by the British among the Indian nations against the American factories."

Irwin also pointed out to McKenney that many Indian agents were "openly" extorting as much as fifty dollars from each trader, British or American, before they would issue a license.

"This is considered a prerequisite of office," Irwin advised McKenney.[13]

McKenney's reply revealed how closely he was watching the financial reports of all "factors." He advised Irwin his arithmetic was poor, in one bill he had found an error of eight dollars. He also pleaded with Irwin to enclose invoices for all goods given to Indian traders along with quarterly accounts, "not only to render them punctually but also to have them faultless and errorless."

Whiskey peddling would always enrage McKenney; his terse order to Irwin was to have smugglers arrested by the army "and make an example of a few of them." He gave Irwin a similar order about Indian agent extortionists; send in their names and he would order their arrest and suspension by the Secretary of War.[14]

When Astor, through his influence in the Senate had a bill passed eliminating foreign Indian traders, McKenney distributed a terse circular order to all his factors, warning them that by law they were now:

> . . . to aid the agency by your vigilance in detecting any movements among traders contrary thereof—as it is presumed some frauds will be practiced upon his excellency, [Governor Cass] even in his exertion to prevent them.

As McKenney's letter pointed out to the factors, all foreigners "were odious to our citizens on account of their activity and cruelty in the late war and are now positively excluded from all intercourse and every capacity . . ."[15]

Obviously Irwin, deep in the wilderness, and possibly even McKenney, was unaware of the machinations then going on behind the Washington political scene. To maintain his hold on the fur trade during the war, Astor had merged with the Canadian interests in what was known as the Southwest Fur Company. This lasted until peace, when the financier set out to realize his fondest dream—the monopoly of the fur trade. Instead of withdrawing from the Montreal firm and engaging in an all-out war, Astor shrewdly manipulated his Washington contacts and had a bill passed which eliminated foreign Indian traders from the American fur trade. However, Astor knew he would need French boatmen and interpreters so the bill provided a loophole: the President had the sole power to decide who could trade. And Astor always had a friend in the White House.[16]

In the summer of 1817 the bewildered Irwin wrote McKenney demanding to know whose orders should he obey—Washington's or Astor's? McKenney, who by this time must have realized what was going on, sent Irwin an uncomfortable reply suggesting he reread his last circular which advised all factors that foreign traders were forbidden on the frontier by an act passed by Congress.

In September 1817 Irwin's long, bitter letter to McKenney disclosed how he had followed his superintendent's advice and encouraged two young American traders to move into the Indian country and establish posts on the Wisconsin River and on Winnebago Lake. A few days before they left Green Bay for the interior, Irwin learned that a number of British traders licensed by the Indian agent at Mackinac were hurrying to the same area.

When Irwin protested to the Mackinac agent, he learned Astor had bought out the Southwest Company and Governor Cass had issued orders that all traders working for Astor were to be granted licenses.

Irwin wrote, he was bewildered by the government's "contrary orders"; General Clark at St. Louis had forbidden licenses to be granted to British traders as had McKenney; Illinois Governor Edwards had requested Chicago factor Varnum to prevent them from trading with the tribes in his area, yet in the north country because they worked for Astor, they had not only been granted licenses by the territorial governor but were depriving native-born Americans of a livelihood. As for the reasons, the angry Irwin wrote McKenney, "I am at a loss to say . . . there appears to be a palpable incongruity in the [government's] manner of conducting the Indian trade . . ."

He stiffly ended his long letter with the suggestion that unless the Secretary of War could "correct these irregularities" it would be useless for McKenney to forward any more goods to Green Bay.[17]

By now McKenney should have suspected the reasons for his factor's frustrations—Astor's political influence. But what the Indian superintendent did not know was that the financier had brazenly written Secretary of War Crawford demanding a book of blank licenses. Crawford had not replied but had issued an order to his chief clerk, George Graham, to write Governor Cass and ask him to give Astor all the cooperation "in your power consistent with the laws and regulations." Cass, a politically ambitious man, didn't need a suggestion rammed down his throat. His urgent order to the Indian agent at Michilmackinac—the headquarters of Ramsay Crooks—was to allow Crooks all the licenses he needed and to aid only the American Fur Company.

When rival smaller traders protested, President Monroe was forced to tighten restrictions on foreigners in the Indian trade. This lasted only until Ramsay Crooks warned Astor that the American Fur Company needed to expand their teams of interpreters and French bateaumen. Astor again wrote to the White House and Monroe issued an order to the War Department allowing the use of foreign boatmen.

Major Irwin, who had no political influence, who refused to deal in whiskey, and who had half the number of traders employed by the American Fur Company, was hopelessly outclassed.

McKenney lamely replied he was sure Congress would soon issue new restrictions to limit foreigners in the Indian trade and then Irwin could "calculate on success in the future."

Irwin was not put off so easily. In the early summer of 1818 he told McKenney he was amazed that the federal government considered Astor's Southwest Fur Company "strictly an American company and consequently some privileges in trade has [sic] been granted to it."

Irwin then went on to tell McKenney what had happened at Mackinac shortly before the War of 1812:

Previous to the declaration of war, Mr. Astor obtained from the then Secretary of the Treasury [Albert Gallatin] an order directing the Collector of Customs at Mackinac to suffer Mr. Astor to have his furs [which were at the British post, St. Joseph's] landed at Mackinac. The agent employed on that business was a British subject. On his way to St. Joseph's he communicated with the British at Malden that war had been or would be declared. The British made corresponding arrangements and landed on the Island of Mackinac with regulars, Canadians and Indians, before the commanding officer there had been given notice that war had been declared.

The same course was about to be taken before the arrival of troops under General Hull, who having been on the march there, frustrated it [the attack].

The giving Mr. Astor, the order to suffer his furs to be landed at, and be shipped from, Mackinac had, it was believed for its object, to secure them from capture or detention, should they have been shipped from St. Joseph's after the declaration of war had been known.

The collector read the order in the presence of several persons. Mr. Astor's agent brought the furs to Mackinac *in company with the British troops* [Irwin's emphasis] and the whole transaction is well known at Mackinac and in Detroit.[18]

Evidently McKenney did not answer this furious letter. While he would continue to confiscate the American Fur Company's supplies if he suspected they contained whiskey, and urge Congress in his yearly report to enforce vigorously the laws forbidding the sale of alcohol by all traders, McKenney had no desire at this late date to charge one of the richest men in the world and a former Cabinet member with connivance during the War of 1812.

That summer Irwin wrote a terse note to McKenney advising the Indian Trade Superintendent that "because of

the various fluctuations which occurred in the Indian Trade" he had reduced the prices of much of his goods to compete with the British traders who had now introduced a new plan "to undersell the Factory."[19]

Irwin continued to hammer away at Astor. As he advised McKenney, Astor was hiring "discharged soldiers" as a front to buy the goods for his British traders and increasing his whiskey trade.

The Indians are frequently kept in a state of intoxication, giving their furs at great sacrifice for whiskey he wrote in 1819.

A return to reason will induce many of them to mention who sold them the whiskey, but it is deemed illegal to accept Indian testimony, so that the British and American traders may deal in whiskey without the slighest chance of detection.

The agents of Mr. Astor have held out the idea that they will before long, be able to break down the Factories; and they menace the Indian agents and others who may interfere with them, with demission from office through Mr. Astor.

They say that a representation from Crooks led to the dismissal of the Indian agent at Mackinac and they say that the agent here is also to be dismissed.

It is said that the commanding officer at Prairie du Chien undertook at the instigation of the Indian Agent, to stop and send on to St. Louis some of Mr. Astor's British trading subjects. For this act, it is said, the agent will be dismissed from the public service.

Irwin ended his letter to McKenney with the sarcastic observation:

We now have the novel spectacle before us of a British subject [Mr. Crooks] travelling to the Prairie, with a passport from Governor Cass, said to have been given by the authority of the War Department, to inquire into the conduct of the Indian Agent and commanding officer.[20]

Colonel McKenney tried to persuade Irwin he was doing all he could to force the War Department to stop the sale of whiskey on the frontier and to cancel the license of British officers who had led Indian raids during the war, but Irwin wasn't impressed.

The Indian trade, he wrote bitterly in the winter of 1820 was now almost completely dominated by Astor's traders who had gained control of the tribes by "selling whiskey privately."

"The Indians are altogether led away by the British traders, and while the American traders are insulted by the Indians at a distance from the [American fort] these traders are cherished and caressed."[21]

5.

HAMSTRUNG BY Astor's political influence, Colonel McKenney turned to his old friend Rev. Philip Milledoler, chairman of the influential American Board of Commissioners for Foreign Missions and president of New Jersey's Rutgers College. The missionary board had established an Indian school at Cornwall, Connecticut, another on the outskirts of present Chattanooga, Tennessee, called Brainerd, and a series of smaller schools among the southern tribes, McKenney, always a strong supporter of the board's work, had been principally responsible for the passage of the Indian Civilization Act of 1819 whereby

Congress voted annually $10,000 for the support of Indian schools.

In the summer of 1821 he urged Milledoler to have the board start a letter campaign to make Congress aware that the "worse species of white men are dealing with the Indians." He undoubtedly meant Astor. As he advised the clergyman, the only way to help the tribes was through the public's influence on Congress:

"The public must speak for the Indians and only then will Congress hear."[22]

Milledoler, who evidently had no desire to get into a quarrel with Astor or Congress, apparently ignored Mc-Kenney's suggestions.

While he expertly juggled Major Irwin's bitter complaints from Green Bay, Astor's influence at the White House and in the Senate, and the suggested letter-writing campaigns, McKenney took time out to boom his friend Calhoun for the Presidency. In the summer and fall of 1821 he used his clergyman friend Milledoler as a political sounding board.

"Adams cannot stand his remarkable popularity. His youth is the only thing on which a harp [sic] can be made. But he will soon reach his 40th birthday, but in experience and profound wisdom and in morals with the true principals [sic] of govt. he is as old as the oldest . . ."

He cautioned Milledoler not "to speak of him as a candidate but as a man picked for the highest office by his countrymen . . . if you like you can do much without stepping into the department of electory campaigning . . . Write me."[23]

6.

THERE IS no evidence, but McKenney, Dr. Milledoler, and the American Board of Commissioners for Foreign Missions may have had a voice in Calhoun's selection of a missionary to make a tour of the Indian Nations and submit a report to the Secretary of War.

Jedidiah Morse, the so-called Father of Geography and author of the first American gazetteer, was selected by Calhoun with the blessings of McKenney and the board. In 1822 Morse submitted a lengthy report on his fifteen hundred mile journey to the West. He mentioned many obvious grievances such as poverty, whiskey peddlers, abuse by traders, and the growing hordes of white invaders into Indian lands. He also complimented the missionary board for their Connecticut Indian School and suggested that government funds be made available to expand the school "so that it could become known as the Indian College of our country."[24]

An important part of Morse's two hundred page report was his shrewd observation that a "revolution" as he called it was slowly gaining strength both among the Indian nations and in the public, for "the general improvement of the welfare of the Indians . . ."

The law that had to be enforced on the frontier, Morse declared, was the one prohibiting the sale of whiskey to the Indians, "the source of quarrels and wars between them and us."[25]

In his investigation of frontier conditions, Morse had extensive correspondence—probably at McKenney's suggestion—with Jacob Varnum in Chicago and Major Irwin at Green Bay.

One can almost see Irwin gleefully picking up his pen in his Green Bay office when Morse asked for his personal view of the Indian trading system on the frontier.[26]

Indian agents, he declared, had to be given more power by Congress "to keep out dishonest and unprincipled traders from entering the country for the purpose of carrying on trade with the Indians. Hence the many impositions that are practiced on the poor Indians, principally in selling whiskey to them . . . it is known that Indians sell their guns, kettles, clothing, horses, etc., for that article, the excessive use of which leads to the destruction of property and the loss of lives."[27]

From Chicago Varnum charged that Astor's American Fur Company with its sale of whiskey and constant campaign against the United States factories in the West had reduced the Chicago post to a trickle of business with the tribes, "not sufficient to clear the wages of my interpreter."

Morse's report was gratefully accepted by the Secretary of War who wrote the usual complimentary letters to the clergymen. It was published and then forgotten.

As McKenney observed the following year, Astor's whiskey peddlers were still doing business at Chicago and Green Bay.

7.

POLITICAL SPARRING, careful infighting with those who had influence in high places, conferences with fervent clergymen and warily answering the pleas and complaints from his disgruntled, frustrated factors in the West had their allotted time in McKenney's long days. It appears, however, there were intervals when he would close his eyes and dream of his "design," as he called it in June 1818, "to bring before the American people the story of the Indians and their claims . . ."

He didn't specify what his "design" was but it could have been the inception of his great portrait gallery; the first portraits would be painted within three years.

There is a curious letter among McKenney's correspondence of that period. Governor Cass was his friend but in June of that year he was hoping that Cass "has considered them [the tribes] as Human Beings . . ." In an irritable letter to an unknown correspondent, he wrote:

As the Good Book says, "of one blood, God made all the Nations to dwell upon the face of the Earth. . ." And were this not satisfactory, an Anatomical examination might prove it—and it might be an affair of Mercy to let the skeptical have a few Indians for inspection. . . I earnestly desire to see the Good Rule in universal operation, "as you would [sic] as men should do to you, do you even so to them," and of course it must reach the Indians. . .[28]

McKenney was also corresponding with English-speaking Indian leaders, soliciting their views on removal. One was Captain David Folsom, a Choctaw chief who would accompany the great Pushmataha to Washington in the fall of 1824. A few years later he was made chief of his nation after the question of Choctaw removal split his people into two hostile factions, pro- and anti-American. Folsom later signed the famous treaty of Dancing Rabbit Creek in 1830 at which the Choctaw yielded up most of their lands in Mississippi and finally were moved west to Indian Territory (Oklahoma).

In the fall of 1818, writing from "Pigeon Roost" in central or eastern Tennessee, Folsom informed McKenney of his nation's "anxious desire" to have schools built in the Choctaw country "so our children can be taught to read and write like our White Brethren." He added that the council of his people wished to send ten Choctaw boys to a missionary school "so they can be useful men to our nation."

Folsom's long letter was warm and friendly but its conclusion, which deals with the Indian removal question, gradually grew grim:

"I must inform you that it will be a disadvantage to my Nation to ever exchange their lands away, and therefore it will not be done. I know my Nation well, listen to my voice—it shall not be done . . ."[29]

8.

FROM HIS first few days in office, Colonel McKenney had let it be known that major bids of army and Indian contractors would be published in the capital newspapers and that dealers, regardless of political influence, would be treated equally.

"Purchases were made wherever and of whomsoever they could be best made," he wrote. "Nor did it become me to consider how little or how much was purchased of any man; but only whether what was bought of him was the best, the cheapest, and most suitable, which, at the time of buying, the markets could furnish . . . "

One day shortly after he had taken office a contractor walked into his office and introduced himself as Duff Green, representing a group of settlers whose cattle had been wiped out in an Indian raid. He handed McKenney a bill for $60,000 and an additional one for $600 for a herd of cattle he was delivering to the Prairie du Chien garrison.

McKenney approved the smaller bill, the first he passed on to his Senate Committee on Indian Affairs. The chairman, a bitter foe of Green, disapproved the bill. Green stormed into McKenney's office and demanded that the Indian Department pay the bill. When McKenney refused Green left, warning:

"Some day I'll mark you, sir."[30]

They were to meet again.

Disgruntled contractors were only part of McKenney's daily routine. A daily flow of politicians, congressmen, cattle merchants, and dealers, all seeking special favors, streamed into his office. While he tried not to offend anyone it was inevitable he would attract enemies.

One day he became aware of what he called "a kind of invisible agency of the prince of darkness sent to annoy and if possible to wound and destroy."

When he learned he was accused of sharing in profits of the Hall Company, McKenney took further steps to protect himself. In the fall of 1817 he contacted his old partner, J. C. Hall, and had him sign a statement stating that McKenney had dissolved their partnership before he took office and did not participate in any of the firm's profits.

McKenney also had his chief clerk measure and weigh the items of trade purchased during his administration against those supplies bought previously. Independent merchants signed statements that there was no comparison between the articles. McKenney put the affidavits in his file and waited for what he called "the fatal consequence."[31]

CHAPTER V:

The Great Question of Indian Removal

I.

FROM THE beginning of his service in the government's Indian departments until his ouster by President Jackson in 1830, Colonel McKenney was deeply involved with the question of Indian removal, principally centered about the large and important tribes, the Five Civilized Tribes—the Choctaw, Chickasaw, Cherokee, Creek, and Seminole—whose nations occupied a vast domain from which Georgia, Tennessee, Alabama, Mississippi, Florida, and parts of the Carolinas were formed; and in the West, the savage Osage, the Chippewa, the fierce Winnebago, and numerous other smaller tribes.

As early as 1802 land concessions had been forced from these southern and western tribes; some would haunt the White House, Congress, and McKenney for years. In one case the federal government had entered into an agreement with Georgia to "extinguish"—the favorite euphemism of early eighteenth century bureaucrats for stealing Indian land—at Washington's expense all claims by tribes living within the state "as soon as it could be done peaceably and on reasonable terms."

Indian removal is popularly associated with the Cherokee's tragic Trail of Tears—the removal of the tribe at bayonet point on orders of Jackson—but the plan to relocate the Indian nations west of the Mississippi was commonplace to McKenney and the politicians of his time.

One of Jefferson's ideas in the Louisiana Purchase was to persuade the eastern tribes to trade their ancestral lands for territory beyond the Mississippi. He viewed the project with such enthusiasm that he prepared an amendment to the Constitution authorizing this land exchange. The amendment, however, never came to a vote.[1]

Section Fifteen of the Act passed by Congress giving Jefferson authorization to complete the Louisiana Purchase significantly includes the power of the President to bargain with eastern tribes for their removal to western lands, under the stipulation they swear allegiance to the United States and not enter into any treaty with a foreign power.

Before he left office, Jefferson suggested to the Choctaw that they exchange their lands for homes in the west; when they refused he did not press the matter. The reason appears clear: the lack of knowledge of that shadowy western "desert," the apathy of the public, the need of funds to complete such a formidable plan, and, more important at the time, the hostility of the Osage nation. Formidable, terrifying in their ferocity, the Osage warriors had turned back not only Spanish explorers and traders but had pillaged, looted, and raided other Indian tribes from the Mexican Border to the Arkansas. They loved war. Mounted or on foot, their raiding parties had forced at least four smaller nations to leave their homes and seek peace in the Red River country, now Texas.

Like the Iroquois in the East, they were conquerors, but without the diplomatic skill of the Six Nations.

The Chouteau brothers, Auguste and Pierre, of one of the first families of St. Louis, finally persuaded the Spanish government to grant them a monopoly of trade with the Osage and about 1800 built their trading post. Two years later they were replaced by Manuel Lisa, that towering figure in the history of the American fur trade. When the Chouteaus moved their post to Three Forks at the junction of the Verdigris, Grand, and Arkansas rivers, so did the Osage under Pawhuska (Pahuska) or White Hair, a chief created by the Chouteaus who won his name because of the wig he wore, a memento of the American officer he tried to scalp at St. Clair's defeat. When White Hair died, his son not only took over the leadership of the nation but also his father's wig.[2]

Despite the hostility of the Osage nation, voluntary Indian removal slowly increased from the Revolutionary postwar years when the first band of Cherokee left the East for the West.

By the early 1800s the Chickasaw and the Choctaw were no strangers to the West. Dr. John Sibley, agent for the New Orleans Territory, notified the war department at the turn of the nineteenth century that large bands of Choctaw were living on the Red River. Four years later he reported to Washington on a council held with two hundred Choctaw chiefs who had voluntarily yielded their lands to the federal government in exchange for lands across the Mississippi.[3]

One of the largest of the government-owned factories in the west under McKenney's supervision was located on the banks of the Missouri at Fire Prairie, near present Kansas City, Missouri. The post stocked with goods for trade was tempting bait for the Osage: they signed a treaty, yielding to the United States all of the country north of the Arkansas, from which the state of Arkansas and a large section of Missouri were formed.

With Washington's approval inspection bands of Cherokee cautiously ventured across the Mississippi. The Osage grudgingly let them pass, and soon the advance parties returned to the South with glowing reports of the western lands. Until the War of 1812 there were so many Cherokee in the West that the War Department appointed William L. Lovely as their agent.

Lovely, a veteran of many major battles in the revolution, is a little-known but fascinating figure of the early West. His letters to the Indian Bureau and War Department give an excellent description of the West before it knew the creak of the white man's wagons.

It was a land with miles of plum orchards heavy with fruit which Lovely insisted was the sweetest he had ever tasted; with buffalo herds that made the earth tremble with their stampedes; with animals of every description, their fur thick and sleek; with flocks of cranes majestically booming their way across a sky so blue it hurt a man's eyes, while the only sound in the vast silence was the high keening western wind that made the grass billow like a brooding, restless sea.

There was only one harsh note in this frontier Eden: the white man. Whenever he appeared, Lovely wrote bitterly, he slaughtered the buffalo ruthlessly, heedlessly, not for food but for profit. He tore out their tongues and skinned the bear for its oil.

Lovely called them "White banditti." He advised Washington he was "surrounded on all sides by the worst of the white settlers and the Indians betwixt whom they [sic] are daily disturbances arising and against whom there are no possible means in my power to enforce the laws...."[4]

The Indians, particularly the Osage, Lovely reported, were the principal victims of the plundering whites who stole the Indians' herds, thirty ponies at a time.

The Osage in turn blamed the Cherokee for bringing in the whites, and intermittent wars flared up between the two nations. The harassed Lovely finally persuaded the Cherokee and Osage to hold a council at the mouth of the Verdigris and for a time there was peace on that far-off western frontier.

The restless, war-loving Osage were only one of McKenney's problems in the early days of the Indian Trade Bureau. Jefferson had helped the Cherokee to move to the Arkansas country—(they were known as the Arkansas Cherokee or the Western Cherokee)—but the Arkansas Cherokee tribe had no formal land claims. The Missouri legislature ignored the red men and created a white man's county which happened to embrace the lands given to the Cherokee by Jefferson. For years there were clashes between the settlers and the Indians who finally were forced to move for a second time, still farther west.

When settlers began to move into Indian lands under his control, Lovely erected boundaries and warned all trespassers they would be arrested. To help enforce these laws the old soldier demanded troops from General William Clark in St. Louis and funds from Washington to build a blockhouse. He got both and once again an uncertain peace settled along the frontier.

In 1816, shortly after McKenney took office, Lovely advised him that more than two thousand Cherokee were now settled in the Arkansas land. Although these first removals were voluntary, McKenney saw in microcosm the trials and tragedies that would face the federal government if entire nations were uprooted and moved west. His fears were underscored in the winter of 1819 when a number of Cherokee agreed to yield their lands in Tennessee to the government in exchange for equal territory in the west.

Tons of lead, powder and ball, provisions, and horses were loaded aboard a fleet of flatboats along with three hundred Cherokee under Chief John Jolly. Robbed, beaten, their lead, powder, rifles, and horses stolen, their warriors killed by drunken settlers, the Cherokee finally arrived in their promised land—only to be greeted by the rifles and pistols of settlers who had defied the government's orders to leave. It took the soldiers from Lovely's blockhouse to enforce the law.[5]

From the correspondence of McKenney's Indian agent, Major Meigs, it appears the Cherokee gradually changed from the victim to become the oppressor. In a council with Meigs the chiefs warned him they were determined to get by any means the Osage land in what is now Oklahoma. To accomplish this they launched a series of wars with the Osage along the Verdigris and Neosho rivers. They also made secret treaties for military assistance with smaller tribes, like the uprooted Delaware, Chickasaw, and Choctaw. In return the Cherokee promised them large tracts of land.

It was Lovely who again stopped the tribal wars. In the fall of 1818 he notified the Indian Trade Bureau that a treaty had been signed between the Arkansas or Western Cherokee and the Osage in which the government had agreed to pay all claims lodged against the Osage nation for their raids. In return the Osage "extinguished" their claims to all lands between the Verdigris and the Arkansas. This gave the Western Cherokee a hunting ground and, as Lovely advised Washington, once again there was peace.

For the Indian agent, weary and ill, this final treaty had an ironical conclusion: the Osage had stolen his horse.

The long journey across the plains was too much for Lovely. He died a few months after the council. The Osage nation, with whom he had fought, argued, and pleaded, wept for him. The white man quickly forgot his deeds but gave his name to the vast tract of Indian land—Lovely's Purchase.

2.

IN 1819 James Miller of New Hampshire was appointed by Washington as the first governor of the Indian Territory and arrived in that beautiful wild country on horse-back. He reported to Calhoun and McKenney that he had found the Osage to be a happy-go-lucky people who danced a great deal, loved fine horses, admired war, and were extremely courteous. On the other hand the Cherokee, he observed, were "not much different" in their ways from the white man.[6]

Meanwhile McKenney and Calhoun were faced with new Indian removal problems; Mississippi was now demanding that the Choctaw be moved west and their lands be opened for settlement. Twice Washington sent Andy Jackson to conduct the negotiations. The first time the great Choctaw chief Pushmataha, whose portrait one day would hang in McKenney's gallery, passionately informed Jackson his people would never leave their lands; the Choctaw who had voluntarily left for the West were no better than wolves, he contemptuously told the general. When state pressure increased, the government sent Jackson back to the Choctaw. This time, by whiskey and bribes, he forced the chiefs to sign a treaty in which the nation exchanged its lands in Mississippi for territory in the West.

However, five thousand settlers occupied this territory and their outraged protests echoed in furious Congressional debates; Governor Miller immediately issued a public proclamation that the Indians would be settled west of the white settlements.

In the summer of 1820 wagon trains continued to move into the western lands until those two curious allies, the Arkansas legislature and the Arkansas Cherokee, joined in common protest to Washington. The Indians, as always, came out second best. Senator Thomas Hart Benton, McKenney's bitterest enemy, railroaded a bill through Congress establishing new boundary lines that ruthlessly included large sections of lands only recently won by the Cherokee. There were also additional unexpected problems: six thousand cultivated acres assigned as Indian lands included grain mills and cotton gins—all owned by white settlers.

Debates went on in Washington, state legislatures, in small county seats, and in Indian tepees—until finally the chiefs turned to the East.

The Great Father—what did he say . . . ?

CHAPTER VI:

The Bravest of the Brave

I.

THE PRACTICE of bringing Indian delegations to the capital did not begin with Colonel McKenney but rather was part of the founding of the Republic.

After the bloody and decisive defeat of General Arthur St. Clair at Fort Washington (Cincinnati) by the united western tribes under Little Turtle in the winter of 1791, President Washington conceived the idea of entertaining leading chiefs of the Iroquois Confederacy and trying to persuade them to act as his peace envoys to the Ohio Indian nations.[1]

It was not the first time Washington had tried this diplomatic maneuver. The previous winter Cornplanter, the famous Seneca war chief, had visited Philadelphia in the hope of modifying the Iroquois land cession and establishing permanent peace between the infant nation and the still powerful Indian confederacy.

Washington took this opportunity to urge the Seneca to travel to the Shawnee country and offer them a peace proposal. The President told the Indian chief:

"You will render these mistaken people a great service and probably prevent their being swept off the face of the earth."[2]

Cornplanter had agreed to make the trip to the Ohio but was prevented by the hostility of his fellow chiefs.

Now, after St. Clair's shattering defeat, Washington was eager to have representatives of the Iroquois Confederacy act as his envoys to the Shawnee and Miami.

The influence of the Iroquois chiefs was obvious; for over a hundred years the Confederacy had not only been the masters of war but also of eloquence and diplomacy. There was no match among the red men—and many said this could include the whites—for the oratory of Red Jacket, the Seneca whose cold sarcasm, nimble wit, and dramatic delivery were known and admired among the Indian nations from the Niagara frontier to the Winnebago country of the Great Lakes. There was also Joseph Brant, Thayendanegea, the great Mohawk war captain who had fought for the king in the Revolution. General Washington could never forget Brant; the cry of "Brant's in the valley" had rung out for eight long cruel years, not only in the Mohawk Valley—breadbasket of the Continental Army— but also in the halls of the Continental Congress. The burned-out farms, pastures, and the scalped dead were grim testimony to the skillful guerrilla war Brant had brought to the New York frontier.[3]

Several months before St. Clair's defeat during a council at Painted Post, the United States commissioners had extended an invitation to the leading chiefs of the Six Nations to visit the capital during the 1791–1792 session of Congress. Washington now intended to use this opportunity to advance his peace proposals to Red Jacket, Brant, and the others.

Red Jacket and fifty other chiefs accepted the invitation to come to Philadelphia but to Washington's disappointment the haughty Brant declined.

In March 1792 the major chiefs of the Iroquois Confederacy rode into the nation's first capital escorted, as one early historian reported, "by ye militia with drum and fifes . . ."[4]

Evidently with this first visit of an Indian delegation to the home of the Great Father, the government started the distribution of presents and the free flow of whiskey.

Down through the years whiskey would prove to be one of the federal government's strongest inducements for Indians to sign treaties, whether in the smallest council on a windblown plain or amid the formal trappings of Philadelphia and later Washington.

Upon their arrival in Philadelphia, General Knox, rotund, cherubic, and jovial, presented each chief with a military uniform and a cocked hat. The delegation stayed until May and was entertained with so much rich food and whiskey that two of them died. One was Peter Jaquette, an Oneida chief and child protégé of Lafayette, who had been educated in the finest French schools.[5]

Four days after Jaquette's elaborate funeral the council with Washington began. Red Jacket outlined with great sagacity the heart of the difficulty the United States was experiencing with the western tribes—the failure of both Americans and the British to provide for their Indian allies after the cessation of hostilities.

The Seneca told Washington and his Cabinet:

> What is more desirable than that we, who live within hearing of each other, should unite for the common good? This is my wish. This is the wish of my nation although I am sorry I cannot say it of every individual in it, for there are differences of opinion among us as there are among the white people . . ."[6]

Red Jacket and the chiefs finally agreed to ask the Shawnee and Miami to call a council at which time they would present Washington's proposal for peace.

At the conclusion of the Philadelphia council, Washington gave Red Jacket a huge silver medal, seven inches long and five inches wide. One side depicted Washington the soldier presenting a peace pipe to an Indian against the background of a white man plowing with a team of oxen. On the reverse side was the motto "E Pluribus Unum."[7]

In his lifetime the Seneca scorned all things belonging to the white man, even chairs. But he proudly displayed this medal on all formal occasions and wore it when his portrait was painted for McKenney's Indian Gallery. The only time it left his possession was when he was forced to put it in temporary pawn for money to buy whiskey.

After Red Jacket and the other chiefs left, Brant arrived, vain, proud, and suspicious. For ten days he was entertained by Washington, Secretary of War Knox, and the Cabinet who desperately tried to win his support for the struggling Republic; they even hinted at bribery which Brant coldly ignored.[8]

In his conferences with Washington and Knox, the Mohawk leader offered to speak at any council to assure the nations of the Ohio the United States wished no land, only a lasting peace. In return Washington promised Brant that old treaties would be renegotiated and appropriations would be made by the United States to the Ohio nations to build schools and bring them the white man's civilization.

While Brant had been impressed by his Philadelphia reception, he was scornful of the bribery attempts by Washington and Knox. From Canada he advised Count de Puisy of the British Service:

> I was offered a thousand guineas down, and to have the half pay and pension I receive from Great Britain doubled, merely on condition that I would use my endeavors to bring about a peace [between the United States and the Ohio Indian Nations].
>
> This I refused. I considered it detrimental to the British interests . . .[9]

In the fall one of the largest councils in the history of the frontier gathered on the Ohio to hear the speeches of Red Jacket, Brant, and the other Six Nations chiefs. Simon Girty, whom the settlers called the White Savage, was there with Colonel McKee, the shadowy half-blood British agent who for years would keep the tribes from warring against the United States.

The efforts of Washington's copper-skinned envoys were unsuccessful. It took General Wayne and the decisive Battle of Fallen Timbers, August 20, 1794, and the

Greenville, Ohio, Treaty signed the following summer, to bring peace finally to the Ohio frontier.

The portraits of Red Jacket, Brant, Cornplanter, and many of the chiefs who had listened to Washington's envoys at the great Ohio council, fought at Fallen Timbers, and then signed the Greenville Treaty would one day hang in Colonel McKenney's famous gallery.

2.

AFTER THE turn of the century, individual Indians and small delegations continued to visit the seat of government. Among the first chiefs to be welcomed by the Great Father in Washington was Shahaka, or Big White, the Mandan chief who had been brought to the world of the white man by Lewis and Clark, and twelve Osage chiefs led by White Hair, who wore his famous wig.[10] The group of chiefs accompanied by Jean Pierre Chouteau, the St. Louis trader, left the Missouri in the early spring of 1804 and arrived in Lexington, Kentucky, the second week in June "creating much excitement" amid reports that Lewis and Clark had been killed by the Osage on the Missouri. On July 13, 1804, the party arrived in Washington, and on the morning of the seventeenth, escorted by President Jefferson, they were given a tour of the navy yard and viewed the frigates *United States*, *Chesapeake*, and *General Green*. A reporter for the *Baltimore American* observed:

> "As they were strangers to anything of this kind, it was expected they would express a great degree of surprise at the sight of a large vessel of war; but it is a trait, very extraordinary, in those men, not to seem surprised at any object, however great, which may have met their eye."

An "Italian Band" met them at the gangplank and serenaded them and Jefferson as they inspected the frigates. They impassively listened to the big guns fire a salvo of salutes and watched midshipmen scamper like monkeys on the yardarms to harbor-furl the sails as signal flags flew up the halyards "but without exciting in them the least emotion."

In the evening the chiefs performed a war dance for Jefferson "and a large concourse of ladies and gentlemen in an open area handsomely lighted by lamps."

The next day they were formally greeted by Jefferson who presented each chief with a formal statement, written on parchment, asking the Osage "and all the Nations of Red People within the territory of the United States to look up to him as their father and friend." The party then proceeded to New York where they stayed for a week.

After leaving New York the Osage continued their tour of the large eastern cities to be entertained by countless displays of fireworks, more guns booming, speeches by mayors, governors, and military leaders; they listened impassively to missionaries tell them about the white man's God as they gave each chief a Bible. Politicians promised that the red men and their white brothers would always live together in peace with each respecting the others' rights, liberty, and pursuit of happiness.

In Philadelphia, White Hair and his fellow chiefs sat for

their portraits by Charles Balthazar Julien Fevret de Saint-Mémin. The artist was born in Dijon in 1770 and after studying painting in France accompanied his father to New York City, their first stopover on a trip to Santo Domingo where the family owned many plantations. They decided to stay in New York after hearing news of the Revolution.

Saint-Mémin was probably the first artist in the United States to make "mechanical" portraits, using a wooden framed drawing device invented by Louis Chrétien in 1786. With a machine known as the physiognotrace, Saint-Mémin did exact, life-size profiles of the Osage chiefs, the earliest known portraits of Plains Indians. Each portrait was finished in crayon. Then using a pantograph he reduced the portrait to a small size which he engraved on a plate. The portraits show the high cheekbones, the bold nose, thin lips, heavy jaw, hair roach, paint, and ornaments of the early western tribes.

After the Osage chiefs returned home, other envious tribes demanded that their representatives be brought to Washington. To keep peace, twenty-seven chiefs and warriors from twelve tribes were escorted to Washington to be greeted by Jefferson in October 1805. They were also given a grand tour of the cities. In Philadelphia, Charles Willson Peale showed them his museum in the State House (Independence Hall) and his gallery of famous Americans.

Shahaka, or Big White, accompanied by his wife and son, met Jefferson in the White House on December 30, 1806. The Great Father, his red hair now streaked with gray, "took Big White by the hand of friendship and welcomed him to the seat of government of the United States."

The President pleaded with the stout, talkative Mandan chief from the alien lands of the upper Missouri to "live in peace and friendship with one another as brothers of the same family should do.[11]

A few days later Big White attended the glittering dinner Jefferson gave for Lewis and Clark in the White House. The Mandan chief patiently did the bidding of the white men. In Philadelphia he sat for his profile portrait by Saint-Mémin, which McKenney would later have copied for his portfolio, and he and his wife willingly played the roles of the "Savage King and Queen of the Mandans" as some people called them. In Washington they entertained the foreign ambassadors with their native dances and with great good humor allowed themselves to be studied, examined, and stared at like some wild animals from the hostile western plains.

When he shyly asked when they would be going home, the answers were always vague. It was only after Clark had been appointed Superintendent of the Western Indian Nations with headquarters in St. Louis that the War Department made plans to return the Mandans and the French interpreter back upriver. It took three years, the guns of the American Fur Company, and seven thousand dollars paid to the Chouteau brothers of St. Louis before this could be accomplished.

Back among his people Big White earnestly tried to describe in the council the awesome sights he had witnessed in the great cities of the white man. But instead of being enthralled, the Mandans scoffed at his tales. They told him he was under the spell of a white witch and lived in a fantasy world.

H. B. Brackenridge in his *Journals of a Voyage up the Missouri Performed in 1811* found Big White "a man of mild and gentle disposition . . . he expressed a wish to come and live amongst the whites and spoke sensibly of the insecurity, the ferocity of manners and ignorance of the state of the society into which he had been placed . . ."[12]

Apparently Big White still had vivid memories of the white man's fabulous cities, his luxurious homes, his inexhaustible supply of whiskey and exotic foods, and the education and solicitude of the men who had escorted him out of the wilderness.

Big White had discovered a man can't go home again . . .

3.

IT WASN'T until the winter of 1820–1821 that the federal government invited the first large Indian delegation to visit Washington. It began with a letter that Benjamin O'Fallon, General Clark's nephew and McKenney's Upper Missouri Indian agent, wrote to Washington in April 1821.

O'Fallon suggested that fifteen of the "principal chiefs and leading men of some of the largest Nations of the Missouri, and high up the Mississippi, be indulged in visiting the seat of Government and some of our largest cities . . ."

O'Fallon's philosophy was that of McKenney's iron below the velvet—let the western nations get a glimpse of the white man's wealth and power to make them pause before starting a war. O'Fallon wrote:

"Our troops have produced much respect and our boats additional astonishment, but many [Indian nations] are still disposed to underrate our strength, and to believe that a detachment of our troops on the Missouri, is not a part, but the whole of our army . . ."[13]

Washington approved O'Fallon's idea and the Indian agent spent that spring and summer on the river gathering together his delegation to visit the Great Father.

4.

IN THE winter of 1820–1821, O'Fallon reported to McKenney at the Indian Trade Bureau with seventeen Pawnee, Omaha, Oto, Kansa, and Missouri chiefs, warriors, orators. His group also included one Indian beauty, Eagle of Delight, a cook, and three interpreters—the vanguard of the hundreds of Indian delegations that would stream into the capital during the next half century.

The *National Intelligencer*'s page one story informed its readers the Indians had come "to visit the Great Father and learn something of that civilization of which they have hitherto remained in total ignorance . . . these red men of the forest are completely in a state of nature . . ."[14]

The Indians were not as commonplace as they became in a few years, and crowds followed them as they walked along Pennsylvania Avenue. One warrior stood out, Petalesharo (Generous Chief), son of Knife Chief, principal chief of the Skidi Pawnee. Six foot, muscular, and handsome as an ancient Roman, clad in buffalo robes painted with birds and horses, an eagle feather headdress dangling to his knees, he never failed to thrill the ladies of Washington.

The women in the party were mostly nondescript, impassive squaws but not Eagle of Delight. She was just eighteen, the wife of the scowling big-nosed Oto half-chief Shaumonekusse (Prairie Wolf). If Petalesharo made the hearts of the Washington females flutter, a shy smile from Eagle of Delight aroused the males from the halls of Congress to the meanest hot potato peddler on Pennsylvania Avenue.

Leading the group was Sharitarish (Angry Chief), second chief of the Grand Pawnee and brother of Tarrarecawaho, head chief of the Pawnee nation who had refused to come to Washington on the grounds it would be too much of a "condescension." His argument to O'Fallon, who passed it on to McKenney, was that the Great Father in Washington could not summon as many braves as he could, did not own as many horses, could not boast a coupstick with as many scalps of his enemies, and did not have as many wives. Therefore he could not call him his Great Father.

McKenney lodged the delegation at Tennison's Hotel because Brown's Indian Queen had no room, then made arrangements to have the Indians meet President Monroe. Monroe was so busy with his budget and annual message he could give them only a brief reception. He told McKenney to send the delegation on a tour of the eastern cities— Baltimore, Philadelphia, and New York—not only to give them an idea of how the white man lived but to demonstrate the strength and power of the United States.

To the regret of the ladies and some of the dashing young Congressmen, Petalesharo and Eagle of Delight left Washington in early December. They returned a few days after Christmas in time for McKenney to make them the outstanding attractions of the annual White House New Year's Reception. The all-day affair began with Congressmen accompanied by their wives, department heads, Cabinet members, foreign dignitaries, officers of the army and navy and, as the *Washington Gazette* called them, "the citizens," streaming into the White House. During the reception the Marine Corps band continuously played "national and appropriate airs."

At the height of the reception McKenney led in his Indians. The copper-skinned chiefs and warriors walked into the crowded room with the air of ancient kings. The Pawnee wore buffalo robes, brilliantly painted with figures of birds and horses and battle scenes. The Omaha chiefs tinkled when they walked from the number of silver bracelets on their arms, and only the fierce dark eyes of the Kansa and Missouri warriors could be seen, so completely were they covered by robes and skins. Their faces, eyebrow to cheekbone, were covered with a thick red paint and the Oto half-chief stalked about the room in a weird headdress of a gold crown from which dangled

vermilion-dyed horsehair from which protruded two buffalo horns.

The guests eagerly crowded about them, shaking their hands and reaching out to touch them. The women whispered enviously among themselves as they eyed Eagle of Delight's scarlet pantaloons, green camlet coat, and moccasins exquisitely decorated with dyed porcupine quills and beads. Her thick black hair was parted in the middle and fashioned into two thick braids from which hung large silver and beaded ornaments.

The *Gazette*'s reporter observed: "The music and hilarity of the scene occasionally relaxed the muscles of their stern countenances and in the place of pensive gravity, a heartfelt joy beamed in the eye of the sullen Indian warrior...."[15]

That January McKenney was busy keeping the Indians occupied while he waited for President Monroe and Secretary of War Calhoun to receive the delegation formally. McKenney had General Mason, his predecessor, give the Indians a tour of the nation's cannon foundry and arranged for a carriage ride about the city which included an inspection of the arsenal, navy yard, and nearby military installations. At the request of Baron Hyde de Neuville, the French Minister, the Indians demonstrated their dances. After the baron's enthusiastic report so many other foreign embassies requested similar performances that McKenney was forced to call a halt to the Indians' "public appearances."

Then in late January a series of events started that would give Petalesharo and McKenney's Indian delegation fleeting national fame.

On January 29 the *National Intelligencer* devoted a half column on its page one to what it called "Anecdote of a Pawnee Chief." The reporter claimed he had discovered the story in a missionary's report on Indian affairs prepared for the President who in turn had sent it on to Congress. The missionary, he wrote, had received the story from a Captain Bell who had accompanied Stephen Long on his famous expedition. The facts, he said, had been confirmed by Indian agent O'Fallon.

During the war between the Comanche and the Pawnee, the story related, several captives were taken. One, a young girl, was selected to be a human sacrifice to the Sun God.

The fatal hour arrived. The trembling victim far from her home and friends, was fastened to the stake. The whole tribe was assembled on the surrounding plain to witness the awful scene. Just when the funeral pyre was about to be kindled and the whole multitude was on tiptoe with expectation, a young Pawnee brave having gone unnoticed, had prepared two fleet horses with necessary provisions, sprang from his seat and ran through the crowd, liberated the victim, seized her in his arms, placed her on one of the horses, mounted the other himself and made the utmost speed toward the nation and the friends of the captive.

The multitude, dumb and nerveless with amazement at the daring deed, made no effort to rescue their victim or her deliverer. They viewed it as an immediate act of the Great Spirit, submitting to it without a murmur and returning to their homes.

The released captive was returned to her home after three days in the wilderness with her deliverer. He then gave her the horse on which she rode with the necessary provisions for the remainder of the journey and they parted. On his return to the village such was his popularity no inquiry was made into his conduct, no censure was passed on it. And since that transaction no human sacrifice has ever again been offered in this or any Pawnee tribe. The practice is now abandoned.16

What the reporter had discovered was a quotation from Bell's *Journal* included in the reports of Long's expedition. The name of the warrior was not mentioned in the *Intelligencer's* article but the news soon flew about the city, probably from O'Fallon to McKenney, that the brave was Petalesharo, now in Washington.

The story was published on a Tuesday. On the following Monday President Monroe, Calhoun, the Vice-President, members of Congress and the Supreme Court formally received the Indian delegation at the White House.

If the President and his official family had hoped to see the chiefs and warriors in their native costume they were disappointed. As the *Intelligencer* reported, the Indians appeared "in completely Americanized costumes," presented to the delegations as gifts of the government. "They were dressed in blue surtouts, red cuffs and capes, blue pantaloons and shiny black boots. On their heads they all wore a coronet decorated with red and blue foil edged with colored feathers." Their faces were painted, but as the *Intelligencer's* reporter noted, "in a less fantastic style than usual." There was a strict caste system in the delegation; the full chiefs were identified by two silver epaulets, the half-chiefs by one.

The women were escorted to a wide sofa but it was Eagle of Delight who held the stage. She sparkled in her scarlet pantaloons and brilliant cape, and her shy smile captivated the room.

The chiefs and the braves were obviously uncomfortable in their white man's dress. Broad shoulders threatened to burst the seams of their velvet coats and, as the formalities continued, one or two slid off their stiff boots and rubbed their aching feet.

Each chief brought a present of a buffalo robe, peace pipes, decorated moccasins, or horned headdresses.

The Indians entered first, followed in a few minutes by the President, members of his Cabinet, Supreme Court justices, Congressmen, and Senators. Monroe, the Vice-President, and Calhoun took seats before the fireplace while the others crowded about the room in a semicircle. President Monroe spoke slowly and paused frequently while the Indians, arms folded in a classic pose, listened impassively. Monroe said the usual things: he was glad his Red Children liked the new clothes which the government had bought for them and he hoped his children had enjoyed their many tours of the Great Father's foundries, army and navy bases and military installations. He also gently but firmly reminded the chiefs of the military strength of the United States.

As Monroe spoke the three interpreters translated every sentence to the various tribes. Each point was greeted by what the *Intelligencer* reporter called "a significant assent, a sort of inarticulate sound or grunt."

After he had finished, McKenney and O'Fallon urged the chiefs to speak "with as much freedom as if they were in their own villages."

The head chief of the Pawnee, probably Sharitarish, stepped forward to shake hands with Monroe and Calhoun, then delivered his speech, "with gestures that while violent were never excessive or ungraceful."

The Pawnee chief assured the President that his words would go into one ear "but would not come out the other." He said he and his people had found the United States to be populous and powerful while they were few and weak in comparison. He paused while the interpreters caught up with him, then slowly and firmly went on:

> But the Great Spirit made some men white and others he made red. The white man could make fine clothing, furniture and carry many guns while the red could make nothing. The white man lived upon the animals he raised at home while the red man hunted the buffalo whose skin he wore and whose meat he ate. Yet the Great Spirit intended that there should be both white men and red men and he looks down and regards them as both his children.

The chief spoke movingly of the vast herds of buffalo thundering across the plains and wisely predicted that the flood of white men would be far greater than the largest herd, which he added sadly, would one day vanish.

He told Monroe that the Indians were pleased with his gifts of clothing. Then he stretched out his arms, paused and stared down at Monroe.

> We have plenty of buffalo, plenty of deer and other wild animals, Great Father. We have an abundance of horses. We have everything we want. We have plenty of land if you will keep your people off of it. Before our intercourse with the white man we could lie down and sleep and when we awoke we would find the buffalo feeding about our camps. But now we are killing them for their skins and feeding the wolves with their flesh to make our children cry over their bones.

He then presented Monroe with a collection of robes, pipes, skins, and necklaces of bear claws.

Petalesharo, the magnificent, was brief; he was more of a warrior than an orator. He simply thanked Monroe for his gifts with the wry comment that he now felt like an animal who had emerged in the spring with a new coat. Then he presented the President with a stunning painted buffalo robe and explained what some of the pictures represented.17

It makes a thrilling scene; the dignified chiefs in their colorful, if lurid, dress, some with their boots off flexing aching toes; the shadows of the soft candlelight playing on the faces of the great men of America; the diminutive Monroe silhouetted by the huge fireplace; Calhoun, his traditional black suit accentuating his slender grace; Chief Justice Marshall, with his shoulder-length hair, nervous blue eyes and quick barklike laughter now stilled, as his fellow justices crowd about him; tall, intent William Crawford, who would soon miss the presidency by a small margin; Daniel Webster, his brooding dark eyes fixed approvingly on the Indian speakers; and Henry Clay who loved fine oratory, nodding in appreciation of the Pawnee's words.

As McKenney would recall later, with typical understatement, it had been "a fine assembly that greeted the President."

At last the speeches were finished. Then O'Fallon, with

a smile, turned to Eagle of Delight and asked her to come forward and meet the President. The Indian girl's brief speech ended the tension in the room, and the President and his Cabinet inspected the gifts which the interpreters had spread out on a table. The chiefs took this opportunity to slip out of their ridiculous cloaks and pantaloons and replace the tinfoil coronets with headdresses of horsehair and buffalo horns, "some as long as those of an ox."

The long evening ended with servants passing plates of cakes and glasses of wine. The Indians quickly finished the wine and polished off the cakes to the last crumb. Then peace pipes were solemnly passed, with even Chief Justice Marshall gingerly taking a puff in the name of peace.

The *Intelligencer*'s anonymous reporter was both prophetic and sensitive. As he pointed out it was impossible to have been in that room and believe

> . . . that these people are destined to soon vanish from the face of the earth . . . they still possess fine traits of character and we can never forget they were the native lords of the very soil which they are gradually yielding to their invaders. . . . Yet I firmly believe all our humane efforts to civilize them will prove to be unavailing. Whether it is [sic] they acquire our bad habits before our good ones or their course of life cannot exist under the restraints of civilization, I know not. But this I do know: it is certain that all the tribes which have remained among us have, or are now dwindling to insignificance or [are] entirely extinct. . . .
>
> You know that every experiment to rear the wild duck has failed, and that they die as certainly by your kindness as your neglect . . .[18]

5.

DURING THE week that followed, the story of Petalesharo's rescue of the Comanche girl became the favorite topic of teas, balls, and meetings, especially at Miss White's seminary where the girls talked of nothing else but the Pawnee's brave act. When they heard Petalesharo was to join in a war dance on the White House lawn they begged Miss White to allow them to go. She finally gave her permission.

When the young ladies arrived they discovered the entire area around the White House was choked with spectators—the capital's newspapers later estimated six to ten thousand were present—with Congress adjourned for the day and almost every business in the city shut down. As one reporter observed, "The lover forgot to call on his mistress . . . the constables did not hunt in droves and neither did the magistrates make out a single mittimus . . ."

Miss White marched her young ladies right into the White House which President Monroe, "as gallant and generous as always," had turned over to them. They soon filled every window to watch the wild dances.

That night back at Miss White's they repeated the thrilling story of Petalesharo and Morning Star, adding the bits and pieces of dramatic invention that were going the rounds of the teas and balls that winter.

"Isn't it perfectly ghastly?" they agreed.

"I believe he deserves a medal," Mary Rapine cried.

"That's it, a medal!" her companions chorused, "to the

Bravest of the Brave. Isn't that what they call him in the tribe? Can't you just see it gleaming on his chest?"

"In silver," Mary said firmly. "It must be in silver like those the President gives the Indians only this one will have his story engraved on it."[19]

The idea grew and Miss White gave her consent after Mary Rapine's wealthy parents had agreed to donate the medal. The story got into print and the *Intelligencer* and *Gazette* reported the plans in detail.

Petalesharo, slightly bewildered, was now a national hero. Two weeks after he had danced in the cold before the White House he was taken by McKenney and Major O'Fallon to the home of Mary Rapine in the shadow of the Capitol. He wore his buffalo robe, while Miss White's young ladies, waiting nervously, wore their Sunday best.

It was Mary's idea, they all agreed, and she should make the presentation.

The tall and muscular Pawnee, arms folded under his robe, faced little Mary Rapine, who stared up into his dark face, her heart beating faster than it had ever done before in her young life.

She began her speech in the traditional fashion with every paragraph beginning with "Brother." It wasn't a long speech but it was sincere. She said very simply that she was presenting him with this medal because "your white Brothers admire and honor such virtue and will always esteem their red brethren in proportion as they display such generosity and heroism. You see we are all young and we admire benevolence and courage, whatever be the color of the skins that cover them . . . your action has filled us with esteem for you and your nation, it is like the odour of sweet flowers."

Petalesharo had no idea of what this frail, pretty white girl was saying but it was obvious it came from her heart. When Mary had finished he bent his head and she slipped the medal around his neck, the shiny silver gleaming against the dark skin.

McKenney's notes of Petalesharo's reply has the Pawnee thanking Mary and the young girls:

> This brings rest to my heart. I feel like the leaf after a storm and when the wind is still. I listen to you, I am glad. I love the palefaces more than I ever did, and will open my ears wider when they speak. I am glad you heard of what I did. I did not know the act was so good. It came from my heart. I was ignorant of its value. I now know how good it was. You make me know by giving me this medal . . .[20]

In between the President's reception and the presentation of Mary Rapine's medal, Colonel McKenney wondered how he could capture for future Americans something of this memorable visit. Who would remember in the next decade what Petalesharo or Eagle of Delight looked like?

It was then that McKenney's idea of his Indian Portrait Gallery was born.

The painter he selected was Charles Bird King who had gained a reputation for his portraits of Calhoun, Clay, and John Howard Payne, who wrote "Home Sweet Home." King had been born in Newport, Rhode Island, in 1785. In the early 1800s he studied under Edward Savage in New

York, then spent seven years in London as the pupil of Benjamin West and the roommate of Thomas Sully. He returned to the United States at the outbreak of the War of 1812, painted in obscurity in Philadelphia for four years, then came to Washington in 1816.

As his reputation as a portraitist grew, King built a studio and gallery on the east side of Twelfth Street NW between E and F streets.

Among the individual portraits King painted were members of the Oto nation, who lived with what remained of the Missouri at the mouth of the Platte, and Shaumonekusse (the Wolf), wearing his buffalo-horned headdress, a necklace of grizzly bear claws, the dress of a renowned warrior. The Comanche, those fierce tigers of the plains, had been routed by the chief the previous summer. Captain Bell's company attached to Long's expedition met them hurrying homeward with their wounded on the Arkansas. The Spaniards also knew and feared the Wolf whose feats in war were so stirring his people called him "Ietan," or Comanche.

King also painted Eagle of Delight, the Wolf's wife, in her figured cloth waist and strings of necklaces which may have been presents from her many admirers. King's portrait of Monchansia (White Plume) shows a handsome painted man wearing a colored turbanlike headdress, strands of necklaces, slender bone pendants, and a presidential peace medal. The artist's portrait of Ongpatonga or Big Elk, the celebrated chief of the Omaha, reveals the piercing black eyes, the large aquiline nose, and the high cheekbones but curiously the pit marks mentioned in Long's journals are missing.

Sharitarish or Angry Chief, second chief of the Grand Pawnee, was painted by King proudly wearing a presidential medal on his broad bare chest.

King's portrait of Petalesharo is believed to be the earliest known representation of a Plains Indian wearing a feathered bonnet and his painting of Eagle of Delight the earliest painting of a Plains woman.[21]

When King painted his portrait of Petalesharo as a singularly handsome young warrior wearing a stunning eagle feather war bonnet the romantic tales about the young Pawnee may have unconsciously guided his brush. John Neagle, the twenty-five-year-old Philadelphia artist, also painted Petalesharo during the delegation's visit to that city. Neagle's full length oil "painted from nature" also shows the Pawnee chief wearing a robe and the feathered bonnet, but the grim, tight face and large aquiline nose are less flattering. Neagle also did oils of Big Elk, Angry Chief, and Big Kansa.

The government paid King for twenty-five portraits. McKenney gave the delegates seventeen and he kept eight, the basis for his famous Indian Gallery. There is also evidence King painted eight portraits for himself, making a total of thirty-three paintings of that 1821–1822 delegation. McKenney now designated King as the official artist for his gallery.

In early March 1822 the Indian delegation left for home by way of Council Bluffs. McKenney ordered a stagecoach which he loaded with boxes bursting with red and blue uniforms, silver epaulets, shells from the far-off Pacific, iron cones, screws, and cowries presented to the Indians by the College of Physicians in New York City, rifles, and King's carefully wrapped copies of their portraits.

As he climbed aboard the stage Petalesharo threw up his arms in a gesture of farewell. The spectators could read the inscription of the silver medal against his dark chest:

"To the Bravest of the Brave."

CHAPTER VII:

McKenney and the Richest Man in America

———— •<•>• ————

I.

THE AMOUNT of work McKenney performed as Superintendent of Indian Trade was prodigious. He was the first to arrive at the Georgetown office and the last to leave. His memoirs are righteous in describing how much he gave of himself to the government—"I am confined to my office until one in the morning," he wrote to a friend in New York City—but his account and letter books are more convincing. Countless letters, bills, memorandums, receipts, official documents detail his many tasks from deciding the case of an upstate New York Mohawk whose horse had been stolen to the sad tale of a Revolutionary soldier vainly pleading for the government to pay him for the lost years he had spent as a Shawnee prisoner.

McKenney also had to fix the rate of items from beeswax to skins the Indians brought into the factories for trade. In the spring of 1820 he was advising William Thompson, his commission agent in Baltimore, to price rough skins at twenty cents and cured at twenty-five.

"The season having come in, it may be safer to sell than to store . . . please sell the beeswax at the price you counted [twenty-nine cents] and inform me what you can get for the beaver and other skins . . .[1]

Then there were supplies needed for the outposts: Chicago wanted more strouding and blankets, Fort Osage begged for a new factor, accounts of Chickasaw Bluffs were missing. Secretaries copied his letters in their beautiful, flowing copperplate handwriting and they went by horse, stage, canalboat, and Indian runner. McKenney also halted whiskey sales to the tribes, passed on recommendations to the War Department for new agents, traders' licenses, carefully studied the latest rumor or bits of gossip about brewing Indian trouble or gleefully opened the latest barrel of Indian "curiosities" sent by one of his factors or dreamed of additional portraits to join Petalesharo and the other chiefs who now stared down at him from the walls of his Georgetown office.

Then McKenney's enemies launched their first attack. One morning he was stunned to read that, if his accounts were called in, $120,000 "would be unaccounted for." McKenney summoned his chief clerk and showed him the newspaper. "Have the Quarterly returns been sent in, Mr. Bronaugh?" he asked.

The clerk replied they had been personally delivered to the Government Auditing Office. McKenney slammed on his hat and drove there with Bronaugh.

"Are my accounts settled, sir?" he asked the clerk.

"They are sir—as far as they can be" was the reply.

McKenney soon learned an "absence of vouchers" left $120,000 unaccounted for in his returns. He indignantly demanded and was given the package of vouchers Bronaugh had delivered. After a close examination he silently showed the package to his clerk, it obviously had been slit open and the cords cut. With the package in Bronaugh's pocket they drove to the War Department. McKenney stalked into the office of Secretary of War Calhoun and gave him a detailed account of what had happened, adding grimly he was prepared to supply a duplicate set of vouchers stored in his safe.

Calhoun summoned the War Department's auditor and ordered him to put his "entire force" on McKenney's accounts until they had been settled.

It wasn't long before a weary Bronaugh reported to McKenney that "the accounts are true to the penny."[2]

As his first year in office passed, McKenney's interest in the culture of the American Indian increased, not only in his primitive combination museum, library, and portrait gallery, but in the Indians themselves. He began to see them as human beings with a vast amount of pride in their heritage and a fear of the white man's civilization that seemed to threaten the life of every tribe, even on the remotest frontier. He began to dream of a day when the Indian would have opportunities equal to those of a white man, when there would be numerous Indian schools and peaceful villages where the red man and his family could live in peace with the white man.

To bring this about, he wrote, it was only necessary that "Indians be looked upon as human beings, having bodies and soul's like ours, possessed of sensibilities and capacities as keen and large as ours, that their misery be inspected and held up to the view of our citizens, that their trophies of reform be pointed to. I say, it needs only this to enlist into their favor the whole civilized population of our country."[3]

Three men would badly dent this idealism: the ruthless John Jacob Astor, "landlord of New York," the aggressive Ramsay Crooks, field manager for Astor's American Fur Company, and Senator Thomas Hart Benton, the man of whom Calhoun would one day bitterly suggest that instead of being a member of the Senate he should have devoted his life to writing advertisements for quack medicines.

Benton was Astor's man in the Senate and Crooks was constantly writing to him with suggestions or demands that certain bills be killed or rewritten so they could not hurt the business of the American Fur Company. Benton never failed to agree with Crooks.[4]

2.

COLONEL MCKENNEY had survived his initial confrontation with Astor in Major Irwin's struggles with the American Fur Company at Green Bay. Although by 1822 he certainly must have discovered Astor's influence was linked to the White House, McKenney doggedly continued to fight the tycoon. He confiscated his company's supplies when he heard they contained whiskey and strongly supported the United States factory system in his yearly reports to Congress.

McKenney was always a strong advocate of the frontier factories. He insisted they were still experimental and should be given another chance after the shattering war years. Rather than be abolished, he told Congress, they should be expanded with an additional $1,000,000 added to the Bureau's budget.

His chief goal was to carry out President Washington's original intentions—protect the Indians "from scoundrels in the fur trade" and from the advancing tidal wave of the white man's civilization. William H. Crawford, Secretary of War during McKenney's early years in the Indian Trade Bureau, agreed with his Indian Superintendent; his theory was that any loss of capital was insignificant compared to keeping peace on the frontier.[5]

By 1822 McKenney had become the hated symbol of the American factory to Astor who viewed him and his bureau as the major obstacles to his American Fur Company's gaining complete control over the fur trade. To destroy both McKenney and the system Astor turned to his voice in the Senate, Thomas Hart Benton.

The Missouri senator not only unleashed a scurrilous campaign against the Indian Superintendent in Congress but also increased his efforts to abolish the office of the Indian Trade Bureau.

McKenney's "day of final consequences" came on April 10, 1822, when Benton forced through a resolution calling for a public hearing on the need for the Indian Trade Bureau and McKenney's administration. On the Senate floor Benton tore into McKenney with such savagery that even the most hardened of observers were shocked. At times he appeared on the very verge of calling McKenney a thief and a purveyor of contractors' kickbacks.[6]

He sneered at McKenney's "eight gross of Jew's harps, suited for a common country grocery store but never for the Indian country." He raked up McKenney's old business associates, the Halls from Pennsylvania Avenue and the Georgetown merchants with whom McKenney had marched to war against the British. With all his half-truths, lies, and twisted facts, Benton brought into play the thundering voice, his superb oratory, his memory for endless detail, the shouted innuendoes accompanied by the raised eyebrow, the cold, questioning sarcasm, and the broad ridicule—all the tricks which made him a favorite of the gallery.

McKenney, not a demonstrative man was filled with seething fury. The slurs and near-charges of fraud were too much. He wrote out a long statement in which he countered Benton's charges step by step. He had only one place to go, the press. Monroe, no stranger to Benton's savage oratory, was furious when he read the charges and may have given his approval to McKenney who turned to the pages of Washington's *National Intelligencer*.

McKenney's reply of April 22 took almost two columns; it was calm, lucid and biting.[7]

He detailed the items offered by his factories, pointing out the Jew's harps had been sent to the frontier "only because it was an item demanded by the Indians themselves." He explained he had inaugurated a new system which allowed each factor "to forward annually a list of supplies wanted for his trading post for this year."

> The annual call is always complied with, so far as the superintendent may be able to command the articles enumerated. It is then submitted to the public, which of the two Mr. Benton or the Indians is best acquainted with the needs and wishes of the latter.

Borrowing some of Benton's sarcasm, he added:

> If the Indians do call for the articles which Mr. Benton has asserted are "unknown to the Indian trade" then it is fair to infer that Mr. Benton is not correctly informed on the subject.

McKenney's one bitter note in his defense was directed at Ramsay Crooks who had testified before Benton's committee but had carefully avoided attacking McKenney's personal integrity. However, Crooks later wrote to Benton charging that McKenney had purchased inferior goods and inferred he was patronizing his old business friends in Georgetown.

Benton had made much of Crooks's information that "cut goods" were being sold instead of "whole goods." McKenney scoffed at this.

"It were strange if a business of twenty years did not accumulate some remnants. The existence of remnants at the factories is therefore admitted . . . it often happens that an entire piece of material is more than supply for any one factory, therefore it will serve three or four. When that is the case the piece is cut up into as many parts."

Another of Benton's charges was concerned with McKenney's purchase of shot at Georgetown for about eight and a half cents a pound; Benton told the Senate the same shot could be purchased for seven cents.

McKenney shattered Benton's information by producing a bill of sale submitted by James Kennerly, brother-in-law of General William Clark and Benton's friend. Kennerly charged the government for two hundred pounds of shot at eleven cents a pound. McKenney also revealed that if the shot had been purchased at St. Louis it would have to travel from Pittsburgh through wild sections of Indian country where there were no agencies or posts.

McKenney slyly noted that Kennerly was an old friend of Benton's but then added he was sure Kennerly "has an integrity which I have not the least reason to doubt."

Benton, he concluded, again was not "correctly informed."

As to gunpowder that Benton insisted could be bought in the West for western trade, McKenney submitted a whole series of orders from factors who stated the Indian nations demanded "Dupont powder."

"But let us compare the price," McKenney wrote, "with that found necessary to pay in St. Louis. For Dupont's best FF glazed rifle powder, I pay twenty-two cents a pound. I have a bill now before me, dated St. Louis, October 1, 1820, in which is a charge of four hundred pounds best gunpowder, at forty-five cents a pound . . ."

One of Benton's more vicious charges was that McKenney was profiting from deals he had made with his old Georgetown friends. The Indian Superintendent, citing long lists of bills, proved the Missouri Senator's accusations were without foundation. He also produced records of his bureau that shattered Benton's image of McKenney as an irresponsible spender of the taxpayers' money on "Indian presents." McKenney revealed the Indian Trade Bureau's budget was $50,185, far less than Benton's estimate of $165,611.

When McKenney finally appeared before the committee he demanded that his accusers be produced as witnesses who would be subject to his cross-examination but Benton refused. McKenney came well prepared; he introduced into evidence the affidavits he had collected from his former partners and Georgetown business friends, all swearing they had not done any business with McKenney in Indian trade goods since he had been appointed head of the Indian Trade Bureau. Some came to Washington to testify for McKenney and to tangle with the rough, bellowing Benton. The calm, dignified merchants proved to be a match for Astor's man in the Senate.

At the conclusion of the Senate hearings, McKenney made a long and impassioned summation to the committee and read a series of letters from his factors around the country confirming the quality of the goods the United States factories were selling to the Indian nations. He also read excerpts from his letter books revealing that items of Indian trade could not be found in New York or Philadelphia but only in the Georgetown market, simply because the Indian Trade Bureau had been transferred from Philadelphia to Georgetown after the War of 1812. In other words, merchants gathered at the selling point.

He scoffed at Benton's charge that no "auctions" had been held to rid the bureau of surplus goods. As Colonel McKenney wryly pointed out, who would attend an auction held in the middle of a wilderness? Once again records proved that inferior or damaged goods had been sold at cost at the posts of Green Bay, Prairie du Chien, and Chicago.[8]

From his extensive testimony and long summation, it is clear that the dignified McKenney only showed signs of anger when he answered Benton's hints that because McKenney maintained an estate in Georgetown on a small salary, he had to be corrupt.

Hundreds of thousands of dollars passed through his hands, McKenney told the committee, yet he challenged "anyone in the nation" to prove he had "kept a penny" for his own good.

McKenney clearly impressed the less hostile members of the committee but, despite his vigorous defense which was commended by President Monroe, the Indian Superintendent knew the days of his bureau and his own government career were coming to a close. Senate friends quietly informed him Benton was soliciting votes to approve a bill he had prepared to abolish the factory system of the United States.

McKenney's letter to Major Irwin in the summer of 1821 reveals his final, desperate plans to preserve the factory system in the West. He advised Irwin that he was "breaking up the trading houses at Green Bay and Chicago" and combining the stock of both posts to establish a new and larger factory on St. Peter's River.

"The government is not yet known in the exercise of its parental capacity in supplying the wants of the Indians in that region," he wrote Irwin. "In addition to the advantages the Indians will derive from the Factory, will be the active and abundant returns which will be received from it."

He gave as a reason for his drastic move "because hordes of private adventurers, availing themselves of the looseness of the [factory] system, have crowded into these parts [Chicago and Green Bay] on account of the superiority of the furs which are taken there, and [they] level all sorts of policy but their own, by the powerful agency which they derive from free use of spirituous liquors as an article of their commerce, and after which the Indians, however afflicting they know the consequences to be, will go."

McKenney's letter did not disclose to Irwin what was to become of him but in February 1822 he wrote Varnum in Chicago that his transfer to the new post at St. Peter's had been canceled, "as it is uncertain whether Congress will renew the law establishing trading houses with the Indian tribes . . ."[9]

McKenney's political intelligence was correct; Benton's campaign finally succeeded and on May 22, 1822, Congress abolished the Indian Trade Bureau and McKenney's post.

Ramsay Crooks jubilantly congratulated Benton "on your decisive victory . . . the result is the best possible proof of the value to the country of your talents, intelligence and perseverance." Benton humbly replied the Senate campaign had "cost me a strenuous exertion."[10]

McKenney had another version; in a letter to former President Madison he estimated Astor had spent "a capital of at least two million dollars" to drive him out of office and destroy the American factory system.

Private enterprise now took over in the form of Astor's American Fur Company. Congress self-righteously limited the issuance of trader's licenses, authorized the appointment of a superintendent in St. Louis, moved to restrict the whiskey trade, and established an accounting system for the fur trade.

The congressional restrictions proved to be at the best haphazard; Astor's agents issued licenses almost at will, whiskey flowed unchecked along the frontier, and the fur trade remained unbridled until 1834 when it was finally regulated. By that time Astor had wrung it dry for a profit of millions.

BOOK TWO

The Wilderness Ambassador

CHAPTER VIII:

The New Superintendent

———————◆•◆•◆———————

I.

AFTER HIS post had been abolished by Congress, Colonel McKenney's financial problems worsened. Probably to avoid embarrassment, he was borrowing, not from Washington friends but from his former Chicago factor, Jacob B. Varnum.[1]

During this period he kept in close touch with the Madisons, now in retirement at Montpelier, and supplied the former President with Washington gossip, political news, and copies of the latest legislative bills.

They corresponded frequently on the subject of Indian removal, and once at Madison's request McKenney sent him "documents connected with the communications of the late President [Jefferson] of the United States on the subject of locating the Indians, now within the State of Tennessee, west of the boundaries of Missouri and Arkansas..."

The slightest encounter in Washington with any member of the Madison clan was enough for McKenney to dispatch a note to Dolley advising her, for example, "your son-in-law as late as the day before yesterday, is well . . ."

McKenney also made sure Madison's name remained before the public; in a sense he had become the former President's public relations representative. Whenever Madison "made a talk" McKenney would forward a copy to the *National Intelligencer*, "with a few remarks of my own." There is little doubt that while McKenney sincerely admired Madison he was also aware that reflected greatness was valuable in official Washington.[2]

Within a short time after he had left the Indian Trade Bureau, McKenney was circulating a prospectus of the *Washington Republican and Congressional Examiner*, a semiweekly newspaper he planned to establish. He sent a copy of his prospectus to Jefferson at Monticello in July 1822. The third President of the United States, now seventy-nine, writing of himself in the third person, replied with a wry, delightful note that "age, debility and an aversion to politics, have for sometime withdrawn him from anything of that character. He reads but one newspaper and that of his own state and for the sake of advertisements, chiefly; giving preference to whatever will tranquilize, rather than disturb the quiet in which he wishes

to pass his remaining years. He salutes Mr. McKenney with respect..."[3]

A month later McKenney and a New York newspaperman, John Agg, put out the first number of the *Washington Republican and Congressional Examiner*. From its very inception the newspaper was an ardent supporter of John C. Calhoun as a candidate in the 1824 Presidential campaign, one of the most exciting in the nation's history. McKenney at the time was almost bankrupt; Calhoun certainly gave the newspaper financial support.

Almost every top-ranking statesman had thrown his beaver into the Presidential ring; the drumroll of candidates now sounds like a schoolboy reciting a roster of America's giants: John Quincy Adams, Daniel Webster, Henry Clay, William H. Crawford, William Lowndes, Andrew Jackson, and John C. Calhoun, who was sure the final race would be between himself, Adams, and Crawford. When Calhoun announced his candidacy, some of the older statesmen who had always hailed him with such superlatives as the youngest and most brilliant cabinet officer since Hamilton now began to hold his youth in question.

The army's men and officers, who had grown to admire Calhoun during his term as Monroe's Secretary of War, came to his aid. McKenney was quick to use their support in his editorials; Calhoun was "father of the army," "a brilliant strategist," a political genius with great "stability" of mind, "a brilliant star in America's political firmament."

The campaign of 1824 was bitter and dirty. Monroe's famous "era of good feeling" was swept aside by the incredible deluge of personal abuse against the Presidential candidates by the nation's press.

In Washington the popular *National Intelligencer* spoke for Clay and the *Gazette* was for Crawford. Only McKenney's semiweekly *Republican* was completely devoted to the candidacy of Calhoun. His editorial support appeared at a vital time, for the *Gazette*'s abuse of Calhoun had become so violent that even Adams, not a great admirer of the South Carolinian, was revolted by the "foulest abuse upon Calhoun personally."

Calhoun supplied the *Republican* with a great deal of

research revealing how Crawford's Treasury Department had been operated with waste and inefficiency; Crawford replied with personal abuse in the *Gazette,* even including Calhoun's mother-in-law.

In February 1824 Calhoun's forces suffered their first setback when the Philadelphia political leaders met to endorse a Presidential candidate. To Calhoun's and McKenney's dismay, the delegation endorsed Jackson. McKenney continued to keep his columns filled with Calhoun news: the handsome statesman sitting with Monroe— "at the side of the last of the cocked hats," as they said—in the luxurious Presidential barge, or escorting the legendary Lafayette on his triumphal tour of the United States. From Yorktown to Williamsburg, Calhoun was at the side of the aging Marquis, a fact which McKenney made sure was known to his readers.

The *Intelligencer* was vulnerable because of its position as the printer to Congress and McKenney kept up his editorial attack on the newspaper's patronage that went back to Madison's administration. The only reason why the *Intelligencer* was against Calhoun, McKenney trumpeted, was that its owners knew they would lose the government contract to record and publish the Congressional debates. McKenney evidently did some investigative reporting and uncovered the various sums the government had paid the *Intelligencer* for publishing the Congressional reports. The disclousures were impressive but the *Intelligencer* ignored its smaller semiweekly rival and continued its deadly editorial barrage against Calhoun, contemptuously reviewing his career from the first day he arrived at the capital.[4] The *Gazette,* meanwhile, denounced McKenney, who their editorials claimed had to be run out of office "by a special act of Congress" because of his dishonesty and mismanagement. The paper also questioned how McKenney, a Georgetown shopkeeper, could buy an estate like Weston.

Then Crawford was stricken and his campaign collapsed. But the elimination of Crawford failed to help Calhoun. At the age of forty-two he went down to defeat in Philadelphia when delegates to the state convention endorsed Jackson.

Calhoun was finished as a Presidential candidate but he was still Secretary of War and in a position to repay McKenney for his friendship and loyalty. In February 1824 he announced the formation of a new Bureau of Indian Affairs to be established within the War Department; its first Superintendent would be Thomas Loraine McKenney.

McKenney at the time had left the newspaper and was planning a trip to Mexico. When Calhoun informed him the annual salary would be $1,600, McKenney thanked him but refused. The salary, he told Calhoun, was not enough to support his family. There was another reason, McKenney's pride. Calhoun's staff was fixed by law; before he could appoint McKenney he had to have a vacancy. That came when his chief clerk, whose annual salary was $1,600, died. Although McKenney would be the Indian Superintendent, technically he was "chief clerk" of the new bureau.

After a meeting with Monroe, Calhoun returned to McKenney with a second offer: the President had promised he would recommend to Congress the establishment of a new Indian Bureau and the salary of its superintendent "would be equal to that of an auditor."[5]

McKenney agreed and on March 11, 1824, he was sworn in by Calhoun as the first Superintendent of the new Bureau of Indian Affairs. His official duties as outlined by the Secretary of War required him

to take charge of appropriations for annuities and current expenses and all warrants on the same to be issued to you on your requisitions to the Secretary of War, taking special care that no requisition be issued, but in cases where the money has been satisfactorily accounted for, and on estimates in detail approved by you, for the sum required. You will receive and examine the accounts and vouchers for the expenditure thereof and will pass them over to the proper auditor's office for settlement and examination and approval by you; submitting such items for the sanction of this department as may require its approval.

The administration of the funds for the civilization of the Indians, is also committed to your charge, under the regulations established by this [Department of War] office. You are also charged with the examination of the claims arising out of the laws regulating the intercourse with Indian tribes, and will, after examining and briefing the same, report them to this department, endorsing a recommendation for their allowance or disallowance. The ordinary correspondence with the superintendents, agents and sub-agents will pass through your Bureau . . .[6]

2.

IN FEBRUARY 1825 the House elected John Quincy Adams President and on March 4 Calhoun rose in the crowded Senate Chamber to announce he had "been called to the vice-presidency by my fellow citizens." The new President and the new Vice President were old friends of McKenney; the Superintendent of Indian Affairs now had impressive support in high places.

McKenney, an intense, dedicated man, spent the next year organizing his complex department. He worked to the utmost, mentally and physically. Year after year he was slowly enveloped in a regimen of constant hard work in which Washington's busy social life was only a muffled echo. Because the most intimate secrets of McKenney's family belong to him alone, we do not know what pleasures he enjoyed away from his beloved Indian Affairs Bureau. When spring was greening the hills about the city, did he walk along thawing, rutted Pennsylvania Avenue under the winter-darkened branches of budding yellow leaves no bigger than teardrops? Or join his wife, son, and neighbors in their Georgetown gardens at dusk when the lazy air was filled with the scent of new flowers? We do not know but what we do know is that McKenney was occupied with an incredible number of varied tasks which poured into the Indian Affairs Bureau. From his voluminous correspondence it appears as if every government bureau automatically sent on to him anything that mentioned Indians. As he liked to boast, "When addressed to the Secretary of War, all communications on Indian Affairs are referred to this Bureau."

Some of the fading, scribbled notes he received give a glimpse of a fascinating early frontier. William Scott,

Justice of the Peace of Logan County in Ohio, sent in a disposition from Robert Armstrong who could not sign it but had "made his mark," testifying that "in my early days" he had been "taken prisoner by the Indians and carried away with them and at various times [was] employed as an interpreter of their language" and would the government pay him for all those lost years of hardship and indignity?

Elizabeth, who also made her mark, once owned a small frontier trading post and wanted the government to reimburse her for the goods stolen by Indians. A last poignant sentence reveals a great deal of her times: "Many of the Indians are now dead and gone from these parts..."

Or the missionary from "the Cherokee Nation" who begged McKenney to have "a small hymn book and a few chapters from the New Testament" printed in Sequoyah's new Cherokee alphabet, "so it can be read by every Cherokee and would be considered by them a very great treasure..." This was later done and the books forwarded to the clergyman.[7]

In June 1825 McKenney, at the request of Secretary James Barbour, outlined his duties during a typical week. They included: trying to change the mind of a veteran and valuable Choctaw agent who wanted to return to the North; examining, cutting, and reorganizing bills submitted by hotelmen, livery stable operators, shopkeepers, and so on, for the care of Indian delegations who came to Washington; placating Indian agents when their bills were returned trimmed of what McKenney considered "unnecessary expenses"; ordering Indian presents; writing an analysis of the 1812 treaty between the Choctaw and the United States government for Congress; addressing an Indian delegation for seven hours; writing a "talk" for one of his agents who was to address an important council of the Creek; protesting a bill submitted by a Washington doctor who had treated a member of an Indian delegation; examining a warehouse of trade goods on their way to a frontier post; working on the annual "estimate" (budget) of Indian affairs; preparing the quarterly report of his department for the President; reading and answering each letter received by his department; preparing a report for The Committee on Indian Affairs; escorting an Indian delegation to the White House; planning an Indian census to be taken in the fall and writing the circular for all agents that would guide them in gathering vital statistics for that census which would include the number of Indians in each nation, village, band as well as the locations of towns, villages, and settlements and their distances from the Agency...[8]

The list went on and on. It was said that Barbour, after reading the list, was reportedly "left reeling" by the strenuousness of McKenney's schedule.

A case selected at random from his massive correspondence—at least one letter is forty pages long—reveals the enormous amount of paper work attached to his bureau: it involved a horse stolen from a Tuscarora warrior in New York State near the Canadian border. A tedious stream of letters and dispatches passed from the Iroquois agent to McKenney's office before a voucher was finally

approved, signed, and sent to the Indian who had insisted he could not work his fields until he received another horse from his Great Father.

Indian crimes from drunken assault to murder occupied McKenney's long days. Once he pleaded with Henry Clay, Adams's Secretary of State, to commute the death sentence "of Little Beaver, an unfortunate Indian as an act of mercy." Clay accepted his recommendations and the brave was released. Sometimes white men were surprisingly found guilty of crimes against Indians. In the spring of 1825, John Johnson, McKenney's agent at the Piqua Agency, forced the trial of three white men charged with the brutal murder of some Indians. After the trio was found guilty, Johnson informed McKenney he had arranged for fifty Indians to witness the triple execution "which indicated the character and justice of this country" in the minds of the tribes. McKenney replied to Johnson that he approved his actions.

Countless Indian claims from the Upper Missouri to Florida flowed across McKenney's desk. They could prove complex, wearisome, and sometimes maddening when lazy or incompetent agents simply accepted the statements of warriors or chiefs demanding damages and sent them on to Washington with recommendations that they be approved by McKenney and paid.

Superintendents also could be troublesome, even the legendary hero, General William Clark, whose constant carelessness forced McKenney to write a long tart note demanding the general examine claims "more carefully" before presenting them to the government.[9]

The question of black slaves who had escaped from Choctaw or Creek masters to Florida Territory to live with the Seminole—some bands gave them equality—became a delicate controversial matter in 1825 when John McIntosh, the Creek chief, demanded that Washington take action against the Seminole who refused to return runaway slaves. The War Department quickly turned the matter over to McKenney, who pointed out to McIntosh that the executive branch of the government had no power "to establish a rule of identity by which property situated as some of yours appears to be, can be restored to its rightful owner."[10]

Seminole warriors going to Cuba to sell slaves was another of McKenney's problems. In the summer of 1824 Florida's Governor Duval, with McKenney's approval, set up a post at Tampa Bay "to prevent any such intercourse with the Spaniards in the future."

3.

THE COMPLEX finances of the Bureau of Indian Affairs, particularly the preparation of budgets even for agencies on the far reaches of the Upper Missouri, plagued McKenney for all of his years in office. The bureau's annual disbursements amounted to more than $1,000,000. From 1825 to 1830 his yearly budgets ranged from $150,000 to $156,000. In the summer of 1825 he was writing to General Clark requesting his annual "estimate" and those of Indian agent Taliaferro now stationed among the wild tribes across the Mississippi. Clark, evidently delayed working out his budget for his western superintendency until the ultimate deadline. When it arrived McKenney was stunned by the increase in operating expenses and lack of detail.

He held a conference with Secretary of War Barbour, then sent a sharp reply to Clark demanding a revised estimate. Clark had just attended a huge council of western tribes during which he had negotiated several important treaties, and was in no mood for penny pinching. He ignored McKenney and replied directly to Barbour, charging McKenney with "casting reflections" on his "zeal and intelligence."

Barbour, who had no desire to test the notorious temper of the redheaded national hero, promptly ordered McKenney to answer Clark.

One can almost hear McKenney sigh as he started his reply. He knew that while it had to contain tact, diplomacy, and not a little flattery, it also had to persuade Clark to send in facts to support his budget. McKenney, who was still smarting from the mauling he had received from Senator Benton's committee three years before, was well aware of the vulnerability of the Indian Department.

"Every credit was given to both your zeal and your intelligence," McKenney informed the touchy Clark. "There was no reason for any apprehension to believe that you had procured those treaties from the Osage and Kansa at an expense which the government would find any hesitation in meeting. You were told *your bills would be paid*." (McKenney's emphasis)

McKenney patiently explained the mechanics of Washington politics to Clark; his budget had increased over the previous year and it is "necessary to have the reason for the increase, *for the information of Congress* should these reasons be called."

He then directed Clark "on orders of the Secretary of War" to have each agent on the Missouri fill out "a letter of reference" detailing the reasons for the increase of their annual budget "and your own recommendations for its allowance.

"This then will be the data upon which the Congress can receive information should the Committee, as is often the case, ask for the reasons for it . . . "

McKenney closed by assuring Clark of his "high estimate of your zeal and intelligence in the management of your Superintendency . . . "[11]

The letter apparently smoothed Clark's ruffled feathers. A few weeks later he revised his "estimate" and broke it down by departments, listing each increase and the reasons for it. But Clark and his haphazard estimates were only part of McKenney's annual struggle to get from Congress the necessary appropriations to operate the Office of Indian Affairs.

That November, on the orders of Barbour, he submitted his budget. Unlike his frontier superintendents, he supplied Barbour with detailed accounts of monies drawn from the Treasury for the first, second, and third quarters, how much had been settled by accounts and how much had to be accounted for.

A total of $780,827.24 had been drawn, $535,017.87 had been accounted for, with $245,809.37 remaining to be accounted.

McKenney proudly pointed out to Barbour that his statement contained the operations of thirty-eight schools operating in the nations with eleven hundred fifty-nine pupils.

"On comparing this with last year's report," he wrote, "it will be found that four new schools have been established, and the increase in the number of children is two hundred and forty-nine."

McKenney's report includes some fascinating details on the federal government's early nineteenth century activities in the deep West and its progress in persuading some of the Indian nations to yield their ancestral lands and move across the Mississippi.

He noted to Barbour that his department was now following two Congressional directives, one of May 25, 1824, that treaties made with the wild tribes beyond the Mississippi be "for the establishment of peace," and the second of March 3, 1825, authorizing the President to "mark out a road" from the western frontier of Missouri to New Mexico and to "negotiate treaties with the tribes for the purpose of obtaining their permission for the marking of this road and the unmolested use, thereof, by the citizens of the United States and the Mexican Republic."

The Indian Superintendent included a partial report of General Atkinson and Indian agent O'Fallon who had escorted the large Indian delegation to Washington in the winter of 1821. He had been selected by the War Department the previous year to chart the road under McKenney's supervision.

Colonel McKenney informed Barbour that only two days before (November 28, 1825) he had received a report from Atkinson and O'Fallon that they had reached Fort Atkinson on the Missouri "after having penetrated the country as far as the Two Thousand Mile Creek, and fully accomplished so far, the objects of their commission. It only remained for them to treat with a few tribes, in which they expect to accomplish in twelve days, when they were to descend to St. Louis and report more in detail . . . it is understood that General Atkinson is on his way to this city bringing with him the Treaties . . . "

McKenney also reported to Barbour that Clark and Governor Cass had successfully mediated the boundary disputes between the Sioux, Sauk, Fox, Chippewa, Iowa, Menominee, and Winnebago tribes and "in this work of mercy these two Commissioners have been successful. The long and bloody wars have been terminated."

Three newly appointed commissioners, Reeves, Sibley, and Mathew—the names to become famous in frontier history—assigned by McKenney to lay out the new road to New Mexico were already in the interior, McKenney wrote, and "engaged in the performance of obtaining treaties with the intervening Indian Tribes."

The ticklish problems of the Shawnee claims for land they had exchanged for their ancestral tract at Cape Girardeau in Missouri had also been settled by Clark, McKenney revealed. The Shawnee had been at war for years with the

Osage and their allies, the Kansa, and McKenney informed Barbour that Clark had the difficult assignment of getting them to give up their titles to the land assigned to the Shawnee. But the Osage and Kansa had refused, and for a time Osage raiding parties were burning Shawnee villages and collecting prisoners.

Clark, after a series of councils, had finally persuaded the Osage and Kansa "to smoke a pipe" with the Shawnee and, at least for a time, an uneasy peace had settled over the frontier.

McKenney was always conscious of the menacing shadow of Indian removal which hung over his office, the War Department, Congress, and the White House. As he advised Barbour, Clark had negotiated the treaties

following up the view of the Executive, for providing a country for such tribes of Indians that may think proper to immigrate and join their friends in the West, but especially to secure a country for the Creek in pursuance of the obligation of the general Government in its compact with Georgia, the commissioner very judiciously embraced in his negotiations for the accommodation of the Shawnee, at that meeting, an extinguishment of the Indian Titles to three or four million acres of land in Missouri and Arkansas, and nearly one hundred million acres beyond the western boundaries of Missouri and Arkansas.

Reservations are secured to the Osages and Kanzas [Kansa] to the first tract of fifty miles front, parallel to and about twenty-five miles west of the Western Boundary of the Missouri, and to the Kanzas a tract of thirty miles front, parallel also to the Western Boundary of the Missouri and about fifty miles west of it; both running back to the Spanish Line.

"A judicious arrangement of land had been made between both Nations," McKenney added.

As he proudly noted:

Thus, all titles to Indian lands within Missouri, except for a few reservations have been extinguished, and a country represented to be fertile, and in all respects, desirable, provided within sufficient extent beyond the boundaries of Missouri and Arkansas for the accommodations of all the tribes within the States, which, should they incline to occupy it, it is the policy of the government to guarantee to them lasting and undisturbed possession.

McKenney also reported that many of the tribes were considering moving to lands in the West where they would no longer be encircled by the whites. The Shawnee and Cherokee of the Arkansas, who had visited the Indian lands in the West in February, "believe, that if they can hold councils with their friends in Ohio, Indiana, and Illinois, they could induce them to immigrate and join them on their possessions in the West. This was the great object of their visit, directions were issued to Governor Cass to meet them at Wapaghkonetto in Ohio, but nothing was accomplished except, that deputations of some of the tribes intend, in the following Spring, to meet their brothers in the West. It is probable that the object of that meeting may in the course of the next year, be in part at least realized."

The Quapaw (a southwestern Siouan tribe), he wrote, will start their "removal" from their ancestral homes on the Arkansas to the Red River country conforming to the terms of the November 15, 1824, treaty, while in the coming January the Choctaw would begin to leave their lands for the West.

In McKenney's long and detailed "estimate" it is significant that the budget for the "civilization of Indians" was $11,032.90 as compared to the $43,318.19 for the Indian agents' payroll, and the $18,728 for "Indian presents."[12] The finances of the Indian Bureau were a favorite target for McKenney's old enemy in the Senate, Thomas Hart Benton. In April 1826 Benton demanded that the Indian Superintendent list every Indian annuity from the date of the treaty, the names of the tribes, and the amounts they had received from 1804 to 1826. It was a monumental task but the conscientious McKenney prepared the material and sent it to Benton.[13]

A short time later Benton, through Secretary of War Barbour, was after McKenney with a request for a financial survey of all monies paid "in relationship with the tribes for the years 1824–1825." McKenney again assigned the few clerks in his office to dig into the official records of his bureau and then sent the report to Benton.

The Missouri Senator continued to harass McKenney with demands for reports, some going back to Jefferson's administration, details of treaties, annuity payments, cost of maintaining frontier agencies, expenses for bringing Indian delegations to Washington and entertaining them, Indian presents, and copies of ration contracts.

The weary but unruffled McKenney carefully gathered the facts Benton demanded and sent them to the Senate. As he wryly observed, Benton and the government auditing bureau knew how every penny his office had been spent, "down to the nail that is driven in an Indian coffin."

4.

McKENNEY's INDIAN portrait gallery and his "archives" continued to be his whole life. Soon after he had been appointed by Calhoun in 1824, he was writing to missionaries, Indian agents, and superintendents like Clark and Cass to send him books, manuscripts, and original journals, "with the view of preserving in the archives of the Government whatever of the aboriginal man can be rescued from the destruction which awaits his race."

McKenney also helped former Treasury Secretary Albert Gallatin with his celebrated work on the American Indian. From 1827 to 1829 he requested missionaries to send him "an Alphabet or a Grammar, and as far as you may be able, a chapter on some subject in the language of the tribe or tribes among whom you and your associates are located." During the years there was a steady flow of Sauk, Cherokee, Shawnee, Osage, Choctaw vocabularies into the Indian Bureau. Some were extensive, others simply a listing of words. He also asked his agents to send him examples of fine Indian oratory, and herbs, roots, and plants medicine men used to treat their patients.[14]

His library continued to grow. Book dealers in New York, Philadelphia, Baltimore, and Boston found him an enthusiastic collector of any books "as relate to the Aborigines of the Country and are deemed to be standard histories —Memoirs—Travels—& such as Heckewelders, Hunters,

Longs, Schoolcrafts—&c &c [sic]—and any theories of the Origin of the Indians; also such works as relate to the Geology of the Western Country."

However, it was the gallery of Indian portraits that was his particular pride. Every visitor was given a tour of the collection and told a story about each painting. In later years Nicholas Biddle, the financier and litterateur, recalled for Daniel Webster how he had met McKenney in his office "surrounded by uncouth portraits of savages of both sexes, whose merits he explained with as much unction as a Roman Cicerone—how nearly extremes touch when so civilized a gentleman was in contact with so wild & aboriginal a set . . . "

The archives and Indian portrait gallery were now part of the Bureau of Indian Affairs in the old War Department Building on Seventeenth Street and Pennsylvania Avenue, a short distance west of the White House.

McKenney's office was on the second floor. The carpet was worn and the drafty fireplace often filled the rooms with smoke. It took McKenney two years to get a new carpet and a potbelly stove. Glass cases containing his Indian artifacts lined the walls. There were pipes, moccasins, British peace medals, arrows, bows, baskets, fringed buckskin leggings, books, journals, manuscripts, and of course row after row of the grim-faced warriors and chiefs who had visited their Great Father. The proper atmosphere was suggested by a large birchbark which hung over the front door.

Apparently it became known on the frontier that McKenney was collecting anything to do with Indian culture; there was always a letter from an old frontiersman offering a "manuscript" or "a journal" of Indian captivity or a missionary with "a scholarly work on the tribes."[15]

The long hours, pressure, and responsibility finally took their toll of his health. As he recalled, "I would have died at my post" had not President Adams and Secretary of War Barbour selected him in 1826 for an important mission to the distant frontier.

CHAPTER IX:

The Augustic Treaties

I.

In the winter and early spring of 1826 when Colonel McKenney received his first Presidential mission to the western frontier, the problem of Indian removal haunted the halls of Congress and the executive branch like a brooding specter whose presence was an omen of evil days to come.

The events that troubled the America of the 1820s did not happen overnight but were the culmination of years of treachery and double-dealing between state and federal government in which the Indian nations were tragic pawns. Before the year ended McKenney traveled seven thousand miles on horseback, canalboat, steamboat, stagecoach, and by canoe to negotiate treaties with the tribes in the south and northwest, agreements that would influence the shape of the frontier for generations. Ironically his reward was the same ingratitude that was so commonplace to the Indian nations, north, south, east, and west.

From Jefferson's administration the question of uprooting the tribes from their homelands had simmered beneath Washington's political surface, only occasionally erupting, then slowly cooling as the Presidents and Congress watched uneasily.

In the dying months of Monroe's administration, Secretary of War Calhoun, under pressure from Georgia, appointed James Meriwether and Duncan G. Campbell of Georgia as Indian Commissioners to negotiate with the Creek on plans "for extinction of all titles to their lands" and for the removal west of the Mississippi.[1]

John Ross, the great Cherokee leader—he was one eighth Indian—campaigned among the Creek chiefs advising them to oppose the Georgia commissioners and to join the Cherokee in fighting Washington. For the first time since their homelands were threatened, two Indian nations united in fighting off the white man. Meriwether and Campbell reported back to Washington they had been unsuccessful but they advised Calhoun they had found a weak link in the chain of chiefs who had barred their path—William McIntosh, the Creek half-breed. Son of a Scotch trader and a Creek woman, McIntosh lived on the Chattahoochee River with two wives, one a Creek the other a Cherokee. He also maintained a plantation forty miles away on the

west branch of the Tallapoosa with another wife.

He was known to be a "white man's chief" and had signed away Creek lands in 1821 in a treaty negotiated by a group of Georgia citizens acting as representatives of the United States. Thirty-eight other chiefs who were present at that council had refused to sign. In a series of thundering angry speeches they pointed out to the commissioners the fraud and deceit in the negotiations; the white men were dealing with only a tenth of the nation in defiance of their ancient tribal law that required the consent of the entire nation assembled in council.

McIntosh ignored the protests of the other chiefs and signed. Two years later when he attempted to sign away more land, the Creek council passed a law that any chief who yielded Creek land would be punished by death. By this time McIntosh had signed away fifteen million acres of land; ten million more remained in the possession of the Creek Nation.

In the winter of 1825 Meriwether and Campbell returned to the Creek country with $50,000 "for presents" to deal with McIntosh and a small group of his followers. Their sordid formula of divide and conquer would be repeated again and again in the federal government's dealings with the Indian nations for over a half century; select the weakest chief and through bribery, flattery, or persuasion get him and his followers to sign the treaty desired by the United States.[2]

The commissioners called a council at Indian Springs in the winter of 1825 which was attended by McIntosh, forty of his followers described as "chiefs of inferior rank," and Creek leaders who represented the majority of the nation. It is to Calhoun's credit that he warned the commissioners a treaty signed alone by McIntosh would not be respected; all the chiefs had to sign.

It was an explosive council. Tuckhabatchee, an important chief, bitterly told the commissioners:

"You asked us to sell more land at Broken Arrow [a previous council] and we told you then we had none to spare. I told McIntosh at that time that he knew no land could be sold except in full council and by consent of the Creek Nation."

The chief added coldly: "We have met here at a short notice, only a few chiefs are present from the Upper Towns; many are absent from the Lower Towns. That's all the talk I have to make and now I shall go home."

Another chief bluntly warned McIntosh he would be killed if he signed any treaty. Despite this warning McIntosh and the lesser chiefs signed what would be known as the Treaty of Indian Springs, one of the more infamous agreements entered into between the United States and the Indian nation. It is obvious from the letters of the commissioners and McIntosh that bribery was resorted to.

The exultant commissioners hurried back to Washington but Calhoun, who had been warned by McKenney, was disturbed; John Crowell, the Creek agent, had alerted the Indian Superintendent that the Creek chiefs were outraged and if the treaty was accepted by Washington violence could be expected.

Monroe, who explained he didn't want President-elect John Quincy Adams to be "burdened" with the treaty sent it directly to Congress where it was ratified in shockingly short time. When the news reached the Creek their council appointed an execution squad headed by Major Ridge who killed McIntosh and some of the other chiefs who had signed the treaty. Ridge was to suffer the same fate years later, over another treaty.[3]

The tragedy excited the frontier and Georgia's Governor Troup threatened to send soldiers into the Creek country. However, President Adams, convinced of the fraud, promised the Creek chiefs a new treaty.

There was also trouble in the West. Lewis Cass, the able governor of Michigan Territory, had met with the Shawnee at Wapaghkonetta, Ohio. Like the southern tribes they refused to yield up their lands and move across the Mississippi.[4]

Then the news spread along the frontier with the speed of a grass fire fanned by a hot summer wind—a Chippewa war party had killed and scalped a family of four on Lake Pepin.

Secretary of War James Barbour ordered McKenney to inform Cass that the Indian murderers must surrender or troops would be sent to capture them.

Cass received McKenney's dispatches in Detroit and left on June 14, 1825, for Prairie du Chien in Crawford County, Wisconsin, to attend a major council of nine western Indian nations; the purpose was to settle tribal feuds, fix boundaries, establish what Washington hoped would be a lasting peace, and demand that the Chippewa turn over the Lake Pepin war party.

This time he was accompanied by his friend James Otto Lewis, a young Detroit artist, engraver, and printer. Lewis, the first artist in the Michigan Territory, was a member of the tightly knit group of early pioneering Detroit residents who supported Governor Cass politically and knew him socially.

Lewis was descended from a well-known German frontier family named Ludewig, from Swabia. His father, John Andreas Philip Ludewig, emigrated to Philadelphia in 1784 and anglicized his name. He married Sophia Pelletier, granddaughter of John B. Pelletier, a family connected with Detroit almost from its founding and they had seven children. James Otto Lewis was born in Detroit, February 3, 1799.

He ran away to enlist in the army and saw action as a boy in the Battle of Schuylerville. He later joined the militia to fight the Sauk and Fox in the Black Hawk War.

George B. Catlin gives Lewis credit for designing the Seal of Detroit.

"Lewis was never a man to hide his light under a bushel and let it be known that he was an all-round artist and a nifty engraver who was eager to prove his skill," Catlin wrote. "After inspecting Lewis's beautiful, engrossing penmanship the mayor and city council of Detroit commissioned him to design and engrave the city's first official seal."

Lewis soon became friendly with Governor Cass, probably through Thomas Palmer, Detroit's famous pioneer merchant. His nephew, Friend Palmer, who also knew Lewis, recalled in later years that Lewis was a frequent visitor to the governor's house where he painted Cass's official portrait. The engraving from the painting by Lewis was used by Cass in his presidential campaign.[5]

Lewis was present with Cass, General Clark, McKenney, and Henry Rowe Schoolcraft at all the major Indian councils held in the northwest in the 1820s and 1830s. He appears to be the unsung hero of McKenney's famous Indian gallery. He submitted over forty watercolors to the Indian Superintendent which were in turn copied by the more polished Charles Bird King.

Lewis did not possess the artistic background of King who had studied in London under the distinguished Benjamin West but he had accomplished three major objectives which were beyond the desire or ability of King: he had witnessed history in the making and had not only recorded but participated in it—he was a witness to the great Fond du Lac treaty of 1826.

Ironically King, who had never seen an Indian outside of his Washington studio, gained a lasting, international reputation from his Indian portraits while Lewis, the man who "painted them on the spot," as he boasted, lived out his life in comparative obscurity in Detroit.

The winter before the Prairie du Chien council, Cass had sent to McKenney a portrait of Tecumseh's brother, The Prophet, painted by Lewis during the Shawnee's visit to Detroit. In an accompanying letter Cass had suggested to McKenney that the Indian Bureau give Lewis a fund of two hundred dollars to paint portraits for the Indian Gallery of famous or colorful Indians who might visit the city. McKenney enthusiastically agreed but suggested that Lewis enlarge his watercolor sketches to 17½ by 14 inches to match the size of the other paintings.

Cass's idea struck sparks with McKenney. He wrote to Florida Territorial Governor William DuVal for portraits "of a few of your distinguished Indian chiefs, which should be taken in the costume of their respective tribes . . . " He also requested DuVal to have the paintings made the same size as the other oils in his gallery.[6]

Cass, Lewis, and General Clark arrived at Mackinac on June 25, 1825, where they were met by Schoolcraft.

Albert Gallatin
whom McKenney aided in his scientific
research on Indians in the 1820's.

Senator John Randolph of Virginia
Brilliant eccentric who defended McKenney in Congress

Thomas Jefferson

John Quincy Adams

Thomas Hart Benton
A bitter enemy of McKenney.

Henry Clay
Friend of McKenney's in the 1840's.

Schoolcraft had good news for Cass; warned by traders that the Dragoons would come upriver, the Chippewa chiefs had turned over the killers of the Lake Pepin settlers to him. They were now waiting trial.[7]

The Prairie du Chien council held in July 1825 was extraordinary for one feature—the United States did not demand land concessions. Cass told the chiefs:

"We tell you again the Great Father does not want your land. He wants you to establish boundaries among you . . . the peace to be made must be a solid one . . . "[8]

It was one of the longest councils in the history of the frontier; talks went on for more than a month. Cass was friendly but he was also firm when some of the chiefs hinted they would rather fight the white man than listen to his words. The governor's warning was blunt and arrogant:

"The President of the United States will suffer no other war drums but his own to be heard throughout his extensive territories and henceforth your wars shall and must cease . . . "

The treaty was finally signed on August 19, 1825, with Cass dumping kegs of whiskey on the ground and warning the chiefs he would arrest any peddler caught in the Indian country.[9]

Lewis returned to Detroit with several striking portraits of chiefs, warriors, and orators including the celebrated Sioux chief Little Crow, whose great-grandson would be held responsible for the so-called "Minnesota Massacre" during the Civil War. He sent them to Washington to be copied by King.

That winter Cass came to the capital to discuss with President Adams, Secretary of War Barbour, and Colonel McKenney the Indian treaties he had concluded and the growing importance of Indian removal.

One afternoon Cass and McKenney toured the gallery of portraits now lining the walls of the Bureau of Indian Affairs. Cass, who had been in the Indian back country for years, knew many of the chiefs and warriors whose paintings he saw. He was known as a vivid storyteller and it would be fascinating to know some of the anecdotes he told as they walked slowly about the rooms. But Indian portraits were only a footnote to the momentous meetings held in Washington during Cass's visit; there was a crisis over the Indian Springs Treaty, and President Adams, who valued the Michigan governor's experience with the nations, asked him to consult with McKenney and write a new treaty.

Cass agreed and within a few months a delegation of Creek arrived in Washington to sign the new treaty which declared the Indian Springs agreement null and void.

Another question plagued them all that winter. The wealth of minerals in the western Indian lands was a glowing prize all Washington coveted.[10]

Copper deposits particularly had been part of the 1820 reports Cass and Schoolcraft had made of their Michigan Territory explorations; they had found and inspected a large mass of copper that frontiersmen called "The Ontonagon Boulder" on the Ontonagon River. Generations of

Indians had chipped pieces from it for cooking utensils and arrow barbs.

When Schoolcraft's *Narrative* focused the public's attention on the mineral wealth in the region, the frontier newspapers were filled with details of mines and deposits. As the *Detroit Gazette* solemnly declared in the winter of 1825, "copper is an article in building our navy, and we ought not to be dependent on foreign countries for a supply of it."[11]

The Senate formally requested that an examination be made of the Lake Superior copper deposits and which Indian Nations owned them. After Schoolcraft made this report, Senator Benton brutally suggested that Indian claims be "extinguished" and the government take over the lands.

Cass, who knew how fragile was the peace he had helped to bring to the frontier, soothed Benton's copper fever with the explanation that there were not sufficient deposits large enough to warrant extensive mining equipment. In the winter of 1825 Benton, now a fervent mineral advocate as well as the Senate spokesman for Astor's American Fur Company, had the Senate pass a bill giving the Indian Commissioners permission to search for copper in the Lake Superior region. The bill failed to pass the House but Benton managed to get approval of a $10,000 appropriation "to hold talks" with the Chippewa on the subject of minerals.[12]

In May 1826 President Adams appointed McKenney and Cass as joint Indian Commissioners to hold a major treaty council of the western nations at Fond du Lac on the St. Louis River, Michigan Territory (now northeastern Minnesota).

It was a time when the nerves of the frontier were taut. The garrison at Mackinac reported the Lake Pepin murderers had escaped, and McKenney's agents warned him the war-loving Winnebago were meeting in councils with their allies; their goal was total war against the whites.

When he heard the reports Barbour was incensed. To impress the Indian nations "with some proper conception of our power," he wrote McKenney, he was ordering a military force to accompany them to Fond du Lac.

The main goals of the council were to be: the recapture of the prisoners; to gain approval of the tribal boundaries set at the Prairie du Chien meeting; to gain permission from the Chippewa for geologists to search for mineral deposits along the shores of Lake Superior; and to project the image of a militarily powerful United States to the Winnebago and their allies to prevent an Indian war.[13]

2.

COLONEL MCKENNEY'S companion from Washington on his first trip to the Western frontier was Ben, a black man. In his memoirs, McKenney never referred to him as a "slave" but always as "my servant" or "my companion."

The Indian Superintendent's glacial stare stopped any racial slurs; he once refused to let Ben be assigned to a precarious perch on the luggage rack of a stagecoach and on another occasion had two drunken drivers removed from a stage so Ben could be given a seat. McKenney's letters, journals, and memoirs do not reveal much about Ben. He once called him "a muscular, middle-aged man" —but we do know he didn't share the colonel's enthusiasm for Indians and their way of life. Although he was suspicious of all tribes, he refused to be intimidated by their play-acting whoops or evilly painted faces. After two warriors had unsuccessfully tried to frighten him by leaping out of a bush, Ben laconically observed that "the next time I just might blow a hole through them."

Ben, who stayed with McKenney for many years, was very protective of his colonel. He not only pampered him with favorite foods but also made sure the sometimes absentminded Indian Superintendent wore the proper clothing, reminded him of appointments, casually contributed earthy advice, warded off unwelcome visitors, and sought out the choicest bits of political gossip from the White House or Senate help.

McKenney and Ben left Washington on the 6 A.M. Baltimore stage, June 1, 1826. From there a steamboat delivered them to Frenchtown, New Jersey, where another stage "crossed the Jerseys" to New York City. A Hudson River steamboat took them to Albany; Utica was reached by a horse-drawn Erie canalboat. A crowded mail coach transported them to Auburn, New York. During this part of the journey McKenney got into a warm discussion with a missionary who objected to the government's Indian removal policy and advocated keeping the nations on their ancestral lands and turning them into farmers.

As the packed coach lurched along the rutted dusty roads, McKenney lectured the intently interested passengers on the government's Indian policy. He pointed out that plows had been introduced to the Indian tribes a long time ago by his Indian department but the rapidly advancing tide of the white man's civilization now endangered the Indian nations and their culture.

"The plan of the Secretary [Barbour]," he told the missionary and the passengers, "embraces what you say and more. The only difference seems to be in the application of these means upon lands that it is proposed to make theirs forever . . . lands, education, implements of husbandry, domestic animals, and added to all these, protection from their enemies, white or red with a permanent and enduring home, where their facilities may continue to expand with the hope that their future generations will flourish . . . "

It sounded all very glorious and the passengers were enchanted. McKenney sincerely believed in his nation's honor and had a strong desire to protect the Indian tribes but in his lifetime he would see that honor tarnished and that sincerity dissipated by crooked, cruel politicians and the avarice of his countrymen.

3.

FROM BUFFALO a steamboat took McKenney and Ben to Detroit in the Michigan Territory. On the morning of

June 16 they caught their first glimpse of the five spires of the city's famous Ste. Anne's Roman Catholic Church; moments later they were greeted by Major Robert A. Forsyth, personal secretary to Cass and a well-known frontier scout.

McKenney stayed at the executive "mansion," a clapboard house that still showed bullet holes made by Pontiac's warriors. In the cluttered office of Governor Cass they planned their expedition to the land of the Chippewa. He would always recall the piles of frontier newspapers, pamphlets, and the walls covered with peace pipes, bows and arrows, headdresses, medals, tomahawks, and snowshoes. There would be several barges for the sixty-two Dragoons and officers of the 2nd Infantry Regiment, two schooners, *Ghent* and *Young Tiger*, for provisions and supplies, and several birchbarks with crews of voyageurs, those incredible paddlers of the northwest.

Mrs. Cass made McKenney a present of a sleeping bag made of two Mackinac blankets, a roll of oilcloth for the dampness, "two nice sheets," and an indispensable mosquito netting.

They were delayed by the late delivery of the canoes so the enthusiastic McKenney toured the countryside on horseback, collecting "curiosities" from an Indian mound for his archives and interviewing survivors of the Indian and Revolutionary wars and the War of 1812. He was ecstatic when Major Forsyth promised him an ancient Indian skull that had been found many years before.

"It will be excellent for the students of phrenology," he wrote that night to Barbour.

Before the expedition was finished, bales and boxes of Indian costumes, bones, jewelry, beadwork, pipes, medals, tomahawks, and weapons, including a Chippewa deerskin dress, a collection that today would be priceless, had been sent back to Washington.

There were days when he overtaxed his frail health and the worried Cass wondered if it would be wise for him to continue on into the wilderness but McKenney waved away his protests and informed Cass he would rather die in the forest than behind a desk in Washington.

McKenney's daily letters also reveal a fascinating, early Detroit, the last outpost before the wild Indian country. He reported visiting the main thoroughfare, Jefferson Street, a statehouse, "a few brick buildings," and the fort commanded by the ill-fated General William Hull during the War of 1812. Lewis gave McKenney a map of the city which he used to explore the streets and surrounding districts. He wrote prophetically:

> I entertain the kindest feelings towards him [the architect of Detroit] but I think for his sake, that it never should have been conceived by him. It looks pretty on paper but it is fanciful; and resembles one of those octagonal spider webs which you see on a dewy morning with a center and lines leading out to the points round the circumference and fastened to spires of grass . . . the citizens of Detroit would do well, in my opinion, and their posterity would thank them for it, were they to reduce the network of that plan to something more practical and regular . . .

The expedition finally left Detroit on the morning of June 23. Aboard the *Ghent* with McKenney and Cass were

Colonel George Croghan, the frontiersman; Richard Connor, a celebrated Detroit Indian trader and interpreter for the council; A. Edwards, secretary for the council; George F. Porter, a government geologist; and the artist James Otto Lewis. As he stood on the deck of the *Ghent* and watched the spires of Ste. Anne's slowly fade away in the distance, McKenney felt apprehensive, but he shook off his fears by an hour's reading of Cowper's poems and the excitement of dragging in "eight fine bass and a pickerel." The star-shot night was so calm and beautiful he decided to sleep on deck, so he rolled himself into the folds of the mainsail and slept like a drugged man until dawn.

On legendary Drummond's Island, the last remaining British outpost on the frontier, McKenney witnessed for the first time what whiskey had done to the American Indian.

They landed in the early hours of the morning to be greeted by a long line of wavering torches, wild cries, whoops, and scattered musketry. At first he was puzzled, then in the glare of the flickering, garish light he saw the reeling, staggering, drunken warriors falling into bushes, crawling along the road, or shaking their arms in a frenzy, the silver bells attached to their wrists making a grotesque tinkling background music to the shrieks, gunfire, wild laughter, and howling gibberish.

In the morning McKenney sadly counted the empty whiskey barrels; there were seventeen. He later learned the Indians had traded the blankets, kettles, tomahawks, rifles, and ornaments they had received the day before from the British at the fort to the whiskey peddlers for a cup at a time of the raw colored alcohol.

By the time they reached the Sault, McKenney was at home in the thiry-foot canoe and could join the voyageurs as they sent the light craft skimming across Superior's long heaving swells.

As they passed St. Joseph's Island, Croghan described for McKenney how he had destroyed the British ammunition depot during the War of 1812 and pointed out the stark white stone chimneys, all that was left of the famous post. Then they entered St. Mary's River, to ride the savage Nibish Rapids. They reached Sault St. Marie to the booming of the garrison's guns celebrating Independence Day.

Croghan asked McKenney, that old soldier, to assist him in an inspection of the troops. Guided by a veteran noncom who bore powder stains on his face "from a sortie on the Erie," they went through the barracks "to examine every kettle, knife and spoon."

McKenney also spent a great deal of time with Jane Johnson Schoolcraft, wife of the ethnologist and explorer and daughter of the famous John Johnson, the colorful squaw man of the early northwestern frontier. The Johnsons had a strong influence over the tribes and a few years before at a council had prevented an infuriated chief from murdering Cass. When McKenney met Johnson he was sixty-four and feeble. Johnson's wife fascinated the Indian Superintendent. She wore a Chippewa costume, deerskin leggings, and beaded moccasins. She had high cheekbones and penetrating black eyes. Although she understood and

could write English, she spoke only in Chippewa. More than once, Cass told McKenney, she had persuaded the Chippewa not to wage war against the whites. She had been educated in Europe and her daughter, Mrs. Schoolcraft, had attended private schools.

On McKenney's orders Lewis sketched her and, as McKenney wrote Barbour, "he has been happy in catching the spirit as well as the form of her face."

McKenney talked at length with Mrs. Schoolcraft about the culture of the northwest tribes and evidently made many notes, at one point copying war chants and courtship songs both in Chippewa and English translations.

Mrs. Johnson also helped McKenney collect plants, Indian medicinal root specimens, and "mohocks"—small wicker baskets—of native maple sugar which he reported to Barbour "is as white as the Havana sugar and richer." He also made a listing of winter, spring, summer, and fall temperatures which showed that on January 29, 1825, the mercury had "stayed in the bulb" at 25° below zero and snow fell as late as April and as deep as twenty-seven inches. He had Lewis make sketches of the Indian snowshoe, dog travois, and sleds and a white fisher or Wa-ba-jick, a species of marten, which Johnson had skinned and given to McKenney for his museum. Before he left, Mrs. Schoolcraft made McKenney a shoulder-length veil of green gauze and thick buckskin gloves to ward off the terrifying hordes of mosquitoes and blackflies.

Without his veil, gloves, and the sleeping net given to him by Mrs. Cass, McKenney wrote, it would have been impossible for him to go on. The Dragoons suffered terribly in the woods; in the morning their eyes were slits and their faces swollen and covered with blood.

By mid-July they were deep into the Lake Superior wilderness; McKenney insisted on exploring everything —lakes, bays, and coves. He put Lewis in his canoe and had the artist sketching from dawn to dusk. Cass, he found, was "a man of all energy who can go to sleep in less time than he can turn over." The governor kept sending out runners to the chiefs and nations, conferring with McKenney on the details of the pending council, studying Lewis's sketches, climbing high points to survey the lake and shores, and constantly inspecting the troops, supplies, and canoes in between studying the weather.

The rugged days improved McKenney's health. With Ben, Lewis, or some of the voyageurs he explored the shoreline and interior, gathering herbs, flowers, or plants or bartering with passing Indians for their ornaments, weapons, or parts of clothing.

On the afternoon of Thursday, July 27 McKenney's canoe reached the sandy beach, the *fond* or bottom of Lake Superior and the entrance of the St. Louis River. After holding a council with the Fond du Lac band, McKenney sent a runner back to Cass on the *Young Tiger*, a day's journey behind them. He also wrote a report for Barbour in which he made a schedule of the miles he had canoed from Sault Ste. Marie; there were still twenty-four miles more to travel up the river to the council meeting site or a grand total of five hundred fifty-three miles. From Washington he and Ben had covered two thousand miles by stagecoach, steamboat, canalboat, schooner, and birch-bark canoe.[14]

4.

THE COUNCIL opened on the morning of August 2, with the expedition approaching the site "in squadron" as Cass had suggested. McKenney's canoe was in the lead, the governor's barge followed, then came a fleet of canoes and the barges loaded to the gunwales with Dragoons. McKenney recalled the line stretched along the river for almost a quarter of a mile. Flags rippled in the warm breeze and the regiment band crashed into "Yankee Doodle" as Indian canoes shot out from the beach like swarms of waterbugs. The shoreline in front of the stockaded American Fur Company post was thick with painted Indians who watched silently as the line of boats, barges, and canoes swung out into a wide line and moved toward them like an invasion fleet. McKenney's canoe ground up on the rocky beach and he stepped out as the hills and valleys reechoed to "Hail Columbia." The fur company's small six pounder crashed in salute and the greasy black powder smoke hung like a haze over the pointed log palisade.

The first Indian to step out of the closely packed lines of stone-faced red men made McKenney feel at home; it was a chief he had met a few years before in Washington. The Indian held up his hand in a sign of peace and called out: "Washigton . . . Washington . . ."

McKenney shook hands with the chief and nodded to Lewis but the artist had already started to sketch.

5.

THE FOND du Lac council lasted for eight days. It ran smoothly until McKenney brought up the government's demand for the surrender of the escaped prisoners.

There were lengthy speeches from the chiefs and principal orators but McKenney and Cass were adamant; murder had been committed and those responsible had to be tried by the white man's law. One wonders why the chiefs didn't ask the two commissioners when white murderers of Indians would be turned over to the Indian nations to be tried under their tribal law.

The impasse was finally broken when the chiefs of the Chippewa Lac de Flambeau band finally agreed to deliver the prisoners to either the Sault or Prairie du Chien. The treaty was signed August 5, 1826, the first McKenney had negotiated in the field. James Otto Lewis was one of the witnesses. The tribes approved the terms of the treaty of Prairie du Chien between the Chippewa and the Sioux which established their tribal boundaries. They gave Washington permission to explore and remove copper and ore; promised the delivery of the Lake Pepin murderers; and agreed on a future council to settle the age-old boundary claims between the Winnebago and the Menominee.

Before the council ended George F. Porter, the government geologist, with a party of twenty-five voyageurs and Indian guides found the famous copper boulder on the Ontonagon River. Porter's official report to McKenney and Cass described the boulder as "a remarkable specimen of virgin copper" lying just below the watermark on the west bank about thirty-five miles from the mouth of the river. Porter and his crew tried for days to move the boulder but found it impossible. He estimated the mass to weigh over a ton. He then explored the riverbed which he found to consist of impassable sandstone ledges. The boulder, he reported, was at least "two-thirds pure metal."

On Tuesday September 12 the *Detroit Gazette* noted the arrival of Cass and McKenney "from the Indian country in a birch canoe."

The story ended with a prophetic paragraph:

A cession has been made to the United States, of the right to search for and take away any minerals or metal which may be found in that country. We consider this grant highly important to the government. Pure copper has been found in so many places in that region as to leave little doubt as to its abundance scattered through the whole country and it will not be long before the procuring of it will become a national object.[15]

The frontier press was unanimous in its praise of Cass and McKenney. McKenney, as the senior in command and Washington's representative, was singled out for his leadership, boldness, and command. The *Indianapolis Journal* reprinted the *National Journal*'s account which pointed out that McKenney had traveled over four thousand miles "half of that in a birchbark canoe."

A great scope of country has been traversed by the commissioners, [the editor wrote] which is entirely unknown to us from any information which may be relied on. It is therefore to be supposed that a great deal of information relative to the country itself, and the manners, characters and customs of the tribes who dwell there, must have been obtained. We are assured by Colonel McKenney that a great variety of many interesting materials have been collected. . . .[16]

Soon after his return to Washington, McKenney, as he put it, "threw together" a volume of five hundred pages of his frontier adventures under the title *Sketches of a Tour to the Lakes*, which he dedicated to Secretary of War Barbour. The book had a large sale and helped to create his image as a noted Indian authority.

McKenney's negotiations were praised in Congress, although Benton grumbled publicly at the expense of the expeditions. But this time his colleagues ignored him, probably aware of the columns filled with eulogistic reports of the Fond du Lac treaty and the peace, uneasy as it might be, that it brought to the frontier.

In the late fall Cass wrote to McKenney reporting on another important treaty that he and Schoolcraft had concluded with the Potawatomi and Miami nations at the confluence of the Mississinewa and Wabash rivers in Indiana. Again he had been accompanied by Lewis who sent on several Indian portraits to Washington. Cass had bluntly told the chiefs there was nothing left for them but to "move on." The game was gone and their people were starving. By moving west they could avoid their greatest plague, the whiskey peddlers who were corrupting not only their young men but their women and even their children. The western lands were their only refuge.

One wonders why Cass didn't explain why the government hadn't prevented, or why it couldn't prevent, the whiskey peddlers from corrupting both nations.

This was now one of the most important periods of McKenney's long career. Unhappy with his salary and the tangled conditions within his complex and far-flung Indian office, he had given Secretary of War Barbour a detailed plan for the creation of a new bureau, an individual office unattached to the War Department "with a responsible head" who would have the authority under the law to fire, hire, and create policy.

Both the President and Barbour accepted his plan; in his first State of the Union message, Adams asked Congress to establish a Home Department, and a Select Committee, headed by Daniel Webster, was assigned to examine the presidential proposals. Barbour wrote to Webster recommending McKenney's plan; later the House Committee on Indian Affairs also considered it, with Chairman John Coche interviewing McKenney at length and making a tour of his office.

Coche asked McKenney to write a bill detailing his proposals. The lamps burned late in the Indian Bureau as the colonel eagerly fulfilled Coche's request. He left a blank space for the annual salary, which Barbour filled in at $3,000. The Secretary of War wrote a terse, penciled scrawl: "Alter not a word."

Coche introduced the bill before the House in March 1826 but it failed to pass despite two readings. When McKenney's friend John McLean took over the chairmanship of the committee, the bill was brought back again to the House. The bill again floundered, and it was held up until General Porter became Secretary of War.

Porter informed Congress he found all Indian affairs to be so complex and detailed they usually interfered with his more important duties; he also recommended a new and separate Indian Bureau.

Porter summoned Governor Cass and General William Clark to Washington to join Colonel McKenney in drawing up a new set of regulations for the reorganization of the Indian office. The report was then submitted to the House in February 1829, incorporating a major part of McKenney's original proposals, codes, and laws. The Twentieth Congress, however, adjourned before it could take any action on the bill which Porter and McKenney had hoped would pass with the added push of General Clark's and Governor Cass's national reputation.

Two years later, when McKenney was out of office, the bill passed without any difficulty. It called for the appointment of an Indian Superintendent at the annual salary of $3,000.

McKenney, and not without reason, always blamed Senator Benton for the constant defeat of his bill which would have seen him in the post he always coveted, the head of an Indian Department unattached to the bureaucratic War Department.

In an unusually bitter letter to Madison, McKenney recalled how Benton had for years represented Astor's "private interests" in the Senate and had fought him until he had successfully abolished not only his post but the entire Bureau of Indian Trade.

> When you first appointed me, the Indian Trade System was too feeble to sustain itself against active interests of the private systems who controlled the tribes by means of ardent spirits which were by law—and properly so—excluded with any intercourse with the Indian nations and the government factories. I think it was my duty to propose remedies for what I considered to be evil, and I suggested to the Congress, from time to time or on calls made on the various committees, such checks of what appeared to me to be private influences. Those concerned as companies and private traders, became alarmed and a resolve was adopted to move upon the [Indian trade] system through the Congress and abolish it. It was carried. This was in opposition to those, who in all Humanity and Justice towards the Indians and those who know how bloody the track has been, from the landing of our Fathers at Plymouth and Jamestown and those who hold personal and interested intercourse with the Indians.
> But it was a powerful array of interests, working a capital of at least *two million* [McKenney's emphasis] and spread all over our northern and western regions. . . .

Then McKenney recalled Benton's vicious attacks on him, and the "fashionable cry of corruption."

> It certainly affords me pleasure [he concluded] to be able after all the noise and bustle which has been going on about this Indian question, to point to its close in the manner I now do, and if it shall tend further to confirm your good opinion of me, I shall be additionally grateful.[17]

Madison may have tried but certainly he knew that once Benton's mind had settled on a person or a subject nothing could change it. The Missouri senator had never forgiven McKenney for his attacks on Astor and the American Fur Company. Calhoun also knew how futile it would be for him to intercede with Benton. The Missouri senator and the vice-president hated each other; a hate to be climaxed on the floor of the Senate with Benton shouting Calhoun was a liar. However, Calhoun expressed his sentiments to McKenney shortly before the Indian Superintendent took off for the west:

> No one knows better than myself how inadequate your salary is, as a compensation for the varied and important duties of your office. There is no branch of the War Department which requires more minute and laborious attention, or to which greater responsibility is attached. I would rejoice to see your compensation placed on a more respectable footing . . .[18]

It was glowing praise but the bill still continued to gather dust.

6.

INDIAN REMOVAL—in the winter of 1826–1827, the subject was heard everywhere, in the eastern cities and in the smallest frontier settlements. How could the federal government confiscate the lands of the Indian nations—the favorite bureaucratic term that season in Washington was "extinguish"—and force them to move into the alien western lands across the Mississippi? Was it right or was it wrong? The debates were not without violence: in New York a brawl took place when a public discussion was held and in a southern saloon two men died in a gun battle after one called the other an "injun lover."

In January 1827 a dozen prominent senators and Congressmen proposed to President Adams that Colonel McKenney be sent among the western tribes "to make a favorable impression on them as to their settlement west of the river Mississippi."

In a letter to the White House signed by all, including William Henry Harrison, a future President, the committee advised Adams:

> Colonel McKenney is not only fully possessed with the views of the government, but in our opinion, he possesses more the confidence of the Indians than any person in the United States, who could so easily be employed for this desirable object. He has, perhaps, likewise equal, if not a superior knowledge of the Indian character and disposition than any person who would likely undertake this work. We would therefore, suggest the propriety and expediency of directing him under proper instructions to visit the Chickasaws, Choctaws and other southern tribes after he has completed his work in the North with Governor Cass this summer.

On March 28, 1827, Secretary of War James Barbour forwarded to McKenney his presidential orders to join Governor Cass in planning and organizing an Indian council at La Petite Butte des Morts (Little Hill of the Dead) on the Fox River, Wisconsin, then to travel down the Mississippi to the country of the Chickasaw, Choctaw, and Cherokee to "ascertain the disposition of the tribes and to note whatever incidents you may esteem valuable, and that in any way may be connected with our Indian relations, and that may tend to enlighten the department in matters pertaining to their judicious disposition and application."

Barbour's instructions to McKenney were to learn and report back to him and the President:

"The nature and extent of the terms on which they will consent to emigrate, which may be made binding on them, on being approved by the President and thrown afterwards into a treaty form."

McKenney was also ordered by Barbour to visit "all the Indian agencies and the schools as may be within your reach, and inform yourself of their conditions and prospects, and generally collect such information as may be necessary to a prompt and efficient discharge of the duties rising out of our Indian relations."

There was one fatal paragraph, relating to who would pay McKenney's expenses:

> Your compensation will be fixed upon your return, and made equivalent to the extent and value of your services . . . your expense (together with any reasonable amount, not exceeding one thousand dollars which you may find it necessary to expend among the Indians for the promotion of the objects in view) will be borne and a requisition will issue on your estimate of what they may probably be, for which you will, as is usual, account on your return . . .

This governmental promise of money should have flashed a danger signal and made McKenney pause; after three years he was still waiting for his full salary which had been promised by another President and another Secretary of War.

But McKenney, glowing with the responsibility of his presidential mission, readily accepted Adams's assignment to the western and southern tribes.

In April Barbour gave him an additional presidential request. By the treaties of 1816–1817 the Creek, now in Alabama, had yielded their lands in Georgia to the United States, except for one remaining strip which they had kept. Since Adams had entered the White House Georgia's senators and congressmen had pressured him to force the Creek to give up that piece of land. The Creek had been adamant in their refusal. Through Barbour, Adams asked McKenney to "employ all proper means at your discretion" to persuade the Creek to surrender that solitary tract. Again McKenney accepted and promised to "do my best to fulfill the wishes of the President."

McKenney joined Cass at Detroit in June 1827. In the ten months since they had conducted the Fond du Lac treaty council the frontier city had expanded. Boards were stacked along the roads and the days were filled with the sounds of hammering as new homes were built; the streets were rutted from heavy traffic of horses and wagons and now there was a small wharf. The Green Bay schooner *Henry Clay* was to make the first ascent of the Ste. Marie River, and McKenney, Cass, and their official party were to be the pioneering passengers. This time there were no troops.

The *Clay* witnessed a great deal of frontier history in the making but was one of the most undependable vessels in the West. It was not unusual for passengers to leave Detroit in June and arrive at Chicago in September "due to long detentions on the St. Clair Flats, furious headwinds off Thunder Bay or interminable calms at Mackinac or Manitous . . ." [19]

The *Clay* rolled like a bowl in the slightest sea and, when the rains came, torrents poured through the deck seams forcing passengers to carry umbrellas and eat their meals off pillows which they carried under their coats to keep dry.

After a stormy trip the steamboat followed its tradition and went aground on the rocks five miles from Green Bay. The passengers reached Fort Howard on the west bank of the Fox River by canoe.

The council site was about thirty miles above the fort, just below the river's opening into Lake Winnebago. Here the land rose from the shoreline to form a hill which commanded the river for several miles. [20] McKenney said "a more beautiful position could not be found."

7.

A FEW days after McKenney and Cass joined Schoolcraft at Butte des Morts, a Winnebago war party attacked the large settlement of Prairie du Chien and massacred a French trader's family. Later they killed the crew of a riverboat. Cass made a forced march down the Mississippi to St. Louis to alert General Henry Atkinson, commanding the troops in the west. Schoolcraft went to Mackinac, and McKenney remained behind to hold the council together and prevent the nations from declaring war on the frontier settlements. McKenney knew he was in a dangerous position. Friendly Indians warned him that Four Legs, a powerful Winnebago chief, was boasting he would soon have McKenney's scalp hanging from his coupstick. McKenney's answer was swift and formidable: he ordered a six pounder rolled in front of his lodge. In addition, while warriors belonging to Four Legs' band carried supplies around the portage, McKenney sat under a tree "in a conspicuous spot" carefully cleaning a brace of pistols. When a warrior sent by Four Legs contemptuously told the others the white man's "short guns" could not hurt anyone, McKenney quietly suggested he canoe across the river and set himself up as a target. When the warrior ignored his invitation and continued to harangue the other braves, McKenney stuck a small piece of bark into the ground across the cleared area. An excellent shot, he casually aimed and fired. The bark shattered. The warrior picked up the target, silently fingered the hole made by the bullet, stared at McKenney who ignored him as he reloaded his pistols, then walked away. As McKenney recalled, that was the end of the haranguing.

But the news from the camps was ominous; young warriors were painted and calling on their chiefs to lead them into war against the whites. Settlements were being abandoned and all along the Wisconsin frontier men, red and white, were arming.

Some bands were becoming arrogant and insulting; to impress them McKenney anchored a barrel in midstream and invited the braves to use it as a target. Spurts dotted the water but none hit the barrel. McKenney carefully sighted the six pounder and touched a match to the vent. The barrel disappeared in a burst of spray and wood. McKenney walked back to his lodge; he knew any comment was unnecessary. McKenney's position continued to remain precarious as the days passed. Scouts warned him that the Winnebago were trying to induce the Potawatomi to join in a war. If it came, the Indian Superintendent was aware that he and the few white men at the council site would be the first victims.[21]

8.

WHILE COLONEL McKenney was impressing the Winnebago with the white man's firepower, Cass was escaping two more assassination attempts. During his journey down the Wisconsin River to the Mississippi the Michigan governor had stopped at a secluded Indian village to talk to a chief. As Cass walked over the peak of a small hill a brave aimed a rifle at his chest. Before he could pull the trigger an older Indian knocked up the weapon, crying out:

"What are you doing? You will ruin us all!"

As the old warrior told Cass, his death would have brought the Dragoons and General Wilkinson whom the Winnebago feared "as the man who could unlock any Indian nation if he was forced to."

As Cass walked down to his canoe which was pulled up on the riverbank, another young warrior jumped out of the bushes, aimed his rifle at Cass, and this time pulled the trigger. The gun misfired and Cass calmly got into his canoe and paddled off.

In the village the old chief warned his people that Cass was under the protection of the Great Spirit and to try to kill him was useless.[22]

When Cass arrived in Prairie du Chien, he found most of the inhabitants preparing to flee to Fort Crawford. John Marsh, the subagent, described the attack which he said had been led by Red Bird, a well-known Winnebago war chief, and several braves. A French-Canadian family was killed but an infant boy survived scalping and a cut throat. Crews of two boats coming down the river from St. Peters had also been killed. March warned Cass that if Red Bird and the warriors were not apprehended the hostilities could spread and a bloody frontier war was inevitable. Cass sent a courier with the news to McKenney who forwarded a report to Secretary of War Barbour. Cass, meanwhile, continued on to Galena, Illinois, the lead mining district. Here the governor also found hysteria among the settlements. Miners and their families were moving into the garrison at Galena while reports told of the Winnebago burning and looting settlements along the Mississippi.

When Cass asked for volunteers to defend Prairie du Chien until troops could arrive, William Stephen Hamilton, sixth child of Alexander, gathered a hundred miners and went back upriver in canoes and barges.[23] At Rock Island Cass also recruited a hundred Sauk and Fox warriors to join Hamilton's men. Obviously this move was more diplomatic than military. Cass knew that word would quickly reach the Winnebago that the powerful Sauk and Fox Nation had joined Cass and could not be relied upon as allies.

It took Cass seven days of constant paddling to reach St. Louis from Prairie du Chien. He immediately conferred with General Clark and General Henry Atkinson at Jefferson Barracks, and it was agreed that six hundred Dragoons would make a forced march upriver to the portage between the Wisconsin and Fox rivers where they would be joined by other troops from Fort Howard on Green Bay.

The next day Cass left St. Louis for Green Bay by way of Peoria and Chicago to rejoin McKenney and Schoolcraft. This swift display of power had clearly impressed Four Legs and his chiefs—when they met with Cass, McKenney, and Schoolcraft to make arrangements for the opening of the council. Four Legs started to bluster and make threats but McKenney told him bluntly that when any nation kills the innocent they must expect to be met with rifles and not peace pipes.

Four Legs, a handsome war chief called "the Dandy" because of his elaborate headdress and beaded buckskins, understood this language. It would be foolish to start a war, he told McKenney, especially with men who had a cannon that could shatter a barrel anchored in midstream. He promised that Red Bird and his war party of warriors would surrender at the Wisconsin and Fox rivers portage after the council.

9.

THE CRASHING salute of McKenney's six pounder was the signal that the great council of Butte des Morts had opened. From the forest, river, and lake more than a thousand Winnebago, Chippewa, Menominee, and other nations hurried to gather about the base of the sacred hill. It was an unforgettable sight that hot sultry day: deep in the west the coming rain rumbled like a disturbed giant; warriors, chiefs, orators, war captains, all hideously painted black and vermilion, waved coupsticks from which hung scalps combed like glossy stallions' tails; hats dripped with strips of weasel skins; tiny trade bells tinked with every warrior's step measured by the drums. They were followed by the women and children carrying pots of steaming pork and beans, of wild rice and puppy stew while all about them was the hideous clamor of the dogs, an indispensable part of every Indian village.

The principal chiefs joined Cass, McKenney, and Schoolcraft under a "bower" of sweet-smelling evergreens and the formalities began.

After the first day's meeting, the nations danced all night in their villages. McKenney would recall the incongrous "sweet hymn singing of some hundred Christian Indians" rising at intervals amid the wild whoops, war cries, rattle of musketry, and the stirring beat of the drums.

For five weary days McKenney and Cass talked to the chiefs from noon to late afternoon. Boundary lines were established after numerous peace pipes had passed between the nations. More than once the chiefs hinted their throats were dry as sticks but Cass and McKenney ignored them; McKenney had issued the warning before the council had opened—whiskey peddlers could expect the consequences if they were captured.

The treaty was finally signed and presents distributed.[24] By dawn of the last day hundreds of canoes were overturned on the shore to be caulked with pitch by the squaws, and the pungent odor of boiling green cedar and spruce boughs lay heavy on the fresh morning air. Columns of smoke from cook fires rose lazily through the trees and across the river came the faint whoops of farewell from the departing western Sioux. The hundreds of lodges vanished quickly; bark strips were rolled into balls by the women who lined canoe bottoms with the poles. Before the sun was over the treetops, the nations were moving down the Fox, molten silver dripping from their paddles.

The departure of the Winnebago was interrupted by the screams of a woman who was almost slashed to death by her drunken husband.

When McKenney brought her to his tent he found one arm almost severed. They searched the forest for the whiskey peddler but he had fled.

McKenney's comment was bitter:

Who can account for the apathy which pervades the councils of this great nation upon this subject? What is the solution of the almost universal indifference with which a great portion of our race, Christian as we profess to be, listen to the wails that reach us from the wilderness homes of these abused and cast-off people? The cry from the forest, from the beginning, and that which is heard to this hour [in 1827] and which has never been hushed in this, "protect us . . . pity us . . ." But where are the practical responses which show that this cry has ever been properly regarded?

10.

THERE WAS still one final aspect of the control to be completed, the surrender of Red Bird at the portage. McKenney also faced the long dangerous journey to the southern tribes. Cass was doubtful, as he pointed out to McKenney, how one man could accomplish what General Clark equipped with large congressional appropriation had failed to do a few years before.

McKenney shrugged off Cass's gloomy predictions.

"I have only one answer, Governor," he replied. "I must go."

They were now joined by the Green Bay garrison of troops and a hundred Menominee warriors. Hampered by the army barges the journey up the Fox River was slow. The heat was exhausting and clouds of blackflies bit the faces of the soldiers cordelling the heavy boats until they resembled men storing chestnuts in their mouths. The Fox twisted like a tossed rope; one time they camped on the northwestern shore of Lake Rush, three miles in a straight line from the Fox and Wisconsin, but there had been so many winding curves it had taken them twenty miles to reach the lake. It was a laborious but inspiring journey for McKenney through the unspoiled wilderness. Giant cranes boomed majestically over their camps, flocks of pigeons and blackbirds darkened the sky, and savannas of wild rice choked the river leaving channels so narrow the barges could barely squeeze through.

The surrender took place soon after their arrival at the Portage. One afternoon at three o'clock Cass and McKenney heard a far-off wailing and the beat of drums. Through a glass the Indian Superintendent saw a number of Indians approaching the opposite shore, some mounted, others walking. The group paused on the riverbank and a solitary mournful chant rose.

"It's Red Bird singing his death song," the interpreter explained.

On orders of Cass and McKenney, the troops were withdrawn. The Menominee warriors painted for war, squatted on their haunches, "eyeing the scene with careless indifference." Barges sent across the river returned with over a hundred Winnebago chiefs and braves surrounding Red Bird and We-Kaw, one of his warriors.

They marched slowly up the bank to where Cass and McKenney were waiting with Major Whistler, the army commander from Fort Howard on Green Bay.

The Indian Superintendent, who knew how much the Indians liked the army's brass band, suggested to Whistler that his men strike up a tune. White men and Indians in the middle of a trackless wilderness waited solemnly until the last martial note died away. Then Caraminie, a chief, advanced to McKenney and told him Red Bird and We-Kaw were prepared to surrender and stand trial under the white man's law.

"They came like warriors to you," the chief said, "do not put them in irons."

When Cass and McKenney gave their promise, Caraminie turned and waved to Red Bird.

The war chief, as McKenney remembered him, was tall and straight as an arrow shaft—"exact and perfect to the very ends of his fingertips"—with his face painted red on one side and green and white on the other. He wore a collar of blue and white wampum and the claws of a large wildcat, the points inward. He was dressed in the Yankton style of dressed elk skin, almost a pure white, with a long fringe continued down the seams of his leggings. A sash of scarlet cloth was thrown carelessly over one shoulder with an ornamented white feather. On the other shoulder was a cluster of porcupine quills dyed yellow, red, and blue and a plume of red-dyed horsehair. Across his chest he wore his three-foot war pipe richly ornamented with feathers, horsehair, and the bills of birds. In one hand he held a white flag, in the other a peace pipe. For a long moment he stood motionless in the center of the council then slowly sat down.

The army band played "Pleyel's Hymn" and the forest echoed with the blare of trumpets and the crash of drums. The Indians appeared to be enchanted and kept nodding to the rhythm of the music. When it ended Red Bird, using a flint, lighted his pipe which made a full circle before the surrender ceremonies formally opened. One by one the chiefs rose and made a speech. McKenney, who took notes, recalled "in substance" they stressed that Red Bird and We-Kaw had surrendered voluntarily to keep peace on the frontier. They had accompanied their brothers to the representatives of the Great Father to ask that the warriors "be treated as men." They also had brought twenty of the finest ponies in the hope the families of the victims would accept them as compensation in the Indian way.

McKenney and Cass both spoke; they praised the Winnebago chiefs for urging Red Bird and his companion to surrender and—"turn away the guns and save your people." They solemnly promised that the Indian defendants would receive a fair trial under the same law that judged the white man. In the future, they told the Winnebago, instead of murder to settle grievances they must go to the Indian agent "who would send their petition to the Great Father and he would redress them . . ."

It would be fascinating to know the thoughts behind the dark copper faces of those listening chiefs; was this the white man's justice that brought the whiskey peddlers to their forest? That demanded year after year new treaties be made and each time more land be taken away? That forts be erected on their land although they had not been consulted?

The Winnebago would say this years later but at this council they only begged the white man not to disgrace one of their chiefs before his people by putting his legs and hands into irons.

Red Bird was the most dignified of all. He stood up and walked to Cass and McKenney and said: "I am ready. I do not wish to be put into irons. I have given my life, it is gone [blowing some dust from between his finger and thumb] like this. I would not have it back. It is gone . . ."

He then threw his hands behind him "to indicate his life was now at his back." Major Whistler gave a sharp command. A platoon wheeled about and Red Bird and We-Kaw marched away between the file of infantrymen. The chiefs and warriors slowly returned to their camp. McKenney, Cass, and Schoolcraft rejoined their expedition and the canoes and barges started toward Prairie du Chien.

That night in his tent McKenney wrote a long report of the surrender formalities to Secretary of War Barbour. Peace, he said, had at last come to the Wisconsin frontier and the country could now be opened for settlement.

Not many miles away in his tent, guarded by Major Whistler's troops, Red Bird sang his death chant. He had predicted to his fellow chiefs he would never again see a spring when the Great Spirit awakened Mother Earth.[25]

Within a year a delegation of Winnebago chiefs would come to Washington to plead for the life of Red Bird, We-Kaw, and other warriors who had been imprisoned for the Prairie du Chien massacre. All had been found guilty of murder and sentenced to hang. After McKenney and Cass recommended the sentence of the Indians be commuted, President Adams advised the chiefs that a presidential pardon was forwarded to St. Louis releasing all the Indian prisoners.

It came too late for Red Bird; he died in his cell. But the great "Augustic Treaties," as Schoolcraft called them— that is, the treaties of Fond du Lac and Butte des Morts, both signed in August—that had formulated a new course in the government's policy in dealing with the Indian nations of the northwest had been signed "and now the tribes were at peace."

CHAPTER X:

Journey Among the Southern Tribes

❧

I.

THE WINNEBAGO war party of two hundred braves that crouched along the banks of the Wisconsin was almost anticlimactic to Colonel McKenney after the long tense hours of the Butte des Morts council and the surrender of Red Bird. The Indians had suddenly appeared out of the forest where the river narrowed and now, silent and ominous, they aimed their trade guns and arrows. As the colonel recalled, Ben's "glossy black face" was now pale.

McKenney strapped on his brace of pistols, filled his pocket with trinkets and twists of tobacco, and ordered Ben to pull their canoe up on the shore. It was during his council with the chiefs that he discovered the Winnebago and Sauk and Fox had gone to war.[1]

After he had distributed his presents and unsuccessfully tried to persuade the Winnebago to return to their villages, the Indian Superintendent continued down the Wisconsin, "a river the color of brandy."

Twilight was fading into darkness when he joined up with General Atkinson's command from St. Louis, forty-five miles from the portage. Years later he pictured the scene; pulled up on the shore were thirty-foot riverboats shallow enough to draw only twelve to eighteen inches of water, their sails hanging limp in the sultry heat; cook fires flickering through the trees, smoke curling upward to the full moon; the quiet was broken by the measured thud of an ax, and all about the camp were the Dragoons, smoking, eating, gossiping, or playing cards.

McKenney found Atkinson recovering from a fever in his tent. Over a glass of claret he sketched the events of the council, the surrender of Red Bird, and the latest outbreak of hostilities between the Winnebago and the Sauk and Fox. Later that night, using the full moon and taking advantage of the coolness to escape the hordes of mosquitoes, McKenney and Ben continued down the Wisconsin to Prairie du Chien where McKenney spent the next few days interviewing survivors of Red Bird's raid.

Here for the first time he understood the motivation of the Winnebago. He discovered there had been numerous reports, later found to be false, that Winnebago warriors had been beaten to death by soldiers at Fort Snelling for the reported murder of a white family gathering maple sugar.

As McKenney wrote Barbour, the Winnebago had resorted to the only law they knew—retaliation; Red Bird had been selected as his nation's executioner. In his report he denounced the savage murders of the French trader's family but suggested that leniency "be considered" for the Indian prisoners.

McKenney now hired a crew of voyageurs and they moved down the Mississippi stopping off at Galena, Illinois, where Governor Cass had recruited Hamilton's small army of miners to protect Prairie du Chien. He was given a tour of the smelting pots by the foreman who proudly boasted they had smelted eight hundred thousand pounds of lead but expected to reach the record of a million within the next month.

McKenney found Galena an early booming frontier town with the usual riffraff of whores, whiskey peddlers, gamblers, and log cabin taverns. He was shocked at the exorbitant rents which he called "the certain index of prosperous times." A one-story log cabin, sixteen by twenty feet, McKenney learned rented for thirty dollars a month while a log tavern's yearly rent was a thousand dollars. But more important to McKenney than the smelting records and frontier rent gougers was the disturbing report of the Winnebago agent. Indian families had been forced off their land by white entrepreneurs who hired miners to improve and work the primitive Indian lead-mining works.

There were now two thousand miners on Indian lands, the agent told McKenney. He had been warned not to interfere and was told, "We go where we please."

Two days before McKenney had arrived the Winnebago chiefs had sent a terse message to the agent: "We will not see you anymore." This, the worried agent told McKenney, could mean war.

McKenney first threw the whiskey peddlers off the Indian lands, then warned the Galena mine owners that if they continued to trespass he would demand that martial law be declared and troops from Jefferson Barracks take over control of the town. He held numerous councils with the Winnebago, placating them with presents and promises, "until a general return to peaceful order of things ensued . . ."

He wrote years later:

> This overt act, this trespass on their [Winnebago] land was the egg from which the Black Hawk War was hatched. There was no necessity for that war, when some years later it did break out. It was only needed that the same justice should be continued to the Indians the same regard shown to their rights (as to white men), and the war would never have occurred . . .[2]

August turned into September. McKenney left Galena a quieter and more subdued town when he and Ben and the chanting voyageurs moved downriver. He noted in his journal that his Canadians paddled twenty-six miles in three hours in the cool invigorating morning. They passed bluffs that reminded McKenney of the turrets of ancient castles; sand islands in the river were covered so thickly with pelicans they appeared to be deep in snow. Sauk and Fox villages were built on terraces like Roman gardens, hunting eagles glided over the treetops and small boys and Indian women called out greetings as they passed. Their first hint of civilization was Fort Edward and the endless acres of farmland along the Illinois side of the river. McKenney celebrated their arrival at the mouth of the Missouri with a bottle of wine which he passed among the voyageurs as they dodged the uprooted trees, roots, and limbs swirling about their fragile bark canoe in the swift Mississippi current.

In St. Louis McKenney stayed with General Clark and was guest of honor at a dinner given by General Leavenworth, then commanding the troops in the West. Benjamin O'Fallon, who had escorted the Indian delegation to Washington several years before, gave McKenney a tour of the bustling frontier city which McKenney predicted would "become great and populous."

He left St. Louis for Memphis on the steamboat *Crusader* which turned out to be a veritable Noah's Ark. The decks were crowded with crates of poultry, tethered oxen, bullocks, mules, cows, and horses which cackled, bellowed, brayed, and mooed from dawn to dusk. McKenney wryly recalled: "Then there was the ammonia..."

From the steamboat's deck he saw the one log house that remained of New Madrid; three-quarters of the bluff containing the town had been swept into the river by the famous 1805 earthquake. Curious he dropped a line overboard but failed to touch bottom.

In Memphis he bought a fringed buckskin jacket, provisions, a riding horse, a horse and wagon for Ben and hired a guide. As he wrote: "A shabbier set of travelers had never left the bluffs..."

His destination was the farm of the Chickasaw chief Levi Colbert on the Tombigbee where the council would be held. In the first week of October 1827, McKenney faced the largest gathering of Chickasaw in the memory of the oldest chief. Violent thunderstorms had shaken the forest the evening before but the morning of the council broke bright and clear. McKenney, who knew his Indians,

was quick to point out the symbolic significance. As he wrote:

"The confusion and the storm, the restlessness and unsettled character, the suffering which everything around appeared to endure, was a symbol of their own lives. They had never been a composed and set people, they were always restless and in a constant state of excitement."

When the chiefs were assembled he told them:

"The Great Spirit has sent the beautiful morning as a symbol of what your lives are to be . . ."

As the interpreter translated McKenney's words a murmur rose from the intently listening Indians. "We know you well," one called out, "now we listen to your words." McKenney carefully spread a map before him then packed and lighted a beautiful carved pipe, a present from a Fox chief. Cries of appreciation rose from the council; it was another coup for McKenney, the words of a white man would be spoken over the smoke of an Indian pipe.

McKenney spoke most of the morning. He reviewed the relationship between the Chickasaw and Washington and brought them up to the present, a new day, a new time when they were no longer one of the most powerful Indian nations in the south but were encircled by land-hungry white men who were supported by their state government "so that the Great Father has much trouble to keep you from being crushed by them . . . need I tell you that your friends everywhere are filled with anxiety about you . . . you all know this and you feel it in your heart and you are sad . . ."

The Chickasaw chiefs doggedly replied with their age-old argument:

"Here lie the bones of our fathers . . . this is the home of our infancy and we love our country . . . we cannot give it up . . ."

McKenney's last speech was blunt and appealed to the Indian's sense of realism and their traditional love of children.

"Your fathers are not here. What remains of them is dust. They feel not, nor care not whether the foot of the white man or the red man treads on their graves. But your children live and they must be clothed and fed. And after them will come other generations of children. Forget not to provide for them. Never stop for a moment but hasten with all speed to place them in a situation that will secure them from the evils that their fathers had to endure and the sorrows that fill your own hearts. That, Brother, is Wisdom."

Then McKenney went on to the heart of his argument. As he said, he was "not for the Indian taking the white man's word in any affair or bargain or sale." The Chickasaw would have to examine for themselves the western land and the proposition he was to set before them.

He studied the stoical copper faces for a long moment. "Say to me for the sake of your children and your children's children that you will go quick and look at this country. Fix the day. Let it be the first of next May. Now let me tell you, it is your time. The time for such terms never came before and they may never come again, take hold of it, and if you think I know anything and am your friend, put such a paper in my hands for me to take home...

"Brothers, I have done. I pray the Great Spirit direct you."

Tishomingo, the celebrated Chickasaw, Levi Colbert, and William McGillivray addressed the council. McKenney's emphasis on the future of their children had decided the Chickasaw: they would consider emigration, provided, as McKenney had pointed out, they could first examine the land.[3]

The government would defray the expenses of the exploring group to be composed of twelve members of the tribe accompanied by three white commissioners, and a physician. They agreed with McKenney to go, by May 1828, by steamboat from Memphis to St. Louis, then overland to the western lands.

2.

A FEW WEEKS later McKenney arrived in the land of the Choctaw and held a council with the principal chiefs, most of whom had been newly elected and were firmly against selling their lands and moving west.

McKenney spoke all day but the interminable Indian answers were summed up in the terse reply of a young chief:

"Tell the Great Father we do not wish to give up our country."

Late that night McKenney was visited by one of the deposed chiefs who told him it was not possible for any of the chiefs to make a decision on the lands; the murder of McIntosh, the pro-American chief, had divided the nation into two hostile factions; and until they were reunited no binding decision could be made on any major question.

It would be wiser, the chief advised, to suggest the appointment of a committee with representatives from both sides to join the Chickasaw when they went west to inspect the territory offered by the federal government.

The following day McKenney followed the chief's advice and the Choctaw council through his old friend, David Folsom informed him they had voted to send a committee of six chiefs "to accompany their elder brothers, the Chickasaw and inspect their western lands."

Folsom and Greenwood Leflore, another influential chief, were secretly in favor of removal and told McKenney in confidence they would endorse his proposal of removal in the council after the return of the exploring party.

McKenney left the Choctaw and Chickasaw teams playing one of their wild ball games and continued on horseback to the Tuscaloosa and the Creek country. As he explained to Barbour he bypassed the Cherokee because he had learned that two United States Indian Commissioners had arrived and were negotiating with the nation for permission to open a canal linking two rivers.

McKenney, now a veteran of Washington's political infighting, explained:

"If the attempt [the canal opening treaty] would prove to be a failure, it might be inferred [by the commissioners] I was the cause of it."[4]

3.

THE JOURNEY to the Creek country was long and dangerous; twenty-five miles were over narrow mountain trails and impassable roads. McKenney wrote that he and Ben had to feel their way "in the blackness so great I could not see my horse's mane although it was white."

The horse and wagon, driven by the "intrepid Ben" as McKenney called him, floundered in "one mud hole after the other," and white man and black were forced to put their shoulders to the wheels. McKenney estimated they traveled about a mile an hour. They camped in the darkness and started out again at dawn to inch their way along the trails. Twilight was fading when McKenney heard a distant, muffled roar and noticed a reddish tinge in the sky; they reached the Black Warrior River, crimson from the glare of a raging forest fire. They were ferried across and continued on to reach Tuscaloosa late that night, "horses jaded and almost broken down, Ben in a condition not much better and myself ready for rest."

After a weekend's rest at Tuscaloosa they crossed the Cahaba, then later the Alabama River, to arrive finally in Montgomery.

But the saddle-weary McKenney forgot his fatigue when he came upon a copy of the *North American Review*, one of the best reviews of its kind in the nation at the time, and read a glowing critical account of his book, *Sketches of a Tour to the Lakes.*

McKenney was a typical first book author. He was so overjoyed at the review's "commendations" that he forgot his saddle sores and celebrated with a hot bath and a glass of the best claret the local public house could offer. When he arrived at the Creek Indian Agency, Fort Mitchell on the Chattahoochee, he sent runners to the chiefs requesting a council be held on the riverbank. At this first meeting the chiefs refused to commit their nation to any proposal.

A second council was held at the Indian capital Tuckabatchee, which McKenney attended accompanied by his agent Colonel John Crowell. Before McKenney's arrival, the chiefs had met in secrecy for three days; the Indian Superintendent addressed a tense, obviously hostile council.

The opposition was led by the two half-breed Cherokee chiefs, David Vann and John Ridge who were acting as advisers to Opothole Yoholo, one of the principal Creek leaders. An angry Ridge later described McKenney's long speech as full of "gross Indian and disgusting flattery."

This was the same chief who in a few years would be executed by his own people for advocating the very policy he denounced in the Tuckabatchee council.

By the second morning of the council, McKenney knew that he would never win approval of the Creek nation if Ridge continued to act as its adviser. The cold, contemptuous, educated young half-breed was ready for any confrontation, even violence. As he later wrote in the *Cherokee Phoenix,* he came to the morning council armed with a "pipe tomahawk to be ready in the case of assault of the white men."

McKenney, of course, used words, not tomahawks. When the council reached an impasse he stood up, dramatically pointed to Ridge and charged the half-breed with working against the federal government.

He ordered Ridge out of the council "in the name of the United States" and warned the chiefs that if Ridge continued to remain, all communication with the nation and Washington would be discontinued.

Ridge silently departed from the council. That same day the Creek leaders voted to sign a treaty with Washington, selling their last strip of land in Georgia for $42,951 of which $10,000 was to be used for their "civilization" or schools.[5] From that day on the Creek nation remained in Alabama.

Before he left McKenney agreed to "adopt," at the request of their parents and the Creek Council, two Indian boys, William Barnard, the ten-year-old son of a well-known chief who had led the Creek against Jackson at the Battle of the Horseshoe, and a thirteen-year-old Yuchi, Lee Compere.

"We wish them to go to the white man's schools and then come back and help their people," the chiefs told the Indian Superintendent.

In Augusta McKenney had their hair cut and "both boys were given a thorough cleaning and were brought to me, dressed not only in handsome suits but in smiles . . ."

The following morning at breakfast Colonel McKenney received a severe jolt. He had sent the two boys to the dining room for breakfast while he finished shaving. When he arrived he found the youths in tears and standing off to one side of the room in a dark passageway. When he was asked what was wrong they told him a lady at the table had sent them out of the dining room "because she did not allow Indians to eat near her . . ."

The outraged McKenney stalked into the dining room "firmly put the boys in chairs on either side of the woman, who sprang to her feet, gave the chair a push backwards, threw her head well up, with her arm extended and her fist clenched, accompanied by a wild and vengeful expression with her lips compressed."

"Sir,' she told Colonel McKenney, "I will not allow Indians to come to my table."

"Madam, I am sorry but on this occasion I must trespass your rules," McKenney replied. "These little boys must have their breakfast and just as they are now—seated with me. At this table, your table, or any other table in Georgia."

"I'll send for my husband," the woman shouted and ran out of the dining room.

In a moment her husband arrived, accompanied by the innkeeper.

"Sir, this is against my rules," the innkeeper said sternly.

McKenney calmly poured a cup of coffee. "Yours is a public house," he informed the innkeeper. "We are travelers. These little boys are under my protection. I shall see, wherever I go, that they occupy the same level as I do. My advice to you as a friend is to keep cool and leave the room. I shall pay you for our fare."

The landlord glared at the dignified McKenney who ignored him as he served the two frightened Indian boys.

"Very well, sir," he said after the woman guest and her husband had indignantly stalked from the dining room, "I suppose it must be."

"It will be," McKenney replied quietly and firmly.[6]

McKenney sent a detailed report of the councils to Barbour, then with the two Indian boys traveled night and day by stagecoach to reach Washington before the President sent his message to Congress.

News of the settlement of the long-smoldering bitterness between the Creek and Georgia over the strip of land stirred Washington. When McKenney arrived at the War Department the first one he saw was Barbour. The Secretary of War hurried down the corridor to embrace McKenney.

"It is true, sir, that you have concluded a treaty with the Creek?"

"It is, sir," McKenney replied.

"Then, sir, there is not enough money in the treasury to pay you for what you have accomplished," the exuberant Barbour cried as he hurried to the White House.

The Senate ratified McKenney's treaty and the "troubles" which had existed for generations between Georgia, the Creek, and the federal government "were finally put to rest."

The Chickasaw and the Choctaw still clung tenaciously to their land but McKenney had returned to Washington with a partial triumph. The tribes at least had agreed to send their representatives to examine the western lands offered to them by their Great Father. This was a coup that not even General Clark with his wagonloads of presents and money belt stuffed with bills had been able to accomplish in his month-long council of October 1826.

4.

McKENNEY DISCOVERED that in Washington a hero's laurels soon fade under what he once described as the capital's "invisible agency of the prince of darkness sent in to annoy and if possible to destroy . . ."

The Devil's own, in McKenney's case, was the government's Second Comptroller, Richard Cutts, who publicly announced that McKenney's accounts were not in order, that he had failed to produce proper vouchers, and had been paid double mileage from Green Bay to Washington. Rumors mushroomed into a broadening scandal until the Congressional Committee on Retrenchment with Cutts as a witness charged the bewildered Superintendent with "wasting public funds" and defrauding the government of six hundred dollars for mileage from the Wisconsin treaty to the capital.

McKenney was stunned, then furious at the obviously distorted and unfair charges. He had made out his accounts with Governor Cass and Schoolcraft and they had been approved for payment by Secretary of War Barbour. What particularly distressed him was the committee's charge that he had failed to produce vouchers with "proper

A View of the Butte des Morts Treaty Ground
with the arrival of Gov. Lewis Cass and Colonel McKenney.

Governor Lewis Cass

General William Clark
Superintendent of Indians in the West under McKenney.

signatures" for two thousand dollars' worth of presents he had distributed among the nations at the southern councils.

"My God, what am I to do—produce Indian marks on a government voucher?" he stormed. "Don't they know I traveled two thousand miles to visit the Southern Tribes and obtain treaties?"

He immediately went to see Cutts who confirmed that an order had been received from the comptroller's office debiting his accounts for six hundred dollars. McKenney demanded and received a certified copy of the order. His anger increased when he learned from Secretary of War Barbour that Cutts had sent the charges against him to the War Department days before McKenney returned to the capital. Barbour's explanation of why he had not contacted his loyal Indian Superintendent was simple: at first he had not paid any attention to Cutts's findings but after he had been alerted that the administration's enemies in Congress were fanning the tiny fire into a roaring political conflagration, he began his own independent investigation. Cass was brought to Washington and signed a deposition that he, Schoolcraft, and McKenney had made out their expense accounts; that McKenney had been paid eight dollars per diem "while employed on Indian duty" and eight dollars per twenty miles, the same rate paid to Cass and Schoolcraft. Barbour pointed out to the committee in his statement and review of the case, it was the rate of payment which had been set by Calhoun.

McKenney was normally a calm, composed, almost aloof man who like his copper-skinned charges rarely displayed bursts of emotion. After the initial wave of anger had subsided his orderly mind took over. He first canvassed his many friends in Congress and obtained statements praising his integrity and devotion to his office; among those who came to his defense were the twelve Congressmen who had originally requested Barbour to send McKenney on a tour of the southern tribes.

McKenney next hired a "scientific and experienced accountant" who he recalled had been given "high and special testimonials" from Calhoun to map his journey from Washington to Wisconsin, down the Mississippi across the south and back to the capital. The clerk reported to McKenney that even including the disputed six hundred dollars, he had been underpaid and in fact the government owed him an additional four hundred and fifty-five dollars.

A grim and determined McKenney submitted to Barbour the clerk's sworn statements and detailed findings including the map he had used. The Secretary of War reviewed the report and ordered the additional funds paid to his Indian Superintendent.

Under pressure from the Secretary of War, Cutts approved the revised accounting "and even waiving the voucher and Indian marks for the Indian presents" but stubbornly insisted McKenney should be still charged for the "double mileage," as he called it, from Green Bay back to Washington. He refused to consider McKenney's explanation that his return route was hundreds of miles longer because of his missions to the southern tribes.

Cutts, who was either an infuriating bureaucratic ass or was being used by McKenney's foes in Congress to smear him, would not budge.

One of the last letters Secretary of War Barbour wrote, before he left Washington for the Court of St. James's as the United States Ambassador to England, was to Secretary of the Navy Southard completely absolving McKenney of any intent to defraud and praising him as one of the most intelligent and faithful bureau heads in all of Washington.

Cutts, he hinted, had ulterior motives in filing his claims against McKenney. He concluded:

> During my continuance of office he has performed his duty with a zeal and assidinity, and, I will add, with an ability, that were worthy of great praise. He inspired me with confidence with every official act.

The congressional committee assigned to investigate McKenney's expense account received scores of letters praising the Indian Superintendent, such as one written by Florida's congressman J. M. White who stated bluntly: "Colonel McKenney has accomplished more in a few months for a small sum than the other [Indian] Commissioners could have done with the Public Treasury at their disposal. I have had much intercourse with the Indian Office and I think that no man in this country has been so wantonly assailed. The United States Government never could have made any progress in their system of colonization without him. . . ."

In addition to White, eight powerful congressional leaders including William McLean, Chairman of the Committee on Indian Affairs, wrote to the War Department insisting that McKenney's accounts "be allowed," and describing them as "reasonable" and made within the stipulation made to him by Barbour.

The committee's two-member minority congressmen, John Sergeant of Philadelphia and Edward Everett of Massachusetts, also filed a vigorous defense of McKenney and praised him as a "meritorious and valuable public officer."

The bitter fight gradually died away but apparently the six hundred dollars remained debited to McKenney's accounts. As the Indian Superintendent bitterly observed:

> Mr. Cutts cannot now pass the account as corrected in my favor, and as allowed by the Secretary of War without admitting he erred and to do this, would be to require, if not the exertion of moral courage, at least the exercise of magnanimity—every man is not gifted with the first, and few put in requisition for the last. . .
>
> To those who devote their time to such [Public] Employment, I have nothing to say, except to wish them a more honorable calling than that which seeks to wound private feelings and degrade the Republic by traducing and vilifying its citizens . . .

5.

COLONEL MCKENNEY's journeys through the territories of the western tribes drastically changed his views toward Indian removal. During his early years in the Indian Trade Bureau, he had firmly advocated the civilization of the Indians in their homelands, but what he had witnessed convinced him that removal was the only way to save the tribes from absolute destruction.

In his official report of November 29, 1827, McKenney condemned the whiskey peddlers who were reducing the once proud nations to a debauched people:

"No man who has the feelings of a man can go through their country and see the total abandonment to this vice [whiskey] without emotion of a most painful kind. I doubt their recovery from its long train of miseries *whilst they retain their present relations to the states to be hopeless.*"[7]

He strongly urged the federal government to move quickly and remove the tribes to the West. The first thing that was needed, he pointed out, was the quick approval by Congress of a $15,000 appropriation to pay the expenses of the Choctaw and Chickasaw exploration party.

A Mississippi congressman introduced a resolution calling on the House Committee on Indian Affairs to consider the money which would enable the Indians to look over the land that their government insisted should be their new homes.[8]

McKenney impatiently paced his office and dispatched his usual lengthy letters to his agents as the weeks passed without congressional action. Then the year turned. May 1, 1828, the date when the Indians were to gather at St. Louis, approached. In late April the Senate passed the bill and returned it to the House. A bloc of New England congressmen—there were no Indian problems in their states—fought the bill against representatives of the southern and western states with heavy Indian population who insisted that it should be passed. It was finally approved in late May and McKenney sent the news by courier to the Indian nations.

In June he was nervously advising a bored General Clerk in St. Louis to "omit nothing that should be thought of and add nothing that might be deemed superfluous," and instructing his agents to "move quickly, let no time be lost."[9]

Now it was the Indians who delayed. The Chickasaw decided they didn't want to go. The tribes were confused. Some of the warriors charged in open council that their chiefs had already sold their lands to the white man. McKenney dispatched a letter to the Choctaw and Chickasaw chiefs pleading with them to keep the promises they had made to him in their councils.

"Let a Red Man anywhere stand up and say I promised and did not perform," he wrote," He cannot. Fail not. It is not too late if you move quickly." He advised the chiefs "not to disappoint me . . . I am your friend and laboring to promote your happiness . . . if they do not mind my words I shall think they are tired of me."[10]

The Indian nations respected McKenney, pleading for his advice and wisdom years after he left the Indian Bureau; this time his plea was effective. His message was read in the councils and both nations voted to send their chiefs to explore the western lands. In the fall Clark reported to McKenney that the first groups had arrived in St. Louis.

McKenney also used two members of a delegation of Cherokee visiting Washington during this period to act as his secret agents; their mission was to try to persuade the southern Cherokee to join the western Cherokee in Arkansas Territory.

Their role was revealed when a notice appeared in the *Cherokee Phoenix* warning them that their heads would be placed on exhibit.[11]

McKenney's efforts to influence the Cherokee to go West gained few recruits. Some emigrants, mostly half-breeds or squaw men, moved into Arkansas in 1828. The news that passed across McKenney's desk was discouraging. Emigrants were beaching their boats and selling the equipment to local farmers. There was another and more deadly obstacle: that fall and winter the fierce western tribes, like the Pawnee and Osage, were lifting Cherokee scalps. There was only blood and war, Indian against Indian, one weary emigrant reported to his family.

All along the border in the fall, winter, and spring of 1827–1828 there was bewilderment, confusion, and anger among the Indian tribes. The Quapaw protested to McKenney that they had been forced to move from their ancient homelands to make room for the immigrating Cherokee. Other smaller tribes became virtually homeless wanderers in the West as the tide of invading families from the southern tribes increased.

The whites also protested to McKenney and the War Department. For years they had struggled with the land, cultivated, farmed it, built mills and homes. Were they now supposed to give it up to some dirty Indian?

Missionary groups who had labored for years among the southern tribes joined in the clamor, protesting to McKenney that the federal government should not abandon its traditional role of civilizing the Indian nations on their homelands. However, there were some who agreed with McKenney that the only way to save the Indians was to move the nations to the primitive lands in the West, far away from the vices of the white man.

McKenney now had a new, if friendly, foe; the powerful American Board of Commissioners for Foreign Missions. He tried in vain to explain to the board the shocking sights he had witnessed on his tours. They listened politely but always returned to their familiar arguments.

As for McKenney, he never forgot the sight of the singing, whooping drunken Indians staggering about the beach at Drummond's Island in the torchlight and the rows of empty barrels in the morning.[12]

The *Cherokee Phoenix*, once his strongest supporter, now became his severest critic. Still McKenney continued to advocate the then unpopular program of Indian removal.

"It is for your sake and not mine," he warned the editor of the *Phoenix* in the fall of 1828, "I deplore to see the vindicity of your spirit and I advise you—think of it as you may treat persons who are your friends, for you have need of all their counsel and their wisdom."

The *Phoenix* editor coldly replied that "this Gentleman [McKenney] would have been welcomed in the Cherokee country a few years before but now a more unpopular Commissioner could not be sent."[13]

CHAPTER XI:

The Great Father's Red Children Come Calling

I.

FROM THE winter of 1821–1822 to near the turn of the century the nation's capital was a paradoxical symbol to the Indian nations of hope and despair, sweet dreams and bitter disillusionment. They came to Washington in their fringed elkskin jackets and leggings, beaded moccasins, feathered headdresses that flowed behind them like wings, or crowns of buffalo skulls with great, menacing, curved horns. They painted their faces, acted with great dignity, performed their dances in front of the White House, and spoke and listened to a long succession of Great Fathers, only to learn their promises were written with water for ink and smoke for parchment.

As their hotel bills reveal, they drank an incredible amount of whiskey, and more than one devastated the white man's furniture and his chinaware in drunken frolics. One wild evening cost the government $250 "for damage to house, bedding, carpeting, tables, etc." as the hotel owner wrote across his bill.[1]

Superintendent of the Bureau of Indian Affairs Thomas Loraine McKenney was responsible to the President and Secretary of War for planning and bringing to Washington the many delegations representing nations from the Florida Territory to the Far West. During the sixteen years he served under Presidents Madison, Monroe, Adams, and Jackson he witnessed many treaties signed not only in the wilderness but also at the White House.

The object of the government in bringing the Indian delegations to the nation's capital was almost childishly clear: to impress the primitives from the Great Plains or the forests with the white man's awesome power and thus avoid a bloody, costly frontier war.

McKenney, an early champion of Indian rights, was a strong supporter of this diplomacy. As he suggested to Secretary of War Barbour, a year after he and Governor Cass had concluded the famous Fond du Lac and Butte des Morts treaties, the best way to avoid a war with the "restless" Winnebago was to invite a delegation of their chiefs to Washington.

After the two big councils, conditions had deteriorated on the northwestern frontier. The reasons included the death sentences imposed on Red Bird and the other Winnebago warriors for the Prairie du Chien massacre and the mounting number of settlers. The two hundred whites in the lead mining districts had increased to almost six thousand by the winter of 1828. The garrison of Fort Crawford at Prairie du Chien whose guns had made the Winnebago pause before they decided to take to the warpath, was in ruins; floods had undermined the walls of the post so severely it had to be abandoned. With the soldiers gone, settlers pouring into the land to work the mines, and the Winnebago waiting to be executed, war drums had begun to thump in the villages.

To avoid a brush-fire war, Cass had urged the federal government to pay $20,000 to the tribe for the occupied land.

When Barbour asked McKenney for his opinion, the Indian Superintendent pointed out the hopelessness of constantly buying Indian land; it brought only a temporary peace. Then acre by acre, mile by mile, settlers nibbled away at the land still held by the tribes until blood was spilled. If the army was summoned it had a traditional solution—"settle the disturbance" as the generals called it, with the musket and the sword. When the gunpowder smoke drifted away there were always more copper-skinned bodies than dead men in blue uniforms, and less Indian land and more future hostility.

McKenney repeated his request of leniency for Red Bird and the Winnebago warriors and suggested to Barbour:

> It is true they [the Indians] have never seen, and therefore (having no medium through which they can perceive our superiority) have no conception of their comparative feebleness. They count upon strength for reasons which are apparent; they have mastered their neighboring tribes and think they know the power of the white man . . . this conclusion is derived from the intercourse they have with the few traders, and sometimes the sight of only detachments of our army.

McKenney reviewed the two treaties he and Cass had concluded in the summers of 1826 and 1827, emphasizing to the Secretary of War the Winnebago were a proud, fearless people to whom war was second nature. He added that his backwoods intelligence had disclosed the Winnebago hunters were killing large numbers of deer and stocking the meat for provisions.

"My opinion is they mean to strike," McKenney warned. He recalled for Barbour that when he was at the Butte des Morts council "one woman followed her man, a chief, like a shadow . . . the reason for her fear, as I found on inquiry, was *her knowledge of our power* (McKenney's emphasis). She had been as far east as New York.

"This mode of conquering these people [bringing representatives to Washington] is merciful and it is cheap in comparison to what a war on the frontier would cost, to say nothing of the loss of human life. It has also been practiced [by our government] and as far as I am informed, never without beneficial effects."[2]

McKenney, always a precise man about his finances, had prepared a cost analysis of bringing the Winnebago to Washington. When he totaled the bill for Barbour, the cost of a delegation of twenty chiefs came to $12,000—including their board and presumably their bar bill.

Barbour agreed with McKenney's proposal and ordered him to make plans for the delegation to be received at the White House. But it took a great deal of letter writing by McKenney, plus personal interviews with the chairman and members of the Senate Appropriation Committee to get approval of the money.

The government's policy was to pay for the expense of the delegations if the trips were on official business but if it was for pleasure, payment came out of the tribe's annuity. In a letter to the Secretary of War in April 1825 McKenney explained: "The rule of the Department in regard to paying the expenses of Agents and Indians visiting the Seat of Government is this—when the object of the visit is one in which the Government is interested; and when a visit is deemed essential to a better understanding of that object, and which could not be done so well by correspondence—and when permission to make that trip is given by the Department."

The delegation variously estimated from sixteen to twenty Winnebago chiefs and warriors headed by Nawkaw or Wood, their ancient chief, set out for Washington in the fall of 1828.[3] They were accompanied by Captain John Kinzie, the Indian agent who would later work for John Jacob Astor's American Fur Company, Major Forsyth, and an interpreter named Paquette. Other chiefs were the one-eyed White Crow, Little Elk, Old Dandy (who undoubtedly was Four Legs, McKenney's formidable opponent at the Butte des Morts treaty council the previous summer), his son, called Young Dandy, War Eagle, Yellow Thunder, and his wife, described as a "remarkable, handsome, powerful woman."

Their route to the capital was by way of Detroit, the lakes, and then the Erie Canal. In early October they arrived in New York City with the newspapers describing them as members of a "remote tribe who had avoided as much as possible all intercourse with the Americans . . . they know less of them and are less known by them, than any Indians, east of the Rocky Mountains."

They were given the usual tour of the military installations, the navy yard, and ships, and like the Osage who had visited Manhattan many years before, they reviewed a parade and were received by the New York mayor and his city officials.

As spokesman for his chiefs, Nawkaw thanked the mayor and his aides and they set off for Washington where McKenney put them up at Tennison's Hotel. While they waited to see their Great Father, the Indian Superintendent handsomely entertained the visiting Winnebago. They were given a tour of the city and were fascinated by three trained dogs and birds who played dominoes at Carusi's Assembly Room. Nawkaw was so enchanted he insisted on playing a match with the dog while one of the other chiefs challenged the bird. Unfortunately the reporter for the *National Intelligencer* who described their visit, apparently thought naming the winner of the bizarre match was unimportant. They were visited by Secretary of State Henry Clay who selected Little Elk as the most talented of the group. Clay had made a shrewd choice: Little Elk was not only a talented leader of his nation but was also a gifted orator.

McKenney also had the Washington Guard's band regale them with a concert and in return the Winnebago did their war dance in front of the White House.

On the afternoon of November 29, 1828, the Winnebago finally saw their Great Father. The harassed and embittered President Adams, still reeling from his vicious mudslinging presidential campaign with Jackson, politely received the chiefs, painted and wearing feathered headdresses, and accompanied by Governor Cass, Major Forsyth, and Colonel McKenney.

Adams and Secretary of War Barbour, flanked by senators and congressmen, shook hands with the chiefs as they filed past to group together under the portrait of General Washington. It was a chilly day and a fire crackled while the beautiful chandeliers sparkled with the rays of the dying afternoon sun.

Nawkaw was resplendent in a brown and cream striped shirt with long loose sleeves held tight to his upper arms by silver bands. The ridge of his nose and cheeks were painted crimson and from his neck hung three peace medals bearing the likenesses of three different Great Fathers.

Four Legs was the peacock of the group. He literally jangled from rows of silver brooches and armbands as he walked. His leggings and moccasins were elaborately decorated with dyed porcupine quills and his clubbed hair flashed with silver ornaments. In one hand he carried a feathered fan.

One-eyed White Crow wore a black silk handkerchief over his empty socket, which gave him the appearance of a pirate. Madeira wine and macaroons were served; when the last drop and crumb had disappeared, Nawkaw advanced to Adams holding aloft a peace pipe and the ceremony began.

But it was Little Elk, the orator, who captured the admiration of Adams and the others. His speech was brief and to the point: the Winnebago had come from their

John Quincy Adams
Indian Peace Medal
Courtesy, Gilcrease Institute, Tulsa, Okla.

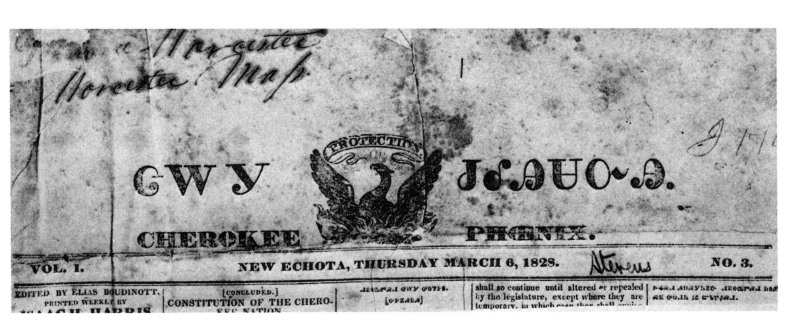

Masthead of the *Cherokee Phoenix*

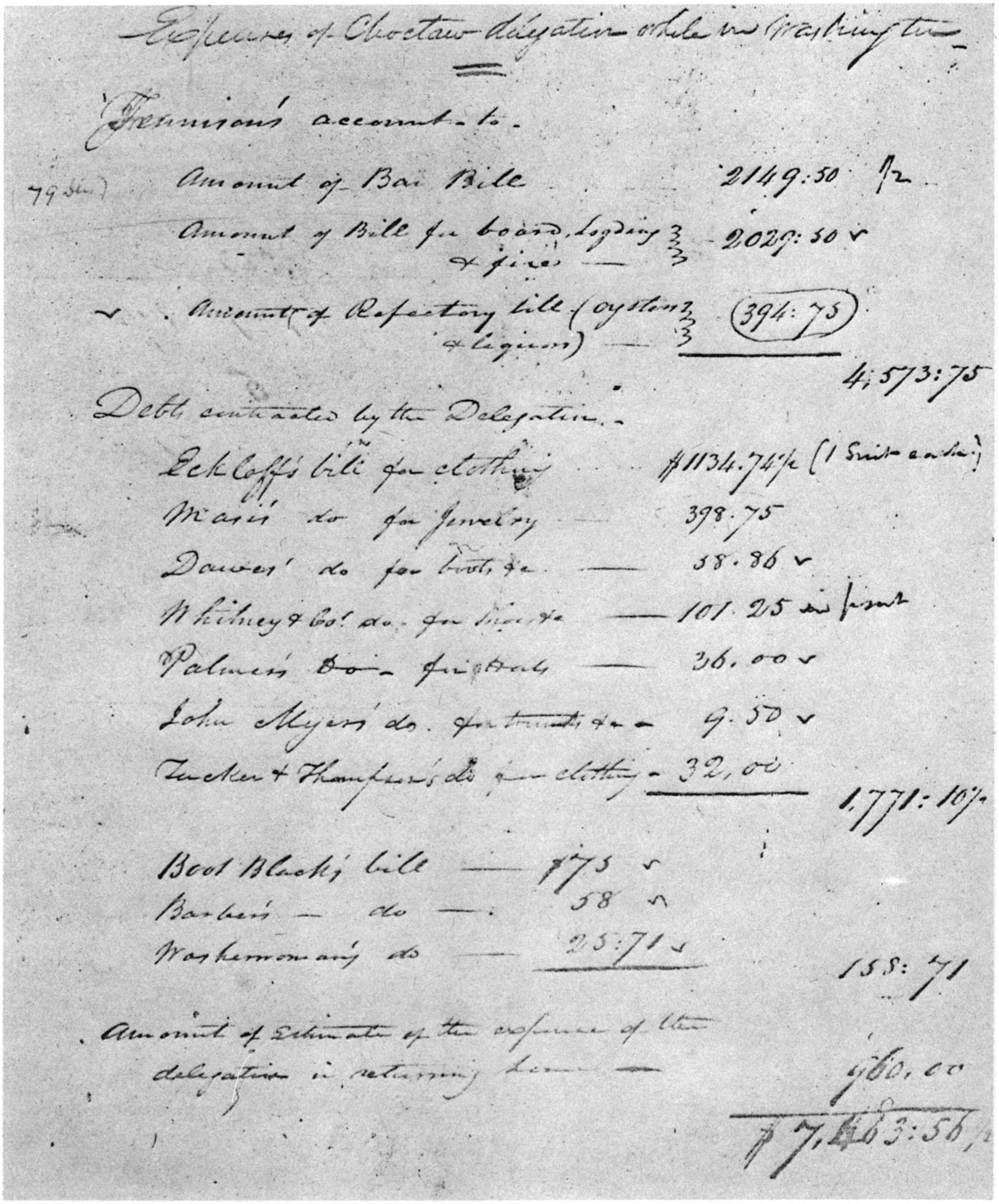

Expenses of Choctaw delegation while in Washington —

Trenison's account to.

79th)   Amount of Bar Bill   2149:50 1/2

    Amount of Bill for board, lodging } — 2029:50

        & fires }

    Amount of Refectory bill (oysters }   (394:75)

       & liquors) — }

                                  4,573:75

Debt contracted by the Delegation —

    Eckloff's bill for clothing — $1134.74 1/2 (1 Suit each)

    Mason's do for Jewelry — 398.75

    Davies' do for boots &c — 58.86

    Whitney & Co! do for hats &c — 101.25 in part

    Palmer's do for fruit &c — 36.00

    John Myers' do for trunks &c — 9.50

    Tucker & Thompson's do for clothing — 32,00

                                   1,771:10 1/2

    Boot Black's bill — $75

    Barber's — do — 58

    Washerwoman's do — 25:71

                                    158:71

Amount of Estimate of the expense of the
delegation in returning home —   960.00

                                $7,463:56 1/2

Part of the liquor bill of the
Choctaw delegation while in Washington.

homes with heavy hearts, they wished the Great Father to pardon his red children at Prairie du Chien.

Adams in turn spoke at length and finally agreed to release the imprisoned Winnebago chiefs. Then he paused and the Winnebago knew what was coming; the white man never granted a request without asking one in return. This time Adams gently suggested that while the lead mining district appeared to be the basis of all their trouble with the settlers, perhaps it would be better for them to yield up that territory.

Nawkaw replied that it was against their law for any one group to make a decision that affected the destiny of the nation but in recognition of the Great Father's mercy they would return home and recommend to an entire council that the Winnebago release a small portion to the white man.

The dignified old chief then begged Adams to consider carefully the Americans he would send among them:

"If you send commissioners to treat with us, let them be good men; if agents to dwell among us, let them be honest men. And do not try and convert us to the habits of your children . . . we wish to live as we have lived, and to follow and abide by the customs of our forefathers."

They filed out of the White House and McKenney and Cass led them back to Tennison's.

Later McKenney gave the Winnebago a tour of his Indian portrait gallery. The tall, dignified superintendent, with his shock of grizzled white hair, slowly led the impassive Indians from portrait to portrait. When the tour was finished it was obvious the chiefs were impressed but as one told McKenney: "We see no Winnebago here."

McKenney had anticipated their reaction. He informed the chiefs he had arranged with Charles Bird King to paint their portraits, which he assured them would soon be hanging on the walls of his office alongside the other famous Indian leaders.

There was also the question of presents. The Winnebago had seen the Sauk and Fox chiefs swaggering about their councils dressed in tricorns, frock coats, and brightly colored pantaloons, with ceremonial swords dangling at their sides.

McKenney was again prepared. Before the delegation had arrived he had urged the War Department to give him permission to buy the same presents:

"I have already ascertained," he wrote, "that the articles can be had on the faith of a Congressional appropriation. It will take some time to prepare these things [the clothes and portraits by King at twenty dollars a bust with an additional charge of $1.50 for the frame] and therefore I respectfully submit my proposition."

It was approved and McKenney, always the guardian of the government's purse, hastened to assure the Secretary of War, "The cost will be kept within that paid for the presents and the portraits for the Sac and Fox in 1824."

From his correspondence McKenney appeared to be a man whose firm rule was: if you want something done right, do it yourself. He not only wrote a series of letters to Washington and Georgetown merchants ordering boots, hats, coats, and swords, but insisted on personally inspect-ing each article before it was accepted by his Bureau of Indian Affairs.

There was also the question of the Indians' luggage which McKenney observed seemed to be getting larger and larger with each passing year. When the first delegation came to Washington in the winter of 1821–1822, the Indians had carried their belongings in buckskin bags, but with the government's presents of clothes, gorgets, pipes, and rifles, the stage companies were demanding that something be done.

McKenney decided on trunks. He ordered twenty "two or three different sizes" from a Georgetown merchant to be sent to Tennison's.

The Winnebago gave McKenney an additional headache with another request; they had seen the fops on Pennsylvania Avenue wearing their fashionable bright yellow shoes and each chief demanded a pair.

After a weary Secretary of War approved the money, McKenney sent his instructions to a Georgetown boot-maker:

"Have the Indians at Tennison's measured for a pair of shoes each. The shoes must be of yellow buckskin and must have thin soles."[4]

When the Winnebago left Washington they told Mc-Kenney they were happy, they had seen their Great Father. But there was another reason why they were content—they had outwitted the white man on a few occasions.

In one eastern city, possibly New York, the wife of Yellow Thunder noticed Major Forsyth paid a fee for them to enter a show, circus, or theatre.

"Does the White Father always pay?" she asked.

"It is the white man's way," the agent explained.

"How much do you pay?" she pressed him.

"Two shillings," he replied.

The chief's wife imitated him. "Two shillin'—hump! [good]"

The next morning the Winnebago gathered for break-fast in the hotel dining room. As usual there was a crowd of spectators but this time the chief's wife slammed shut the door. A few minutes later there was a knock. She edged open the door and held out her hand.

"Two shillin'," she said.

The spectator paid and she let him in. Juliet Kinzie, wife of the agent, and author of the delightful *Wau-Bun*, her recollections of the early frontier and the Winnebago, wrote:

"The game went on until she had accumulated a con-siderable sum . . ."[5]

2.

COLONEL MCKENNEY, under fire many times by congressional committees who selected him as a favorite political target, grew understandably expense conscious. Before any delegation left for the nation's capital he demanded that his agents or superintendents give him the exact number of chiefs, warriors and women in the delegation and the cost of transporting them across the country including the return trip.

When their replies were unsatisfactory he would contact the stage companies himself and wasn't above haggling for a group rate.

Richard Burgess, owner of the Washington-Baltimore Stage Company, was always in McKenney's office arguing over his rates. McKenney finally got him down to three dollars per Indian with baggage included, "even if the baggage is believed to be more than customary . . ."[6]

He also personally checked the prices of flag manufacturers, gunsmiths, and bootmakers for presents to be presented to the visiting Indian delegations, prepared the nation's peace medal, and made sure the red man's health was protected during the time he was a guest of the government.

When General Clark and Indian Agent Lawrence Taliaferro accompanied a large delegation of Sioux and Chippewa chiefs to Washington, McKenney decided the President should present each one with a rifle.

He wrote the nation's number one gunsmith, Henry Deringer, in Philadelphia, "to prepare and have ready for delivery . . . five handsome and well furnished fowling pieces and twenty tomahawks of the pipe pattern. The pipe is to be made of brass and the hatchet part to be made of highly polished steel.[7]

McKenney also ordered flags for this delegation at the cost of $148, a custom which would be followed by subsequent superintendents of the Bureau of Indian Affairs until the post–Civil War years.

The health of the Indian delegates was another problem for McKenney. After one of the chiefs died in a Washington hotel "from effects of the croup" and another fell off a cliff, the War Department adopted McKenney's suggestion that the Surgeon General's office be ordered to care for all visiting Indians. This, he insisted, would not only save a private physician's fee but he would always have a doctor available.

McKenney took this action after an angry exchange of letters between himself and a group of Washington doctors whose bills for treating Indians had gradually increased, year after year. In the winter of 1825 when a Choctaw chief became ill McKenney summoned Doctor Cousin. A month later the physician sent in his bills; one was for three thousand dollars, the second for three hundred dollars. A furious McKenney reminded Cousin he had agreed to accept the "standard rate and therefore it is not possible for me to recommend an increased allowance for you."[8] A year later an angry Doctor Cousin was still writing to McKenney demanding that his bill be paid.

3.

DURING THEIR stay in Washington, the Indian delegations were the guests at the best hotels but apparently, like the indignant southern woman who refused to eat at the same table with McKenney's two Indian boys, the capital's residents might stare fascinated at America's painted aborigines but didn't care to be their table mates.

After an Indian delegation had complained to McKenney that they had not been permitted to sit with the other guests at Williamson's Hotel's dining table where food was served family style, McKenney complained to the owner, Basil Williamson, that not only was his bill higher than usual but he had discriminated against the chiefs and warriors.

Williamson, one of the best known of the Pennsylvania Avenue hotel owners, offered a vague explanation that the delegation was so large, "I could not furnish them in any other manner than a private table" to maintain the "character of the house."

The policy of Williamson, Jesse Brown, owner of the famous Indian Queen, and the other hotel men was to charge the government as much as they thought they could slip past McKenney. Their usual fee was $1.25 to $1.50 per Indian in a room that included candles, a fire, and apples. Liquor was always extra and the best customers the hotel bars ever had were the Indians. McKenney was constantly battling with innkeepers over their padded bills for the incredible amounts of whiskey the Indians consumed, as well as the tables, chairs, rugs, and mirrors they smashed in their drunken brawls. The itemized bills reveal a fascinating picture of how the chiefs and warriors spent their time in Washington.

The great Choctaw chief, Pushmataha, for example, arrived in Washington on the morning of December 15, 1824. He was accompanied by eight chiefs and warriors and McKenney made arrangements for the delegation to stay at Tennison's Hotel. They were soon ordering oysters on the half shell along with ale and brandy, first by the glass then by the bottle. Later in the day they all switched to gin slings and bottles of wine. This diet lasted two days. Gin and bar whiskey followed, to be replaced by bottles of porter.

When they discovered that Christmas Eve was a white man's honored holiday devoted to much merriment, laughter, and song, the Choctaw decided that what was good enough for the white man was good enough for the red man, and they ordered a bowl of eggnog sent up by room service. Probably as an afterthought they informed the bartender that wine chasers would be desirable.

But oysters and whiskey continued to be their favorite fare; waiters were constantly running up and down from the bar to their rooms with bottles and trays.

They celebrated New Year's Eve in grand style, as quick to lift a glass in a toast at the bar as their white brothers. New Year's Day was devoted to testing "cyder" with brandy and porter chasers. For the rest of their stay it was back again to oysters and brandy.

The chiefs spent over five thousand dollars which included $2,149.50 for liquor, $75 for bootblacks, $1,134 for clothing, $400 for laundry, and $58 for the barbershop.[9] Their generous government only charged them half the bill to be paid out of their annual annuity. The Indians also had to pay for their transportation; fares came to $960. The grand total charged to the Choctaw nation was $7,463.56 at Washington prices, circa 1825.

Only death was a bargain for the Indians. When a western chief died suddenly in a Washington hotel, the government agreed to supply the delegation with five yards of cloth for a shroud, a dollar's worth of music, a barber for a dollar, and a seven dollar wooden coffin. There was no charge for the Congressional cemetery plot.[10]

John Ross, the great Cherokee chief, came to Washington to dispute the amount of annuity money divided between his nation and the so-called "Western Cherokee," or those bands that had moved west of the Mississippi. He spent a great deal of time with President Monroe, Colonel McKenney, and Secretary of War Calhoun.

Despite these hours with the President and important Cabinet members, the government refused to pay his transportation and board bills. Calhoun pointed out that he had not come to the capital at the "government's invitation but only for the prosecution of your objects, in the success of which your nation alone will benefit."

But Ross was sophisticated in the ways of Washington politics. When he increased the pressure Calhoun finally ruled after months of exchanging letters that the bills would be charged against the annuity of the Western Cherokee. It is not known what their reaction was to this political expediency.[11]

4.

THE INDIAN delegations continued to arrive and depart. McKenney's problems were both humorous and tragic but none more bizarre than the case of the Osage warrior who was held as a hostage—not by an enemy tribe but by an indignant boardinghouse keeper in Norfolk.[12]

The Osage was one of several who had been lured downriver by a French entrepreneur who promised to escort them to Washington to see the Great Father. Instead the Indians found themselves on a ship crossing the ocean. The Frenchmen informed them they were going to the home of the Great Father by way of Europe.

In Le Havre, Paris, and Holland they were put on exhibition as "Savages from the American Wilderness." For years they were moved across the cities of Europe. When the exhibit had run its course the owners divided the Indians into two groups. Each was placed in the steerage of a ship bound for the United States.

On a bitterly cold day in January 1830 the first group, bewildered, half-starved, penniless, and completely lost, was dumped on the Norfolk wharfs. Two had died aboard from smallpox and their bodies had been buried at sea, to the horror of the Indians.

Somehow they arrived at the boardinghouse of Mrs. Rachel Anderson, a kindhearted but peppery widow. While she fed and housed the red men, city officials wrote to Washington describing the Indians' plight and asking what should they do.

Letters shuttled from bureau to bureau, while Mrs. Anderson thoughtfully totaled up the bill for her Indian boarders—it was quite impressive.

One of the letters finally reached McKenney. After consulting with the War Department, Quartermaster General T. S. Jesup was ordered to deliver the Osage travelers to Washington. Jesup followed orders and some weeks later the weary Indians, dressed in tattered blankets, walked into the office of the Bureau of Indian Affairs. The Osage listened impassively to McKenney's speech of greeting. When he had finished the Superintendent waited for the usual recital of grievances against the white man but instead the spokesman, through an interpreter, told McKenney that not only was there another group of their warriors on the high seas but a white woman was holding one of their chiefs as a hostage.

The perplexed McKenney finally found out the whole story: Mrs. Anderson had turned her boarders over to the army but had kept one of the chiefs as hostage for her bill. As McKenney wrote to the War Department, he was "held as kind of a hostage for the forthcoming of the pay for their expenses and to take care of their baggage."

McKenney assured Mrs. Anderson her bill would be paid by the War Department after she had released her hostage, "who is to be sent to Annapolis, from which place the steamboat runs."

The first group was clothed, dined, given presents, and the profuse apologies of the Great Father who carefully pointed out to the Indians that it had been the French and not the Americans who had caused their difficulties. Then they were sent to General Clark in St. Louis with instruction to return them to their nation.

The Osage were uneasy at leaving Washington without their brothers who were somewhere on the Atlantic bouncing and tossing in the hold of a trading vessel. McKenney assured them many times that he would be personally responsible for their safety.

In April 1830, the *New York Post* published an article about the arrival of some Osage Indians aboard a French ship but neglected to say what had happened to them. Somewhere in the city were several homesick, bewildered, penniless Osage warriors. McKenney suggested to General Jesup that he do the obvious:

"I am not able to tell you at what place [in New York City] the Indians may be found but the notice of their arrival being published in the New York Post, the editor of that newspaper no doubt can give you the information . . . "

The *Post*'s editor and his ship news reporter, along with Jesup's army officers, finally found the Osage Indians in a waterfront inn. They were returned to Washington where they were given gifts of blue coats with white lace, boots, hats, swords—and of course, yellow shoes with thin soles—and then returned by stagecoach to St. Louis and General Clark.

5.

WASHINGTON'S MOST celebrated Indian visitor during the 1830s was undoubtedly Black Hawk. He came to the capital on April 23, 1833, as a prisoner of war but was welcomed as a conquering hero.

In June the delegation of Sauk and Fox chiefs, led by The Prophet who had been instrumental in persuading

Black Hawk to wage his celebrated guerrilla war, visited Norfolk, Boston, Philadelphia, and New York City.

In Norfolk's navy yard they went aboard the 74-gun frigate, *Delaware*. They felt honored, they told the officers because the "great canoe" had an Indian figurehead on its bow. Huge crowds massed outside the hotel for hours chanting for Black Hawk. The Indian finally appeared, tipped his hat, and called out greeting to "all our white friends."[13]

In Baltimore they met President Jackson who was also making a tour of the eastern cities and again Black Hawk promised to bury the tomahawk "so deep it will never be resurrected."

Black Hawk liked Philadelphia, the town, he said, "where they make money and medals." They attended an opera performance which Black Hawk said he didn't understand but enjoyed anyway, toured the United States mint, and like all tourists were given shiny coins. The chiefs also reviewed the troops before they took the stage for New York.

On June 14 Black Hawk and his delegation were guests of honor at a balloon ascension in Battery Park. A reporter for the *New York Gazette* quoted the Indian chief as calling the aeronaut "a brave man who could go to heaven to see the Great Spirit." Pa-Maah-hooh, Black Hawk's adopted son, gravely informed the press he was sure the balloonist "could even see the English country across the Great Sea."

Crowds followed the Sauk and Fox chief—he wasn't a chief in the elected or hereditary sense but a popular warrior who attracted a large following of young warriors —and again stood outside his lower Broadway hotel demanding that he appear. Black Hawk finally came out on a balcony, raised his hat, and called out:

"How do you do? How do you do all? The Great Spirit knows I love you, and that my heart is with you."

He was the star attraction in the crowded and popular Niblo's Gardens where ladies fought to kiss him, was mobbed at Castle Garden, and was presented with a pair of topaz earrings for his wife.[14]

He finally returned to the West where he died many years later, never too weary to recall his trip to Washington and the white man's fabulous cities.

By 1837 Indian delegations had lost their glamour for the citizens of the large eastern cities, particularly Washington, where residents now complained of the rough behavior of the red men, especially when a group of Indians, after finishing several bottles of brandy, tried to lift the scalps of some passersby on Pennsylvania Avenue.

The National Intelligencer reported that one gentleman fainted after looking out the window of his carriage into the painted face of a brave who held out his hand for some silver.

One fall day Indian agent Major Taliaferro escorted a large delegation of Sioux warriors and chiefs to the capital. They were bigger and more muscular than the smaller Pawnee, Creek, Choctaw or Osage the Washington residents were accustomed to seeing. The fierce-looking men from the Great Plains carried bows, arrows, and tomahawks; rather than frighten the citizens, McKenney ordered them put up at the smaller Globe Hotel.

An indication of the times was the letter an indignant reader wrote to the *National Intelligencer*:

"With due deference to the 'powers that be' we doubt the propriety of these Indians being encouraged to walk about our streets 'cap-a-pie' without their attendents..."[15]

6.

PRESENTS FAVORED by the visiting Indian delegations were whiskey, rifles, and medals.[16]

In the late 1820s Colonel McKenney was ordering shipments of fifty rifles at a time from Deringer, his favorite weaponmaker, not only for the chiefs calling at the White House but for agents conducting treaties on the frontier. In July 1826 fifty were shipped to General John Tipton, McKenney's agent at Fort Wayne, Indiana, while "ten strongboxes of rifles" had been sent on to General Clark in St. Louis. Evidently these were only part of the Indian Bureau's order, as Deringer advised McKenney: "I am going on with the other rifles according to order."

In the winter of 1829 McKenney wrote Deringer he was considering a lower bid from Henry, another gunmaker whose rifles became famous on the frontier. Deringer's long, indignant reply reveals something of the gunsmith's industry of that period.

Writing from his Philadelphia shop Deringer told Colonel McKenney:

> I can only say that rifles I make and have made for $12.50 per gun, that the material costs me ten dollars and no gunsmith in the country can supply materials cheaper. I have my own mills and machines for barrel making and for brass forging, in fact every part belonging to a gun is made under my immediate inspection. As for materials or for workmanship, there is no gunsmith here or in the country that can make them cheaper than myself.

Deringer went on to tell McKenney of his earliest days as the frontier's master gunsmith.

> General Mason [McKenney's successor as Superintendent in the Indian Trade Bureau] was hard put for good rifles before I commenced making them in 1810, and [I] have made them to the satisfaction of the Indian agents and the Indians themselves, in fact, agents wrote to General Mason not to send any other rifles after I began making them in 1810 . . . in the 18 or 19 years there has never been any fault found with any of my weapons as to quality or workmanship . . . when General Mason established the price for rifles for the Indian trade at $12.50, the material was considered less than the present. A person not established the same as I am cannot make a living at $12.50 for the same quality of rifle I make . . .

Deringer explained that his barrels are "made of the best iron which costs me forty dollars extra a ton and there is not a speck in them which is more than Mr. Henry can say for his barrels." He closed with a bitter comment that "Mr. Henry is well known to undermine any person he can, whether he finishes the work afterwards or not..."[17]

The letter apparently convinced Colonel McKenney; his terse reply assured Deringer the Bureau of Indian Affairs would continue to deal with him and not Henry.

Brass tomahawks "in pipe paterns" as McKenney called them were also an Indian gift item disbributed both by the Americans and the British. Some came with a silver belt buckle or were engraved with the name of the recipient or a fanciful hunting scene. Tecumseh was wearing a fancy tomahawk when he was killed in the Battle of the Thames and it was removed from his body along with the ornamented belt and silver buckle by his chief warrior, John Naudee. Joseph Brant was presented with a tomahawk, said to be silver and engraved with his name, by King George III when Brant was received at the royal court in 1776.

McKenney also presented the visiting chiefs and warriors with silver hatbands, shiny silver gorgets, and three- to four-inch belt buckles.

However, medals were considered the supreme gift by the Indians. They were status symbols, concrete and undeniable signs they had been received by the Great Father. Many times they were handed down, generation to generation, or were buried with the owners.

The first American Indian peace medal is believed to have been made in 1757 by Edward Duffield, a Philadelphia watchmaker, for a Quaker Society called The Friendly Association for the Regaining and Preserving Peace With the Indians by Pacific Means.[18]

The most interesting of all Indian peace medals was the one Washington presented to Red Jacket during his Philadelphia visit in 1792. (McKenney tried to buy it many many times but the famous Seneca orator always refused.) On one side Washington, in full regimentals has presented a peace pipe to an Indian who is smoking it; the Indian is standing and off to one side is a pine tree, at its foot a tomahawk. On the reverse side is stamped the crest of the United States on the breast of an eagle. In the right talon is an olive branch; in the left a sheaf of arrows. In its beak is a ribbon with the motto *E Pluribus Unum*; above it glory is breaking through the clouds and is surrounded by thirty stars. The size was 6¾ by 3¾ inches. Red Jacket is wearing this medal in his McKenney and Hall portrait.

McKenney had no difficulty with the peace medals bearing the likenesses of Madison and Monroe but was almost driven to distraction by the problems he encountered with the Adams medal.

The maddening correspondence between President Adams, Colonel McKenney, a New York artist named Moritz Furst, whom McKenney had commissioned to do the official portrait for the die, Furst's son, and William Moore, Director of the United States Mint in Philadelphia, began in the spring of 1825 when McKenney wrote to the Secretary of War outlining the history of the Indian Peace medals and proposing that one be struck for President Adams with New York artist Moritz Furst commissioned to do the portrait. Furst had designed several peace and commemorative medals for the government. "The sooner the work is done, the better," McKenney urged, pointing out that Indian delegations would be soon arriving in Washington and it was the custom to distribute medals of the current President, "who the Indians claim for their Great Father."

He went on: "It is the practice for an agent and especially by those on our North Western Frontier, to take medals of the King from the Indians, who receive them from British traders, in which case they present another of the Great Father. . . . The British standards are taken from them and an American given in their stead. . . .[19]

McKenney received approval four days later from the Secretary of War and immediately contacted the White House to arrange for a sitting. On June 25 Furst reported to McKenney that "the likeness of President Adams has been completed and I will forward the impression as soon as all three sizes are finished, for it will save time."[20]

When McKenney saw Furst's portrait he reacted quickly. The tip of the nose, he wrote Furst was so out of line it distorted the President's lower lip while the shoulders were too broad and the forehead too wide.

Letters flew back and forth that summer and fall between the angry McKenney and the distraught Furst who, as delicately as he could, tried to point out to McKenney that he was the artist and McKenney was the Indian Superintendent. But McKenney insisted that the impression "had to be altered or destroyed."

Furst finally advised McKenney he had finished a new portrait and had "done everything in my power to improve the likeness which I believe is as good as the Original. . . ."

The Indian Superintendent grudgingly agreed to send it on to Adams for approval. John Adams, Jr., promptly returned it with a whimsical note pointing out that the impression was better than the others he had seen, but at the same time he wished "Mr. Furst had been more fortunate. It is however, I think, better than either of the medals of Mr. Madison or Mr. Monroe. The family generally coincides with me in opinion."

Undoubtedly with a sigh of relief McKenney sent his approval to the mint accompanied with an order for the medals. In mid-December 1825 he received the first box in time to fulfill a request from Indian Agent O'Fallon who pleaded for "at least a dozen medals" to distribute to the tribes at a council soon to be held on the Upper Missouri.

It was inevitable that politicians would investigate the cost of McKenney's Indian medals. After he had been accused of "wild expenditures" and "large sums spent on Indian medals" McKenney wrote to a friend in Baltimore explaining why the medals were important and who paid for them. Either McKenney or his friend made sure a copy went to the editor of the *National Intelligencer*. He wrote:

There undoubtedly has been created an error in the public minds in regard to this medal business. It has been the usage of the French and British governments and of our own, since Gen. Washington's Presidency, to provide and present medals to Indians; and the practice forms an essential part of our policy in our intercourse with these people; as that of giving them blankets, strouds or tobacco. It appears not to be known to the writers of this subject; (I mean those who amuse themselves by squibbing about it in the newspapers) that we have the Washington, Jefferson, Madison and Monroe, as well as the Adams medal and that the cost has always been paid, as in the present instance, by the government . . .[21]

John H. Eaton
Secretary of War under whom
McKenney served.

Peggy Eaton
Wife of John H. Eaton
Courtesy, Library of Congress

CHAPTER XII:

The Chippewa Who Stole Washington

I.

S HE CAME out of the bitter sleeting night in 1827, a pretty, petite woman who asked Mr. Haller, the Georgetown tinsmith, in a soft, shy whisper, if she could warm herself by his forge. She held out her hands to the glowing coals, shivering uncontrollably under her threadbare blanket, as she explained in broken English mixed with French how she had walked through the winter wilderness from Detroit.[1]

Haller peered at her through the gloom. As he later said, he thought at first his visitor was an old beggar. When he looked closer he could see her glossy black hair, wet, stringy, and hanging to her shoulders under the calico sunbonnet. Her fingers were frostbitten and she wore men's boots caked with slush that was making a pool of water on the floor. She said she was a Chippewa woman.

It was obvious there was only one man in all of Washington who would know what to do with her, Haller told himself. Colonel McKenney. He called his apprentice and ordered him to guide the Chippewa woman to Weston, the McKenney estate, on Georgetown Heights.

It was about eight o'clock when the apprentice knocked on McKenney's door. When it swung open to show the colonel framed in the doorway, the boy gestured to the shivering woman at his side.

"She came to our shop to warm herself," the boy explained, "and when she said she was an Indian, Mr. Haller told me to take her to you, sir."

McKenney thanked the boy and ushered the woman into his kitchen. She said her name was Tshusick.

"Are you hungry?" he asked her.

She nodded and McKenney waved her to a table.

McKenney questioned her while she ate.

"Where are you from?"

"Mackinac."

"Who do you know there?"

"Mother and Father Boyd (George Boyd was McKenney's Indian Agent), Mr. and Mrs. (Robert) Stuart (the American Fur Company Agent), and others." She waved her hand. "All of them are known to me."

McKenney pressed her. "Who else do you know there?"

"Mr. Johnson's family at Sault Ste. Marie . . ."

"Do you know anyone at Detroit?"

Tshusick nodded vigorously. "Father Cass." [Governor Lewis Cass.]

Then she went on to describe in detail the interior of Cass's home. Before she had finished McKenney was sure she was not an imposter.

With tears brimming her large dark eyes, Tshusick told McKenney how after her husband had died she had walked through the snow, rain, and hail from Detroit. She described Agent Boyd's wife, who, she insisted, she loved as a mother, then recited for McKenney the many stories Mrs. Boyd had told her of her sister, Mrs. John Quincy Adams, "who lived in the White House of the Great Father."

After her husband died, she fell to her knees and vowed she would walk to Washington if necessary to seek out the sister of Mrs. Boyd, "who being the wife of the Great Father of the white people, would, she hoped, protect her until she was properly instructed and baptized."

We can assume McKenney became very interested in Tshusick when he heard the name of Harriet Boyd, sister of Louisa Adams, America's First Lady. As an old Washington hand McKenney was familiar with the story of how George Boyd, in a moment of political pique, had resigned his post as head of the government pension board and was unemployed for so long that his family suffered; there was no food, and creditors harassed him. Louisa Adams, unknown to her husband, begged President Monroe to find a post for her brother-in-law.

"Knowing how contrary it is to my husband's principles to assist any member of his family," she wrote to the President, "I again repeat that I am shocked at the necessity of the step which I am now taking; but my religion sanctions it, and I prefer my duty to God to my duty to man."

Soon after he had received Louisa's letter, Monroe arranged for Boyd to be appointed Indian agent at Mackinac.[2]

McKenney knew that Louisa Adams, who had been close to her sister, would be eager to hear any news of the Boyds so he arranged for Tshusick to stay at Holtzman's

Boarding House and then bought her some scarlet and blue cloth, needles, thread, and beads. Now she could discard her rags "and make a costume in the fashion of her people."

Tshusick proved to be a clever dress designer. She worked steadily in her room until she had a striking, colorful dress, a dark blue skirt trimmed with pink, a vivid red jacket and red pantaloons, edged with pink and blue facing. There was enough left over from the goods McKenney had sent to fashion a white blouse. Later the Indian Superintendent presented her with a pair of moccasins and a black hat crowned by waving plumes.[3]

When Tshusick returned to McKenney's office the colonel was startled; as he recalled he had never seen a more beautiful and colorful Indian woman. Always foremost in his mind was the Indian Gallery; obviously Tshusick was a fine subject. He took her to King's studio where he commissioned her portrait for twenty dollars.

While Tshusick was sitting for King, McKenney told the First Lady her romantic story. Louisa Adams was thrilled and arranged to have McKenney bring the beautiful copper-skinned orphan of the storm to the White House. Mrs. Adams was astonished by the Chippewa's wit, her flawless French, her skill as a seamstress and dress designer and, as McKenney later recalled, "her firm address, remarkable manners and her propriety."

Tshusick not only captivated Louisa Adams and the President but the entire White House staff, foreign dignitaries, prominent politicians, and just about everyone who called on the President.

One of her conquests was William Theobald Wolfe Tone, son of the famous Irish patriot and French general. After meeting Tshusick at a party given in his honor by McKenney at Weston, Tone told the colonel he was astonished that "anyone but a native Parisian could speak my language with such fluency and elegance."[4]

The dignified First Lady and the petite Indian squaw spent hours together, Tshusick fascinating Louisa with stories about her sister Harriet's way of life in the wilderness, her husband, their daily chores, the Indians, and how Harriet kept house in a log cabin.

The President was so enchanted with Tshusick that one afternoon he hung a silver medal about her neck.

Louisa Adams was Tshusick's golden key to Washington. Few doors were shut to the First Lady of the land and wherever she went the Indian woman was at her side, dinners at the home of the Secretary of War, receptions for congressmen and senators, teas with the wives of the foreign dignitaries—Tshusick was soon one of the most talked about women in Washington.

Then one day she informed the Indian Superintendent, "she wanted to be made a Christian." McKenney notified the Reverend Mr. Grey of Georgetown of Tshusick's wishes and he went to see her. The clergyman was no less susceptible to her charms than the First Lady, the distinguished foreign visitors, or the Secretary of War. He informed McKenney they had spent an evening conversing in French, "because of the sacredness of the subject and delicacy she felt had to be given the sacrament." There

was no doubt in his mind Tshusick was "a fit subject for Baptism."

The ceremony took place in Christ Church, Georgetown, with McKenney escorting Tshusick to the font and offering her the name of Lucy Cornelia Barbour, in honor of the wife and daughter of the Secretary of War.[5]

The new Lucy Cornelia Barbour stayed in the capital for ten days after her baptism. Stories about her began to appear in the capital's newspapers and her circle of admirers expanded with the stout and formidable Major General Alexander Macomb, soon to be appointed the army's general-in-chief, as her constant escort.

McKenney was an amused observer. But an instinct, sharpened by years of contact with Indians from every corner of the land, began to question this charming, dark-eyed beauty from the wilderness. To McKenney it was beginning to sound almost too romantic, like a chapter from a Scott novel. It was true he had satisfied his early doubts by his severe cross-examination even to where an Indian painting hung in Cass's study, but a lingering doubt still remained. One night on an impulse he wrote to Cass, casually telling him about Tshusick and how she had captured Washington.

While his letter was en route to Detroit by stagecoach, steamboat, and canalboat, McKenney disclosed to Tshusick that he had written to the Michigan Territorial Governor on some official matter but had added how she was visiting Washington. A short time Tshusick abruptly informed McKenney she had to return home "to my people." So many presents from disappointed admirers who begged her to stay poured into the White House, that President Adams told his wife to buy Tshusick a trunk.

Among the boxes and packages were gifts from the Presidential family to the Boyds and their children, which Tshusick promised to deliver. The White House arranged for the Chippewa to travel to the end of the stagecoach line, then buy a horse to continue her journey to Detroit. Major General Macomb also provided a money belt stuffed with currency "and with the gallantry which forms a conspicuous part of his character, fastened it with his own hand, upon the person of the lovely tourist."

It makes a delightful picture: America's First Lady, senators' wives, Mrs. Barbour and her daughter who had given their names, Colonel McKenney, congressmen, William Wolfe Tone who had been impressed by Tshusick's fluency with French, all misty-eyed as they watched the general-in-chief of the Army of the United States gently fastening the money belt about the slim waist of the smiling Indian girl.[6]

In Baltimore she was greeted by Mrs. Barnum, owner of the famous Barnum's Hotel, "who took her into her private apartment, detained her for several days as a guest, and showed her the curiosities of the beautiful city." Tshusick then left for Frederick, Maryland, where the stage owners insisted on giving her free passage to the end of the line.[7]

The dreary winter days passed. Then McKenney received a reply from Cass. As he read it the chagrined Indian Superintendent could almost hear his old friend roaring with laughter; Tshusick was a superb confidence woman.

It was true she was married but her husband was very much alive. In fact, Cass wrote, he was at that very moment "a short squat Frenchman who officiated as a scullion" in the Boyd household at Mackinac.

Tshusick, Cass revealed to McKenney, was a professional swindler, who had duped the great and near-great "in her wanderings through the whole length of the Canadas, from Montreal to St. Louis and from Quebeck to the Falls of St. Anthony and many times in the interior."[8]

Washington had been her supreme and most successful effort. As Cass gleefully pointed out, she had taken in McKenney, the supposed Indian expert, the President of the United States and his First Lady, the Secretary of War and his family, a good part of Congress, hard-nosed politicians, foreign ambassadors, dignitaries and that man of the world and revolutions, William Theobald Wolfe Tone.

McKenney, a determined man, vowed he would find Tshusick. He stalked her all over the West but her backwoods intelligence was flawless; when he came to Detroit to visit Cass, she had left for Mackinac; when he wrote the Boyds, she had left for Fort Howard or Green Bay or Pittsburgh; it was always the same, Tshusick was as elusive as quicksilver.[9]

Kentucky's Senator Wickliffe, who became a new McKenney enemy in 1828, attacked him from the Senate floor for spending large sums on Tshusick's entertainment and giving the Indian woman the names of the wife and daughter of the Secretary of War. McKenney's Indian gallery also came under attack when Wickliffe questioned why the government should pay twenty dollars for the "likeness of an Indian woman."

This public and political denunciation of him and his Bureau of Indian Affairs were familiar to McKenney. Once again he used the columns of the *National Intelligencer* for his answer. He wrote:

We have five hundred youths of both sexes, now bearing the names of our most distinguished families, and they are pleased to bear them. There is nothing new, therefore, in this; and certainly no one will suppose that this name was given in derision. It was more to please the Indian than to dishonor anyone.

It is true her likeness was taken. It hangs in the office of Indian Affairs with the rest, and preserving the female costume of the North West and is a fine portrait. She left Washington after collecting the bounty of many, and after about ten days tarrying. (Since which time I have never seen her) and left a name for propriety of conduct in all respects (whatever her real character may be) highly creditable to her . . .[10]

2.

AFTER TSHUSICK'S visit, the Congressional Retrenchment Committee and Representative Thomas T. Moore of Kentucky selected as their target McKenney's portrait gallery and the expenses he had approved for entertaining Indian delegations.

In June 1828 Moore, under the title of "Address of Thomas F. Moore to his Constituents," submitted a voluminous report to the *Louisville Public Advertiser* detailing in eight full columns the work he had done the past winter in Washington. Moore, like the *Advertiser*, was violently

anti-Clay, lukewarm toward Calhoun, and strongly pro-Jackson.

The report reveals Moore to be a frontier demagogue. He denounced the outgoing Adams administration, reviewing the President's expenditures from as far back as the War of 1812 when he was summoned from Russia by Madison to conduct peace negotiations at Ghent.

After five columns of incredible political distortion, Moore reached Colonel McKenney and went on to review the "extraordinary expenditures" in McKenney's Indian department:

Tennison's for boarding McIntosh and his party of Indians	$1,000
Boot and shoe blackening for Indians	$ 216
Morris Furst for his portrait of John Quincy Adams	$1,000
Three years of taking portraits of Indians	$3,190

In an obvious appeal to the anti-Indian philosophy of most frontiersmen, Moore wrote:

I cannot think it was very economical to send a gang of Indians to the most expensive hotel in the city to board, then taking thousands of dollars of your money, to pamper savages who a few years ago were burying tomahawks in the heads of our wives and children . . .

Still less necessary can I see for paying $3,190 for the pictures of these wretches, the use of which would be impossible to tell. I believe they are hung in Mr. McKenney's office to gratify the curiosity of strangers.

It was doubtless just as proper to give $1,000 for Mr. Adams's portrait as $3,190 for the portraits of Indians. But I doubt whether the people care enough for the likeness or the original to squander thousands of dollars on them. Who pays for these pictures? The People!

Yes, my Constituents, of what use are they? None at all! But you have had to pay, not only for the feeding and wining of Indians, teaching them habits destructive to themselves, and for their pictures but also for blackening their shoes.

This caps the climax![11]

The report of the Committee of Retrenchment not only attacked McKenney's Indian Gallery as a wasteful extravagance of the government's money but also included his library which contained manuscripts, rare books, and articles on the American Indian and his culture.[12]

McKenney, in the form of a letter "To A Friend" who conveniently leaked it to the *Intelligencer*, defended his gallery and his expenditures. The gallery, he pointed out, could now be sold for double its original value, "and with it may go, without any regret of mine, of a personal kind, all the little relics which in my travels I have picked up, and at great trouble brought home with me. It is no fancy scheme of mine."[13]

McKenney always found support among the minority members of any Congressional committee that investigated him. The minority report of the Retrenchment Committee scoffed at the majority members' conclusions and insisted that instead of trimming McKenney's budget for his gallery and archives, it should be expanded and the entire bureau be assigned larger offices. In that fashion, they wrote, the portrait gallery "might be more advantageously exhibited, the portraits in question and others which may be added to them, together with ample collections of the arms, costumes, household implements and all the other articles pertaining to Indian life and manners . . ."

Such a large gallery, they concluded, would not only

help to impress the visiting Indian delegations but could also provide "a repository, possessing a high degree of scientific and historical value."[14]

Secretary of War Barbour also felt the pressure of the Retrenchment Committee. He nervously advised McKenney that there were enough Indian portraits, "which it is desirable to obtain." No more expenditures will be permitted, he ruled, "unless the subject be remarkable and have claims to the remembrance of posterity for some deeds or virtue or prowess; or be in figure or in costume very peculiar indeed."

When Red Jacket visited McKenney, the Indian Superintendent quickly claimed the great Seneca chief indeed belonged to posterity and his portrait—at the cost of $51—joined the gallery. Mohongo, the Osage woman who had been kidnapped and taken abroad by the French entrepreneur, was something of a problem but after a deluge of notes and memorandums from the Bureau of Indian Affairs, the Secretary of War wearily surrendered and gave his consent. McKenney sent a brisk note to King advising him that Mohongo was staying at Williamson's Hotel and he should paint her portrait without delay.

"Better do it," he wrote, "I think it may open the door again for more work. The Gallery is growing in popularity." King's fee, as usual, was twenty dollars.[15]

King, who obviously wanted the door to open, painted the Indian mother and her child, born either in Paris or aboard the ship which had taken her and the other Osage to Norfolk, and McKenney triumphantly added her portrait to his gallery.

CHAPTER XIII:

McKenney and Jackson

1.

JOHN QUINCY ADAMS had continued in the tradition of Monroe and nothing was changed. Despite the protesting Jacksonians, he had made Clay his Secretary of State but most of Monroe's old appointments, including Colonel McKenney, had continued in office. President Adams removed only twelve federal officials, not on political grounds, but for incompetence.

This failure to build his own party and machine through patronage—he insisted that only ability was the criterion for appointment to serve the federal government—led to his downfall in the brutal, dirty election of 1828.

There were indications in 1826 that Calhoun was ready to desert Adams and support Jackson when he allowed John Randolph of Roanoke, a bizarre figure even in an age when everything was outsized, to tongue-lash the White House daily. Adams's patience finally snapped and he and his vice-president engaged in a battle of the newspaper columns. While Washington looked on amazed, the President of the United States and his vice-president hurled barrages of charges at each other under the pseudonyms of "Patrick Henry" and "Onslow."

Randolph, whose silver voice never failed to enchant the galleries, continued his attacks on the powerless Adams through the spring, summer, fall, and winter of 1826–1827 while Calhoun, from his vice-presidential platform listened impassively to the Virginian's orations which went on at times from early afternoon until late at night. Since his editorship of the *Washington Republican*, McKenney had always dreamed of the day when Calhoun would walk into the White House. In every presidential election year he launched a personal boom for Calhoun in his letters to men of affairs and high office. Even his old friend Rev. Philip Milledoler, President of Rutgers College, wasn't immune. As McKenney wrote in a letter marked, *"private altogether sir.":*

"What do you think of our excellent friend Calhoun for next President? What a lodgement of power, politically and mentally would be in the Executive Seat! *He is the man.*"[1] (McKenney's emphasis.) McKenney wrote to Milledoler the following day again proposing Calhoun as a presidential candidate: "If you would like this great result to be idealized, and I am sure you would, you can without stepping into the Department of Electioneering campaign *do much*. Write me and tell me what you and your friends think of it all."

In the 1828 campaign Calhoun decided to support Jackson and run for the vice-presidency on the assumption that Jackson, then sixty, would step aside after one term and help him become the next tenant in the White House.

Adams, who had brought to the office a high-minded conception of the national interest, was no match as a politician for the Jacksonians. Charges of corruption were hurled at him and his administration, and the editorial abuse was incredible.

The theory of the Jacksonians was that Adams had won the White House only because he had traded the post of Secretary of State for the support of Henry Clay, while Jackson had in fact won the larger initial vote. The bitterness of the 1828 campaign brought out a record number of voters, five times as many as four years earlier.

Old Hickory's strength came from the West and the South. When the returns came in it was a surging tidal wave for Jackson while Calhoun was an easy victor for the vice-presidency.

2.

IT WAS now President-elect Jackson. The winter of the changeover of administrations was as bitter as the recent campaign. At a time when the city was usually alive with balls and levees, now it was strangely quiet, almost eerie with the freezing wind howling down the deserted streets. Few windows glowed with candlelight; curbs were empty of carriages. The *Intelligencer* and *Gazette* reported the bitterly cold weather was breaking records and the Potomac was frozen solid. After one heavy snowstorm poor families were discovered starving and freezing to death in their unheated shacks. The *Intelligencer* with a spurt of community conscience began a campaign to buy wood for the needy.

Jackson's inauguration was the wildest in presidential history. His army was everywhere; bearded frontiersmen with clay-caked boots, men in buckskins, moccasins, skinning knives in their belts, weather-beaten women in calico and heavy boots, came to see their hero; newspapers estimated that twenty thousand were packed along Pennsylvania Avenue. Jackson finally mounted the steps to the portico, stood behind the table covered with red velvet, and took the oath of office from Chief Justice Marshall. Calhoun had earlier taken his oath in the Senate Chamber. There was a roar from the crowd as it surged toward the White House. Men, women, even children, white and black, climbed through the windows to reach the waiters who were ladling out the punch. Red clay smeared damask-covered chairs and couches were used by the backwoods people to peer over the crowd to cheer Jackson who finally fled to a nearby tavern to enjoy a quiet dinner with friends and Vice-President Calhoun.

Early in Jackson's administration the turnover in federal bureaucracy was about forty percent. The new President was a firm believer in the dictum, to the victor belong the spoils. New names and new faces appeared; among them Martin Van Buren, the short, portly Dutchman from Kinderhook in upstate New York, "The Red Fox of Kinderhook" as he was called during the 1828 election when he effectively marshaled the northern votes for Jackson and received his reward as Secretary of State.

One by one Colonel McKenney saw his old associates in government receive their terse note of dismissal from the White House and slip away from Washington, some disappearing without a ripple.

He still had two powerful friends at court—Secretary of War John Eaton, the former senator from Tennessee who was practically Andrew Jackson's adopted son; and Vice-President Calhoun. He also had a skilled and savage enemy, Duff Green, owner and publisher of the *Washington Telegraph*. Green, the one-time cattle contractor, admitted he had never forgotten that McKenney failed to get approval of his $60,000 bill for a herd stolen by the Indians during the days when McKenney had been Madison's Superintendent of Indian Trade. McKenney called Green "the mouthpiece of the palace"; the publisher had reciprocated by dubbing him, "The Kickapoo Ambassador." Green was also a member of Jackson's so-called Kitchen Cabinet and his advice and opinion carried a great deal of weight with the President.

The Age of Jackson had scarcely begun when it was shaken, not by a war or a major scandal but by a flurry of petticoats. Before it was over, McKenney would feel the first chill draft preceding his dismissal.

The affair revolved about Peggy O'Neill Timberlake, who most observers of the time agreed was the most beautiful and flirtatious woman in Washington. Ben Perley Poore, the capital's newspaperman whose two-volume memoirs contain many shrewd and concise observations of the capital's men and manners from Jefferson's administration to the Civil War, recalled Peggy as a stunning, black-haired Irish beauty, with a sensual smile and white skin "delicately tinged with red."[2] She had been known in the capital since she was a teen-ager. Her friends included Jackson, Dolley Madison, ambassadors, politicians, generals, and senators.

When Timberlake, her husband, committed suicide, she and the handsome red-haired Eaton were married. The first ladies of Washington refused to attend the wedding but Jackson grimly led their husbands to the pews. When Calhoun protested the appointment of Eaton as Secretary of War because it would bring Peggy into Washington's social orbit, Jackson snapped:

"Do you suppose that I have been sent here by the people to consult the ladies of Washington as to the proper persons to compose my Cabinet?"

But Peggy greeted with a whoop the news that she had been made the wife of a Cabinet officer.

"Damn it, I'm off," she cried and kicked off her shoes.[3]

The angry ladies of Washington wondered why Jackson was Peggy's firm defender and gossip had him as her lover. The truth was that when Jackson had thrown himself across the grave of his wife, Rachel, in the driving rain, it had been Rachel's friend Peggy O'Neil Timberlake who had gently led him into her house and had fed and comforted him in his shattering grief.

Jackson, who never forgot a friend, always insisted that Peggy was a virginal, refined gentlewoman; those who disagreed could pack their bags and leave the government's employ. This was not the view of the ladies of Washington. Led by Mrs. Calhoun they refused to receive or visit the persistent Peggy. At the inaugural ball Mrs. Calhoun acted as if Peggy never existed.[4]

This infuriated Jackson; as he coldly informed his Cabinet, any insult to Mrs. Eaton was an insult to him. Van Buren, a masterly politician, carefully stoked the Peggy O'Neill warfare, painting Calhoun as the chief villain. Gradually the friction between the President and the Vice-President began to smolder, then suddenly burst into flame. Jackson became a willing pawn in the battle between Van Buren and Calhoun as each reached for the Presidency. The upstate New York politician scored a major political coup by stepping down to the post of minister to Britain (the Senate later refused his confirmation), jockeying the Cabinet into resigning, and thus getting rid of Calhoun's following.

Colonel McKenney first sensed that he was falling out of favor with the administration when his old friend Postmaster General McLean was fired and a party hack named Barry took his place. Barry's first order was that in the future no government letters would be sealed with wax; economy was the reason.

The puzzled McKenney took the copy of the order to Eaton.

"Does this apply to the Bureau of Indian Affairs?" he asked.

"Why not?" Eaton replied.

"Because most of our correspondence must traverse the wilderness and portions must swim rivers tied to heads of Indians and in various other ways be exposed to the weather and to border conditions."

"I suppose the postmaster must know his business," Eaton said formally. "Conform to the order."

McKenney made his own test of how much the wax would actually add to the cost of the mail and discovered that it would be less than five pounds for the daily mail of the combined State, Treasury, War, Navy, and Attorney General's offices.

He wryly observed, "There was a great deal of speculation as to the real object of the order."[5]

McKenney soon learned from the capital's underground intelligence that Green was urging Jackson to fire him; his champion was now Eaton who pointed out to Jackson the complexities and importance of the Indian Affairs Bureau and the potentially explosive dangers which could arise if an incompetent was appointed. Confusion and dissatisfaction could result in a border war, he cautioned. Evidently this warning brought back many stark memories to Jackson who knew at first hand the horrors of Indian warfare and he agreed to let McKenney remain at his post.

When Green heard that Eaton had blocked his attempts to get Jackson to remove McKenney, he stalked into the War Department and demanded that Eaton join him in a request to the President that a new Superintendent of the Bureau of Indian Affairs be appointed. Eaton dismissed Green and suggested he "return to his own business."

However, one day Eaton summoned McKenney and suggested he see the Presdient. The bewildered McKenney replied there wasn't any reason why he should visit the White House.

"In these uncertain times," Eaton elaborately explained, "it is well to cultivate those personal relations which go far toward securing the goodwill of those in power."

Sensing the growing anger of the tall white-haired man who sat across his desk, Eaton hurriedly explained that Jackson had received some "disparaging reports" about McKenney.

"What are these things disparaging of me?" McKenney demanded.

When the Secretary of War insisted he didn't know the details McKenney decided to find out for himself.

In the White House interview McKenney matched Jackson's legendary bluntness.

"You know, McKenney, I am a candid man—" Jackson started.

"I beg your pardon, sir," McKenney said holding up his hand; "but I am not here to question that but to hear charges which it appears have been made to you affecting my character, either as an officer of this government or as a man."

Jackson, momentarily startled by the terse interruption, went on to list the "charges."

They included the report that McKenney had been the "principal promoter" of the paper "We the People," which had scandalized Jackson's wife, and he had helped to circulate handbills known to history as the "coffin handbills" that depicted Jackson as a heartless general who had sent his troops to needless slaughter.

Then Jackson stopped, crossed his legs and, as Mc-

Kenney recalled, "glared at me as if he had already convicted and prostrated me."

"Well, sir, what else?" McKenney calmly asked.

Jackson snapped, "I think that conduct is highly unbecoming in one who fills an office in our government such as you do."

"I request, if this is all you have heard?" McKenney said quietly. "Are there any more charges?"

"There is," Jackson exploded.

"What are they?"

"I am told your office is not in the condition it should be."

McKenney relentlessly demanded, "What else, sir?"

"Nothing, but they are all serious charges," Jackson shouted.

McKenney then informed the President he didn't intend to answer any of the charges "with the idea of retaining my office, nor do I intend to reply at all, except under the solemnity of an oath." McKenney, who all his life had a flair for the dramatic, suddenly raised his right hand and intoned: "I solemnly swear what I say is the truth, the whole truth and nothing but the truth."

Jackson, taken aback, said, "You are making quite a serious matter of this, sir."

"It is, sir," McKenney said.

He went on to deny vigorously that he had any connection with the newspaper or the handbills. In fact, he told Jackson, one had been sent to him through the mails and he had immediately torn it up.

"As to my office," he said, "that is my monument and my records are my inscription. Let it be examined. I invite a commission for that purpose, nor will I return to it to put a paper into place or in any way prepare for an ordeal. If there is any flaw in it, or any just grounds for complaint, either on the part of the white or the red man, you have my free consent to put any mark on me you may think proper."

There was a long moment of silence during which Jackson studied McKenney. The President, who had always boasted he could read a man's soul in five minutes, at last said softly: "Colonel McKenney, I am satisfied and I will not push the matter any further." He got up and linked his arm with that of the Indian Superintendent and said, "Come down and let me introduce you to my family."[6]

If Jackson was temporarily satisfied, Duff Green was not and his editorials about the "Kickapoo Ambassador" continued. It was also soon evident that Jackson, for all his show of friendship for McKenney, was beginning to listen to Green.

Not long after the White House interview McKenney was proudly giving a well-known politician a tour of his Indian gallery.

"And which is the Kickapoo Ambassador?" the visitor asked innocently. McKenney smiled. "You have the honor of standing before him."

"Tell me, McKenney, who writes the treaties with the Indians?" the politician asked.

"I do."

"And who gives instructions to the commissions and in

general carries on the affairs and correspondence of this office?"

"Well, I do," the puzzled McKenney replied. The visitor shook his head. "Then this office is not for me."

McKenney was shocked. "What office?"

"This office," the visitor repeated. "General Jackson saw me this morning and said it was mine if I wanted it but before I saw the Secretary of War I thought I would first have a chat with you."

"Take it then, my dear sir, take it," McKenney said angrily.

"No, it's not for me," the visitor said, "I prefer the auditor's office where the forms are established."

With a casual wave of his hand he left the bitter, heartsick McKenney.

McKenney claimed in his memoirs that the visitor had presented Jackson with a pair of valuable pistols Washington had carried during the Revolution and Jackson in an outburst of gratitude and offered him McKenney's post.

McKenney was calculating the remainder of his days as Superintendent of the Bureau of Indian Affairs when a strange new champion appeared in the form of a frock-coated Dutch Reform minister from New York City. He was conjured up by the familiar, still tragic Cherokee removal, now emerging as a major problem of the Age of Jackson.

3.

THE CHAIN of events began in the spring of 1829 when a delegation of Cherokee chiefs visited McKenney, whom they called White Eagle, and Secretary of War Eaton to complain about white trespassers and Georgia's refusal to deal with them. Eaton, echoing Jackson's sentiments, refused to give them any hope that the federal government would interfere with state's rights in their case. Eaton bluntly suggested they should accept the inevitable—yield their lands and move West where they would never again be faced by the white man's infringements of their rights.

The Cherokee took their case to their friends, the influential American Board of Commissioners for Foreign Missions. Composed largely of Congregational and Presbyterian membership, the board had been active among the Cherokee Nation for many years, especially in education. By 1829 they had twenty-one schools compared with seven of other denominations combined.

The American Board turned to the large newspapers in the eastern cities and produced a public outcry and a demand that the Cherokee be allowed to remain on their ancestral lands.

It soon became apparent to the leaders of the Jackson administration that they needed a similar organization to convince the public of their goodness of heart, their concern for the Indians, and the integrity and humanity of their removal plan.

Gradually, out of the chaotic newspaper stories, angry Indian delegations, political statements, charges and countercharges, there emerged a new organization, the Indian Board for the Emigration, Preservation, and Im-

provement of the Aboriginals of America. The organization, staggering under this ponderous name, was formed behind the scenes by Thomas Loraine McKenney in the summer of 1829. Its genesis is not certain; it could have come from McKenney himself, Eaton, or Jackson.

Despite their differences in philosophy over Indian removal, McKenney had maintained a friendly relationship with the Rev. Philip Milledoler, who in addition to being president of Rutgers College was also chairman of the American Board. Correspondence between them during the 1820s and 1830s was warm and friendly, with McKenney a strong supporter of the Board's educational system among the Cherokee.[7]

But now McKenney favored Indian removal which was in direct contrast to the Board's and Dr. Milledoler's policy of insisting that the federal government permit the Indian Nations to remain on their ancestral lands.

During this period McKenney was walking a political tightrope. For sixteen years he had enjoyed prestige and power in a federal post to which he had given a great deal of his loyalty, talents, time, and energy. He obviously did not want to give it up but, hardened by Washington politics, he knew it would be only a matter of time before he was dismissed.

He had also declared many times he would never support or endorse any administration that tried to uproot the Indian nations by force. As he had written his old friend David Folsom, the Cherokee chief, a few years before: "This I tell you—*you will never be pushed off your land. If you go it will be by your own consent and free will.*"

It may have been Eaton who tried to help him by pointing out that Jackson desperately needed a big city sounding board that could appear to be nonpartisan. Perhaps it was McKenney's own fertile imagination but whatever the source the newly formed Board reached out for the comparatively obscure Reverend Eli Baldwin of the Dutch Reformed Church and his small board of laymen. The New York City church group was small but McKenney was desperate; in a warm, urgent letter to Baldwin he outlined his program of promoting the security, preservation, and happiness of the tribes by standing behind the government's policy of Indian removal as the first step in saving them. He wrote of public committees, of groups traveling to Washington to support Jackson's plans and even going among the tribes to explain the wisdom of emigration, pointing out the advantages of their homes in the West where they would be safe from the white man and the tangle of his laws. Only Public Opinion, "the great force in the country," he warned Baldwin could bring this about.

On May 21, 1829, McKenney sent a speech Eaton had made to the Cherokee to Baldwin. In his accompanying letter McKenney stressed Jackson's one firm, inflexible rule: Georgia had the right to expel its Indians and the federal government would not interfere with this state's authority.[8]

The letter put McKenney with both feet in Jackson's camp. It was apparent he had decided to obey the ancient law of power politics—flexibility is the first principle.

Baldwin accepted McKenney's proposal and the Indian Superintendent exuberantly urged him to try to join forces with Episcopal Bishop Hobart.

"He is a host," McKenney wrote, "and your two churches, whether formally or informally united I would consider adequate to carry this great measure through. All this ought to be ripe before the meeting of the next Congress. There is no time to be lost."[9]

But Baldwin proved to be a cautious organizer. McKenney impatiently coached him how to do it; he organized the first meeting and had Baldwin invite General Stephen Van Rensselaer, perhaps the wealthiest and the most socially prominent figure in the state. Baldwin then called together his clergymen and laymen—there were only ten—and read McKenney's letters and proposals to them. It was an obvious rubber-stamp group; they quickly consented to adopt the organization with the ponderous name. What was more important to McKenney was their resolution approving Jackson's policy of Indian removal. McKenney, of course, sent an effusive letter of praise to Baldwin.

The Indian Superintendent came to New York in mid-July and met with Baldwin and his committee to discuss the constitution. He suggested that all hints of "bigotry and sectarianism" be excluded so it would in no way sound partisan.

Back in Washington he gave Eaton an enthusiastic report which he undoubtedly hoped would reach Jackson.

"I confess I never had such hopes of the Indians before," he wrote Eaton. "I am utterly mistaken if this body of men (they are in three churches, Dutch Reformed—Episcopal & Presbyterian) does not carry all before it."[10]

On July 29, 1829, the Board was formally born. Van Rensselaer, although not present, was elected president and Baldwin corresponding secretary. The constitution which strongly supported· Jackson's policy of Indian removal appears to have been practically dictated by McKenney.

A letter to Eaton, marked "private," reveals that McKenney was playing politics not only to support the program of Indian removal which he sincerely believed in, but also to retain his government post. However, his cynical use of the naive clergymen and the Indians was unworthy of him. He wrote Eaton he thought his "divines are the most through-going Jacksonites in the nation . . . I found myself in the midst of a hot-bed. From considerations of policy, I found it necessary, knowing their object to be pure, & to embrace only the rescue of the Indians, to suggest, for the sake of giving power to the undertaking, & relieving it from all liability of being suspected as a political machine, that a general invitation be worked up, & in the Constitution, to all Citizens, without respect to sects, or parties, to unite, etc. It was adopted. A merrier, or better tempered, or happier set of folks, it would be hard to find . . . "[11]

The Board's first meeting in August was attended by six hundred at McKenney's estimate. His address like his letters was long, it ran for fifty minutes and faithfully incorporated the entire Jackson-Eaton policy of Indian removal. Three thousand copies of his speech were printed and distributed, the War Department paying the cost of two hundred dollars. McKenney now boldly suggested to Eaton that he should get Jackson's approval of the organization's constitution and this should be included in the pamphlet. There is little doubt that McKenney hoped the President would read and applaud his speech.

In late August Eaton replied in Jackson's name, giving presidential approval to the group and in passing taking a slap at the nation's press for the "many inaccuracies both to object and to motive [of Jackson's Indian Removal Plan]." He hastened to assure Baldwin that Jackson would never consider "anything of a compulsory nature" in removing the Cherokee. The future tragic developments of the Cherokee forceful removal makes Eaton's promise cheap political expediency.

The forty-eight-page pamphlet was finally published, containing a great deal of McKenney—his address, his letters, and Eaton's and Jackson's letters.[12]

Undoubtedly through his friendship with Governor Lewis Cass, McKenney persuaded the Michigan Territorial Governor to write a favorable review of the pamphlet in the popular *North American Review* in the winter of 1829. Under McKenney's direction, the Rev. Mr. Baldwin became a busy publicity man for the group and got many of McKenney's letters published in New York City, particularly in the pro-Jackson *New York Post*, which used several.[13]

Among the glowing tributes there were some harsh comments. The *Cherokee Phoenix* sadly reported McKenney's address in New York and strongly refuted his charges that some chiefs were holding back their people from emigration by threats.

"The Great body of the tribe are not anxious to remove," the *Phoenix* thundered.

But the *Phoenix*'s tiny backwoods voice of disapproval was lost in the chorus of favorable publicity about the new board and Superintendent McKenney. When Cass's article appeared the *Post* used large extracts.

Baldwin became a problem for the first time when McKenney suggested the committee come to Washington to lobby for Jackson's Removal Bill. The clergyman warned McKenney it was impossible to expect the members to give their own time along with their money.[14]

McKenney urged Baldwin to try to raise the funds telling him he and his group were "indispensable." Finally in the winter of 1830 Baldwin and three members of the board did appear in Washington to present their "memorial" to the House. There is no government record to show that the Indian Bureau paid the bills so apparently McKenney's flattering letters had again influenced Mr. Baldwin.

This mild and very ineffectual storming of the gates of Congress was the last official act of the group. McKenney's prediction of a great public sentiment, growing larger and larger as it snowballed through the eastern states, failed to materialize.

As McKenney later recalled the group had been "struck by paralysis." In his *Memoirs* he gives as the reason for the failure of the group his growing realization that Jackson,

Eaton, and their congressional supporters had lied when they promised that no force would ever be used to remove the Indians from their land.[15]

After gold was discovered on Indian land few politicians were ready to accept McKenney's policy that the Indians should be removed peacefully and gradually. When white men moved in on Indian land, they were supported by their state leaders who waved aloft the treaty they had signed with the federal government many years before, giving them power over the tribes.

The United States Supreme Court upheld the rights of the Cherokee but Jackson only shrugged and commented that now that Chief Justice Marshall had rendered the verdict it was up to him to enforce it.

In the late 1820s McKenney had played a dangerous game with Eaton and Jackson, now in the winter of 1830 he found himself swinging more wildly than ever on his political tightrope which in the past he had found very reliable in crossing from one administration to another.

As he struggled to survive he knew that the most expert of political tightrope walkers could not maintain this balance for very long.

CHAPTER XIV:

The Eagle and the Raven

I.

THE RAVEN, as the Cherokee called him, had come home. Flamboyant and theatrical as ever, Sam Houston arrived in Washington in January 1830 in the ebb time of his colorful life. He had resigned as Tennessee's governor at the time President Jackson was about to endorse him for reelection, separated from his wife after a brief honeymoon while the frontier buzzed with gossip over the reason, then vanished into the Cherokee country near Fort Gibson, Arkansas Territory, to open a store he called The Wigwam.

He arrived to find the Cherokee about to launch a bloody war against the Pawnee and the Red River Comanche. Houston, who boasted of his power among the Cherokee, addressed one of the largest war councils in the nation's history at Bayou Menard. He advised the nation against war and made many promises but the young warriors ignored him. That summer they joined the forces of Dutch, the famous Red River Cherokee war chief, massacred the inhabitants of a large Comanche village, and returned to Arkansas with over two hundred scalps.[1]

During the fall and winter of 1829–1830 the "mortified" Houston endorsed a Cherokee memorial to Jackson and promised the nation's leaders he would have Old Hickory's ear when he went to see the Great Father. The grateful Cherokee adopted him as a son and he began wearing buckskins, blankets, and a turban that made him look like a shabby actor in a bad frontier melodrama.

On his way to Washington the Raven, or Tah-lou-tusky as he signed his articles in the *Arkansas Gazette*, had dinner with Major E. W. DuVal, the Cherokee agent, in his home near Fort Smith. While they were having after-dinner bourbon and cigars, a messenger appeared at Du-Val's house with a letter advising the agent to "beware of Houston," that he was on his way to Washington to press charges against him.

The grim-faced DuVal handed the letter to Houston who read it.

"Is this true?" DuVal asked.

"Substantially," replied Houston.

"Put your charges then in writing," DuVal snapped and handed Houston a pen, paper, and ink. Houston wrote out the charges then left for Washington.[2]

DuVal, an old friend of Colonel McKenney, had spent many years among the Cherokee and had a reputation for honesty and integrity. However, he wasn't the only Indian agent who had encountered the often impulsive enmity of the restless, ambitious, frustrated Houston.

Earlier, Houston had been successful in forcing the War Department to fire J. F. Hamtramck, another close friend of McKenney, as the Osage agent. But this time Houston wasn't aware of the forces he had unleashed in distant Washington; while Houston was threatening DuVal as he sipped his bourbon, Major Hamtramck was in Washington telling his father-in-law, Duff Green, how Houston had him fired. Green quietly spoke to the Vice-President of the United States, John Calhoun, who was also vitally interested; Mrs. Hamtramck was a relation. DuVal didn't possess the political leverage of Agent Hamtramck but he had a sincere champion in his corner in Colonel McKenney.

Houston swept into Washington charming the ladies with his new-found stoical Indian stance, his brilliant blue blanket, and his tinkling silver ornaments. For the first several days of his visit the Washington gossips whispered excitedly behind their fans. Houston's former in-laws, friends of President Jackson, had decided Houston was not an honorable man and were ready to force him into political oblivion.

The capital held its breath while Houston's enemies advised Jackson that the former Tennessee governor was nothing but a scoundrel who should have been horse-whipped for his treatment of his bride. For three months Houston waited for presidential benediction or condemnation; the decision finally came when Jackson invited him to a White House reception. Washington cheered and Houston became the glamorous, much sought after guest of honor.[3]

The curtain slowly rose on the first act of what history would know as the Indian Removal Ration Scandal. Before it ended, the sordid details would be uncovered by a congressional investigation, and McKenney's enemies would include Houston, Eaton, and Jackson. Ironically, and not without ulterior motives, a temporary supporter was his old foe Duff Green.

2.

IN EARLY February 1830 Sam Houston, clad in blanket and buckskins, entered Colonel McKenney's office with a rush. He pushed a chair next to the Superintendent's desk and without any preliminaries began to talk about the proposed bid for the government rations which would be issued to the emigrating southern tribes, particularly the Cherokee, if Congress voted that the southern nations had to yield their land claims and move across the Mississippi. The complex and highly important contract would entail feeding eighty thousand Indians, men, women, and children, not only from the moment the tribes started on their long trek westward but for a year after they had been settled in their new homes in the Indian Territory. Whoever gained the contract had to be an experienced army or Indian ration dealer, wise to the problems of herding cattle, sheltering them in pens overnight, knowledgeable in the trails that the early drovers used in moving herds through the wilderness, and he had to be equipped with the names of settlers who could supply large amounts of corn and who had areas with water for Indian camps and lodging. Boats and barges also had to be available with rivermen who knew the currents and the ways of the treacherous cattle crossings.

McKenney had estimated the total cost would be $4,400,000.[4]

He later called it one of the largest undertakings in the history of the Bureau of Indian Affairs and possibly the model for later Indian emigrations.

Houston came to the point very quickly.

"It is my intention to engage in this [ration contracting] business, McKenney. I wish you to aid me. You can do a lot in accomplishing my intentions. Everybody knows your acquaintanceship with this business; you can have it pretty much as you please."

McKenney stiffly replied : "General, I regret your mode of approaching this subject and the terms you have in presenting it. I have no power over this subject."

Houston leaned back in his chair and smiled. "Colonel, I'm still of the opinion that if you chose you could be useful to me. Why don't you see me at my lodgings?"

McKenney gave him a cool good-bye but Houston appeared the next day asking McKenney if he had seen Secretary of War Eaton. When the Indian Superintendent said he had, Houston quickly wanted to know what Eaton had said about the Indian ration contract. McKenney tersely replied that there had been no discussion on that subject.

Houston looked surprised and muttered, "That's damn queer."[5]

He was back the next day and as McKenney recalled, "sometimes two and three times a day." Once he casually gave McKenney his charges against Indian Agent DuVal and suggested that they be forwarded to the Secretary of War. McKenney realized Houston was now trying to intimidate him.

After about the fourth or fifth visit Houston told McKenney that Eaton had assured him McKenney would be given orders to publish notice of the ration contract in the *Washington Telegraph*.

"The Secretary has not discussed this matter with me," McKenney told him.

"Why don't you go and see him then?" Houston demanded.

"My place is subordinate," McKenney snapped. "I cannot with propriety move on the Secretary of War. I must wait for his movements upon me."

Houston then became "vexatious" and stormed out of the office.

He returned the next morning and this time "with vehemence" insisted McKenney see Eaton.

McKenney declined giving the same reasons. Houston exploded and shook his finger at the Indian Superintendent.

"McKenney, you have sustained Major DuVal too long. You issued to the delegation [the last Cherokee Delegation to visit McKenney and the President] fifteen hundred dollars without proper or justifiable reason." He shouted, "I know certain things, of which, however, I have said nothing."

Fighting to control himself McKenney told Houston he had as much authority as "my doorman" to pay out such a sum. Houston angrily left the office.

Apparently McKenney seethed all day; that night he decided to put on the record an account of Houston's many visits and demands. He wrote a letter to Houston in which he detailed the former governor's visits, his demands, his insinuations of misconduct, and his denunciation of McKenney for refusing to take action against Major DuVal or the Osage Agent Major Hamtramck.

"I hereby relax any feelings of delicacy toward me which you appear to indicate, and assure you with the utmost frankness, of my perfect readiness to have any part of my conduct, as an officer or as a man, examined into and acted upon."[6]

McKenney waited but Houston did not appear again nor did he answer his letter. A few days later McKenney was summoned to the office of Secretary of War Eaton who asked him if he had seen Houston.

"I have but our interviews have not been agreeable," was his wry reply.

Eaton ignored this and then took a paper from inside his pocket. It was the newspaper copy for the ration specifications written as McKenney would recall "in Houston's hand" when the Secretary of War asked McKenney to "read and examine it." McKenney glanced at the copy and informed Eaton it was "imperfect and incorrect," because Houston had failed to list any depots where the rations for the Cherokee would be stored.

"If these are not specified [in the published specifications] those who may incline to bid will not be able to say at what price the rations can be supplied."

Eaton waved aside his objections and insisted he "take it home, examine it, and put it in the proper form for publication."

McKenney did as he was ordered and wrote out the government's specifications for the Cherokee ration contract to be published in the *Washington Telegraph*, February 18, 1830. But he left blank the time for receiving the bids. Eaton called this to his attention and McKenney said he did this deliberately to "call your attention" to the time limit that would exclude distant contractors. McKenney also warned Eaton that the fiery Colonel A. H. Sevier, Senator from Arkansas, would surely protest on the part of his constituents and embarrass the administration.

Eaton snapped: "I don't think it's important, Colonel, if the supplies come from Ohio or Kentucky. Thirty days is sufficient for the proposal to circulate through the country."

McKenney protested but Eaton shut him off; make it thirty days, he ordered.

He then sat down at his desk and wrote "an alteration" to McKenney's copy:

> The right to be reserved by the Secretary of War to enlarge or alter the quantity of the rations to be issued, and the right of continuing the contract to any period of time he may think proper, and to determine it at his pleasure when any of the conditions shall be broken. The points of delivery not to exceed three in the country of either of the tribes, to be designated by the Secretary of War.[7]

McKenney was appalled. But Eaton ignored his protest. "Houston is waiting," he said. "Few men are so well qualified for the discharge of such a trust."

McKenney and Eaton met several times after that without further discussion of the contract. But unknown to the Indian Superintendent developments were taking place in all parts of the capital.

In the White House, Eaton, Houston, and Jackson were "sitting together in earnest conversation" when Duff Green entered. Eaton waved him over.

"What time should the copy for an advertisement intended for publication the next day, be at your office?" he asked Green.

"Any time before ten o'clock," Green replied.

"I'll send you one tomorrow," Eaton said.

"Oh, no, I'll take it there myself," Houston put in quickly.

The following morning Houston delivered the copy for the Indian Ration contract to Green's *Telegraph* and it was published. A few weeks after the White House conference, Eaton told Green he was "about to close an important ration contract for supplying the emigrant Indians with rations." He had learned that the rations in the past had cost the government twenty-five cents but Houston had a wealthy New York City partner who had decided to take the contract for eighteen cents an Indian. He estimated the rations would feed from 60,000 to 80,000 Indians.

Green was shocked and insisted that instead of a saving to the government the Houston contract would mean a tremendous loss because, as a former contractor, he knew that beef on the hoof could be purchased in Missouri or Illinois for one dollar to one dollar and fifty cents per hundred pounds; from a rough estimate he believed the rations could cost not more than six cents.

As Green later said, Eaton "impatiently dismissed my arguments and seemed unwilling to listen to me."

Green strongly suggested that a new bid should be advertised "to give the western people a chance to bid thus assuring the government a great saving." Green left Eaton "under a firm conviction he was determined to give Houston the contract."[8]

Green unsuccessfully tried to get an old friend to put in a low bid, then went directly to President Jackson and warned him Houston's bid was far too high and it could be made lower by a routine check of the corn and beef prices.

Jackson said quickly: "Will you take it for ten cents?"

"No sir," said Green.

"Will you take it at twelve? You will have it now." Jackson snapped.

"I'm not a bidder for the contract, Mr. President," Green said, "but who ever gets it will make a handsome profit . . . my own purpose in coming here is a desire to serve you and the administration and not to speculate." Green might have added he had privately vowed to wreck Houston's bid for his role in forcing Major Hamtramck to resign as the Osage agent.

When he returned home Green decided to make a formal protest to Eaton. Like McKenney he wrote a letter to the Secretary of War reviewing their conversation and warning him there could be serious criticism of the administration if Houston was given the bid.[9]

Houston was also busy. After he had learned that Ben Hawkins, a Texas cattle dealer had put in a bid of nine cents a ration, Houston persuaded him that the contract was far beyond his means and to turn it over to him. Hawkins, a half-breed who appears to have been intimidated by Houston and his Indian regalia, agreed and wrote a note, dictated by Houston, that he had turned his bid over to Houston.

Houston next met with Luther Blake, a well known Indian agent who had the government contract for the Creek who had moved west the year before. Blake had entered a bid of eight cents a ration, "after he had seen an advertisement signed by Colonel McKenney asking for bids for the government contract."

Houston astonished Blake by informing him that he knew his bid and those submitted by Prentiss Butler and Thomas Crowell, two former Indian agents. After Blake admitted he had bid eight cents Houston suggested Blake withdraw his bid and buy out the others and join him, "because myself, himself, and his wealthy friend could get it at a higher price and that a big fortune could be made."

Houston kept after Blake, visiting him regularly as he had McKenney.

Blake finally told Houston "some sort of an agreement had to be between us before I would withdraw my bid and buy out the others."

"Oh, that can be done very easily," Houston said.

A few days later Blake was abruptly summoned to the

War Department and assigned by Eaton to the West as an Indian agent.

In an interview with Colonel McKenney, Blake said he was mystified how Houston had found out the details of the bids, sealed by federal law—"to peek behind the curtain," as he put it. But Colonel McKenney was not mystified. During the period when the closed bids were being received by his office to be forwarded to Richard Randolph, Eaton's chief clerk, brother-in-law, and sometimes acting Secretary of War, the Indian Superintendent arrived one morning to find his chief clerk waiting to tell him that Houston had removed sealed bids from the office.

An angry McKenney ordered him not to give Houston "or anyone else without authorization from the Secretary of War to examine any papers in this department."

The next morning Houston rushed into McKenney's office.

"Did you forbid me the use of any papers I might want?" he shouted.

"I did, sir," McKenney said quietly.

Houston blustered and threatened but McKenney not only refused to allow him to see the bids which had come into his office but also summoned his chief clerk and reiterated his order.

An "excited" Houston left, warning McKenney that he would never forget what he had done.

McKenney then went to see Eaton and gave the Secretary of War an account of what had taken place. When he had finished Eaton silently pointed to a pile of papers on the sofa.

"There are some papers and a letter book, you had better take them."

McKenney silently gathered up the papers; he saw at a glance they were all from his office and were the supposedly "sealed" bids, but the wax seals were broken.[10]

Houston now joined forces with another contractor, R. L. Rose, and met with General John Van Fossen, a wealthy New York financier. After a series of meetings with Houston, Van Fossen agreed to join him and Rose in a bid for the Indian rations contract. Each man put in a separate bid; Houston's was thirteen cents per ration, Rose's twelve, and Van Fossen's eleven cents.[11]

During this period when he was supposedly considering each bid Eaton took Van Fossen to the White House to meet Jackson. The President assured him that he agreed with Eaton; the government didn't want the ration contractor "to suffer a loss because it would result in an injury to the business of emigration."

While Houston and Van Fossen were preparing to capture the huge ration contract, Congress passed a resolution calling on the Secretary of War to submit a report analyzing the cost of Indian rations based on the removal of the Creek in 1829. Eaton summoned McKenney and ordered him to prepare the information.

McKenney and his small staff gathered together the bills and old contracts and prepared a cost analysis; to remove each Creek cost the government thirty-three dollars, and six cents a day to support each Creek for a year in the Indian Territory. McKenney wrote:

The entire cost of removing each Creek and supporting him has been fifteen cents per day, or fifty-four dollars per year. But subsequent experience in taking over the last party has shown that under the present system, it need not amount to more than half the cost of the first movement; and it may be, as I stated [in his annual report, 1829, McKenney had suggested a system of contracts which would have reduced the government's cost considerably] be still reduced by a system of contracts. . . .

If fifty-four dollars be assumed as the cost attending the removal of each Indian and supporting him for a year after his removal and if there are, as it is presumed to be, eighty thousand Indians east of the Mississippi, the entire cost will be for removing them and for supporting them for a year, four million, four hundred thousand dollars. If from this be reduced the difference between the actual cost of the first and last party [of Creek] it would cost two million, eight hundred thousand dollars; and if one third of this be deducted under a system of contracts which I think would be a fair reduction, it would be two million, two hundred and ninety-four thousand dollars.

It is proper to remark that this estimate is based on the removal of eighty thousand Indians. If however, it is confined to the Indians which is assumed may have been intended to be embraced, viz. the four southern tribes, the Chickasaw, Choctaw, Creek and the Cherokee, the Seminole in Florida and the remnants of bands in Ohio, Indiana, etc. those numbering about fifty thousand, it would be proper to deduct one-fourth, which would leave one million, seven hundred and twenty thousand dollars.

As for the method of reimbursing the government, McKenney suggested that the sale of the Indian lands left by the nations would not only pay for their removal "but could furnish a fund for their improvement in the West, for many years."

McKenney gave his report to Eaton who forwarded it to Congress; the Indian Superintendent heard no more about it.

Houston had now left Washington for Baltimore and from there advised his partner, General Van Fossen, that he had seen Ross, the other contractor, who he revealed was now "ready to start buying" and gathering the herds in preparation for the granting of their bid. Van Fossen later insisted to a Congressional Committee that Houston's concern for him was only altruistic but Houston's letter states flatly he had intended to be the general's partner from the very beginning.

"When I advised you to put in your bid," he wrote, "I did expect to be fully concerned with you in this business. [Luther] Blake told me he would withdraw his bid. If these things have been done, ascertain if these [the bids] are less than twelve or thirteen cents. If all others are withdrawn under twelve cents, and you can get the contract at twelve, it is a safe business. It may be you can't get it at twelve, if so take it at thirteen!"[12]

Houston again wrote Van Fossen from the "Wigwam, Neosho Territory," advising the financier that the Commissary General in the Indian Territory was preparing cattle pens for the Indian rations contracts. His "fortune," he swore, "must not wane . . . it must full [sic] if I live and meet with my deserts (in my humble opinion)."

He ended by suggesting to Van Fossen that he read the "chapters signed Tah-lou-tus-ky in the northern papers… The author you may guess at."

Van Fossen replied that he was "determined to have the contract even if I have to bid much lower than you proposed." As he predicted, "a handsome fortune may be made of it . . ."[13]

Thirty days, the time period for the bid, finally passed. The morning after the expiration date, the contractors who had entered their bids appeared in McKenney's office. Headed by Luther Blake who had resigned from the Indian Bureau and William Prentiss they included former Indian agents, frontiersmen, and experienced cattle contractors. They ranged in bids from eight to twenty cents per ration. Blake was lowest at eight; General Van Fossen and Houston had bid thirteen cents. Their letters were dated from February 18 to March 20, all within the specified time period.

Each batch of bids had been daily turned over to P. G. Randolph, Eaton's chief clerk by Colonel McKenney.

When they gathered in McKenney's office, Blake and the others asked for the name of the contract winner. There was an uproar when McKenney informed them he didn't know.

"You as the head of this department, don't know who is to supply the Indian rations?" Prentiss said unbelievingly.

"It is the Secretary of War who makes the decision, not me," McKenney told them. "I would suggest you see him."[14]

They did as McKenney suggested but learned nothing. Prentiss then received an unexpected visit from Van Fossen who told him Secretary of War Eaton was ready to declare his (Prentiss's) bid illegal because he was "joined with Blake." The shocked Prentiss immediately sent a note to Eaton denying he was Blake's partner. Eaton promptly replied insisting he had never told this to General Van Fossen.

Van Fossen then tried to buy out Prentiss but the contractor refused. Instead the contractor kept visiting the War Department until he saw Eaton who refused to let him see the other· bids, although Prentiss pointed out that contractors under federal law were permitted to view the bids after the expiration date. A testy Eaton still refused and advised Prentiss "the business" was now before President Jackson.

Fifteen days passed. Prentiss sent another letter to Eaton this time in the name of all the contractors and demanding to know the name of the lowest bidder.

On April 30, long after the expiration date, Eaton sent Prentiss a terse note informing him his bid was "not the lowest but if it were the lowest, it would not impose an obligation [upon me] to enter into a contract upon it." Eaton then went on to discuss the federal law which gave the Secretary of War final authority for granting any contract but now that "circumstances" had arisen a new bid was to be advertised.[15]

Prentiss and the other angry contractors continued to badger Eaton until November 1, 1830, when Eaton advised Prentiss that "there are no Indians now emigrating" and until Congress had taken action on the Indian Removal Bill, the question of ration contracts would not be advertised.

Blake, Prentiss, and the outraged contractors then went to Arkansas Senator Sevier and told him the whole story.

Sevier, a short-tempered former frontier prosecutor, exposed the ripening scandal when he berated Jackson and Eaton "for shutting out the people of Arkansas because they knew it would take thirty days for the news of the government's proposals to reach the people of Arkansas."

Sevier, who considered Houston a flamboyant troublemaker who constantly stirred up the Cherokee in his state, also swore he would do "all in my power to defeat the Houston contract."

McKenney's early warnings to Eaton now came true; Sevier marshaled his supporters in Congress, the administration's foes took up the cry, and Houston, Eaton, and President Jackson were denounced for treachery, fraud, and deceit. Duff Green not only openly supported Calhoun in the raging feud between Jackson and Calhoun but became McKenney's strange bedfellow. His *Telegraph* berated Houston, Eaton, and the White House.

The embarrassed Eaton was forced publicly to cancel Houston's and Van Fossen's bid. He suffered an additional humiliation when an angry Jackson ordered all future bids to be transferred from the War Department to the office of General George Gibson, Commissary General of Subsistence.

For weeks the "ration business" as Green's *Telegraph* called it, raged in Congress. Houston and Eaton became bitter enemies, the news of the scandalous bids reached the Indian country and agents warned the War Department that the tribes were "restless" over the knowledge they were being swindled even before they left their homelands. The scapegoat, of course, was McKenney. Weeks passed before Eaton would even bid his Indian Superintendent good morning. McKenney tried to remain aloof from the savage political infighting and continued working his usual long days, "his lamp the last to go out in all of Washington."

He knew now it was only a matter of time before his "sword of Damocles," as he called it, would fall.

One morning McKenney entered his office to find his chief clerk in tears.

"You are to be replaced today by Congressman Thompson from Georgia," the man told him.

When McKenney asked how he could know such a confidential matter, the clerk looked about, then whispered:

"He boards at my mother's house and I have it from himself. He says I shall remain but he will dismiss all the others to make room for the President's friends."

McKenney soon discovered that while the angry Eaton blamed him for his troubles, he was still an honorable man. When Thompson arrived with a letter from Jackson appointing him the new head of the Bureau of Indian Affairs, Eaton refused to accept his appointment. Instead he went over to the White House and demanded that Jackson reconsider.

The fuming Thompson was sitting in Eaton's outer office when a letter arrived for him from the White House canceling his appointment.

McKenney recalled that Thompson, "in a rage," left the War Department, shouting, "It's a pretty business indeed when Eaton thinks he can command a frigate and I can't manage a cockboat."[16]

On August 16, 1830, McKenney was in New York. On his return to Washington he stopped off at Philadelphia where he found a letter from the War Department waiting for him. It was from Randolph, Eaton's chief clerk, who also blamed McKenney for his public embarrassment. The brief note simply said his services were no longer required as Superintendent of the Bureau of Indian Affairs after October 1, 1830.

McKenney had expected it but he was still stunned at the cold, abrupt dismissal after sixteen loyal, dedicated years to a department that was now emerging as one of the most important in the federal government. Duff Green evidently considered his temporary truce with McKenney was ended. His *Telegraph* gleefully fired its last shot, hailing McKenney's dismissal as "an act of justice to the people."

To McKenney's credit there are no bitter recriminations or savage denunciations in his *Memoirs;* he says simply he went back to Washington and cleaned out his desk. He said a silent last good-bye to the row after row of the stoical Indians whose portraits he had gathered with such intenseness and loved so dearly, then left. In the corridor he met Randolph. More out of curiosity as to how the other man would reply, he asked the reason for his dismissal.

Randolph shrugged. "Oh, everyone in Washington knows your qualifications but General Jackson has long been satisfied that you are not in harmony with him in views in regards to the Indians."[17]

Then he turned and entered his office. McKenney slowly walked down the corridor and left the old War Department Building for the last time.

He was far from defeated. The tiny idea which had been growing for a long time in his imagination had blossomed into flower; he would publish the Indian portraits in a magnificent portfolio for all Americans to view and cherish.

House at Lafayette and Prince Streets in New York City
where McKenney visited the dying President Monroe.
Courtesy, Library of Congress

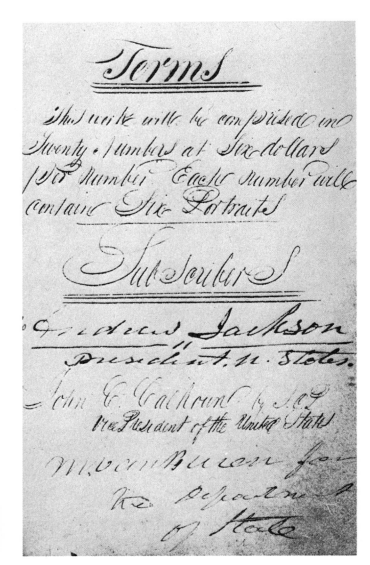

The History
of the
INDIAN TRIBES
of North America,
with Biographical Sketches & Anecdotes
of the
Principal Chiefs
embellished with 120 Portraits
from the
Indian Gallery in the
Department of
War
at Washington

Terms

This work will be comprised in
Twenty Numbers at Six dollars
per Number. Each Number will
contain Six Portraits

Subscribers

Andrew Jackson
President U. States.

John C. Calhoun by S. C.
Vice President of the United States

M. van Buren for
the Department
of State

Draft of prospectus for
McKenney-Hall's *History of the Indian Tribes of North America.*

James Hall

Henry Inman

CHAPTER XV:

The Last Act: The Great Portfolio

1.

THERE IS NO exact date but it is definite that Colonel McKenney was still in office when he first made plans to publish his Elephant Portfolio of lithographic reproductions of the Indian Portrait Gallery.

His *Memoirs* reveal that he was in Philadelphia discussing the project with Samuel Bradford, a printer and lithographer; he had tried to persuade Jared Sparks, the eminent historian, to become his coauthor and had asked his western superintendents and Indian agents to help him gather material, "historical and biographical," which could "accompany" the published portraits.[1]

He was also prepared to drive away any poachers, such as the two entrepreneurs who appeared in Washington seeking permission to copy the portraits of the chiefs and warriors.

To protect his idea McKenney became dissembling and oblique. He advised the pair the portraits were a national treasure and could not be used for personal gain. Their publication, he wrote, would not "be proper unless it was connected with some great national object; and this could be realized only by uniting the Gallery with the work on the Aborigines of this Country and descriptions and history of the Tribes, and the individuals, that might be represented in this Gallery. An undertaking upon such a basis would be national." At the time McKenney wrote this he was discussing terms with Philadelphia printer for what could only be described as a personally profitable venture.[2]

While he waited for Bradford to prepare a prospectus for the portfolio, McKenney issued a circular announcing his plan to establish a New York firm to supply goods for the Indian trade.

When he heard of this, Henry Rowe Schoolcraft commented sadly in his journal, "This appears to me to be a striking mistake of judgement. Colonel McKenney of all things is not suited for a merchant."[3]

Schoolcraft had made a prophetic observation; McKenney hadn't been in business for sixteen years and while he had many friends and admirers among the Indian nations and agents, the fur companies hated him, especially Astor's American Fur, and would try to drive him into bank-ruptcy. This firm failed. McKenney and one of his brothers, probably Samuel, went into at least two other commercial ventures which wiped out their fortunes and forced McKenney to sell Weston at a severe loss.

After his substantial financial reverses McKenney and his wife moved into a boardinghouse at 287 Chestnut Street, Philadelphia. Probably for free board he began writing to his friends, asking them "to circulate among your friends a high opinion of this sweet and delightful boarding house. . . . Mrs. McKenney and myself find a delightful home in it."[4]

It is one of the few times in all his voluminous correspondence stretching across sixteen years that McKenney mentioned his wife or his son William, who, as he wrote to his old friend, the Rev. Philip Milledoler, "has gone out in the Frigate *Potomac* and is attached to the surgical department."

Evidently the colonel and his wife were now alone. He was forty-five years old.

He remained an avid observer of Washington politics and once offered to act as mediator between the Cherokee chiefs and Jackson's administration, which was refused. Eaton had left Washington and died soon after. Lewis Cass, McKenney's partner in the northwestern Indian councils, was now Secretary of War.

2.

JARED SPARKS was one of Colonel McKenney's oldest and undoubtedly his most patient friend. Their correspondence of the 1830s and 1840s often sad, sometimes humorous, reveals the trials, tribulations and at times abject poverty McKenney experienced to make his dream of the Indian portfolio become a reality.

Sparks was editor of *The North American Review*, one of the nation's most respected reviews and literary journals, and was later president of Harvard. Their friendship began when Sparks was chaplain to Congress shortly after the War of 1812 and McKenney was the new Superintendent of Indian Trade.

In the first several months after his dismissal by Jackson and before his financial debacle, McKenney continued to visit and dine with old friends, giving each one a glowing description of his future plans. Men who had been associated with the Indian nations and early explorations of the American West continued to seek him out.[5]

During the winter of 1831–1832, McKenney had written some of the text for the portfolio or at least a rough outline because he asked Sparks "to read and edit the outline of this history, cut up and mangled in more places than one . . ."[6]

That spring McKenney disclosed to Sparks that he had commissioned Henry Inman, the artist, to make copies of the Indian portraits in the Washington gallery. Twenty-nine-year-old Inman, a founder of the American Academy of Design and a recent bridegroom, had moved from New York to Philadelphia where he met McKenney. His task was to make the copies which McKenney would use for the lithographic engravings done on stone for the portfolio.

The problem that faced the colonel was both difficult and intriguing. Should he send Inman to Washington or somehow sneak out the original portraits to Philadelphia? McKenney knew the unforgiving Jackson would never give his permission. Then came the disturbing news that the President was about to grant the rights to someone else to use the gallery for a portfolio.

McKenney turned to his old friend Secretary of War Cass. One of the colonel's letters hints that Cass may have given him permission without Jackson's knowledge to take the original paintings portrait by portrait to Philadelphia where they were copied and then returned, "so I can engrave them at leisure from Inman's copies."

It makes a delightful scene to imagine McKenney clutching several of the framed paintings, tiptoeing out of his old office, then several days later replacing them on their hooks.

McKenney warned Sparks this information "must be kept strictly confidential." He explained he was forced to do it this way "because of Jackson's lack of principle."

Inman, he said, had "hand copied" each portrait but instead of the original "medium size" he made them "full portrait size." McKenney added proudly: "The effect of thirty or forty is more imposing than any I ever saw."

As for Bradford, the frustrated McKenney was ready to "choke" his publisher for not moving fast enough to get the portfolio published.

"For six months he was dumb, telling me some fib now and then," McKenney wrote, "then he came bustling in with the declaration that he was ready to go."[7]

In the summer of 1831, McKenney hurried from Philadelphia to New York to visit the dying James Monroe. The former President had sent word he wanted to see him on a matter "of great personal urgency."

McKenney was ushered to the deathbed and the emaciated, wasted man whispered his dying request. It was for McKenney to describe to him the exact events of the Georgetown "mutiny" of officers who had refused to fight unless Armstrong was removed; how McKenney had been selected by his commander to seek out Madison in the smoldering capital to inform him of the events, and his return to Georgetown with the news of the President's dismissal of Armstrong. Monroe, then Secretary of State, was named Secretary of War in Armstrong's stead. The reason was to answer the longtime Washington gossip that Monroe had "undermined" Armstrong's reputation and to "hand down a spotless reputation" to the Monroe family.

In the small sweltering room with Monroe's family hovering about the bed, Colonel McKenney recalled in precise detail the events of that far-off day. He paused from time to time when the last of the great Virginians was shaken by spasms of coughing which left him gasping for breath. Finally McKenney finished. Monroe, his eyes closed, whispered:

"This is all I want."

A few days later the nation's church bells tolled for the fifth President of the United States.

The following summer Jackson's congressional foes resurrected the Houston-Eaton ration scandal and a Select Committee was appointed to determine "whether an attempt was made by the late Secretary of War John H. Eaton, fraudulently to give to Samuel H. Houston, or any other persons, or person concerned with Samuel Houston, a contract for supplying rations to such Indians as might emigrate to the lands West of Arkansas and Missouri and whether Samuel Houston made a fraudulent attempt to obtain such contract."[8]

The committee held public hearings during the spring and summer of 1832 with Colonel McKenney as a key witness. It was clear from the voluminous pages of testimony that McKenney's honesty had upset the arrangements and he later became the administration's scapegoat.

The committee of five Jacksonians and two Whigs filed its report in July 1832 with the majority following party lines. It absolved Jackson, Houston, and the dead Eaton. Whig Congressman John Leeds Kerr filed a strong individual minority report, stating that the evidence he had heard "establishes the fact that strong endeavors were used by Samuel Houston to obtain from the late Secretary of War Eaton, the contract for supplying the Indian rations . . . and that he was concerned with other persons, at divers times to obtain such a contract disadvantageous to the government."

Kerr's statement pointed out that "President Jackson certainly knew of the proposals of Samuel Houston and at one time approved of his having the contract at the highest terms proposed by him . . ."[9]

Minority members of the committee in their report concluded that Houston had "wrongfully" tried to obtain the contract and that Eaton did "attempt, wrongfully" to give it to him, but it was Kerr's strong opinion that vindicated McKenney and produced a stir in the capital.

Indian rations, political feuds, and noisy politicians soon faded from McKenney's life. In the spring of 1833 he wrote Sparks a joyful letter with the news that Lafayette had asked him to send copies of the portfolio to Paris and "he has sent over several names as subscribers."

Bradford at last reported to McKenney that he had a

total of one hundred and four subscribers but McKenney shrugged this off commenting to Sparks, "they are all voluntary, Bradford had done nothing on this score, in fact he has done nothing on any other score."[10]

The year 1833 was one of frustration for McKenney. He and Bradford were no longer on speaking terms and the angry colonel informed Sparks he and Bradford had dissolved their partnership and a new printing firm, Key & Biddle, also of Philadelphia, had taken over the project.[11]

McKenney never gave up hope that Sparks would join him as coeditor of the portfolio. In the winter of 1833 he suggested to the historian that he "go to Washington to lay the foundation for the materials, work them up and go West," with expenses to be paid by Key & Biddle, all profits to be divided equally between them.[12]

By the following spring McKenney grudgingly accepted Sparks's firm refusal. It was then that he began to search for another coauthor. He found him in James Hall, author of several popular nonfiction books about the western frontier.

3.

THE MYSTERY of how Colonel McKenney in Philadelphia met James Hall of Cincinnati may be explained by Jared Sparks's correspondence. In the fall of 1835 Hall had been corresponding for the first time with Sparks who wanted him to write an article for the *North American Review* on the life of Daniel Boone, which the Boston historian had heard was to be the subject of Hall's next book.

Writing from Cincinnati, Hall thanked Sparks for his offer to write for the prestigious *Review* but made it clear he did not intend to accept prestige for hard coin. He wrote:

"I cannot write such a work for the compensation mentioned. It would not amount to what I actually paid in travelling and other expenses." Then Hall went on to describe in fascinating detail, the financial problems of a researching historian, circa 1835.

> It cost me fifty dollars last year to visit several old men in distant places, the companions of Boone, for the purpose of collecting unpublished facts from their lips; and I have given to one individual thirty dollars for a collection of letters and an old diary, all bearing dates in the wilderness about the year 1775. I intend to write the life of Boone and I am sure if well done it will be a valuable and popular work. If your publisher will give me anything like fair compensation, I will cheerfully contribute to your work and be proud of the company in which I have been placed.[13]

Old letters and a diary of Boone's companions with "dates in the wilderness about the year 1775" may have whetted Sparks's scholarly appetite; obviously it would be a coup for the *Review* to publish an article rich in new, fascinating material on a popular hero such as Boone. To help persuade Hall to do the article, he brought the Cincinnati writer and Colonel McKenney together. It was a successful meeting. The former Indian Superintendent and the celebrated midwestern author agreed to work together on the portfolio. McKenney's next letter to Sparks happily informed him that Hall was "working hard at the material."

McKenney may have been impressed by Hall's prolific literary output which numbered several histories of the West including his popular two-volume *Sketches of the History, Life and Manners in the West; Containing Descriptions of the Country and the Modes of Life in the Western States and Territories of America.*

At the time of his meeting with McKenney, Hall had just turned forty. He was a stocky, intense, somewhat egotistical man, ambitious and personally courageous. To obtain material for one book he took a dangerous keelboat trip down the Missouri.

He came from a family of lawmen, poets, and educators. His grandfather had accompanied Lord Baltimore to Maryland.

Three of Hall's brothers were lawyers, editors, and publishers; the fourth, a naval surgeon, was lost at sea. James Hall, the youngest, "reared in a literary atmosphere" in Philadelphia and New Jersey villages, studied law but abandoned his clerkship to enlist at nineteen as a rifleman in the army during the War of 1812. He commanded a detachment at the Battle of Chippewa, fought at Lundy's Lane, and received commendations as a lieutenant of artillery during the siege of Fort Erie. He was stationed at Fort Mifflin where he was selected to accompany Stephen Decatur aboard the *Enterprise* on the expedition against the Barbary pirates. In 1816 he was back in the States as an officer in the army's Ordnance Department and served at various posts in Rhode Island and on the Pennsylvania frontier.

In 1817 he was court-martialed at Pittsburgh; he had committed a military mortal sin: he had knocked out a fellow officer during a public brawl. He was found guilty and sentenced to be publicly cashiered from the service but Hall decided to fight the verdict of the court-martial board. He took his appeal to Washington where it was finally decided that in view of Hall's "brave and meritorious service during the late war [1812]" he was reinstated. His honor satisfied, he immediately resigned his commission and returned to his law studies. That same year he was admitted to the bar and hung out his shingle in Shawneetown on the Illinois frontier.

Hall soon made his reputation in the rough, colorful, backwoods circuit courts. Three years after he had opened his law office he was appointed Illinois State Attorney, serving a judicial circuit of ten counties in the southeastern part of the state, then terrorized by the toughest bands of cutthroats and outlaws in the history of the Midwest.

The young lawyer who had fought the British, Barbary pirates, and Indians was not intimidated by the train and stagecoach robbers. He not only personally led posses to clean out the gangs in their hideaways but prosecuted them until they received long prison sentences. For the first time law and order came to the territory; a few years later the grateful communities voted Hall in as judge of the judicial circuit.

In 1827 the Illinois legislature abolished Hall's judicial

circuit and he joined Robert Blackwell, the state printer, in publishing *The Illinois Intelligencer*. He was next elected Illinois State Treasurer but continued to retain his editorship. It appears 1830 was a busy year for Hall. Again with Blackwell he founded the state's first literary magazine, *The Illinois Monthly Magazine*, and his sketches of the western frontier were later published in book form. The scarcity of type, ink, and paper forced him and Blackwell to print the magazine in sections in St. Louis and Cincinnati. These were delivered by riverboat to the frontier town of Vandalia where the two publishers worked nights stitching the parts together.

In 1833 Hall, then known as "Judge" Hall, bought out Blackwell's interest and moved the magazine to Cincinnati where it was published under the elaborate title of *The Western Monthly Magazine, a Continuation of the Illinois Monthly Magazine*.

The publication was many times in danger of foundering but Hall stubbornly refused to close its doors; his vast energies and his book royalties kept it in print.

Hall had now selected Cincinnati as his home town. He slowly gained a reputation as a combined frontier historian, novelist, essayist, editor, and publisher. A survey of his works reveals his pen was never still; there was a steady flow of manuscripts from Cincinnati to New York and Philadelphia publishers. He married Mary Harrison Posey, daughter of the famous Revolutionary major general and governor of the Indiana Territory. A year later the indefatigable Hall produced the biography of his father-in-law. When William Henry Harrison, first governor of the Indiana Territory and hero of Tippecanoe, then living in North Bend, Ohio, was being mentioned as a presidential candidate, he turned to Hall, an old friend, and soon his biography appeared, *A Memoir of the Public Services of William Henry Harrison*.

The first Mrs. Hall died in 1832. Seven years later Hall married the daughter of another prominent Revolutionary hero, Richard Clough Anderson.[14]

4.

IN 1832 Henry Inman, who had painted the copies from the Washington gallery, and Cephas Childs his partner, engraved one of the portfolio's first plates, Shingaba W'Ossin, the Chippewa chief, which was printed in Volume I. The following year Key & Biddle entered the first copyright for the plates. Two years later, almost on the very brink of the publication of the portfolio, they were all startled to learn that James Otto Lewis, the frontier artist who had accompanied McKenney to the Fond du Lac and Butte des Morts treaty councils, was announcing the publication of his *Aboriginal Port-Folio*. Obviously an embittered Lewis had heard about McKenney's work based on his own sketches and had decided to get his book out first.

The lithography on the Lewis portfolio was done by Lehman & Duval of Philadelphia.

Peter Duval had been brought to the United States only

two years before by Inman and Childs. Following the success of his first print, "Grandpa's Pet," he had been persuaded to join Lehman's new firm. Duval was a brilliant lithographer, credited with the chrome process but his work on the Lewis portfolio was inferior with the color washed in by hand. Rare copies reveal no title page or text, simply a flimsy paper cover and an advertisement signed by Lewis on July 20, 1835, which pointed out the "disadvantages" of an artist traveling in a wilderness—clearly a thrust at King who had copied Lewis's works in his comfortable Washington studio or tree-shaded yard.

The first three sections of Lewis's *Port-Folio*, which Schoolcraft considered "a valuable contribution," were issued in June and July of 1835.[15]

In the winter of 1836 Hall met Catlin in Cincinnati and put before him a proposition that the Catlin Indian Gallery be merged with McKenney's collection so a "complete monopoly" could be created and "immense profits be realized."

He detailed the portfolio as consisting of twenty numbers "each to contain six portraits and twenty or thirty pages of text and would be known as McKenney and Hall's *History of the Indian Tribes of North America*. One section would be devoted to a general history of the tribes and the rest would consist of individual biographies," the never modest Hall boasted. His material for this part of the work

is very voluminous and of the most authentic nature, having been collected from a great number of Indian agents and other gentlemen who are personally acquainted with the Indians . . .

Should you think proper to join us, we shall have in our hands a complete monopoly; no other work can compete with what we could make. We shall begin to print within a few days. As soon as two numbers are complete my agent may be sent to Europe, where the sale will probably be very extensive.

Your object, I presume, will be to make money by the exhibition of your gallery, and it will doubtless be a fortune to you. But you could in no way enhance the value of your gallery more than publishing a part of it in such a work as ours, which would naturally excite the public attention toward it.

My part of the work is to do the writing . . .[16]

This one line must have caused Catlin to smile since he was embarked upon his historic work on the same subject.

This was the year Catlin made his celebrated journey to the pipestone quarries in Minnesota and an expedition to the upper Great Lakes and Upper Missouri. Later, in a letter to the American Turf Register he contemptuously dismissed Hall's proposition; he either found Hall too aggressive or considered all other western painters as poachers in a territory he felt he had won by hard work and great personal risks.

5.

DEATH AND triumph marked McKenney's year of 1836; he buried his wife, still only a name and a shadow in his correspondence, and saw the first volume of his portfolio published. As usual he was in financial difficulties and in a hurry to collect his royalties. He wasn't shy about taking advantage of his friendship with people who might help the sale of his books. After Lewis Cass resigned as Secretary of War to accept an appointment as minister to Great Britain, McKenney gave him a number of copies of the prospectus for the portfolio and casually asked him to make sure they were read "by the right people." In between royal receptions the United States minister to the Court of St. James's became a book salesman! Jared Sparks was ordered to write a series of letters "to such persons as you can address in England, France and Germany, on the merits of the fidelity of the work as history and as illustrating [the] true character of the American aboriginals. These are highly important to me."

McKenney also asked the historian's assistance in helping him organize a lecture series on the American Indian.

"Now if I could have a skeleton [format] from you, it would give me confidence and all the filling up that you could impart would add to my pleasure in giving such a course. I have thought of dividing the course [of lectures] into 12 parts. But first let me hear from you . . . "[17]

McKenney kept after Sparks until a review appeared in the *North American Review;* then he was jubilant. He predicted the portfolio was on its way to becoming one of the most famous books in America's literary history "with over 200,000 sold and about 75,000 of that within the last four months and a half." The profits, he predicted, would reach almost a half million dollars.[18]

Then came the bitter panic of 1837 in which every bank in the nation suspended specie payments; the firm of Key & Biddle was taken over by Frederick W. Greenbough, a well known Philadelphia lithographer who reissued Volume I in 1838. But now there were few subscribers for the $120 set.

A relentless fate continued to pursue McKenney from the spring of 1839 to the early 1840s. He was a frightened, penniless, aging man, desperately trying to maintain his dignity and pride.

His beloved portfolio, once a soaring eagle, now hung about his neck like an albatross. But years of frustration, disappointment, and disillusionment failed to defeat him. He was always writing to Jared Sparks or other friends that his hour of triumph over adversity would burst upon him at the next tick of the clock.

In the late 1830s he set out on a tour along the eastern seaboard from Maine to Boston, lecturing on the history and the tragic plight of the American Indian. His only asset now was his gallery of Inman's portraits. There is evidence he sold them twice to pay his bills.

William D. Lewis, chief cashier of a Philadelphia bank which held two of McKenney's notes of an undetermined sum, was now the target of the prolific letter-writing McKenney.

The banker was clearly intrigued by McKenney's stories and anecdotes and his Indian gallery. McKenney quickly took advantage of this whenever the banker summoned him to ask when the bank could expect another payment on the loans. It wasn't long before McKenney was trying to interest Lewis in buying an interest in the gallery. As

he confided to Lewis, he was "ready to take in a friend who shall own jointly with me, this valuable property."

His plan was to first exhibit the portraits in London and then sell the entire collection. He wrote: "I have been told that the strife between noblemen for a collection of *such paintings* [McKenney's emphasis] representing faithfully, parts of twenty of the North American Tribes would raise it up to an enormous sum, less in anybody's estimation of $100,000."[19]

Lewis appears to be an unusually kind and generous early nineteenth-century banker. Probably more out of friendship and respect for the former Indian Superintendent, he wrote back that he would "entertain" the proposal. That was all McKenney needed; within a day Lewis was reading a brisk businesslike letter outlining the colonel's terms of a sale.

> Under written and legal form I will divide the ownership [of the gallery] retaining one half for myself with all its interests, and emoluments and transferring the other half to you with all its benefits. For this half I will take five thousand dollars in modes of payment, most convenient to yourself, in stocks or whatever else may be converted into money, bringing me that sum of money.
>
> I will then possess you of my half, that may secure you against any possible loss that may attend upon our plans to make the whole productive. Of these $5,000 I will leave five hundred dollars in your hand, applicable on my part to the joint enterprises that we may agree upon for the exhibition, or sale, or both of this Gallery, with the understanding that all profits, whether of exhibition, or sale, or both, after deducting the expenses, are to be equally divided between us.

A week passed. Apparently Lewis sent back a friendly note but stayed clear from getting into any business entanglements with the colonel. McKenney's next letter was exuberant. He was going to lecture "some 20 miles off" but would soon return to Philadelphia to "talk about the future of 1 or 2 hundred thousand dollars that I shall be happy to put into your pocket as well as in mine . . . "

In between trying to sell Lewis an interest in his gallery, McKenney persuaded the banker to grant him another loan. The following fall after vainly trying to get McKenney to pay up, Lewis reluctantly put one of the notes for $220 into the hands of a Philadelphia lawyer.

McKenney begged Lewis to let him renew his note. ". . . after the war [Jackson's fight against the Bank of America] is over and our victory is achieved, I will have time to look up your affairs and the country's as well as mine and to attend to my own business . . . "

A year later, almost to the day, Lewis was again writing to McKenney about the notes which he had renewed with two cosigners.

This time McKenney revealed he had been summoned to Washington by his old friend William Henry Harrison, the ninth President, "who had assigned me, tho, informally, to my old bureau. He died, before his will could be consummated in this and in other matters."

Of his two cosigners, one was in a "flurry" and the colonel asked Lewis to inform him "the matter will remain as is, until my return." The other cosigner, he added, was a relative, "as good as gold."

Two years later the incredibly patient banker was still pressing McKenney about the notes. McKenney sadly pointed out to Lewis that he "had been met by counter-currents which have borne me away from my object—and who has not? If I have desire which is all absorbing, and which gives me greater pleasure than any or all earthly things, it is that *to pay what I owe to the last dollar.*" (McKenney's emphasis.)

He was full of plans for the gallery and still delivering his "addresses on Indian subjects," he told Lewis, with two to be delivered that very night in Germantown. Lewis continued to hold the unpaid notes, but possibly had a lien on the gallery. McKenney's letters hint that eventually Lewis helped to persuade a Philadelphia physician named Clark to buy a three-quarter interest in the gallery and McKenney may have tried to resell those same interests. In the fall of 1843 Lewis protested to McKenney who replied, "I have forgotten that you had any of the Indian Portraits . . . there appears to be a mistake in the matter between Doctor Clark and myself, which I think when we come together will be easily corrected . . . "

Lewis replied accusing McKenney of "avarice" but the colonel wryly replied that "a little dash of that ingredient would do me good."

As the year turned McKeneny was hopelessly entangled in the many deals he had made, selling off parts of the Indian gallery, sometimes twice. He finally turned to Lewis for advice; the banker proposed that the entire collection be sold so that McKenney could satisfy his many debts.

McKenney warned Lewis, the banker, and Clark, the physician, that the collection was "valuable only as a whole" and should not be sold in segments.

Speaking of himself in the third person, he advanced this proposal to Clark:

> McKenney has a right, you know, to a fourth of the Indian Gallery of Portraits. The design came from his head. It is right he should profit by whatever is done to them. He tells me he wishes you to have charge of them and to take them with you to Europe with the expectation of mutual benefit, the sale of them or whatever else you may esteem at best to do with them.
>
> He confides in you. Now if the whole can be got together I will deliver over those [portraits] in my possession, cheerfully to aid the collection. . . .

The correspondence between the three men abruptly breaks off in 1843 and there is no way of knowing the fate of the portraits. It can be assumed that the gallery was not sold because McKenney kept sinking deeper and deeper into his financial mire.

McKenney was not entirely a fraud; he was more a declining Mr. Micawber who would be satisfied with nothing less than the grandiose. He had too much a sense of style to be a common cheat. The gallery was his only asset, his remaining link to the great days of his lost glory. It was also his talisman, his shield against the cold, bitter world of unpaid bills, loans from embarrassed friends, and the humiliation of the Chestnut Street boardinghouse after the luxury of Weston. He was sincere when he proudly predicted to his investors that all of them would soon be showered with unbelievable riches. If there was a principal victim, it was McKenney himself.

6.

AS THE years passed, Colonel McKenney fought hard to keep his gallery in print. Every dollar he could beg or borrow went to the printers. The lithographer Greenbough was now replaced by the printing firm of Daniel Rice and James G. Clark who republished Volume I and Volume II and the final volume in 1844. Curiously, some of the stunning plates were engraved by Lehman & Duval who had done such a shoddy job with the unfortunate James Otto Lewis's *Aboriginal Port-Folio* almost ten years before.

Rice & Clark were taken over by a new firm, Rice & Hart, who published the first royal octave volumes 1842–1843. The portfolio continued to be published in various forms through the 1840s, 1850s, and almost to the year of Appomattox.

Hall and McKenney suffered the pains of coauthorship and parted. On the title pages of some editions, McKenney's name is listed solely as the author and at times he referred to himself as the "author of the History of the Indian Tribes of North America."[20]

The 1840s were desperate times for Colonel McKenney. He was now fifty-eight, almost penniless, and forced to beg loans of small sums from his loyal, patient old friend Jared Sparks.

In May 1843, covered with embarrassment, the colonel confessed to Sparks that he was without funds, and would need "fifty dollars for some thirty days until my remittance arrives."[21]

Sparks wrote on the bottom of the letter: "May 29th, sent a check for $50 on the New England Bank of Boston."

McKenney proved he was no deadbeat. In July he wrote a note of thanks enclosing an order for fifty dollars. He apologized for not being able to deliver the payment personally and to have "the opportunity for a long talk but my speaking engagements will not permit it."

A short time later McKenney was writing again to Sparks asking "for the loan of $40 from an old fashioned friend" so that he could continue his speaking tour "from Portsmouth and then further on."[22]

McKenney just couldn't face Sparks and ask for the money. This time he sent a messenger with an elaborate explanation that he had injured his knee, "but by the use of Leeches and a little rest it will soon be itself again."

Sparks wearily wrote on the bottom of the note: "Oct. 5, sent the $40."

A month later McKenney was explaining that his "remittance" had failed to arrive and he was "mortified." He finally repaid the $40 loan with profuse thanks, explaining how the "remittance has been following me from city to city and you should know how very annoying such things are . . ."[23]

In the fall of 1844 McKenney asked for another small loan. This time it was for $50 to cover his publishing expenses. His last bill for the portfolio had come to $287.64, he wrote, "and to settle it took the very scrapings from my wallet."[24]

Sparks sent the money "by Hales Express" and it was

repaid three weeks later. In the winter and spring of 1845 Sparks evidently helped McKenney edit his *Memoirs* which were published the following year. But before the book came out there was another note delivered to Sparks's office. The historian must have known what it was without opening it. The loan this time was for $50, to be repaid "at the very salient moment."

That following summer McKenney wrote a melancholy note to Sparks on the bottom of his prospectus for his *Memoirs*. He was penniless and instead of seeing his friends he "expected a sheriff's summons." We can assume Sparks noted with dismay McKenney's postscript:

"But such a disaster cannot happen because the control of such a matter is in your hands . . . "25

Sparks continued to loan McKenney small sums from twenty dollars to fifty dollars which the colonel faithfully repaid whenever he received his "remittance" or "letters of claim," as he called them.

In the winter of 1847 McKenney was engaged in a furious battle of letters to the newspapers and privately printed pamphlets with the son of Secretary of War Armstrong, commander of Washington's defenses during the War of 1812. McKenney had charged in his *Memoirs* that Armstrong's incompetency had led to the burning of the capital, a charge which history confirms.

Armstrong's son published a pamphlet defending his father's memory and denouncing McKenney. The colonel "scraped the bottom of my wallet" to pay for a pamphlet answering Armstrong.26

But the long-dead war and forgotten generals were not foremost on McKenney's mind during those raw March days of 1847. As he wrote Sparks, despite the fine reviews his *Memoirs* were "profitless . . . " But McKenney, who always saw the silver lining in the gray clouds of gloom cheerfully predicted that the book "would soon find its way into wider circulation. . . ."

But the *Memoirs* slowly died and for the first time McKenney appeared defeated.

"The past few years," he wrote Sparks "have been filled with hard knocks . . . everybody seems to fall on me . . . I may be able to get up . . . when I shall you will hear from me. . . ."27

Personal adversity failed to halt his championing the cause of the American Indian. He was almost penniless but he insisted that a share of the proceeds of his lectures must go to the poverty-stricken tribes. His whole object in appearing before the public, he once wrote a friend, was to "awaken the public's attention to the condition of the Indian tribes and to call forth an effort for the preservation of these unhappy people . . . a portion of the income [from the sale of his lecture tickets] is to lay the foundation for the rescue of the remnants of the Red Race from annihilation. . . ."

He had been a guest of honor at the unveiling of a monument over the grave of Red Jacket and in 1846, when he was sixty-one, he returned to the frontier to visit his old friend, Keokuk, whom he had not seen for over twenty years.

McKenney found the famous Iowa chief a stooped, wrinkled simulacrum of the statuesque, majestic man he had escorted to the White House in Monroe's time. The Iowa Nation was no longer so powerful that it controlled the shifting of a small Republic's frontier. Now, the tribe was dying out, shunted about at the white man's whim, from territory to territory.

They were both old men now and the former Indian Superintendent and one of the greatest of Indian chiefs spent the afternoon on the Kansas River recalling old battles, forgotten generals, rogues and heroes, red and white.28

7.

THE LETTERS to Jared Sparks finally dwindled away. The historian had been elected to the presidency of Harvard in 1849, and three years later when his last major book was published, *Correspondence of the American Revolution, Being Letters of Eminent Men to George Washington,* he retired to his home in Cambridge.

One by one the great men McKenney had been associated with all his lifetime died. The sound and fury of the events which had shaken all their lives were now history. As McKenney had predicted in the early part of the century, many of the tribes on the eastern side of the Mississippi had vanished or were now shabby, drunken remnants of great races. Indian delegations occasionally came to Washington but only the chiefs and warriors of the fierce wild tribes from the deep west like the Sioux were treated with any respect; even the great Cherokee John Ross, who pleaded from the Indian territory to the Great Father to carry out the promises and treaties the white man had made many years before, was treated with contempt.

It was 1859 and the shadow of a terrifying Civil War was edging across the land. Colonel McKenney was now seventy-four, still tall and erect, but frail and with fading eyesight. In February 1859 he was living in New York City. On a Saturday night he died alone. His four-line obituary listed no survivors.

"Washington papers, please copy," it ended.29

Only the *Intelligencer* briefly and sadly commented on his passing. But Colonel Thomas Loraine McKenney, champion of the American Indian, was beyond caring. He had joined the Grandfathers.

Joseph Brant, Thayendanegea

HEN THE smoke of wood fires and burning leaves clings to the November mists in the Mohawk Valley, men still talk about Joseph Brant, the great Mohawk war captain who tried all his life to keep a foot in two worlds, the red and the white.

He refused to bend his knee to King George but gallantly kissed the hand of his queen. He had his portrait painted by the famous English painter George Romney. He was at ease drinking tea from fragile china cups, but could hurl a tomahawk with deadly accuracy. He was a graduate of the Indian school that later became Dartmouth College, and he translated the Bible into the Mohawk language, yet he could leave the Mohawk a blazing ruin from Fort Stanwix, near Rome, to the very outskirts of Schenectady. He was one of the greatest of American Indians; had he given his support to the struggling Continental army the course of our history would certainly have been changed.

But it would have been improbable if not impossible for Brant to wear a Continental tricorn; he was too vain and too closely allied with the Lords of the Valley to consider casting his lot with the humble Palatine Dutch farmers who talked so much of freedom. For Brant, they had the stink of cow dung about them; he was more familiar with buckled shoes and cologne.

His decision to side with the British was tragic for the Iroquois Confederacy or Six Nations as it was called. That ancient confederation bound together by wisdom, skill at war, and diplomacy became helplessly divided when it was agreed that each nation should go its own way. In the past a declaration of war had to be voted unanimously. Some nations like the Oneida went with the Americans, others tried to stay neutral, or like Brant's Mohawk fought for the British.

Brant joined Colonel Barry St. Leger's invasion of the Mohawk, one of the prongs of Burgoyne's doomed campaign. The famous Battle of Oriskany, undoubtedly the bloodiest and most ferocious of the Revolution, was fought with Herkimer's gallant farmers standing musket to musket with the King's Own, the best of his Hessian gamekeeper-sharpshooters, and Brant's painted warriors. Brant, who despised defeat, led his Indans back to Fort Niagara, bitterly advising the British high command in Montreal that from now on he would fight his way.

For six years he led his Indian raiders into the Mohawk, again and again leaving the beautiful valley a sea of flames while the alarm bells in the tiny forts clanged frantically.

Some raids became classic atrocity stories of American wars: Cherry Valley, where women and children lay dead in the snow with Brant protesting fiercely that Walter Butler, who led Butler's Rangers, was to blame; Wyoming, which gave birth to the celebrated eighteenth-century poem "Gertrude of Wyoming," which pictures Brant as a murderous fiend who slaughtered the innocent. But as it developed Brant was never there.

Following the Revolution Brant led his people—the first American DPs—across the border to settle in Canada.

He came in solitary glory to Philadelphia in 1792 to see Washington and his cabinet, but only after the other Iroquois chiefs, like Cornplanter and Red Jacket, had already left the capital. It was typical of Brant. Humility was alien to the Mohawk; in fact, pride and arrogance were his major flaws.

Brant was no wigwam, storybook Indian dressed in buckskins stained with bear grease and smelling of a thousand campfires. He was educated, he wrote with the grace and lucidity that was far beyond many of the farmers he had fought against. His clothes were of the finest material, and in his luxurious home elaborate meals were served on crisp Irish linen. He had a host of slaves, as many as the aristocratic Virginians who would later rule the United States.

He died in his fine home on Grand River, Ontario, November 24, 1807, whispering with his last breath: "Have pity on the poor Indians."

Painter: Brant was painted by many famous artists; among them were Romney, Charles Willson Peale, George Catlin, and Wilhelm Berezy. It is not certain who painted this post-revolutionary portrait.

Joseph Brant

Red Jacket

ED JACKET was no fabled warrior; his favorite weapon was his eloquence, never a musket. Colonel McKenney compared him to Cicero, a man who better understood how to lead his countrymen to war instead of leading them into battle.

He first appeared as the spokesman of his people during the 1786 great council of the confederated Indians held at the mouth of the Detroit River. The Six Nations above all Indian nations were lovers of intelligence and eloquence. The notes of that treaty described his address as a "masterpiece of oratory," and the oratorical powers of Red Jacket were compared to the Virginian John Randolph, whose silver voice and brilliance never failed to cast a spell over the Senate.

In March 1792, Red Jacket led fifty Iroquois chiefs into Philadelphia as guests of Washington and his cabinet. General St. Clair had been routed in a bloody defeat in the previous fall, a bitter reverse to the hopes of the young Republic. It was feared that the British might again arm the still powerful Iroquois Confederacy and its warriors would fall on the feeble settlements of the Niagara frontier and again leave the Mohawk in flames. Red Jacket was the principal speaker at this lengthy council in which the Iroquois chiefs finally, reluctantly, agreed to act as mediators between the United States and the warring tribes of the west.

Several years later Red Jacket led his chiefs to Connecticut where he appeared in a dispute with the Connecticut Land Company, which claimed a large section of the present state of Ohio, then called New Connecticut. The Six Nations insisted it was their territory by right of conquest. A man who was there recalled for William L. Stone, the Seneca's biographer, how Red Jacket ended:

"We stand a small Island in the bosom of the great waters. We are encircled—we are encompassed. The evil spirits ride upon the blast and the waters are disturbed. They rise, they press upon us and the waves will settle over us and we shall disappear forever. Who then lives to mourn us, white man? None. What marks our extermination? Nothing. We are mingled with the common elements."

Once, an agent of the Missionary Society of Albany led a group of missionaries to the land of the Seneca. Red Jacket finally agreed to listen to their arguments as to why they should become Christians. After hours of talk to which he listened with a great deal of courtesy, he rose and faced the Black Coats as he called them. His reply was long, but he said in part:

Brother: You think us ignorant and uninformed. Go then and teach the whites. Select for example the people of Buffalo. We will be the spectators and remain silent. Improve their morals and refine their habits. Make them less disposed to cheat the Indians. Make the whites less inclined to make the Indian drunk and to take away their lands. Let us know the tree by the blossoms and the blossoms by the fruit. When this shall be made clear to our minds we may be more willing to listen to you. I have spoken.

He died January 20, 1830, in a small clapboard house in the Seneca village. He was about seventy-four.

When the local missionary heard that the chiefs intended to bury Red Jacket with pagan ceremonies he indignantly "assembled his party, took possession of the body, and conveyed it to their meeting house." Services were completed, and the missionary asked the chiefs if they wished to say a last word. One old man rose and in a quivering voice replied: "This house was built for the white man, the friends of Red Jacket cannot be heard in it."

The Black Coats had pursued the old Seneca to his grave.

Painter: Charles Bird King, Washington, 1828.

Red Jacket

Cornplanter, Kiontwogky, or Handsome Lake

I T WAS agreed by the Schoharie settlers in this summer of 1780 that they had never seen finer fields of grain. It would be one of the prosperous harvests on the frontier.

Times had been better during the past year. Frame houses had replaced some of the early crude log cabins; there were plenty of horses, and the herds of cows had increased so that there was scarcely a pasture that didn't have several good milkers.

The long war was fading. For more than a year the dread cry of "Butler and Brant's in the Valley" had not been heard. There was even talk of peace, and some said the Lobsterbacks were only too happy to go home.

There was one lingering doubt: the Seneca. The nation was reported still licking its wounds from General Sullivan's scorched earth invasion. Scouts predicted they would return under Cornplanter, the Seneca's capable young war captain.

This time they came from all directions; Indians under Brant, Regulars and Butler's Rangers under old Colonel John. They received reinforcements along the Tioga route and headed for Schoharie. On September 17, Cornplanter led his single file of painted braves to Unadilla to join Sir John Johnson's forces. Crossing Summit Lake they swooped down on the settlements.

Stone Arabia was sacked by Cornplanter's braves who put the lush fields to the torch. There was a strong west wind to fan the flames and the Seneca were delirious with revenge, whooping, howling, and firing off their muskets. Great columns of smoke cast shadows on the slowly rising hunter's moon.

Then at Fort Plain occurred one of those events in war that is so melodramatic it is almost trite. A batch of white prisoners, men, women, and children, were being herded together when one of the men spoke quietly to a Seneca guard in his own tongue and asked what they intended to do with them. The surprised guard summoned Brant who stared hard at the tall, sinewy man of about fifty-five with a weather-beaten face. The Mohawk knew him to be John O'Bail (also spelled in colonial documents O'Beal, O'Ball, and Abeel), and they talked for a few moments. In his youth O'Bail had lived with the Indians and at one time had a Seneca wife. After she died he had returned to the Mohawk and made a haphazard living as a farmer, trapper, Indian interpreter, and scout. Brant hurried to find Cornplanter.

Before they left the valley, Cornplanter came up to the prisoners and studied O'Bail closely.

"Are you the white man called John O'Bail?" he asked at last.

"I am John O'Bail," the settler replied.

"Did you have a wife in the Seneca Castle?" Cornplanter asked.

"I had a Seneca woman but that was a long time ago," was the reply.

The Seneca war captain, his face streaked with red and black paint, put his hand on O'Bail's shoulder.

"That woman was my mother, I am your son." He took O'Bail aside and told him: "If you now choose to follow me and live with my people I will promise to cherish your old age with plenty of venison and you shall live easy. But if it is your choice to return to your people and live with your white children I will send a party of my young men to escort you to safety."

"I am a white man. I have a wife and children. I will return to my own people," O'Bail said.

Cornplanter nodded. "I respect you, my father." Before they left the Mohawk, Cornplanter assigned several young warriors as an escort for O'Bail, his wife, and children.

Red Jacket, Brant, and Cornplanter comprised the great triumvirate of Iroquois chiefs who led their people in the trying postwar period of the Revolution. In later years Cornplanter became a religious zealot and a bitter enemy of Red Jacket. In the winter of 1801–1802, he traveled to Washington as the guest of Jefferson who became his frequent correspondent. He died February 18, 1836, "aged about 100 years" on a reservation of over nine hundred acres in Pennsylvania.

Painter: F. Bartoli, 1796. In his 1836 catalogue McKenney has this painting "taken in New York forty years ago by Barton and copied from the original by Otis in Philadelphia." Obviously he misspelled Bartoli's name (the signed painting is now in the possession of the New-York Historical Society) and Otis is Bass Otis who has been credited with producing America's first lithograph. Otis also lived in Philadelphia in the 1830s.

Cornplanter

Ahyouwaighs, or John Brant

ISITORS TO the home of John Brant, chief of the Six Nations, found him a charming host who spoke perfect English and dressed in the latest London fashion, except for beaded moccasins. James Buchanan, British consul general in New York, who expected to find a family of painted savages sitting about a cook fire in their wigwam, was astonished, as he wrote, to discover Brant and his sisters ready to enter any English drawing room.

Francis Hall, a British officer, remembered Brant's young sister Elizabeth for her elegant dress and manners, but was more impressed by her "softness approaching to Oriental languor." Hall, who visited the Brants in 1816, wrote in his *Travels in Canada and the United States*:

"She retains so much of her native dress as to identify her with her people, over whom she affects no superiority, but seems pleased to preserve all the ties and duties of relationship."

The mother of John Brant was Catherine, widow of Joseph Brant the famous Thayendanegea, war captain and chief of the Iroquois Confederacy, or Six Nations, during the Revolution. Catherine, eldest daughter of the head of the Turtle clan, the first in rank in the Mohawk nation, had the honor of selecting one of her sons to be chief. She picked John, her fourth and youngest, who had been born on September 24, 1794.

Like his father, John had strong loyalty to the Crown and led his warriors against the United States in the War of 1812. He later lived with his sister Elizabeth in grand English style on Lake Ontario. Ironically, his mother had returned to her native village "and resumed the customs of her fathers."

In 1821, young Brant, following in the footsteps of his famous father, traveled to London to argue the authenticity of his land claims before Parliament. His strongest supporter was the Duke of Northumberland. Their ties were traditional; when Joseph Brant had visited London to see King George in 1776 the elder duke had been his friend and sponsor before the royal court.

During his visit to England John wrote to Thomas Campbell, the nineteenth-century poet, asking him to correct his celebrated "Gertrude of Wyoming," which calumnized Thayendanegea as a bloodthirsty slayer of innocents at the massacre of Wyoming. Historical evidence had proved Brant was not present at the tragedy.

Campbell later admitted in a magazine article that he had been mistaken and lamely described his Brant as a fictional character. Chief Justice John Marshall, however, refused to correct the second edition of his *The Life of George Washington*, published in 1834, despite John Brant's letters and pleas.

In 1821, Brant was elected as a member of the Canadian provincial parliament for the county of Haldimand, which included many Mohawk. Landowners contested the election on the grounds that the Indians were not actually landowners and the seat was vacated. During the campaign to regain the seat, both Brant and his political opponent died of cholera.

After her brother's death Elizabeth Brant married William Johnson Kerr, a grandson of Sir William, and for a time it seemed that the great colonial dynasty that began with Molly Brant, Joseph's sister, and Johnson, the great Empire Builder, would continue. The last survivor of the Brant children, Catherine B. Johnson, died in 1867.

Painter: Unknown.

Ahyouwaighs

McIntosh

HE STORY of McIntosh, the handsome Creek who looked like a swarthy-skinned Scots Highland chief is tragedy as Eugene O'Neill and Euripides knew it; the story of a noble man, neither villainous nor perfectly virtuous, who is defeated by forces too powerful for him to cope with.

McIntosh (Macintosh) first appears in the history of his people when South Carolina General John Floyd mentioned him in his dispatches during the battle of Atasi (also spelled Autossee) on November 29, 1813.

McIntosh, who signed his name "Wm. McIntosh," was also praised by General Jackson for his courage during two of Jackson's campaigns: the Battle of the Horseshoe Bend of Tallapoosa River, in Tallapoosa County, Alabama, March 27, 1814, in which more than a thousand Creeks were killed, and the American war against the Seminole. A large part of the territory of the conquered tribe was confiscated and opened to white settlers.

McIntosh is linked to history not by his exploits in war but by his stand on the question of Indian removal, which both canonized and condemned him in the Creek nation.

The shadow of the land-hungry white man first fell over the Creek in 1802 when an agreement was signed by Georgia and the federal government, in which both sides stipulated that the United States "shall, at their own expense, extinguish, for the use of Georgia, as early as the same can be *peaceably* effected, on *reasonable* terms, the Indian title to the lands within the forks of the Oconnee and Oakmulgee Rivers...and that the United States shall...also extinguish the Indian title to *all* the other lands within the State of Georgia."

It was a deadly land grab, a contract that would eventually deprive the Creek of their ancestral land. Of course, they were not consulted.

From 1803 to 1821 many Indian delegations came to Washington to "extinguish"—the favorite euphemism of early nineteenth-century politicians for stealing land from the American Indians—the titles to their homes.

Year after year the acres disappeared. In one treaty council fifteen million acres of Indian land were signed away; the United States government paid $1,250,000 for the lands. The Creek became alarmed. In 1811, at the famous Broken Arrow council they passed a tribal law forbidding, under penalty of death, any Creek chief from selling the nation's land.

The state of Georgia became impatient and pressured Washington into calling more councils and forcing the Creek to give up more land. But after Broken Arrow the chiefs refused to meet.

An emotional whirlwind engulfed all three: the federal government torn between state pressure and the realistic view of some of its leaders that it would only be a question of time before the Indian nations were inundated and absorbed by the tidal wave of white civilization; Georgia faced by the increasing traffic of settlers pushing into forbidden Indian land and ready to provoke a frontier war; the Creek, pinned between land-hungry whites, the need for money for cattle, crops, and schools for their children, and the intense love of their land.

The United States answered Georgia that it was doing all it could peaceably. As Colonel McKenney wrote at the time, the improvements for the Creek that Georgia complained so bitterly about was "only a continuation of the policy adopted by Washington...one would think [this policy] needed no defence before a civilised and Christian people..."

Under pressure—and obvious bribery—McIntosh and some lesser chiefs signed the treaty of Indian Springs on February 12, 1825, giving Georgia large tracts of Indian land.

Creek Agent John Crowell advised McKenney of the treaty and the Indian superintendent forwarded it to Calhoun. The secretary of war refused to send it on to Congress for ratification. Monroe, however, who did not want President-elect Adams to be burdened with the treaty, sent it to Congress where a bloc of senators rammed it through in the record time of twenty-four days.

The Creek, whom McKenney described as "greatly excited," sent out an execution squad searching for McIntosh who claimed protection promised by Georgia. On May 1, McIntosh was shot and killed with Etomie Tustennuggee, another chief. A half-breed, Sam Hawkins, was hanged and his brother Ben severely wounded.

McIntosh

McIntosh left behind him a divided tribe. One faction believed he had done right and followed his son, Chilly McIntosh, to the west after they had signed away their lands in Washington on January 24, 1826, for $100,000. The other faction soon gave up their lands to Georgia and crossed into Alabama. That state also demanded they be removed. At last "this wretched people," as McKenney called them, also followed Chilly McIntosh to the west. There was still no immediate peace; both factions fought until a bitter peace was finally hammered out.

Painter: Charles Bird King, Washington, 1825(?).

Apauly Tustennuggee

THE SECTION of country [Indian territory] set apart for the Creeks and Seminoles, is about the same in extent with that of the Choctaws, but not so mountainous. The soil is considered to be equal in fertility, to any in the south-western section of the country. It is well watered, and has plenty of timber; there are some prairies, which however are of great advantage to the settler, the soil being rich and easy to cultivate, and they are very profitable for raising stock.

The Creeks are a corn-growing people. Those that have been in the country some years, raise corn in large quantities; some of the principal farmers crib from five to ten thousand bushels in a season. They do not raise much stock, nor are they, as a people, so far advanced in civilisation as the Cherokees and Choctaws, though, as agriculturists, so far as raising corn, they excel either of the above named tribes. They raise stock sufficient for their own consumption, but none of any consequence for sale.

This is part of a report sent from the Indian territory to the War Department by a Creek Indian agent in 1837. Instead of wigwams or tepees, the Creek, he wrote, lived in "good, comfortable farm houses, have fine gardens, orchards....Two of these traders are natives, who do considerable business, selling eighteen or twenty thousand dollars' worth of goods annually."

This was one year after the removal of the Creek had begun; it would take three more years for the United States to transfer what one early Alabama historian had called "a nation that is proud, arrogant and haughty, brave and valiant in war," from its ancient homelands to the West.

One large Creek delegation visited Washington in the winter of 1825–1826 and forced the United States to declare the infamous Indian Springs treaty "to be null and void to every intent and purpose whatever. . . ." However, it proved to be a Pyrrhic victory; as with the Cherokee, the white man's treaty, obtained by trickery, had split the Creek and brought about the murder of their chief, McIntosh. In 1827, Colonel McKenney negotiated with the Creek for the sale of the remainder of their land in Georgia. The nation was then confined to their lands in Alabama. Still, there was no peace when that state demanded they be removed. Finally, the first families boarded the steamboats for the alien western lands, the promised land as the exuberant War Department called it.

McKenney's brief description of Apauly Tustennuggee was "a chief and a warrior...a firm, brave man—and of good sense."

Painter: Charles Bird King, Washington, 1826.

Apauly Tustennuggee

Ledagie

EDAGIE, A CREEK chief, played a small role in the struggles of his people to retain their lands in the 1830s. His village was one of many on the eastern side of the Mississippi, in Georgia, and Alabama that were called the Upper and Lower towns.

The principal chief at the time was Big Warrior under whom Opothle-Yoholo was the principal "speaker of the councils." The important council house of the Upper towns was at Tuckabatchee, home of Big Warrior.

The portrait of Ledagie was probably painted when he was a member of one of the Creek delegations that visited Washington to protest their removal. Their pleas were futile. A treaty was finally concluded in Washington on March 24, 1832, by which they were forced to yield up their homes, and ratified by Congress on April 4. By 1836, most of the Creek nation had moved west.

Painter: Charles Bird King, Washington, 1825.

Ledagie

Oche Finceco

OLONEL MC KENNEY only hints at the story behind the suicide of this celebrated chief who signed the treaty between his nation and the federal government in Washington, 1826.

Apparently he had received $10,000 at the signing, either as a bribe or part payment for an agreed annuity for his people.

"He was followed by certain blacklegs who won the money where upon he went to his loft and hung himself" is all that McKenney wrote.

In 1827 when McKenney was in the country of the Creek following the Butte des Morts treaty council in the northwest, he saw how the people still mourned Oche Finceco; women cared for his grave and warriors were building a roof of split shingles over his resting place. "A man held in much esteem by his people" the Indian superintendent concluded.

Oche Finceco was a half-breed and known to the settlements as Charles Cornell.

Painter: Charles Bird King, Washington, 1826.

Oche Finceco

Selocta

T FORT MIMS, the entire garrison from the oldest man to the youngest child had been massacred by Creek warriors under William Weatherford, the half-breed chief. When General Jackson moved into the land of the Creek, he found the nation divided into pro- and anti-American factions.

Chinnaby, a leading chief, and his son, Selocta, led the warriors who favored the Americans, while Weatherford swore to his council that he would never sell an acre of land to the Americans and would drive them into the sea.

Jackson's first contact with Selocta was when the young warrior appeared in his camp begging for soldiers to help fight off Weatherford's forces that had surrounded his father's small log fort on the Coosa River.

Jackson gave him some light infantry and the siege was lifted. Selocta then became Jackson's principal guide and Indian adviser. He was the government interpreter when Weatherford surrendered to Jackson.

"I am in your power, do with me as you please," Weatherford calmly told the general. "I have done the white people all the harm I could; I have fought them, and fought them bravely; if I had any warriors left, I would still fight, and contend to the last. But I have none; my people are all gone; and now I can only mourn over the misfortunes of my nation."

Jackson, no Indian lover, always respected a courageous enemy. He told Weatherford that he was free to leave the camp, but Jackson warned him that if he were retaken he would be hanged.

The half-breed shook his head and through Selocta told Jackson: "There was a time when I could have answered you; I then had a choice, but now I have none—even hope has ended. . . . I cannot call the dead to life. My warriors can no longer hear my voice...While there was a chance of success, I never left my post, nor asked for peace. But my people are gone, and I now ask for peace for my nation and for myself. . . .Those who would still hold out, can be influenced only by a spirit of revenge, and to this they must not, and shall not, sacrifice the last remnant of their nation. You have told us where we must go, and be safe. This is a good talk, and they ought to listen to it. They shall listen to it."

Shortly after Weatherford's surrender, Jackson urged a united council of chiefs to remove their nation to western lands offered by the United States.

This time it was Selocta who pleaded with Jackson, reminding the general of how he and his father had fought with the Americans against their own people, and for the sake of peace had rejoined Weatherford and the other chiefs. John Henry Eaton in his *Life of General Jackson*, published in 1824, recalled the Creek's speech and added:

"There were, indeed, none whose voice ought sooner to have been heard than Selocta's. None had rendered greater services, and none had been more faithful. He had claims growing out of his fidelity that few others had."

Selocta soon discovered that fidelity meant little to the white man. In the winter of 1825–1826 he was among the Creek chiefs who were finally forced to sign away their lands and move west.

Painter: Charles Bird King, Washington, 1825.

Selocta

Menawa, the Great Warrior

OR A LONG time Menawa stared out over the grand sweep of the land and the tiny town. His people called him, but he stood there like a stone man until the sun had set. At last he turned away. When his warriors asked why he had stayed in one spot so long he replied:

"Last evening I saw the sun set for the last time, and its light shine upon the tree-tops, and the land, and the water, that I am never to look upon again. No other evening will come, bringing to Menawa's eyes the rays of the setting sun upon the home he has left *forever!*"

Menawa, whose personal bravery in war had earned him the title of the Crazy War Hunter, was leading his people across Alabama's Tallapoosa River for the last time, headed for the dark lands beyond the Mississippi where the Great Father had insisted they must now live.

For years the great Creek chief had resisted the government's removal plan. To buy time for his people he had even fought on the side of the white man he despised and distrusted. Finally, he bowed to the pressures of the state and the government; there was no other alternative, he told the council, they must leave and survive or be ground under the boots of the white man or die under their guns.

Menawa was the strong man of the Creek. Colonel McKenney called him the Indian Rob Roy of the southern frontier of the early 1800s. Drover, marauder, crafty trader, warrior, and skillful war captain, he was hated, feared, but respected by the white settlers along the Cumberland River.

In the Battle of the Horseshoe, March 27, 1814, he was wounded seven times but fought until he collapsed. At twilight the battle was over; a thousand warriors had gone to war, only seventy survived. Menawa advised his men to return to their homes and "submit to the victors, and each man make his own peace as best he might."

When the Creek nation was split over the Indian removal question, Menawa led the anti-American faction against William McIntosh, the Creek chief who supported Washington. After McIntosh signed the treaty of Indian Springs on February 12, 1825, in which the Creek sold their lands, the Creek council ordered the death of McIntosh and the other chiefs who had signed the treaty. Menawa was selected as executioner. Seventy-five days after the treaty signing, Menawa and a band of warriors killed McIntosh and his followers.

In an attempt to heal his nation's wounds, Menawa led a delegation of Creek to Washington in January 1826 to sign a new treaty with Secretary of War James Barbour. Colonel McKenney was the witness.

During this visit McKenney persuaded Menawa to pose for his portrait. The Creek chief agreed but only on the condition that a copy be given to him.

During the Seminole War, General Thomas Sidney Jesup, a former aide to Jackson, asked Menawa to serve with another Creek chief, Opothe-Yoholo, as mediator in the Seminole War. After both chiefs were unsuccessful as arbitrators, Menawa led his warriors into the swamps to fight at the side of the white men he detested. Like Opothe-Yoholo he had one request, that he and his family be permitted to remain on their land and not be forced to travel across the Mississippi.

He returned to find his lands confiscated, his herds gone, his family moved west. Menawa quietly packed his few belongings and prepared to join his wife and children. The night before he left he gave the copy of his portrait to an old friend, a white man.

"I am going away," he said, "I have brought you this picture—I wish you to take it and hang it up in your house, that when your children look at it you can tell them what I have been. I have always found you true to me, but great as my regard for you is, I never wish to see you in that new country to which I am going—for when I cross the great river, my desire is that I may never again see the face of a white man!"

Painter: Charles Bird King, Washington, 1826.

Menawa

Tustennuggee Emathla

OR HOURS this Creek chief sat in Colonel McKenney's office in the War Department and impassively recited the broken promises and treachery that he had suffered from the United States, a country he had served faithfully in both war and peace.

When his nation was helplessly split over the question of Creek removal, he joined the followers of the pro-American chief William McIntosh and spoke at numerous councils in favor of moving to the western lands.

In 1838, he joined General Thomas Sidney Jesup to fight in Florida against the Seminole on condition that his family would not be removed to the West and his property be allowed to remain intact while he fought in the swamps.

Jesup, who knew the young chief was one of the nation's most charismatic leaders, quickly agreed, and Tustennuggee raised a war party of seven hundred warriors.

Tustennuggee's first role with the army was as mediator when Jesup asked him to arrange a truce between the Seminole and the Americans. The Creek chief and a select group of warriors trailed the Seminole for weeks, but their shouted pleas for a council were never answered by the shadows that slipped ahead of them through the dank wilderness. Finally he returned to Tampa to join General Richard Keith Call, former aide to Jackson, governor of Florida, and commander of all troops in Florida.

The Creek chief and his warriors fought in numerous campaigns with Call's men. The Florida governor praised his courage and leadership and told the War Department that Tustennuggee was one of the best guerrilla fighters in the Florida swamps.

The chief returned to the Creek country to find the army had broken its promise; his wife and nine children and their household goods had been loaded on a steamboat along with thirty-six Creek women and children—all whose husbands were fighting for the Americans in the Florida swamps—and removed to the West.

Tustennuggee set out for the Indian territory. At an army post he heard the news that shattered his life. The ancient boilers of the steamboat *Monmouth* had exploded, and all the women and children had been drowned or scalded to death.

Colonel McKenney wrote only a few lines about Tustennuggee's "melancholy" tragedy, but they reveal strikingly Washington's attitude toward the Indian tribes of the early eighteenth century:

"So far as the chief before us has any claim upon the justice or benevolence of our country, there can be no doubt that the Government will maintain its faith inviolate. Whatever may be thought of our policy towards the Indian tribes, as such, we are not chargeable, as a people, with any backwardness in the discharge of our obligations to individual claimants."

In other words, good single Indians yes, nations no.

John Mix Stanley, the great artist of the American West who painted him in 1843, described the Creek:

"He is and always has been a firm and undeviating friend of the whites . . . first as mediator, to induce the Seminoles to abandon the bloody and fruitless contest in which they were engaged, but was unsuccessful."

One bitter memory may have always stayed with Tustennuggee—some Seminole never surrendered.

Painter: Charles Bird King, Washington, 1826.

Tustennuggee Emathla

Paddy Carr

T THE age of nineteen, Paddy Carr was principal interpreter for the Creek chiefs when they visited President John Quincy Adams in 1826 to protest bitterly the infamous Indian Springs treaty. Colonel McKenney, who later witnessed the new treaty with Secretary of War James Barbour, found the young half-breed to have "a quick perception of the human character, which enabled him to manage and control the Indians with more success than many who were his seniors . . . in rapidly interpreting the speeches of the Indian orators . . . he often gave it additional vigour and clearness. . . . He possessed the entire confidence of the whole delegation, who regarded him as a youth of superior talents."

It was clear that Paddy Carr, son of an Irish trader and a Creek woman, did not intend to remain an interpreter for occasional traders, horse dealers, and infrequent Indian commissioners who only appeared when the government wanted to buy more land. Shortly after his return from Washington he wooed and married the pretty daughter of a wealthy half-breed farmer, who presented his new son-in-law with a generous dowry. In ten years Paddy owned considerable land, herds of horses and cattle, and seventy to eighty slaves—many more than a Virginia aristocrat.

In 1826, he defied his neighbors and became interpreter for General Thomas Sidney Jesup in the Creek country. Later he served as second in command of a large force of Creek warriors who fought as mercenaries against the Seminole.

Racehorses became his passion, and in later years the former Indian interpreter owned a large stable of blooded ponies. McKenney wrote that "when he has a trial of speed . . . he cannot suit himself with a rider, he rides his own horse."

Paddy Carr was now one of the lords of his valley and the chief source of employment for many poor Creek families. McKenney called him a man of "a liberal and generous disposition, hospitable to strangers, and kind to the poor."

Evidently the handsome half-breed not only had a fine eye for blooded horses but also for pretty women. In the 1830s he had three wives, all described as attractive.

Painter: Charles Bird King, Washington, 1826.

Mistippee

Opothle-Yaholo

I T WAS 1824 and the Creek nation was almost helplessly divided over the question of Indian removal. Years before the federal government had entered into an agreement with the state of Georgia to "remove" from within its borders all Indians and transport them to wilderness lands beyond the Mississippi.

Indian commissioners sent south to bargain with the Creek returned empty-handed. But their arguments, bribery, flattery—and whiskey—gradually recruited converts. Among the leaders who advocated removal to the western lands was McIntosh, head chief of the Lower towns; opposing him was Big Warrior, head chief of the Upper towns. In between was Little Prince, ruler of the entire nation, once a famed warrior-chief but now a feeble, sick, and apprehensive old man.

In the summer of 1824 Washington sent two more commissioners to the abortive treaty council of Broken Arrow where Big Warrior thundered that he would not "take a houseful of money for his interest in the land." Once again the commissioners returned to Washington with unsigned treaties.

The following year, February 1825, the adamant War Department sent two more commissioners to Indian Springs for another treaty council. This time a new Creek leader, Opothle-Yaholo, led the young warriors of the Upper towns.

He was a handsome man who wore a beautiful blue tunic, an incongruous dark cravat like a white man, and an embroidered hat topped with feathers.

His deep powerful voice filled the council house as he told the commissioners:

"We met you at the Broken Arrow, and then told you we had no land to sell. . . . We have met you here upon a very short notice, and I do not think the chiefs present have any authority to treat. General McIntosh knows that . . . what is not done in public council is not binding. Can the council be public if all the chiefs have not had notice, and many of them are absent? I am, therefore under the necessity of repeating what I told you at the Broken Arrow, that we have no lands to sell. . . ."

At the conclusion of a long bitter speech the young chief spun about and pointed a finger at McIntosh.

"I have told you your fate if you sign that paper. I once more say, beware!"

But McIntosh signed the treaty giving his nation's land to the white man in return for tracts of wild, uncultivated territory across the Mississippi. The council issued McIntosh's death warrant, and he and some of his followers were executed.

In the winter of 1826 Opothle-Yaholo led a large delegation of Creek chiefs and warriors to Washington to protest the Indian Springs treaty, which had been rushed through Congress and ratified. Colonel McKenney described him as "cool, cautious, and sagacious; and with a tact which would have done credit to a more refined diplomatist . . ."

The Indian Springs treaty was declared null and void by President John Quincy Adams and a new treaty was signed by Opothle-Yaholo and his chiefs on January 24, 1826, with Secretary of War Barbour and Colonel McKenney as witnesses. It was ratified by Congress in April.

Painter: Charles Bird King, Washington, 1825.

Opothle-Yaholo

Waapashaw

HIS SON of a famous Sioux chief was celebrated as an outstanding Indian diplomat. He was known to the French as La Feuille (the Leaf), but various translations and the twisted versions of Indian names in the logbooks of explorers, especially Pike and Long, finally resulted in the name of Waapashaw or the more popular Wabasha. There were three chiefs of the same name, father, son, and grandson. The original Wabasha held a balance of power in the West during the last years of the Revolution when British agents tried to incite an Indian border war to divert some of Washington's troops. Wabasha successfully juggled both sides until peace arrived, then calmly claimed presents from the British and Americans for not declaring war. The chief was described by General Henry Whiting in 1820 as a small man with a patch over one eye, but who walked about with the air of an ancient king.

"He never moved, or was seen, without his pipe-bearer," Whiting wrote. "His people treated him with reverence. Unlike all other speakers in council, he spoke sitting, considering, it was said, that he was called upon to stand only in the presence of his great father at Washington. . . ."

Wabasha was not a warlike chief and advised his tribe to live in peace with the white man. As he boasted to Whiting, he had never been at war with the whites, "though many of his young men, against his advice, had been led astray in the war of 1812."

Pike considered him a chief of the entire Sioux nation, but in fact he was only chief of the Kiowa band of the Mdewakanton Sioux, a subtribe of the Santee. After the Sioux War in Minnesota they were removed to the Missouri River, then later to the Niobrara Reservation in Nebraska.

Wabasha's importance is underscored by the number one position of his name above all the twenty-six chiefs at the signing of the Prairie du Chien treaty. He was also first on behalf of the "Sioux of the Mississippi" of another treaty made at Prairie du Chien.

After the siege of Fort Meigs by Tecumseh and the British under General Proctor, Wabasha, still neutral, had stopped at Fort Malden on the way with his band to Quebec. After his arrival a trader informed John Renville, a well-known interpreter, that the Winnebago wished to see Wabasha.

The Sioux, accompanied by Renville, visited the Winnebago council. There they were shocked to find that the Winnebago had killed a young white prisoner and after roasting him had sliced up his body. Wabasha was invited to join the feast.

The chief glared at the Winnebago and then said:

"My friends, we came here, not to eat the Americans, but to wage war against them; that will suffice for us; and could we even do that if left to our own forces? We are poor and destitute, while they possess the means of supplying themselves with all that they require. . . . We thought that you, who live near to white men, were wiser and more refined than we are who live at a distance; but it must indeed be otherwise if you do such deeds."

Then he walked away.

At the Prairie du Chien council the Winnebago made secret plans to massacre the United States commissioner. When Wabasha heard about it he summoned the Winnebago.

In the council house the warriors formed a wide circle about their chiefs as Wabasha entered. He stared down at them in silence, then plucked a hair from his long scalp lock and held it up.

"Winnebagoes! do you see this hair? Look at it. You threaten to massacre the white people at the Prairie. They are your friends and mine. You wish to drink their blood. Is that your purpose?"

His voice rose, cold and grim.

"Dare to lay a finger upon one of them, and I will blow you from the face of the earth, as I now"—he blew the hair from his fingers—blow this hair with my breath, where none can find it."

The short, dignified, and obviously angry Sioux chief slowly searched the circle of dark impassive faces but no one answered him. Then with a look of contempt he stalked out. The next morning not a single Winnebago was left in camp.

Painter: Original by James Otto Lewis, Prairie du Chien council, 1825. Copied by Charles Bird King in Washington. Catlin also painted Wabasha in 1835.

Waapashaw

Wanata, or the Charger

AJOR STEPHEN H. LONG, in his account of his expedition to the source of St. Peter's River, gives an excellent description of this Sioux chief upon their first meeting.

> The most prominent part of his apparel was a splendid cloak or mantle of buffalo skins, dressed so as to be of a fine white colour; it was decorated with small tufts of owl's feathers, and others of various hues, probably a remnant of a fabric once in general use among the aborigines of our territory, and still worn in the north-east and the north-west parts of this continent, as well as in the South Sea Islands; it is what was called by the first European visitors of North America the feather mantles and feather blankets, which were by them much admired. A splendid necklace, formed of about sixty claws of the grizzly bear, imparted a manly character to his whole appearance. His leggings, jacket, and moccasins, were in the real Dakota fashion, being made of white skins, profusely decorated with human hair; his moccasins were variegated with the plumage of several birds. In his hair he wore nine sticks, neatly cut and smoothed, and painted with vermilion; these designated the number of gunshot wounds which he had received; they were secured by a strip of red cloth; two plaited tresses of his hair were allowed to hang forward; his face was tastefully painted with vermilion; in his hand he wore [bore] a large fan of the feathers of the turkey; this he frequently used.
>
> We have never seen a nobler face, or a more impressive character, than that of the Dakota chief, as he stood that afternoon...

Long was courteously received by Wanata and his people who prepared a sumptuous feast of three roasted dogs, which they served on bark plates under a pavilion formed of several skin lodges joined together. Before the guests sat down the air had been perfumed by burning sweet grass.

Wanata was chief of the Yanktonai tribe whose principal village was on the St. Peter's River which emptied into the Mississippi just below the falls of St. Anthony.

During the War of 1812 the young chief fought with the British and was wounded many times.

According to McKenney, several years before Wanata came to Washington he made a vow to the Sun God that if he returned safe from a war against the Chippewa, he would fast for four days and nights. On his return he performed the Solitary Sun Dance of the Dakotas, making deep incisions in the skin of his chest and suspending himself by buckskin thongs from a pole erected in front of his lodge. He hung there for four days and nights, at times swinging back and forth as he recited the sacred chants. When he finished he distributed his lodges, horses, dogs, and furs among the people of the tribe and with his two wives began a new life. He had been reborn by the sun.

Wanata was visited by Long in 1835. He died in 1848 at about fifty-three years of age.

Painter: Charles Bird King, Washington, 1826.

Wanata

Little Crow

FTER THE War of 1812 had ended, the British commander of Drummond's island in Lake Erie on the northern peninsula of Michigan invited the Sioux to visit his post for a council.

When they arrived the commander thanked the Indians for fighting with the British against the United States. He pointed to some clothing and cheap trinkets piled on the floor and said these were gifts from the king.

Little Crow contemptuously kicked the pile and the trinkets scattered over the floor.

"Now after we have fought for you, endured many hardships, lost some of our people, and awakened the vengeance of a powerful nation, our neighbours, you make a peace for yourselves, and leave us to get such terms as we can," the Sioux chief told the garrison commander. "You no longer need our services, and offer us these goods as a compensation for having deserted us. But, no — we will not take them; we hold them and yourselves in equal contempt."

Then he walked out with great dignity, followed by his silent warriors.

Little Crow, or Chetañ wakan mañi (The Sacred Pigeon-hawk Which Comes Walking), was one of the hereditary chiefs of the Kaposia band who formed a dynasty among the Sioux. His grandson was the celebrated Little Crow who would lead the Indians during the Minnesota outbreak of 1862.

Little Crow's village of Kaposia was on the east bank of the Mississippi below the mouth of the Minnesota River where St. Paul now stands. Henry R. Schoolcraft, the explorer and ethnologist, and Michigan's Governor Lewis Cass, who visited it in 1820, described the village as consisting of twelve large lodges, housing about two hundred families.

James Doty, Cass's secretary, recalled Little Crow as a man with "a great deal of fire in his eyes, which are black and piercing. His nose is prominent and has an aquiline curve, his forehead falling a little from the facial angle . . . his whole countenance animated and expressive of a shrewd mind."

McKenney saw Little Crow as "cunning, artful, and treacherous," but Schoolcraft thought him magnanimous. In his memoirs the ethnologist tells the story of how the Sioux chief had discovered a Chippewa robbing his traps. In the deep woods the penalty for this crime was death, but Little Crow handed the thief his traps and rifle.

"I come to present you the trap, of which I see you stand in need," he said. "Take my gun also . . . and return to the land of your countrymen . . . linger not here, lest some of my young men should discover your footsteps."

Little Crow came to Washington in 1824 as head of the Sioux delegation.

Painter: Charles Bird King, Washington, 1824.

Little Crow

Eshtahumbah, or Sleepy Eyes

SIOUX WARRIOR, Sleepy Eyes came to Washington in the summer of 1824 as a member of the Sioux delegation led by the celebrated chief She-tah-wah-coe-wah-mene, or Little Crow. McKenney's description of Little Crow is "cunning, artful, and treacherous; is not much distinguished as a warrior, but is very successful as a hunter, especially of beaver."

This Sioux was born on the Minnesota River near present Mankato, Brown County, Minnesota. He died in Roberts County, South Dakota, but his remains were removed to the Minnesota town that today bears his name. His Indian name is probably taken from *ishta* (eye) and *hba* (dreamy, sleepy, or drowsy).

Evidently Sleepy Eyes was a leading member of the tribe. His name can be found on the treaties of August 19, 1825, and July 15, 1830, signed at Prairie du Chien, and St. Peters, of November 30, 1836. His name as well as his son's, also Sleepy Eyes, is found on the treaty of Traverse des Sioux, July 23, 1851. They were members of the Sisseton band of Sioux.

Painter: Charles Bird King, Washington, 1824.

Eshtahumbah

Moukaushka, or the Trembling Earth

SINGLE, RECKLESS act raised Trembling Earth (or Earthquake) from a lowly horseholder to a warrior of distinction who represented his people before the Great Father in Washington.

As Colonel McKenney heard the story, the series of events that affected the young brave's life began when a party of voyagers on their way to a trading post met a band of warriors from Trembling Earth's village. When a Frenchman refused to share his horse he was murdered by one of the Indians. The rest of the trappers fled to the Yankton village to inform the chiefs and demand the killer be executed.

The ancient code of the Sioux permitted a victim's relative to seek revenge; if no relative was willing, a friend was allowed to take his place.

The tribe laughed when Trembling Earth publicly announced that he would satisfy the honor of the unknown white man, but the boy who had never been on a war party silenced them when he returned with the warrior's scalp.

McKenney claimed that the motivation for Trembling Earth was not pity for the white man he never knew nor to wipe out the stain of dishonor on the village, but simply ambition. The young warrior, he wrote, "grasped at an opportunity, thus fortuitously presented, to emancipate himself from his humble condition."

Evidently, the chiefs were not concerned with Trembling Earth's motivation; not only had a murderer who had endangered their village been executed but more important, the white men were satisfied and the Dragoons from Jefferson Barracks in St. Louis did not appear.

The former horseholder now became "a good warrior" who was sent to Washington in 1837 as a member of the delegation that signed a treaty with their Great Father.

Trembling Earth was stricken in the capital with what McKenney called a "fever," but he refused to cancel the appointment to have his portrait painted. As McKenney wrote, the Sioux was "suffering under the influence of fever" when he sat for the artist. It was finished three days before his death in October 1837.

Painter: George Cooke (a pupil of Charles Bird King), Washington, 1837.

Tenskwatawa

Catahecassa, or Black Hoof

HIS DISTINGUISHED Shawnee chief was not only present when his warriors annihilated Braddock's expedition in 1755 but also fought in every border conflict until peace was declared in 1795. Like Tecumseh, he hated and feared the white man.

After General Wayne's victory over the Ohio tribes at Fallen Timbers, Black Hoof signed a peace treaty with the American general who admired the Shawnee's military skill. Once he had signed, Black Hoof promised Wayne that he would never again lift his tomahawk against the United States; it was a promise he never broke.

When Tecumseh began his tour of the Indian nations to form an Indian confederacy and make war on the white man, Black Hoof, while agreeing with the famous Shawnee's political philosophy, disagreed with his intense desire for war. Both Tecumseh and his brother, the Prophet, held many meetings with Black Hoof in an attempt to get him to join their forces. British agents came to his village with gifts and whiskey, but the Shawnee smashed their kegs and drove them into the forest.

Black Hoof also gained a singular reputation for his faithfulness to one woman. When he was a young warrior he wooed and finally won the daughter of a chief. He lived with her for forty years and raised a large family. Colonel McKenney, accustomed to chiefs with as many as five wives, was astounded when Black Hoof told him he had lived with one woman all his life.

Black Hoof signed the famous Greenville, Ohio, treaty with General Wayne on August 3, 1795; another at Fort Wayne, June 7, 1803, and a whole series of treaties up to the final one in September 1818.

Although McKenney included the chief's portrait in his Indian Gallery, there is no evidence Black Hoof visted Washington. McKenney claimed that when he died in 1831 at Wapakoneta, Ohio, he was one hundred and twelve years old. This appears to be exaggerated; ninety would be more accurate. He was born about 1740.

Painter: In the 1830s, McKenney described this painting as a portrait representing Black Hoof "when a much younger man." The artist is not known.

[158]

Catahecassa

Paytakootha, or Flying Clouds

FLYING CLOUDS was a wanderer on the plains, a strange ambassador of peace who was called upon many times to arbitrate tribal feuds. Ironically, although he was a Shawnee of the Chillicothe tribe, he had been born in the Creek country. He had fought with distinction in many tribal wars but was known more for his attempts to maintain peace between the Indian nations and the white man.

Like many Shawnee he had adopted the name of a white man he admired. After Captain Reed, a Revolutionary officer, befriended him, Flying Clouds not only took the officer's name but signed it to the treaties he witnessed.

Colonel John Johnston, former quartermaster in Wayne's army and veteran Indian agent at Upper Piqua, Ohio, told McKenney that the Shawnee was "a wandering, unsettled man, often engaged in embassies between the tribes, and frequently journeying to distant villages."

He signed many treaties for his nation; one was the important Greenville, Ohio, treaty with General Wayne; the last was in the fall of 1825 when the Shawnee sold their lands in Ohio. It is possible he gave his name to a small town called Read's Town in Logan County, Ohio.

Painter: Charles Bird King, Washington, date not known.

Paytakootha

Quatawapea, or Colonel Lewis

LEGEND HAS the Shawnee becoming chief of his tribe through a quirk of fate. During the Revolution he and his people had fought on the side of the colonies. After peace was declared the Shawnee were invited to Washington to see Secretary of War Henry Dearborn and President Jefferson. Quatawapea's superior "dress and manners" impressed Jefferson who placed a medal about his neck. The Shawnee regarded this as an indication of the wishes of the United States and made him their chief.

It was not unusual for Indians to adopt the name of favorite white friends and Quatawapea took the name of a Continental officer named John Lewis. The Shawnee chief became known as Colonel Lewis and gave the name to Lewistown, the town where he settled in Logan County, Ohio.

What happened to the Shawnee was typical of the government's fraud and ingratitude: In 1831, the tract of forty thousand acres deeded to Colonel Lewis and his people for their loyalty was taken away by the United States government, which removed the Shawnee to the western lands beyond the Mississippi.

McKenney recalled him as "a sensible and brave Indian."

Painter: Charles Bird King, Washington, 1825.

Quatawapea

Kishkalwa

ISHKALWA, SON of the Shawnee chief, was disgraced. In fleeing from a hostile war party he had lost his jacket. For a Shawnee to lose his rifle, bow and arrows, or any part of his clothing to the enemy was an unforgivable offense. It was compounded when the offender was the son of the chief.

Kishkalwa, only a boy, tried to explain he had lost his buckskin jacket while crawling through the brush, fleeing from a band of Chippewa who had discovered him hunting on their lands. The elders, sucking on their pipes, listened politely but after Kishkalwa had finished he was advised that "none, but an Osage, will thus disencumber himself, that he may run the faster from his foes."

There was only one solution: the disgrace had to be expunged.

As McKenney tells the story which he heard from the tribes' Indian agent, the young boy returned by himself to the country of the Chippewa and came back with three scalps. This was good, the old men told him, but not good enough.

He raised a party of young bucks for another raid and led them along the southern bank of the Ohio and the Mississippi until they reached Iron Banks where they fell on a hunting party of Miami. This time when he returned to his village Kishkalwa raised a coup stick from which dangled the scalp locks of several warriors he had killed and paraded the seventeen women and children prisoners they had taken before the lodges of the old men.

Relatives of warriors killed by the Miami insisted they be tortured but Kishkalwa refused, telling the council that "not a drop of their blood should be spilt" in a Shawnee village.

A pretty young girl caught the eye of one of the old chiefs. When he asked to buy her for a wife, Kishkalwa agreed but only on the condition runners be sent through the Shawnee villages, "declaring in a loud voice" that Kishkalwa had regained his honor.

Legend or truth? There is no way of knowing. It was one of the many tales McKenney gathered from his Indian agents, interpreters, commissioners, and frontiersmen when he was collecting material for his famous portfolio.

Romance aside, there is no doubt of Kishkalwa's importance as a chief. He took part in the battle on the mouth of the Great Kanawha in West Virginia, October 10, 1774, the largest battle ever to take place at the time between the colonists and the Indians. The Shawnee and their allies were led by the celebrated Chief Cornstalk, the settlers by General Andrew Lewis. Cornstalk, who never forgot that savage battle, refused to join the tribes of the Ohio in the 1794 war and turned down the British in the War of 1812.

When the Wea and Piankashaw touched off an Indian war in Missouri, Kishkalwa raised a party of Shawnee and served under General Henry Dodge. Ironically, the Shawnee chief this time protected the lives of Indian prisoners, not from his own people but from the tough Missouri militiamen.

When Kishkalwa saw a Shawnee boy laughing at a white soldier torturing an Indian dog he "instantly checked him, and explained in a few words the impropriety of making sport of the miseries of a helpless brute."

The last major battle Kishkalwa took part in was the 1818 war of the Shawnee, Delaware, and Cherokee against the Osage. He was then eighty, but "displayed his usual bravery and prudence..."

When the Osage, superhorsemen, swept across the plains, Kishkalwa faced his warriors and cried:

"Do not heed their shouts; they are but the yells of cowardly wolves, who, as soon as they come near enough to look you in the eye, will flee..."

During the bloody afternoon the old Shawnee was everywhere on the field encouraging his braves and leading small parties into battle. Before sunset the Osage retreated, "suffering great loss in killed and prisoners."

Kishkalwa was a signer of a treaty at a council between the Shawnee and Indian agents in St. Louis, November 7, 1825. He later led a delegation to Washington where he met McKenney and the President at the White House.

Painter: Charles Bird King, Washington, date uncertain.

Kishkalwa

War Dance

OLONEL MC KENNEY used this painting by Peter Rindisbacher, a member of Lord Selkirk's Red River colony, as the frontispiece to the folio edition of his *The Indian Tribes of North America*. McKenney described the dancers:

> In the war dance the actors are distinguished by a more free use of red and black paint, except in mimic representations in time of peace, when the colours are not so closely adhered to; in the peace dance by a display of white and green; in that for the dead by black; and generally in the other dances, except the *Wabana*, black prevails, mingled with other colours.

The paint, in all the dances, is put on according to the fancy of each individual. A line is sometimes drawn dividing the body, from the forehead, and from the back of the head downwards, on either side of which different figures are drawn, representing beasts, birds, fish, snakes, etc. Frequently the hand is smeared with paint and pressed on either cheek, the breast, and the sides. It rarely happens that two of a group are painted alike.

The music consists of a monotonous thumping with sticks upon a rude drum, accompanied by the voices of the dancers, and mingled with the rattling of gourds containing pebbles, and the jingling of small bells and pieces of tin, worn as ornaments.

The *Wabana* is an offering to the devil, and, like some others, the Green Corn Dance for example, winds up with a feast.

The painting, McKenney noted, "was drawn on the spot as the scene was actually exhibited. The actors are persons of some note, and the faces are faithful likenesses."

He described the songs of the dancers as "short, disjointed sentences, which allude to some victory, or appeal to the passion of revenge, and the object of which is to keep alive the recollection of injury, and excite the hatred of the tribe against their enemies."

The Dance of the *Wabana* may be derived from the Chippewa *waban* (it is twilight), or *biwaban* (daylight is approaching).

The painting also served as the frontispiece to one of the earliest western travel books, *Travels in North America during 1834, 1835, and 1836* (Volume 2), by Charles Augustus Murray, published in London in 1839.

War Dance

Makataimeshekiakiah, or Black Hawk

LACK HAWK gave his name to a war that made a soldier out of a tall, gangling Illinois frontiersman named Abe Lincoln. He was also probably the most popular and honored prisoner of war in American history.

He doffed his hat to thousands of admiring Americans, watched a balloon ascension at New York City's Battery Park, and forced a President to cut short a popularity tour.

Black Hawk's war was born of wild frontier rumor, the unbridled imagination of a politically ambitious governor, and the rifle shots of frightened militiamen. It began in the spring of 1831 when Sauk and Fox women kicked over fences settlers had erected across Indian trails. Stories soon grew that the nation was uniting with their old allies, the Potawatomi, Winnebago, and Kickapoo, to declare war on the whites.

At a council held at Rock Island the Sauk and Fox agreed to be settled west of the Mississippi. Several months later talk of an Indian war flared up again when it was learned that Black Hawk, a leading Sauk chief, had crossed the border to visit the British Fort Malden.

General Atkinson, commanding Fort Armstrong on Rock Island, wrote Governor John Reynolds of Illinois that the Sauk and Fox under Black Hawk were now united with their old allies, the Kickapoo, and the Potawatomi had crossed the Mississippi and were moving up on the east shore of Rock River.

After he received Armstrong's letter, Governor Reynolds issued a proclamation addressed to the "Militia of the North-Western Section of Illinois," which declared an emergency because " 'the British band' of Sauk, and other hostile Indians, headed by Black Hawk" were preparing to ravage the frontier.

An advance guard sent out by Reynolds encountered six Indians walking up a road, all holding up their hands in the sign of peace. The frightened citizen-soldiers opened fire, killing five. The only survivor found Black Hawk who later recalled that "he was engaged in entertaining some visitors with a dog feast" and warned him the army was approaching.

Reynolds blundered into the ambush Black Hawk had set up. Encountering a withering cross fire, the governor led a wild retreat leaving behind fourteen dead. Black Hawk, who realized that he had reached the point of no return, now launched the war that was to bear his name. For two years he conducted a skillful frontier guerrilla campaign until the white man's army finally reduced his warriors to a pitiful handful. Dressed in white deerskin, the tribe's symbol of peace, he surrendered at Fort Crawford, Prairie du Chien, August 27, 1832.

He spent the winter in the Jefferson Barracks prison where Washington Irving described him and his followers as a "forlorn crew—emaciated and dejected." In the spring Jackson brought him to the White House; his reception should have given the President second thoughts. Instead of a bloodthirsty mob calling for his death, he was welcomed by "a grand melee of Washington," as a Washington newspaper called it.

Norfolk, Baltimore, Philadelphia, they all lionized the Indian chief. When crowds outside his hotel chanted their demands that he come out and talk to them, Black Hawk would appear on the balcony, take off the top hat that rested on his scalp lock, wave it above his head, and repeat again and again:

"How do you do? How do you do all? The Great Spirit knows that I love you and that my heart is with you."

For some bizarre reason Jackson, who was touring the East to test his popularity, had decided to visit the cities at the same time Black Hawk was present. If his motive was based on a frontiersman's opinion that a humiliated Indian chief would enhance his charisma, the President's plan backfired badly.

At a balloon ascension in New York, Black Hawk, rather than the daring, pioneering aeronaut, was the attraction. Crowds fought to touch him and police had to use their clubs so the Indian chief could reach his carriage. Jackson apparently realized he could not compete with his prisoner of war so he sent Black Hawk back to the West. Political writers wondered if Jackson was afraid of "being Black-hawked."

Curiously Colonel McKenney was not attracted by the chief's courage, integrity, or popularity, but by his attitude toward women. McKenney wrote:

"The strongest evidence of his good sense is found in an assertion contained in his autobiography that he has never had but one wife."

Painter: Charles Bird King, Washington, 1837.

Keesheswa

Keesheewaa

Despite the slight variation in the spelling of his name, this is a portrait of Keesheewaa, The Sun, a noted Fox warrior and medicine man. It was probably painted during his visit to Washington in 1824 as a member of the Sauk and Fox delegation.

In 1836 Colonel McKenney described Keesheewaa as a friend of the great Fox chief, Keokuk.

"He is a firm, onward, fearless chief, and of good character and gave proof by his conduct that in war or in peace, he was to be trusted," McKenney wrote.

Painter: Charles Bird King, Washington, probably 1824.

Keesheewaa

Wakechai, or Crouching Eagle

T HE ORAL history of the Indian nations, myths, legends, and tales handed down from father to son, were told by old men to young boys around the winter fires. Colonel McKenney heard them from the visiting chiefs, from Indian agents, from factors in the old government frontier factories. Some were woven in the very fabric of a nation, others were mere incidents about men and events—like the day Crouching Eagle had his great vision.

The Sauk and Fox war chief had been dying for days in his village near the mouth of the Rock River in Illinois. The chanting, rattles, and herbs of the medicine men had failed to shake the raging fever that had reduced the short, powerfully built chief to a wasted feeble man who could barely move.

Suddenly the Great Spirit appeared and commanded Crouching Eagle to throw himself into the Mississippi at the mouth of the Rock River where he would meet a messenger who would guide him to Grandfather Land.

Crouching Eagle dragged himself to the edge of a bluff overlooking the river and threw himself in. The shock of the cold water revived him and although he paddled about for some time no messenger appeared. The disappointed chief swam back to shore and crawled to his lodge where he died the next day.

His people buried him on the bluff overlooking the river, waiting, they explained, for the messenger who was delayed in coming to take Crouching Eagle to the Great Spirit.

The chief signed the treaty between the Sauk and Fox and the United States on August 4, 1824, as "Wash-kee-chai, or Crouching Eagle." His importance in the nation was underscored by the position of his name—third after the famed chief Keokuk.

Painter: Charles Bird King, Washington, 1824.

Wakechai

Kaipolequa, or White-nosed Fox

HIS SAUK and Fox chief was leader of the Oshkosh, or the Brave, one of the two main bands in his nation; the other was called the Kishko, or the Long Hairs, led by the famous chief Keokuk.

Red was the standard of the Long Hairs, blue the color of the Oshkosh. Membership in these important soldier society groups took place at birth. The first male child born to a Kishko was marked with a tiny spot of white clay and belonged by law to that party; the next male of the same family was marked with a black spot designating him as a member of the Oshkosh group. The first son always belonged to the band of his father. Other males in the same family were alternately assigned to either group.

They were friendly rivals on the ball field, on the hunt, and in council when tribal policy was formulated. In war games warriors were either painted white or blackened with charcoal. Colonel McKenney wrote:

"From early youth each individual is taught to feel, that whether engaged in war, in hunting, or in athletic sports, the honour of his band, as well as his own, is concerned in his success or failure, and thus a sense of responsibility is awakened and kept alive which has the moral force of a constant and rigid discipline."

Kaipolequa, he wrote, "is considered as one of the most distinguished braves of the nation."

Painter: Charles Bird King, Washington, 1824.

Kaipolequa

Powasheek

KEOKUK, WAPELLA, and Powasheek composed the triumvirate of great Sauk and Fox chiefs. The first two became famous on the frontier of the 1820s and 1830s, but Powasheek, who, Colonel McKenney called "a daring warrior, and held a respectable standing in council, as a man of prudence and capacity," remained always in their shadow.

He signed his first important treaty between his nation and the United States in 1832 and his last ten years later. The chief visited Washington in 1837 as a member of the large Sauk and Fox delegation.

Painter: George Cooke, Washington, 1837.

Powasheek

Taiomah

THIS FOX brave was actually dying when his portrait was painted by Charles Bird King during the summer of 1824. He had suffered from tuberculosis for some time, and General William Clark of Lewis and Clark fame, who headed the delegation of Sauk and Fox, urged Taiomah to remain behind but the Indian refused. He not only made the weary journey to the capital by steamboat, stage, and horseback, but sat for many hours in King's studio.

Colonel McKenney may have selected Taiomah for his Indian Gallery after he had learned that the Fox brave was leader of a powerful secret organization called the Great Medicine Society, which the Indian superintendent compared to the Freemasons.

Members were said to be expert in "occult knowledge," and a recruit was carefully screened by the head man who then passed his name to a number of warriors and chiefs. In a few days his application was either accepted or denied. New members were placed on probation for one year.

There were four degrees, or four roads, of the Great Medicine Society. As McKenney wrote: "There are few who have attained . . . the fourth road . . . traders have offered large bribes . . . [to learn] the mysteries of the society; but these temptations and the promises of secrecy failed. . . ."

McKenney's disclosures of the Great Medicine Society were confirmed almost a century later by ethnologists who described the secret rites of the Midewiwin, or Grand Medicine Society, as one of the most important of the Sauk nation. Meetings of the society were held once a year during the spring when the ceremony was conducted by a group of young men and women bound together by its secret laws.

In the 1820s McKenney said that the membership fees were forty dollars; twentieth century ethnologists found that "payment of a fee" was still demanded. The society's rituals were compared in importance to the adoption and death ceremonies of the Sauk and Fox.

Taiomah's name is preserved in the name of a county and town—Tama, Iowa.

Painter: Charles Bird King, Washington, 1824.

Taiomah

Appanoose

WHEN THE delegation of the greatest of Sauk and Fox chiefs was escorted to Boston's Faneuil Hall in the fall of 1837 for the governor's reception, the orator who made the most popular speech was Appanoose, a Sauk chief.

After he had shaken hands with Governor Edward Everett, Appanoose thanked the officials for inviting his people to "the great council house. . . . This we cannot reward you for now, but shall not forget it, and hope the Great Spirit will reward you for it. This is the place which our forefathers once inhabited. I have often heard my father and grandfather say they lived near the sea-coast, where the white man first came. I am glad to hear all this from you. I suppose it is put in a book, where you learn all these things. As far as I can understand the language of the white people, it appears to me that the Americans have attained a very high rank among the white people. It is the same with us, though I say it myself. Where we live, beyond the Mississippi, I am respected by all people, and they consider me the tallest among them. I am happy that two great men meet and shake hands with each other."

Then as the interpreter translated his speech, Appanoose walked over to the governor and shook hands "amid the shouts of applause from the audience, who were not a little amused at the self-complacency of the orator."

Painter: George Cooke, Washington, 1837.

Appanoose

Wapella, or the Prince

NE OCTOBER night in 1837 the house lights in the Washington Theatre dimmed and the curtain rose slowly. The young actress, a favorite, was greeted with waves of applause.

Halfway through the first act a large object sailed out of the darkness and landed on the stage. The actress looked stunned, then gingerly picked up a buffalo robe beautifully trimmed with feathers and porcupine quills, draped it over her arm, and continued her role. Moments later a headdress with tails of feathers like colorful wings floated gently to the stage. The actress calmly put on the headdress, then the buffalo robe, and continued.

Beaded belts, moccasins, and tobacco pouches rained down on the stage "until showers of Indian finery became so thick that she was obliged to seek assistance to remove them."

In the large box the delegation of Fox chiefs and warriors led by Wapella whooped in delight. While the audience cheered, the young actress returned out of the wings with a sheaf of ostrich feathers, which she distributed among the delighted Indians, then made what McKenney called "an *appropriate* address" of appreciation.

Washington Theatre was only one of many theatres, circuses, and sideshows attended by the Fox delegation of 1837 that toured the country after signing their treaty in Washington.

In Philadelphia they had a special box at the celebrated Cooke's Circus; in New York they toured Catlin's Indian gallery where they murmured among themselves at the familiar faces of warriors and chiefs.

Their largest reception was held in Boston's Faneuil Hall where Colonel McKenney claimed that "so great a multitude was never assembled in that city to witness a public spectacle." Before the general public was admitted a ladies' reception was held from ten to noon, and "this ancient hall was crowded in every part, floor and gallery, by the fair citizens."

At noon the Indians, led by Wapella, were escorted to the statehouse where they were received by Governor Edward Everett, the legislature, and distinguished guests. After numerous speeches Governor Everett took the Indians to the balcony of the statehouse where presents were distributed. As one Boston newspaper reported:

"During this ceremony, a mass of at least fifteen acres of people stood below, filling the streets and the common. The chiefs were escorted to the common by the cadets, and began their war dance. The crowd very patiently kept outside the lines, leaving a space of many acres, in the centre of which were the Indians. Their war exercises were not very striking. One beat a drum, to which they hummed monotonously, and jumped about grotesquely. This lasted half an hour, when they moved off in carriages to their lodgings."

Wapella, whose name is derived from *Wapana*, meaning "He of the Morning," signed many treaties between the Fox and the United States, beginning with the Fort Armstrong treaty of September 3, 1822.

Painter: Charles Bird King, Washington, 1837.

Wapella

Kishkekosh

AUK AND Fox delegations of chiefs and braves entered the room in the War Department that warm October day in 1837. They were followed by several Sioux chiefs and orators. The Fox went to the left, the Sioux to the right. They sat on the floor and glared across the room at each other as the nervous secretary of war, Indian commissioners, and interpreters quickly prepared a peace pipe.

One Fox warrior stood out among all the others. He was tall and husky with streaks of paint like black fingers stretching upward from below his mouth to his cheeks. But what made him taller and more terrifying was his crown of a buffalo skull and horns.

The Sioux seemed hypnotized by it. They muttered among themselves as the Fox brave, arms folded, sat on a high bench staring down at the angry dark faces of his people's ancient enemies.

The Indian agents, sensitive to the undercurrents always present at any Indian council, finally discovered why the conference had reached an impasse. The Fox brave, named Kishkekosh, had single-handedly invaded a large Sioux village, scalped several braves, then tore the buffalo crown from the head of a popular chief. The Indian commissioners and agents knew Kishkekosh's arrogant display of contempt could result in a confrontation between the two nations at any moment. Gifts, promises, and threats persuaded Kishkekosh to leave behind his trophy, and both tribes finally signed an uneasy peace treaty.

The portrait of Kishkekosh has been variously labeled as "Kee-o-kuck, The Watchful Fox, principal chief of the confederated tribes" or "Kis-te-kosh."

Colonel McKenney translated his name as The Man with One Leg, but ethnologists say He with a Cut Hoof would be more correct. Curiously, the Fox chief had no deformity.

Painter: George Cooke, Washington, 1837.

Kishkekosh

Nesouaquoit, or the Bear in the Forks of a Tree

ESOUAQUOIT'S REPUTATION came not from his courage in war, his diplomacy, or his skill in hunting, but from his violent hatred of alcohol and tobacco. Colonel McKenney described him as "the only Indian of whom it can be said—*he never tasted a drop of spirituous liquor or smoked a pipe!*"

Nesouaquoit had seen what the whiskey peddlers had done to not only the Sauk and Fox but other nations on the frontier, and he was determined they would not destroy his people. He would beat in the heads of the barrels, pour the stupifying traders' whiskey or high wines on the ground, then, using the barrel staves, would drive the peddlers from his villages.

The Fox chief was the son of the famous Chemakasee (Shemakasi[a]) or He of the Little Lance, friend to the Americans in the War of 1812. McKenney told how the old chief defied the tribes at a council held by the British at Fort Malden by crying out:

"We will not fight *for* the red coats, but we will fight *against* them."

To protect the Fox, General William Clark was ordered by the War Department to escort Little Lance and his people to Fort Edwards on the east side of the Mississippi in what is now Hancock County, Illinois, where they remained until after the war.

In 1815, a treaty was entered into by the government and the Sauk and Fox, in which an annual annuity was to be paid to Chemakasee and his people.

They proved to be the most patient Indians in history. One, two, three years passed and no money or trade goods came from Washington. Chemakasee grew older and his son Nesouaquoit took his place as chief. Finally, twenty years passed and Nesouaquoit told his warriors and subchiefs that he had decided to go to Washington to see the Great Father and collect their annuity.

In St. Louis General Clark agreed he had a just complaint, but informed him that there were no government funds available to send him on that long trip.

Nesouaquoit then visited a French moneylender in St. Louis who agreed to finance the round trip with "*three boxes and a half of silver*"—equivalent to about $3,500. But before the money would be turned over to them, the Fox had to gather enough pelts to put up as collateral.

All that winter Nesouaquoit's hunters filled their lodges with skins. In the spring with Clark's approval the loan was completed, and Nesouaquoit received his box of silver, and the moneylender his furs.

The Fox chief presented his petition to the President and the secretary of war the following year "in a firm and decided manner. The authorities recognised his claim and he was assured that the provisions of the treaty . . . should be scrupulously fulfilled, and respected in future."

Nesouaquoit's warriors could have saved their furs and the St. Louis moneylender his boxes of silver, for nothing was ever done. Year after year the Sauk and Fox chiefs pleaded with Washington but as one chief angrily told Clark it was clear that the Great Father had two sets of ears, one for the whites and the other for the Indians.

When he was in Washington, the Bear in the Forks of a Tree was given the usual tour of the capital and had his portrait painted. Other Sauk and Fox chiefs visited Washington that fall, but for the first time the War Department had trouble persuading them to sit for King. McKenney was now out of office, and there was no one they trusted who could calm their fears that the painter—the Shadow Catcher as the Indians would later call artists and photographers—would imprison their spirit bodies on canvas. As the *National Intelligencer* of September 29, 1837, reported, "the Indian Chiefs [are] under some superstitious impression [and have] declined to sit for their portraits."

King, who had been painting Indians now for sixteen years, somehow got them to sit for him. It would be fascinating to know how he did it, but neither the *Intelligencer* nor Colonel McKenney revealed King's technique.

Painter: Charles Bird King, Washington, 1837.

Nesouaquoit

Peahmuska

OLONEL MC KENNEY described the Fox chief as an inoffensive man who lived a reputable life, but apparently in 1830, despite his peaceful ways, Peahmuska was the wrong man in the wrong place.

The party of hunters he was leading down the Mississippi was attacked by Sioux and Menominee warriors who had set up an elaborate ambush fifteen miles below Prairie du Chien, where the river narrows. A volley of rifle fire and showers of arrows from both sides of the river cut down the Fox chief and most of his hunters.

The killings ignited a tribal war. The following June a large Fox war party discovered a number of Menominee families camped on the eastern shore of the Mississippi below Fort Crawford. An early Wisconsin historian pointed out that "they had obtained whisky enough for all to get socially drunk upon, and it is rare to find a Menomonee who will not get drunk when he has the chance; and they had carried their revels far into the night, until men, women, and children were beastly drunk...."

The Fox warriors launched their attack "about two hours before day," and a savage battle took place with the Fox slaughtering more than thirty men, women, and children.

Peahmuska had signed the first treaty for his people in 1815 as "Pierremaskkin, the Fox Who Walks Crooked" and another in 1825 as "Pee-ar-maski, the Jumping Sturgeon," both examples of the tortured translations of many Indian interpreters.

Painter: Charles Bird King, Washington, 1824.

Tahcoloquoit

Weshcubb, or the Sweet

THIS CHIPPEWA chief was known on the frontier not only for his leadership and prowess as a warrior but for the reputation of his son, a notorious A-go-kwa, or Indian homosexual, who, Colonel McKenney claimed, constantly disgraced his father.

Alexander Henry, the famous Red River Valley trader, describes Weshcubb's son in his journals as "a curious compound between a man and a woman. He is a man both as to members and courage, but pretends to be womanish, and dresses as such. His walk and mode of sitting, his manners, occupation, and language are those of a woman. His father, who is a great chief . . . cannot persuade him to act like a man."

A more vivid description of the chief's son is given by John Tanner, an Indian captive:

"This man was one of those who make themselves women, and are called women by the Indians. . . . they are commonly called A-go-kwa . . . she soon let me know she had come a long distance to see me, and with the hope of living with me. She often offered herself to me, but not being discouraged with one refusal, she repeated her disgusting advances. . . ."

Tanner eagerly joined a hunting party to escape the attentions of the A-go-kwa who kept wandering about the woods "whistling" for him. The other Indians were amused by the advances of the A-go-kwa, but Tanner found them "intolerable."

McKenney described Weshcubb as "a good, fat, comfortable looking Indian."

Painter: Original by James Otto Lewis, Prairie du Chien council, 1825, later copied in Washington by Charles Bird King.

Weshcubb

Metakoosega, or Pure Tobacco

 ENRY ROWE SCHOOLCRAFT, the early eighteenth-century explorer and ethnologist, met Pure Tobacco (probably Mitakosige or I Smoke Pure Tobacco, i.e., without any mixture of bark or of other plants) when he was Indian agent at Sault Saint Marie, Michigan. He found the Chippewa to be a cheerful, unconscionable beggar who insisted that Schoolcraft give him not only tobacco but also whiskey and provisions.

In July 1824 Mitakosige found enough ambition to join a band of Chippewa braves who planned a horse raid on a Sioux village. On their way they discovered John L. Findley, a sutler's clerk at Fort Crawford, Prairie du Chien, and two trappers asleep on the shore of Lake Pepin.

There are two versions of the murders that took place; the white men were drunk and provoked a quarrel with the Indians, the other that the Chippewa butchered the sleeping men.

The so-called "Lake Pepin Massacre" threw the frontier into a turmoil. At Fond du Lac, McKenney finally ordered the warriors to surrender.

Metakoosega surrendered to the council and underwent an "examination," as McKenney called it. Both the Indian Superintendent and Governor Cass were satisfied that while Metakoosega had been a member of the war party he had not taken part in the murder of Findley. Governor Cass's final question was, "will you put your hand on your breast and say that [he did not murder the white man] in the face of the Great Spirit?"

The Chippewa glared at McKenney and Cass.

"Am I a dog that I should lie?" he cried.

Painter: The original portrait was by James Otto Lewis at the Fond du Lac council, 1826, and was later copied in Washington by Charles Bird King.

Metakoosega

Shingaba W'Ossin

HINGABA W'OSSIN, or Image Stone, was one of the most influential chiefs of the Chippewa nation during the years Colonel McKenney was in office. He was a famed war captain, a powerful orator, and a statesman admired by both red and white men.

Frontiersmen and army officers recalled the Chippewa chief as tall with a nose thin and sharp as an ax blade and deep-set penetrating eyes. He had an air of command, almost aloofness, and was a member of the ancient Crane clan. He became a legend for his exploits in the great war between the Chippewa and the Fox, which finally ended the feud between those two nations.

Like his friend, Tecumseh, the Chippewa feared the white man's civilization. When John Johnston, the celebrated Indian trader, asked to marry his daughter O-shaw-ous-go-day-way-gua, Shingaba W'Ossin told the "accomplished Irish gentleman" to go back to Montreal and think seriously over what he had proposed.

"White man, I have noticed your behaviour," he said, "it has been correct. But...*your colour is deceitful.* Of you, may I expect better things? ... If you return I shall be satisfied of your sincerity, and will give you my daughter."

Johnston took the chief's advice and returned to Montreal. In a year he was back and Shingaba W'Ossin kept his word. Johnston and the chief's daughter were married and had several children. One, Jane, "an accomplished woman, who had been educated in Europe," married the explorer-ethnologist Henry Rowe Schoolcraft.

McKenney was a fellow commissioner with Schoolcraft and Lewis Cass, Michigan's governor and Indian superintendent during the famous Augustic treaties with the Winnebago and the Chippewa in 1826 and 1827.

As McKenney later learned, Schoolcraft's wife and her family had prevented the Winnebago from murdering Cass, an act they knew would have plunged the settlers and the tribes into a bloody frontier war.

Shingaba W'Ossin constantly urged his nation to seek peace with the white man. As he told them at one council:

"If my hunters will not take the game, but will leave the chase and join the war parties, our women and children must suffer. If the game is not trapped, where will be our packs of furs? And if we have no furs, how shall we get blankets? Then when winter comes again we shall perish! It is time enough to fight when the war drum sounds near you—when your enemies approach—then it is I shall expect to see you painted for war, and to hear your whoops resound in the mountains; and then you will see me at your head with my arm bared—"

He signed all the treaties drawn between his nation and the United States in the councils held between 1825 and 1827 at Prairie du Chien, Fond du Lac, and Butte des Morts. He also informed McKenney that the thousand dollar annuity that the government agreed to pay the Chippewa nation should go toward starting an Indian school at Sault Sainte Marie on the northern Michigan peninsula.

There was an added attraction for the white man in the Chippewa country. Besides land, there were mineral deposits and the legendary mound of virgin copper located near the mouth of the Ontanagon River. It weighed almost three thousand pounds and would later be famous as the Ontanagon copper boulder.

In 1827, following the Butte des Morts treaty council, Indian crews tried to raise the boulder and to melt its base with fire but couldn't budge it. McKenney later wrote that "specimens were broken from it, some...as pure as a silver dollar...." The mass of copper was probably much larger at one time, McKenney pointed out, since those who had worked on it down through the years with "chisels, axes, and various implements...no doubt took away specimens...."

McKenney later selected the portrait of the chief as the frontispiece for his book, *Sketches of a Tour to the Lakes.*

Painter: Original by James Otto Lewis, Fond du Lac, 1826. Copied in Washington by Charles Bird King.

Peechekir

Waatopenot

OLONEL MC KENNEY described the Chippewa of the 1820s and 1830s as "wandering savages who inhabit the sterile and inhospitable shores of the northern lakes . . . they are the most miserable and degraded of the native tribes . . . exposed to the greatest extremities of climate, and forced by their situation to spend the greater portion of their lives in obtaining a wretched subsistence . . . they have little ambition and few ideas . . ."

This is typical of some of the partisan and inaccurate observations of Colonel McKenney and his co-author, James Hall, in their 1836 portfolio. However, they were writing over a hundred and thirty years ago, long before research in the ethnology of the American Indians made them the best known and most fully described of all primitive peoples.

McKenney—or Hall—probably was not aware that the Chippewa nation was one of the largest and most vigorous of North American tribes and rather than being indolent they were a fierce, aggressive people who had driven the Sioux, skilled in plains warfare and numerous, from the Great Lakes country to the deep west.

A listing of Indian paintings in the Smithsonian Institution, compiled by William J. Rhees in 1859, has Waatopenot (spelled Wautopenot, The Eagle's Bill), a Fox chief. Lewis also used this Indian portrait in his *Aboriginal Portfolio* published in 1835.

Painter: Original by James Otto Lewis, Fond du Lac council, 1826, later copied in Washington by Charles Bird King.

Waatopenot

Jackopa, or the Six

THIS CHIPPEWA chief, according to McKenney, was an "exceedingly active, sprightly fellow, quick in his movements, ardent and fond of his family."

Colonel McKenney met him at the Fond du Lac treaty council in 1826 when the chief introduced him to his fourteen-year-old son.

Through an interpreter McKenney suggested he take the boy back to Washington "and educate him."

Jackopa listened to the interpreter translate McKenney's proposal. Then shaking his head he ran his finger from his forehead down to chest, "indicating," as McKenney recalled, "that to depart from his son would be like cutting him in two..."

Painter: Original by James Otto Lewis, Fond du Lac council, 1826, later copied in Washington by Charles Bird King.

Jackopa

Ongewae

THE CHIPPEWA were not one of Colonel McKenney's favorite tribes; sulking, cowardly, and cunning are some of his descriptions. Curiously, many of his frontier experiences were with the Chippewa who demonstrated to him their bravery, loyalty to the Americans, and wisdom in their councils.

McKenney wrote only a terse description of Ongewae:

"A good looking man, but not with such an overpowering intellect as might be expected from such a fine looking head."

Painter: Charles Bird King, Washington, 1827.

No-Tin

Katawabeda

THIS CHIPPEWA chief whose name is translated as Old Tooth, or Broken Tooth, cried out in many councils that he hated war and would never lead his people into battle unless they were attacked and had no choice.

He was a firm believer in negotiation and justice as a method to avoid war. Colonel McKenney, who had listened to scores of tales of battles, campaigns, and raids, welcomed this "sensible, prudent, politic man" whom he met at the Fond du Lac council in 1826.

Henry R. Schoolcraft, the early nineteenth-century explorer and ethnologist, recalled the Chippewa chief in his journals as "the friend and advocate of peace." He wrote:

"He discountenanced the idea of the Indians taking part in our wars. He said he was a small boy at the taking of *old* Mackinac (1763). The French wished him to take the war-club, but he refused. The English afterwards thanked him for this, and requested him to raise the tomahawk in their favor, but he refused. The Americans afterwards thanked him for his refusal, but they did not ask him to go to war. They all talk of peace, he said, but still, though they talk of peace, the Sioux continue to make war upon us. . . ." Zebulon Pike, who met him in the winter of 1805–1806, called him the "first chief" of his tribe.

Painter: Original by James Otto Lewis, Fond du Lac council, 1826, later copied in Washington by Charles Bird King.

Katawabeda

Wabishkeepenas, or the White Pigeon

I T WAS the summer of 1826 and the tribes had gathered for the important Fond du Lac treaty. Villages of different nations had sprung up in the forest, smoke of cook fires hung in the sultry heat, and the throbbing of drums and the chants of dancers echoed thinly across the water. In his lodge near the cleared space where the council would be held in a few days, Colonel McKenney was writing a report for Secretary of War James Barbour when he suddenly became aware of an Indian standing in the doorway.

He later recalled how shocked he was at the brave's gaunt dark face, sunken cheeks, and eyes glittering with fever. The Indian studied McKenney for a long moment in silence, then slowly raised a bony arm and whispered in Chippewa.

McKenney summoned his interpreter, but before he could appear the Indian had vanished into the forest.

The face of the obviously ill man haunted McKenney, and he ordered the interpreter to find him. On the eve of the opening ceremonies of the council the interpreter appeared with the Chippewa and told his story to McKenney.

Six years before, Governor Lewis Cass and Henry R. Schoolcraft, the early explorer, ethnologist, and one of McKenney's agents, had made a tour of the Upper Lakes region. One of their missions was to find the legendary copper boulder—later known as the Ontonagon copper boulder—and White Pigeon was selected as their guide.

The Chippewa were uneasy; the copper boulder was regarded as a *manito*, a holy place that guided their destiny, and it was considered a sacrilege for a white man to visit this spot.

White Pigeon was aware of his people's feelings and led Cass and Schoolcraft in a bizarre, roundabout fashion that finally left them miles from the boulder.

Cass selected a new guide and White Pigeon returned to his village. A council was held and the ironic conclusion was reached that White Pigeon had not only offended Cass, the representative of the Great Father, but had been led away from the place by the angry gods. The unfortunate warrior was then banished from the village.

Bad luck clung to him; arrows he shot at game missed their mark. His rifle backfired and split the barrel. His family refused to recognize him. His horse vanished. And in his village the people said that they knew it all the time—White Pigeon was a doomed man. For six years he had wandered through the forest living on small game and roots. McKenney wrote:

"Bereft of his usual activity and courage, destitute of confidence and self-respect, he seemed to have scarcely retained the desire or ability to provide himself with food from day to day."

After he heard White Pigeon's story McKenney advised Cass and Schoolcraft who were disturbed to learn that they were the cause of the Chippewa's miserable existence. McKenney recalled years later:

"They determined to restore him to the standing from whcih he had fallen, and having loaded him with presents . . . his offence was forgiven, and his luck changed."

White Pigeon's portrait was used as a plate in McKenney's *Tour to the Lakes*. The medal worn by White Pigeon in the painting was presented to him by Cass during the governor's lake tour.

Painter: Original by James Otto Lewis, Fond du Lac council, 1826, later copied in Washington by Charles Bird King.

Wabishkeepenas

Waemboeshkaa

COLONEL MC KENNEY called this Chippewa chief one of the "most remark-able" he met at the 1826 Fond du Lac treaty council. The Indian superin-tendent reported Waemboeshkaa was the only man present "who seemed to have a right conception of the kingly crown, and to have succeeded in constructing a very successful imitation of that appendage of royalty."

The Chippewa's "crown" was a mixture of feathers, "glossy and very beautiful" from the drake's breast and from the bill and head of the wood-pecker. His wrists were decorated with bracelets of the same mixture, while his neck was encircled with rings of horsehair, dyed vermilion. "His pipe was made gay with the same materials, and his pouch had been the object of his special attentions."

McKenney and the other commissioners noted that Waemboeshkaa was not an outstanding orator or statesman but he certainly was the peacock of the large council. He seemed to have a flair for the dramatic and even came late so he could strut and show off "the ornaments of his person."

However, when reports of the commissioners are closely examined it appears that the Chippewa did not have much competition. The six or seven hundred warriors and chiefs were classified by McKenney and Governor Lewis Cass as "the worst clad and most wretched body of Indians we ever met with." Only the Chippewa chief stood out among the others, parading about "dressed like King Saul."

When the curious Colonel McKenney inquired about the chief through interpreters he was told Waemboeshkaa was a complete nonentity; he didn't even distinguish himself "by much smoking, for all Indians are inveterate smokers..."

Despite the Chippewa's lack of importance, McKenney used his portrait in his *Tour of the Lakes* under the title "Chippeway Chief with his calumet & pouch."

Painter: Original by James Otto Lewis, Fond du Lac Council, 1826; copied by Charles Bird King in Washington.

Waemboeshkaa

Okeemakeequid

OLONEL MCKENNEY first made his acquaintance with this Chippewa chief during the Fond du Lac treaty council in 1826 when he asked one of the interpreters to introduce him to an Indian canoe maker. He was referred to the Chippewa of whom McKenney said: "His countenance was intellectual, and wore an unusually civilised expression." After the "bargain" was struck McKenney wondered if the canoe could be finished before the council ended. When the Chippewa replied that "we should name our own time," the Indian superintendent gave him a deadline.

The chief waved his hand. "It shall be done," he said.

Suddenly out of nowhere appeared a long line of Indian children and women all following Okeemakeequid into the forest. In a short time the chief reappeared, leading the same group now all loaded down with rolls of birchbark and strips of watap, the root of the red cedar or fir tree.

The Chippewa chief was empty handed.

Okeemakeequid first made a rough sketch of the canoe in the dirt, thirty-six feet long and five feet wide, the colonel's dimensions. Then stakes were driven into the ground to form the shape and bark was draped over them. McKenney recalled the scene:

> The bark thus arranged hangs loose and in folds, resembling ... the covers of a book with its back downwards, the edges being up, and the leaves out. Cross pieces are then put in. These press out the rim, and give the upper edges the form of the canoe. Next, the ribs are forced in—thin sheathing being laid between these and the bark. The ribs press out the bark, giving form and figure to the bottom and sides of the canoe. Upon these ribs, and along their whole extent, large stones are placed. The ribs having been previously well soaked, they bear the pressure of these stones, till they become dry. Pressing round the bottom, and up the sides of the canoe to the rim, they resemble hoops cut in two, or half circles. The upper parts furnish mortising places for the rim; around and over which, and through the bark, the wattap is wrapped. The stakes are then removed, the seams gummed, and the fabric is lifted into the water, where it floats like a feather.

While he was at the council McKenney learned that one of the nation's legends centered about the Chippewa canoe maker's mother Oshegwun. When a young girl she had been a member of a large hunting party attacked by the Sioux. Two warriors had torn part of her scalp loose, and her wounded father crawled through the snow and killed both of them. Half scalped and with a badly gashed finger, she was brought back to her village.

The finger became infected and as Okeemakeequid told McKenney his mother cured it very quickly; she placed it on a block of wood and in a single blow with a tomahawk cut it off. When McKenney looked dubious the Chippewa proved it by repeating the tale before several elders who confirmed the details. He also brought his ancient mother to the council and insisted on showing McKenney the scars in her scalp and the missing finger. Not content, he and his brother "went through the blank motions over the head of the mother, to show how the Sioux performed that ceremony [scalping]."

McKenney learned that the original owner of the Chippewa's costume—deerskin dyed almost black—had been a Sioux chief. At the 1825 Prairie du Chien council when peace was declared between the Chippewa and Sioux, Okeemakeequid proposed to a Sioux that they exchange blankets and clothing. "After the exchange had been made, the Sioux, looking Okeemakeequid archly in the face, and pointing to the head-dress, said, 'Brother, when you put that dress on, feel up there—there are five feathers; I have put one in for each scalp I took from your people—remember that!'"

Painter: Original by James Otto Lewis, at the Fond du Lac council, 1826, and later copied by Charles Bird King.

Okeemakeequid

Caatousee

LITTLE IS known of this Chippewa's background but Colonel McKenney described him as "a person of little repute, either with white or red men. He is too idle to hunt, and has no name as a warrior; nor is his character good in other respects. He is, however, an expert fisherman and canoeman, in which capacity he is occasionally employed by the traders. He has never advanced any pretensions to chieftainship, except to be a chief among the dancers, and in his profuse use of paints and ornaments."

Earlier McKenney had called him "a young man of great cleverness and fond of various colors and a spirited warrior."

Painter: Original by James Otto Lewis, Butte des Morts council, 1827, and copied in Washington by Charles Bird King.

Caatousee

Anacamegishca, or Foot Prints

LL THAT is known of this Chippewa chief is Colonel McKenney's terse, stereotyped description: "He is six feet three inches in stature, and well made."

The Indian superintendent first met the chief at the Fond du Lac treaty council in the summer of 1826.

The appearance of the chief was a singular victory for McKenney and Michigan Governor Lewis Cass; both were aware of the long allegiance of the Rainy Lake Chippewa to the British. The close relationship of the tribe and the Crown began with Anacamegishca's great grandfather, the famous Chippewa chief Nittum. (This is McKenney's spelling, but it may be the Chippewa *nitam*, meaning "the first.")

His influence over the nation was so great that the North-West Fur Company wooed him for years with gifts of whiskey, rifles, and powder in order to keep his friendship and maintain their monopoly of the fur trade. When the old man died the officials of the company ordered his burial platform elevated near the Grand Portage trading post in the northeastern corner of Michigan and the Union Jack flown nearby.

In 1803, when the post was abandoned for the new trading center Fort William on the northwest shore of Lake Superior, the chief's bones were removed with great ceremony, as McKenney recalled, and "honoured with distinguished marks of respect . . ."

The respect and trust with which the Indian nations of the frontier of the 1820s regarded Colonel McKenney and Governor Cass undoubtedly helped to influence the Chippewa to abandon the British for the Americans.

Painter: James Otto Lewis, Fond du Lac council, 1826, and later copied in Washington by Charles Bird King.

Anacamegishca

Tshusick

HE PARTY Colonel McKenney gave for William Theobald Wolfe Tone at his Georgetown home in the winter of 1827 was a brilliant affair with its guest list a drum roll of America's great names.

Tone, son of the famous Irish patriot and French general Wolfe Tone, was a social prize for any Washington host or hostess. He was a figure of romance, a character who could have stepped out of a Scott novel. After the death of his famous father he had been adopted as a child by the French government on orders of the Directorate. He served with distinction in the French army, then at twenty-seven came to the United States to study law and later to serve as an American army officer.

After he resigned his commission he retired to Georgetown to write his famous *School of Cavalry* and other works on military tactics. Colonel McKenney, now an author himself, that winter may have given Tone this party to celebrate his latest book.

The guests, particularly the women, flocked about Tone, but he seemed to be fascinated by a tiny, pretty woman dressed in a scarlet jacket, blue skirt, and red and blue pantaloons. She was a Chippewa, whose story was as romantic as Tone's, but this was not what had attracted Tone. Upon McKenney's introduction she immediately began a conversation in French, not in the harsh, labored American style, but with what McKenney called "purity and delicacy."

Tone gently rebuked McKenney. This was surely a joke, he told the Indian superintendent, a masquerade in which a young engineering officer "had gotten up an ingenious scenic representation for the amusement of his guests...."

McKenney told him that this was no farce. Tshusick was a genuine Chippewa, even though she spoke French as purely as any native of Paris. In addition, she was a superb cook, a brilliant conversationalist, an expert seamstress, and a skilled woodsman. How else could this tiny woman have survived the dreadful journey through the winter forest from Detroit and on foot?

Tone insisted on hearing the whole story. McKenney, surrounded by his fascinated guests, recited the tale that was familiar to most of Washington—of how Tshusick had appeared on a bitterly cold night, to warm her hands at the forge of a nearby tinsmith who sent her to Colonel McKenney's home.

Over the dinner table she had told McKenney the strange story of how she had walked through the snowbound Michigan wilderness to Washington. She told him that she had worked in the household of McKenney's old friend Michigan's Governor Lewis Cass in Detroit and knew George Boyd, the Indian agent at Mackinac. Mrs. Boyd had told her many times of the kindness of her sister who lived in the White House as the wife of the Great Father.

It can be assumed that McKenney stiffened in his chair when he heard this; Harriet Adams, sister of the First Lady, had married George Boyd who had been the director of the government bureau of pensions. Some years before he had resigned at the climax of a political feud and for a long time had been unemployed.

Harriet's sister Louisa, wife of John Quincy Adams, without telling her husband, had written to President Monroe begging him to find a post for her brother-in-law. Monroe had quickly arranged for Boyd to enter the Indian service and he became McKenney's agent at Mackinac. The Indian superintendent questioned her closely, but Tshusick provided so many intimate details of the Cass and Boyd homes that McKenney was convinced her story was true.

Colonel McKenney brought Tshusick to the White House where Louisa Adams, eager for news of her sister on the frontier, treated the Chippewa woman as an honored guest. She became the favorite of the capital from President Adams to General Alexander Macomb, general in chief of the army.

One day McKenney told Tshusick he had written about her to his friend Governor Cass. It was then that the Chippewa woman abruptly announced she had to return home. She left, as McKenney said, "loaded [down] with presents," some sent by Mrs. Adams for her nieces and nephews in faraway Mackinac. There was a crowd of good wishers to wave good-bye, and even General Macomb helped to load her gifts on the stage.

Tshusick

Cass's reply told McKenney he had been taken in by a shrewd Indian confidence woman, who had played the same game in other cities as far north as Canada. It was true she worked in the Boyd household, but as the wife of a "short, squat Frenchman, who officiated as a scullion" who was very much alive and waiting to greet his wandering wife.

When he visited the frontier the following year, McKenney tried to find Tshusick, but the pretty redskin swindler was always one jump ahead of him.

Her trip to Washington, McKenney said admiringly, "was a masterpiece of daring and successful enterprise, and will compare well with the most finished efforts of the ablest impostors of modern times."

Painter: Charles Bird King, Washington, 1827.

Chippewa Squaw and Child

NLIKE MANY early nineteenth-century frontier American males, Colonel McKenney was sympathetic toward Indian women whose life he considered "one of continual labour and unmitigated hardship."

The Chippewa were not McKenney's favorite Indians. He frequently described them as "wretched" people whose women, strong and resourceful in times of adversity, were forced to share major hardships of the hunt. He wrote: "The woman who, during the season of plenty, was worn down with the labor of following the hunter to the chase, carrying the game and dressing the food, now becomes the purveyor of the family, roaming the forest in search of berries, burrowing in the earth for roots, or ensnaring the lesser animals. While engaged in these various duties, she discharges also those of the mother, and travels over the icy plains with her infant on her back."

McKenney and his co-author, James Hall, obviously ignored the traditional status of women of other Indian nations who like the Chippewa followed the hunters, skinning, dressing, and even carrying heavy chunks of meat for long distances—many times with a child on their backs.

Big White, the Mandan chief whose portrait was included in McKenney's portfolio, had shocked Lewis and Clark when he calmly loaded a hundred pounds of buffalo meat onto the back of his slender wife Yellow Corn, while he returned to the fort carrying only his rifle and pipe.

This portrait is probably the one entitled "Manner of carrying a child on a journey" used by McKenney in his *Sketches of a Tour to the Lakes,* published in 1827.

Painter: Original by James Otto Lewis, Fond du Lac council, 1826, later copied in Washington by Charles Bird King.

Chippewa Mother and Child

Petalesharo, the Bravest of the Brave

HE LITTLE Washington schoolgirl dressed in crisp crinoline, her pretty face ringed with curls and her young heart thumping in her chest like an imprisoned bird, held up the velvet ribbon from which hung a silver medal.

The handsome Indian, his face streaked with red and black paint, bent down. The girl carefully placed the ribbon about his neck and recited her rehearsed speech. The interpreter, to Colonel McKenney's disgust, clumsily translated the words. Then Petalesharo (Generous Chief) with great dignity thanked the schoolgirl for her kindness.

The scene in the living room of the home of young Mary Rapine, a student in Miss White's Seminary for Select Young Ladies, was a moving climax to the Pawnee's visit to Washington. He and the delegation of Pawnee and their allied tribes would leave the capital in a few days, but it would be years before the wonderful tale connected with Petalesharo's life would be forgotten. Romantic, thrilling, brave, it had touched many female hearts, not only in Washington, but in all the eastern cities.

The story of how he had saved a young Comanche girl from a human sacrifice was first printed in the Washington *National Intelligencer*, then later reprinted by eastern newspapers. In the winter of 1821 the *New York Commercial Advertiser* published a florid eleven-stanza poem entitled "The Pawnee Brave." It became so popular with sentimental New Yorkers that they held parties in their stiff, chilly parlors to read aloud the poem and weep over the gallantry of this wilderness savage.

The Comanche girl was not the first prisoner Petalesharo had saved from the sacrificial pyre. Once before the young chief had defied his people to rescue a young Spanish boy who had been taken prisoner. When the boy's captor demanded he be burned at the stake in a public ceremony as a sacrifice to the Great Star (Morning Star, or Ho-Pir-i-Kuts), Petalesharo warned his father, chief of the Pawnee, "I will take the boy, like a brave, by force."

The old chief knew his son would kill the brave and cause a serious rift in the nation. Instead, he sent criers about the Pawnee villages asking for presents to buy the boy's freedom.

Piles of skins, knives, and trinkets were placed before the old man's wigwam. But the brave still refused to release his young captive. Petalesharo, infuriated, threatened to kill him if he didn't accept the presents. With Petalesharo's knife at his throat the brave not only freed the boy but agreed to let the gifts be sacrificed in his place.

Poles were erected on the spot where the boy was to have been burned, then the skins, strouding (coarse cloth or blankets used in Indian trade), and buckskins were slashed, hung from the piles, and burned.

Petalesharo was not successful in his third attempt to save a prisoner from sacrifice. In May 1833, together with an Indian agent, he tried to free a young Cheyenne girl who had been taken captive in a raid. Petalesharo, then chief, was lifting her to the saddle of the agent's horse when she was killed by a shower of arrows. When she fell, Petalesharo and the agent were overwhelmed by the mob that tore the young girl "limb from limb," and smeared her blood on the bodies of the assembled Pawnee.

Petalesharo was a member of the delegation of sixteen Indians, principally Pawnee, who came to Washington in the winter of 1821–1822 to be greeted by the President, his cabinet, most of Congress, and the entire Supreme Court.

On New Year's Day, 1822, Petalesharo and his braves performed a war dance in front of the White House before six thousand spectators. All businesses were closed for the day and Congress adjourned its session.

This portrait is undoubtedly one of the first McKenney commissioned Charles Bird King to do for his famous Indian Gallery. It was painted during Petalesharo's visit to Washington.

Painter: Charles Bird King, Washington, 1821.

Petalesharo

Peskelechaco

THIS PAWNEE chief was among the delegation that visited Washington in the winter of 1821. Little is known of his background, and only his death is recorded. He was killed in 1826 in a battle with a war party of Osage who raided his village.

"A firm, determined man, an expert hunter and a fearless warrior" is the way McKenney recalled him.

Painter: Charles Bird King, Washington, 1821.

[240]

Peskelechaco

Sharitarish

LARGE delegation of Pawnee, Omaha, Kansa, Oto, and Missouri arrived in Washington on that stormy Wednesday and Thursday, November 28–29, 1821, it was reported by the *National Intelligencer* with the observation that the Indians' mission "is to visit their Great Father and learn something of that civilization of which they hitherto remained in total ignorance."

The chiefs, subchiefs, and warriors, the newspaper noted, "are from the most remote tribes with which we have intercourse and they are believed to be the first of these tribes that have ever been seen in the midst of our settlements. . . ."

One of the chiefs in that famous delegation was Sharitarish, of the Grand Pawnee nation. Colonel McKenney, who escorted the delegation to the White House, recalled him as "a chief of noble form and fine bearing; he was six feet tall, and well proportioned; and when mounted on the fiery steed of the prairie, was a graceful and very imposing personage. His people looked upon him as a great brave, and the young men especially regarded him as a person who was designed to great distinction."

Sharitarish had met Zebulon Pike on the Republican River, in Webster County, Nebraska, on September 25, 1806, with his father and older brother Tarecawawaho, who succeeded his father as chief of the nation. When Indian agent Benjamin O'Fallon invited him to visit the Great Father in Washington, Tarecawawaho refused. As he reminded O'Fallon the Pawnee was the greatest Indian nation on the plains and it would be condescending for him to visit the White House.

O'Fallon suggested a number of his chiefs and warriors be sent as a substitute and Tarecawawaho agreed.

W. Faux, an Englishman touring the United States, stopped off in Washington during the time the Indian delegation was in the capital. In his *Memorable Days in America*, published two years later, he recalled how Sharitarish and the other braves performed a wild war dance "in front of the President's house" before six thousand cheering spectators. The Indians, Faux wrote, "were in a state of perfect nudity, except a piece of red flannel round the waist and passing between the legs. . . ."

Faux described the Indians as "men of large stature, very muscular, having fine countenances, with the real Roman nose, dignified in their manners, and peaceful and quiet in their habits. . . ."

Their portraits, he said, were painted by "Mr King in their native costume, buffalo skins, with the hair inside, turned back at the neck and breast, which looked very handsome, like fur collars. . . ."

King, he said, copied and kept for himself eight of the Indian portraits, including the one he had done of Sharitarish (Angry Chief). He added:

"He [King] received 400 dollars from *Uncle Sam*" for painting the series of portraits commissioned by McKenney to start his famous Indian Gallery.

One of the Indians Faux called "the Otta half-chief" [probably Shaumonekusse, or L'Ietan, who was among the delegation] "and his squaw have taken tea. . . . She was a very good-natured, mild woman, and he showed great readiness in acquiring our language."

Tarecawawaho came to regret that he had refused O'Fallon's invitation. Sharitarish returned home on such a wave of popularity that his brother became bitterly jealous. However, before a feud could break out the older brother died and Sharitarish became chief of the Grand Pawnee nation. His reign was brief; in a few months he also died, probably from cholera.

Painter: Charles Bird King, Washington, 1821.

Sharitarish

Osceola (Aseola)

"WHEN CONVERSING on topics agreeable to him, his countenance manifests more the disposition of the white than of the red man. There is great vivacity in the play of his features, and when excited, his face is lighted up as by a thousand fires of passion, animation, and energy. His nose is Grecian at the base, and would be perfectly Phidean, but that it becomes slightly arched. There are indomitable firmness and withering scorn in the expression of his mouth—though the lips are tremulous from intense emotions, which seem ever boiling up within him...."

This was the way M. M. Cohen, who knew the Seminole War captain, recalled him in his *Notices of Florida and the Campaigns*, a superb account of the Seminole War.

Cohen described Osceola as the best ballplayer, hunter, and wrestler in the Seminole nation.

Woodburn Potter, a former staff officer in the Florida campaign, had a different opinion of the Seminole whom he called a man "not above mediocrity," "perverse and obstinate," whose exploits and influence over the Seminole "are very exaggerated..."

Son of an Englishman named William Powell and a Creek mother, Osceola fought as a boy against General Jackson's troops during the Creek War. Later he moved to Florida with his mother and again fought Jackson's dragoons in the first Seminole War.

He was in his mid-twenties when he became a subchief under Holato Micco, the Blue King, and the leading opponent of Payne's Landing treaty by which a minority of Seminole chiefs had signed away their nation's lands for territory in Arkansas.

In the councils Osceola seemed obsessed with nationalism and race, the deep love of the Seminole for their noble land, and the land-hungry, treacherous whites.

Osceola warned General Wiley Thompson, the Indian commissioner, that he would fight to death before he would allow the Americans to remove him or his people to the West. In an arrogant, swaggering speech he predicted that while he would die he would make sure to take three white men with him. Pro-American chiefs urged Thompson to arrest Osceola, but the commissioner, who liked the young Seminole, refused.

Osceola became a shining symbol of resistance to his people. He traveled from band to band advising the Seminole not to leave their country and denouncing the chiefs who had signed the Payne's Landing treaty as traitors and cowards.

In the autumn of 1835 negotiations with the Seminole reached a critical point; those friendly to the Americans prepared to move to Arkansas, the others had warned that they would fight rather than leave their land.

Civil war within the nation broke out in late November when Osceola killed Charley Amathla, a well-known Seminole leader who was planning to move west. The Dade Massacre followed. Then a few weeks later the frontier was shocked by the news that Osceola and his braves had killed General Thompson.

Guerrilla war now came to the Everglades. The frontier was laid waste from Fort Brooke to Fort King. For two years Osceola led his warriors in swift, ruthless raids, driving off herds of cattle and horses, burning bridges, and attacking patrols and outposts.

Four generals took the field against him. Winfield Scott, Edmund P. Gaines, and Richard K. Call were unsuccessful. It was not until General Thomas Sidney Jesup, who had helped subdue the Creek in Alabama in 1836, took over the army in Florida that Seminole resistance began to weaken.

After Jesup's eight thousand troops had driven Micanopy's bands from his Withlacoochee River country the first Seminole party appeared with a flag of truce. In a council with Jesup, Micanopy declared he was tired of fighting and would lead his people to Arkansas. Jesup, a practical man, took a large band of hostages to bind Micanopy to his word.

There was no spirit of surrender in Osceola. In a daring raid he freed the hostages and forced Micanopy to accompany him into the brush. But now the Dragoons were everywhere. They flushed the Seminole out of their hiding places, killed them, burned their villages, slaughtered their cattle, horses, and oxen, and relentlessly pursued them through the swamps.

Osceola

In September, Osceola was finally betrayed and captured. He was sent in chains to South Carolina where he died in Fort Moultrie in January 1838.

The fort's surgeon gave Catlin, who painted Osceola in prison, an eyewitness account of his death. Imprisonment had slowly killed Osceola. He knew death was approaching so he summoned his two wives, their children, and his chiefs.

When they surrounded him he slowly rose from his mat on the floor, put on his shirt, leggings, and moccasins, and called for his red paint. Using a small hand mirror he painted one half of his face, neck, throat, and wrist, and put on a turban headdress topped with three ostrich plumes. Then "in dead silence" he shook hands with the surgeon, his chiefs, and his family. His chiefs lowered him on the mat and "in a moment [he] smiled away his last breath, without a struggle or a groan."

Many artists besides Catlin were allowed to sketch and paint the Seminole chief while he was at Fort Moultrie. It is not known if this painting was included in McKenney's Indian Gallery in Washington; it was included in his portfolio.

Painter: This is one of the few full-length paintings in McKenney's portfolio; the artist is unknown.

Halpatter-Micco, or Billy Bowlegs

 HISKEY, BRIBERY, and threats, the government's classic persuaders, had forced the Seminole to sign the infamous Payne's Landing treaty on May 9, 1832, by which the nation yielded up its lands and agreed to move west of the Mississippi.

The white men had accomplished what the old chiefs insisted could never happen—Seminole fighting Seminole. It had happened to their cousins the Creek, the Choctaw, and Cherokee, now the great Osceola was leading the resistance of his people against the treaty. As he warned the pro-American chiefs in council, whoever sells our land will die.

The first chief to defy the fiery young leader was Charley Amathla (Emathla) who died under the bullets of Osceola's warriors. Years of guerrilla war in the swamps followed until eight thousand troops led by General Thomas Sidney Jesup, who had subdued the Creek, seized Osceola under a flag of truce, an act condemned as inexcusable treachery by the same public that had urged him to kill or capture the Seminole leader.

After Osceola died in his Fort Moultrie cell, other chiefs continued their guerrilla war in the Florida Everglades.

For a time Coacochu (Coacochee), Wild Cat, slipped in and out of Jesup's traps until disease and starvation forced him to surrender. Dressed in colorful costumes they had stolen from a theatrical group, Wild Cat and his warriors turned in their rifles and were removed to the West. The War Department proudly announced that the power of the nation had been broken and trading could begin; the victory announcement proved to be premature.

General William Selby Harney, who had won fame fighting the Choctaw and Creek, opened the first trading post, and it appeared as if peace had finally come to the Florida territory.

Then one sultry night two hundred Seminole braves slipped over the walls of Harney's stockade. They were under the command of Halpatter-Micco, a skillful young chief known to the frontier as Billy Bowlegs. Most of the garrison was slaughtered with Harney, the so-called greatest of Indian fighters, escaping in a fishing boat.

Billy Bowlegs was now recognized as the principal Seminole War chief. For more than a year his tightly knit band of eighty warriors waged guerrilla war against large numbers of United States troops.

It was a bitter, weary life, and at last Billy Bowlegs told his warriors they could continue no longer; the children were dying and there was no food. He finally surrendered and the government gave him and his people a small amount of land. On August 14, 1842, Washington formally announced the eight-year Seminole War was over—at the cost of the lives of 1,500 Americans and $20,000,000.

Billy Bowlegs

There was peace until 1856 when land-hungry whites demanded the land owned by Billy Bowlegs and his people. Osceola and the great days of resistance were now only memories. Billy told his warriors that he was too old and weary to fight any longer; a keg of whiskey, some money, and veiled threats persuaded him to sign away his land.

He left his native country for the last time, not with honor but to the catcalls and jeers of some of his warriors who had sworn to die before they gave up their lands and moved west.

In New Orleans the Seminole chief was greeted as a conquering hero. Crowds of white men escorted him on a wild tour of the city's saloons; by nightfall he was a mumbling drunk, staggering about the narrow streets while his people searched frantically for him.

He finally brought his band, now reduced by whiskey and disease to thirty-three warriors and eighty women and children, to the land the government had given them on the north and south forks of the Canadian River, Indian territory. Billy Bowlegs did not have time to love his wild new home, which the government had promised would never know the footfall of a white man; he died a short time after he cut down the first logs for his cabin.

The name Billy Bowlegs did not indicate a physical deformity, but was probably from his Indian name Bolek. The correct formal title is Halpuda Mikko, which signifies that the chief (*mikko*) belongs to the Alligator, or Halpuda, clan.

Painter: Charles Bird King, Washington, 1826.

Julcee Mathla

THIS SEMINOLE chief fought in the Everglades for several years and outlasted four American generals. After the death of Osceola, the great Seminole patriot and chief, the savage guerrilla war was continued by Billy Bowlegs who laid waste large sections of the Florida frontier. His surrender ended the Seminole War, but some chiefs and warriors continued to kill white men.

In the winter of 1842, General W. J. Worth, a veteran of the long and bloody campaign in the swamps, recommended to the War Department that one hundred and twelve Seminole warriors and over two hundred women and children be permitted to remain in Florida and not be removed to the Indian territory. Washington approved, and the remnants of the small nation that had fought almost twenty years against an army that at times totaled eight thousand troops returned to their homeland, ironically located on the Peace River.

Painter: Charles Bird King, Washington, 1825.

Micanopy

Foke Luste Hajo

T WAS April 22, 1835, and General Wiley Thompson, agent for the Seminole in the Florida territory, was reading a presidential message to the seven hundred warriors who had gathered to protest the treaty of Payne's Landing, Fort Gibson.

What had happened to the Seminole was a bitter parallel to the events that had divided the nation of their cousins, the Creek. Indian commissioners under pressure from Washington had forced a handful of chiefs to sign the Payne's Landing treaty and yield up their lands in return for territory across the Mississippi.

Prior to the Payne's Landing council in 1833, the Seminole had agreed to send seven chiefs to inspect the western land offered by the United States. General James Gadsden, a former aide to Jackson and a veteran of the 1818 Seminole War, had warned the secretary of war that the Indians had *"most positively refused* to negotiate for their removal west of the Mississippi," but as a mark of good faith were willing to inspect the western territory.

"The final ratification of the treaty," Gadsden added, "will depend upon the opinion of the seven chiefs. . . ."

Gadsden and the Indian agents carefully selected chiefs they knew could be bribed or who would bend under pressure. One, a distinguished war captain, was Foke Luste Hajo, whose name meant Black Dirt.

The seven chiefs returned to Payne's Landing, Fort Gibson, but, instead of reporting back to the council of their people, were persuaded or bribed to sign the treaty that doomed their nation.

The treaty divided the Seminole into two hostile camps. Colonel McKenney, now out of office for five years, condemned the treaty and predicted that if it was ratified by Congress war would break out in the Everglades. Evidently the tragedy of the Creek was still vivid in his memory.

General Thompson committed his first diplomatic blunder when he opened the 1835 council with the hope that the Seminole, who boasted of their honor, would "act like honest men."

He then went on to read Jackson's letter, a mixture of syrupy platitudes and veiled threats. The President cruelly reminded the Seminole that "the white people are settling around you. The game has disappeared from your country. Your people are poor and hungry. . . . And nearly three years ago, you made an agreement with your friend Colonel Gadsden . . . by which you agreed to cede your lands in Florida, and remove and join your brothers, the Creeks, in the country west of the Mississippi. . . ."

Jackson pointed out that the United States had allowed seven of their chiefs "in whom you placed confidence" to examine the western land and then report back to the nation, and that these seven, "satisfied on these heads," had signed the Payne's Landing treaty.

Jackson pleaded with his "children" not to defy the government but to face their situation with reality.

"Even if you had a right to stay," he brutally informed them, "how could you live where you now are? You have sold all your country. You have not a piece as large as a blanket to sit down upon. . . ."

Then came the final blunt warning. Troops had been sent to control the Seminole, and one-third of the nation would immediately be removed to the West.

It was the same sad story. As McKenney had predicted, the Seminole War broke out. The cost of the Payne's Landing treaty would be over a thousand lives, red and white, and millions of dollars.

After the 1835 council Foke Luste Hajo received his death sentence. Unlike McIntosh, the pro-American Creek who had impassively accepted his fate, the Seminole chief fled to Fort Brooke where he and his followers sat out the war.

McKenney described Foke Luste Hajo as "a War Chief, a man of desperate character, and always ready for fight."

Painter: Charles Bird King, Washington, 1826.

Foke Luste Hajo

Neamathla

 ILLIAM P. DUVAL, appointed governor of the Florida territory by President Monroe, once wrote to the War Department that he considered Neamathla "a man of uncommon abilities, of great influence with his nation, and as one of the most eloquent men [I] ever heard. . . . This chief you will find perhaps the greatest man you have ever seen among the Indians..."

But personal views were secondary to Duval, a consummate politician, when he heard Neamathla was advising his people not to accept the government's offer to remove them to lands beyond the Mississippi. Duval immediately deposed this "man of uncommon abilities" as chief of the Seminole.

It was not the first time white men had interfered with Indian tribal policy.

Colonel McKenney wrote: "This [the removal of Neamathla] is a curious instance of the anomalous character of the relation existing between our Government and the Indians; for while the latter are for many purposes considered as independent nations and are treated with as such, they are in all essential respects regarded and governed as subjects..."

It should have been clear to Duval that Neamathla would never be a puppet chief. A year before he was removed by the governor, Neamathla had shocked Washington by refusing the government's annuity payment of one thousand dollars to build a school to teach Seminole children the ways of the white man. The payment was part of the Moultrie Creek treaty, signed by Neamathla and thirty-two members of his tribe on September 18, 1823.

Neamathla told Duval that the Seminole instruct their children in their own way:

"We teach them to procure food by hunting, and to kill their enemies. But we want no schools such as you offer us. We wish our children to remain as the Great Spirit made them, and as their fathers are, Indians. The Great Spirit has made different kinds of men, and given them separate countries to live in; and he has given to each the arts that are suited to his condition. It is not for us to change the designs of the Great Master of Life...."

Painter: Charles Bird King, Washington, 1826.

Neamathla

Chittee-Yoholo

HEN HE was asked by an American general what he had done in the savage battle on the Othlacoochee during the Seminole War, this chief's reply was brief and to the point: kill white men.

He was one of the principal Seminole War chiefs who helped stage the night attack of March 28–29, 1836, when a large force of Dragoons and Creek warriors were surrounded and wiped out.

Chittee-Yoholo was a superb guerrilla fighter, a night raider who slipped in and out of the swamps with small bands to attack outposts and unprotected settlements. He boasted of bringing back so many scalps that he was known as the Snake that makes a noise.

He scouted Fort Mellon on the shore of Lake Monroe by lying in a culvert covered with grass and counting the troops as they passed in and out. A few days later he led the unsuccessful attack on the fort.

He explained to Colonel McKenney that when a garrison was too strong to take by siege he and his warriors would drive off the stock. Then his people would feast for days on the stolen beef, "while the soldiers ate grass."

In several battles, he told McKenney, he had seen the noted Jim Boy (Tustennuggee Emathla) a tall, powerfully built Creek chief, fighting with the American troops. When the Indian superintendent asked why he had not killed the Creek, a conspicuous target, Chittee-Yoholo gave a philosophical shrug:

"He replied that it was not the will of the Great Spirit; and added that he had been in many battles, and not having lost his life, he concluded he should die of sickness, and he supposed that 'Jim Boy' would die in the same way."

The Seminole War captain surrendered to the army garrison at St. Augustine and later agreed with other chiefs to give up their Florida lands and move to Arkansas.

Painter: Charles Bird King, Washington, 1826.

Chittee-Yoholo

Sequoyah, or George Guess

EQUOYAH WAS an authentic Indian genius who gave his people their greatest gift—communication.

Without books, letters, or newspapers, he invented the Cherokee alphabet while living in the deep woods surrounded by Indians and whites, most of whom were as illiterate as himself.

Sequoyah, or George Guess as he was commonly called on the frontier, was the son of an itinerant white farmer named Gist and a half-breed mother.

McKenney, who knew Sequoyah, described him as a dreamer, a moody boy who disliked the favorite game of all Indian youths—war. Instead, he took long walks in the woods and built ingenious toy houses of sticks and mud.

His mother was a struggling, poverty-stricken frontierswoman who owned a few acres, some cows, and wild horses. When he was twelve Sequoyah, to help his mother, was determined to find out all he could about dairy farming. He built a milkshed, learned how to make cheese, and to care for the cows so they became the most productive in the neighborhood. Next came their horses. A Cherokee horse trader taught him all he knew, and Sequoyah broke his herd to the saddle. Later, a white man taught him how to plow; a fine corn harvest was the result.

Hunting then became his passion. He lived in the woods with Cherokee hunters until he returned with bales of skins. Silversmithing caught his fancy also, and he wasn't satisfied until his work was among the finest in the nation. Once when he visited a trading post he discovered the white man had a method "by means of which a name could be impressed upon a hard substance . . ."

Charles Hicks, a Moravian and part Cherokee who years later would become an influential chief, scrawled "George Guess" on a scrap of paper, and Sequoyah laboriously copied his name on a die, then stamped it on all his silverwork. It was probably the first Indian trademark.

Art came next. He sketched from early morning to late at night by the fireplace, in between plowing a field, rounding up the cows, breaking horses, or designing a new piece of silverwork. Up to this time he had never seen an engraving or painting.

In 1820, Sequoyah visited some relatives in a Cherokee village on the Tennessee River. During the afternoon the subject of the white man's skill of writing was discussed. One brave insisted that only the Great Spirit could have given them the magical gift that enabled one man to put down his thoughts on paper so they could be read by another man many miles away. There was a general shaking of heads over the ingenuity of the white man. Guess startled everyone by scoffing at the idea that it was a gift of God. Rather he said, it was an art, and he was sure that he could invent some kind of a written tongue so the Cherokee could express their thoughts and wishes on paper for one another, even though they were separated by great distances.

The next day Sequoyah begged some scraps of paper, which he fashioned into a book and began making "characters."

As McKenney described the method:

"His reflections on the subject had led him to the conclusion that the letters used in writing represented certain words or ideas, and being uniform, would always convey to the reader the same idea intended by the writer—provided the system of characters which had been taught to each was the same."

He polished his work in 1821. That same year he began teaching the alphabet to others. After the Cherokee language could be read and written he toured Arkansas teaching his alphabet to the Cherokee who had been removed to that territory.

In 1823, he left Alabama with the Cherokee who had accepted the government's offer to move them west of the Mississippi. He carried with him a silver medal presented by his people. The inscription read:

"Presented to George Gist, by the General Council of the Cherokee nation, for his ingenuity in the invention of the Cherokee Alphabet." One side was in English, the other in Cherokee.

John Ridge

cultivated many friends, red and white, and made as many enemies.

The Cherokee Trail of Tears led to the Indian territory. Still there was no peace. Jealousy, greed, and shattered pride accomplished the white man's ultimate goal—to force Cherokee to fight Cherokee.

In the struggle for the nation's leadership, John Ridge was dragged from his bed in Park Hill Mission, Indian territory, and slashed to death. His wife ran out and flung herself over his body as three horsemen pounded down the road to vanish into the night.

Major Ridge was also killed, shot down from ambush, along with Elias Boudinot, editor of the *Phoenix*. Boudinot, who had taken the name of a white benefactor, was the brother of Stand Watie, the Cherokee chief who would gain fame in the Civil War.

Ross was finally elected chief of the entire nation by the council that denounced Major Ridge, John Ridge, and Boudinot as outlaws who had betrayed their people.

The wife of John Ridge who had come to the beautiful valley as his bride, who had survived the tribal feuds and power struggles, who had made the terrible crossing to what the white man had called the Promised Land, who had seen her husband butchered, and her father-in-law killed, now sadly packed her belongings and took her children to Arkansas. Her son, John Rollin Ridge, later became a prominent California newspaperman.

Tragedy continued to stalk the Cherokee nation. For the next several years bitterness and hate intensified between the two factions. Men died on lonely roads and houses were burned in the night. Then the white man's Civil War burst upon them. The Cherokee who were slave owners and influenced by southern life joined the Confederacy; others fought for the Union.

One day Stand Watie, who led his famous Cherokee regiment for the Confederacy, marched on Park Hill, Indian territory, and burned the mission buildings. The Cherokee who were there that day recalled how they turned away as the flames devoured their old schoolhouse. But not Stand Watie; he watched grim-faced as one building collapsed in a shower of sparks and charred timbers. It was Ross Hill, the beautiful home of John Ross.

Once again the white man had forced Cherokee to fight Cherokee.

Painter: Charles Bird King, Washington, 1825.

Tahchee, or Dutch

HE LIFE story of this Cherokee chief (Tatsi is probably the correct spelling) is typical of an Indian who was born shortly after the Revolution and lived in the first part of the nineteenth century. His days were occupied with war, raids, horse stealing, scouting and hunting.

Dutch, as he is known to frontier history, was a child when his family joined the first Cherokee removal from the big Indian village called Turkey Town on the Coosa River in what is now Alabama to the St. Francis River in Arkansas, west of the Mississippi. It was a wild country that had not known the white man's presence.

The casual life of the hunter appealed to him, and at about the age of twelve he joined one of those incredible Indian hunting parties that roamed the prairies for as long as three years.

It was a life of feast or famine. The hunter's constant enemy was the weather. Weary hours were spent on horseback, but the hardships were forgotten in the excitement of the hunt and the occasional clash with other tribes.

Dutch roamed beyond the Mississippi and explored the Red River country. Years later a white man asked him how many buffalo he had killed and Dutch answered, "So many I cannot number them."

Tahchee

He lived with other tribes to study the techniques of their hunters, even the Osage, the traditional foe of the Cherokee, and was among the few of his nation who knew the Osage dialect. He became a legend on the plains and the prairies, a lone hunter with three large dogs running on both sides of his horse's flanks. He explored the Arkansas River to the south of the Grand, or Neosho, River, then traveled on foot for hundreds of miles to the Missouri. When he returned downriver his canoe was almost swamped by beaver skins.

The treaty the Cherokee made with the United States in 1828 so infuriated Dutch that he led several families to the Red River country. They were constantly at war with those superb horsemen of the Texas plains, the Comanche. To keep the frontier peaceful, the army ordered both nations to stop their raids, an order Dutch refused to recognize. He was finally declared an outlaw, and the army's wanted poster offered five hundred dollars for him dead or alive.

Dutch fought a one-man war with the army for years, even boldly scalping a Comanche in the shadow of Fort Gibson. Both sides finally grew weary of the hound and hare game. The commander, a shrewd man, hired Dutch to form a group of Indian scouts in the army's campaign against the Comanche. Before he retired to his ranch on the Canadian River, Dutch was known throughout the early Indian fighting army as a tireless tracker and "a man to be relied on."

Catlin who met Dutch in 1834 called him "a guide and hunter for the regiment of dragoons.... The history of this man's life has been very curious and surprising; and I sincerely hope that someone, with more leisure and more talent than myself, will take it up, and do it justice. I promise that the life of this man furnishes the best materials for a popular tale, that are now to be procured on the Western frontier."

The portrait of Dutch, included in Mooney's celebrated "Myths of the Cherokee" in the Nineteenth Report of the Bureau of American Ethnology (Washington 1900), was credited to Catlin, but it is obvious that it is from the McKenney-Hall portfolio. Catlin's portrait of Dutch, painted in 1836, shows a Cherokee with a light beard.

Dutch refused to accompany the Cherokee to Washington in May 1828 to sign the treaty he despised, but he may have been a member of other Cherokee delegations that visited Washington in October 1821, February 1823, and March 1824.

Painter: Charles Bird King, Washington date unknown.

John Ross

 PARE OUR people! Spare the wreck of our prosperity! Let not our deserted homes become the monuments of desolations! But we forbear! We suppress the agonies which wring our hearts, when we look at our wives, our children, and our venerable sires! We restrain our forebodings of anguish and distress, of misery and devastation and death which must be the attendants on the execution of this ruinous compact."

This was the conclusion of the long bitter letter sent by John Ross, the brilliant chief of the Cherokee, to Congress on September 28, 1836, from Red Clay council ground, Cherokee Nation, East.

Ross and his chiefs again were begging the United States to review the treaty of New Echota, made on December 29, 1835, by which the Cherokee had sold all their lands in exchange for territory across the Mississippi.

Ross, in his letter to Congress, pointed out that his people had been by the treaty "stripped of every attribute of freedom and eligibility for legal self-defense. . . . We are denationalised! We are disfranchised! . . . We are deprived of membership in the human family! We have neither land, nor home, nor resting-place, that can be called our own. . . ."

The treaty of New Echota in northern Georgia had been signed by Major Ridge, his son John, and Elias Boudinot, editor of the *Cherokee Phoenix*. Ridge represented a minority of the tribe, less than a hundred Indians; against them was the rest of the Cherokee nation headed by Ross.

The treaty had divided the nation into two hostile factions, one headed by Ridge, the other by Ross.

Congress ignored Ross' plea. On November 3, 1836, General Wool, commanding the troops in the Cherokee nation, warned Ross that the United States was determined to have the treaty "religiously fulfilled in all its parts, terms, and conditions . . . and that no delegation which may be sent to Washington with a view to obtain new terms . . . will be received or recognised. . . ."

John Ross

It was the doom of the Cherokee. In desperation, Ross sent a committee of chiefs to the "Western Cherokees," or that part of the tribe that had moved to the Indian territory under the treaties of 1817 and 1819. Both nations joined together in a resolution that they hoped to present to President Jackson, but Ross and his chiefs found the White House closed to them. The Senate, "owing to the press of business," also sent them away.

Ross's bewildered cry rang out through his nation: *"How have we offended?"*

On March 16, Ross and his chiefs turned to newly elected President Martin Van Buren, pointing out to him that the United States had reviewed and declared invalid two other treaties with the Creek and the Seminole. Why, he asked, are we not given the same justice?

The new President was courteous, but his answer was the same; the treaty must stand—the Cherokee must be removed from their ancient homelands to the Indian territory.

Not mentioned, of course, was that when the white man had found gold near the present Dahlonega, Georgia, within the limits of the Cherokee nation, a powerful agitation had begun for the removal of the people who were then at the peak of their prosperity. Indian cattle and horse herds were extensive, their farms prospering, and many of their children were attending the Foreign Mission School at Cornwall, Connecticut, or Brainerd in Tennessee, both established in 1817 by the Board of Commissioners for Foreign Missions.

The removal of the Cherokee took place in the winter of 1838–1839 after the army had driven Ross's people into stockaded camps. There have been various estimates of the casualties of that long and bitter Trail of Tears; John Ross's figure was 424 men, women, and children, but Grant Foreman, the eminent Oklahoma historian who did some fine pioneering research on the tribe among the official archives in Washington, estimated 4,000, including those who died in the camps as well as on the trail.

The army, the federal government, even Ross and the Cherokee themselves, must share the blame for the tragedy. It must be recalled that Ross insisted the removal not begin until the hot weather had passed and then ran into ice-choked swamps and rivers.

The great Sequoyah played a leading role in trying to unite the western and the eastern Cherokee in 1839 after Ridge, his son, and Boudinot were murdered. It is not to the credit of Ross and his followers that the murders were never solved. In fact, the Cherokee council denounced the Ridges and Boudinot as outlaws who had betrayed their nation.

After several years of killings and house burnings both sides united, but hardly had the old wounds been healed when the white man's Civil War burst upon them. Many of the Cherokee who were slave owners and surrounded by southern influence fought for the Confederacy; others like Ross turned to the Union. Their territory was overrun by both armies and Appomattox found them prostrated. By a treaty of 1866 they were readmitted to the Union but were forced to surrender their slaves and admit them to equal citizenship.

Ross died in Washington on August 1, 1866.

Painter: Charles Bird King, Washington, date not known.

David Vann

AVID VANN was an ally and close friend of Major Ridge, the controversial Cherokee leader. Like Ridge, Vann believed that the only way for the Cherokee to survive was to give up their territory and move to the lands beyond the Mississippi, which the government had solemnly promised would never hear the sound of a white man's voice. The Cherokee, Choctaw, Chickasaw, Creek, and Seminole, the so-called Five Civilized Tribes, would discover that the Great Father's promises were written on water or in smoke.

Vann was an educated Cherokee and a supporter of Ridge. They both risked their lives when they denounced a half-breed prophet from the mountains who appeared among the Cherokee in the 1830s. This prophet promised survival if the Cherokee would abandon the ways of the white man. It was the same, sad Indian dream of a return to the old ways that would be repeated in the Ghost Dance of the plains, and scattered forever at Wounded Knee.

Colonel McKenney, who knew Ridge, Vann and the other Cherokee chiefs, wrote:

Red Bird

This display of strength convinced the Winnebago chiefs that war was futile. A council of chiefs forced Red Bird and his warriors to surrender to McKenney, Cass, and the army commander.

McKenney called Red Bird (Zitkaduta), who won his name from the preserved red bird he wore on a shoulder, "perfect in form, in face, and gesture." When he faced the Indian superintendent the chief's face was painted one side red, the other blue and white. Around his neck he wore a necklace of blue and white wampum and the claws of a wildcat "with their points inward." His leggings were pure white deerskin and embroidered with blue beads. Tied to his chest with buckskin thongs was his war pipe, three feet long and dripping with streamers of dyed horsehair and feathers.

Like all Indians, Red Bird was a realist who accepted but never questioned his fate.

" 'I am ready,' " he told McKenney. " '...I have given away my life—it is gone—(stooping and taking some dust between his finger and thumb, and blowing it away)—like that'...'I would not take it back. It is gone.' "

His words were prophetic. He died in a cell within a year, shortly before President John Quincy Adams pardoned him and his warriors.

Painter: Original by James Otto Lewis, at the Portage, 1827, later copied in Washington by Charles Bird King.

Nawkaw, or Wood

 T WAS a strange mission for Nawkaw, the ancient Winnebago chief. The previous year in an attempt to maintain peace on the frontier, he had ordered three of his warriors to surrender to the white man and be tried for murder. They all had been found guilty in St. Louis and sentenced to hang. Now, in the fall of 1828, Nawkaw was in Washington to beg the Great Father to spare the lives of his people.

The chief made a vigorous plea for mercy. President Adams, short, squat, weather-beaten, listened intently, then after conferring with McKenney and the secretary of war agreed to pardon the three Indians.

It was too late for Red Bird, one of the warriors. A year's imprisonment was a horrendous existence for an Indian who had been raised on the broad sweep of the plains and the great lake country of Wisconsin. A frontier newspaper reported that the "privations of imprisonment destroyed his health, broke his spirit and hurried him to a premature grave."

The Winnebago had arrived in the capital accompanied by Major Thomas Forsyth, an Indian trader and agent for the tribe, and John H. Kinzie, who worked at Prairie du Chien for John Jacob Astor's American Fur Company. Kinzie's father was the founder of Chicago; his wife, Juliette, years later would write *Wau-Bun*, that delightful book on the frontier that includes many fascinating anecdotes about the Winnebago.

When Colonel McKenney learned the Winnebago, embittered over Red Bird's death, were arming, he ordered Forsyth and Kinzie to take the Indian delegation on a tour of the major eastern cities to let them "witness the highest evidences of our wealth, power, and civilisation." McKenney always believed in the whispered warning rather than the angry war whoop.

Nawkaw proved to be a terror to hotelmen. In New York when the same piece of roast beef was placed before him for the second time, he demanded — and got — chicken. In Baltimore he ordered one of his braves to spear a roast turkey from a sideboard before the other guests had a chance to serve themselves. Nawkaw's explanation to the angry innkeeper was simple; now the white man would know what his people were doing to the Indians.

In another city Nawkaw questioned the agents. Were all meals they ate paid for by the Great Father? Kinzie said they were. At the next meal Nawkaw and his warriors calmly dumped the remaining food on the table into a buckskin bag. When the agent protested, Nawkaw shrugged.

"You said the Great Father paid for all the food. Why should we leave it for the dogs?" he replied.

When he arrived in Washington, Nawkaw told McKenney he was ninety-four "winters." The Indian superintendent described the Winnebago as six feet tall, muscular, and looking many years younger.

Painter: Original by James Otto Lewis, Butte des Morts council, 1827, later copied in Washington by Charles Bird King.

Nawkaw

Tshizunhaukau

HEN THE Winnebago warrior appeared in Colonel McKenney's office in the War Department he carried a tall staff covered with strange symbols.

"What is this staff?" the Indian superintendent asked.

"It is the staff of life," Tshizunhaukau replied, and then explained what the marks and figures represented. McKenney recalled that they were "divisions of time, and certain changes of the seasons, to which were added signs indicating the results of certain calculations he had made respecting the weather. It was a curious and original invention, the fruit of an inquisitive and active mind. . . . He had noticed the phenomena which took place around him with deep attention, and had recorded upon the tablet of a retentive memory all that seemed worthy of remark."

The Winnebago, whose translated Indian name meant He Who Runs with the Deer, had accompanied Nawkaw, head chief of the Winnebago nation, to Washington in the fall of 1828. McKenney discovered Tshizunhaukau was both a medicine man and a magician, who "practised the art when it suited his convenience... He was a sagacious man, who knew and thought more than those around him."

When the Indian superintendent brought the Winnebago to the artist's Washington studio to have his portrait painted, he ordered the artist to paint the part-time medicine man holding what McKenney called his staff, "an almanac, and doubtless as complete a one, in reference to his wants, as our common almanacs are to the enlightened astronomer."

McKenney called him a "warrior of remarkable genius and singular character."

Painter: Original by James Otto Lewis, Butte des Morts council, 1827, later copied in Washington by Charles Bird King.

Wakaunhaka

Amisquam, or Wooden Ladle

S THIS celebrated war captain explained to Colonel McKenney, a leader of an Indian war party seldom carried weapons or took part in the conflict. His responsibility was to direct "like the general in the army of a civilised people...the efforts of others..."

Amisquam told the Indian superintendent open discussion prevailed at every Winnebago war council:

"All who are of sufficient age may speak, and the decision is usually unanimous..."

Details were left to the war chief who in turn conferred with his favorite captains. Orders were given to them on the eve of the battle; if the raid was small and only a few warriors engaged, plans were disclosed to the entire party. In rare cases, Amisquam told McKenney, a war chief would personally lead his braves into battle, always at the head of his men.

When McKenney asked the significance of his necklace, the Winnebago war chief explained that the string of beads was a trophy always given to the first warrior who brought back the head of an enemy.

"The trophy was always given on the spot," McKenney observed.

The Winnebago were known to the whites since the French found them living on Green Bay in 1634. The name Winnebago is derived from the Algonkian, meaning "people of the filthy or bad-smelling water."

Painter: Original by James Otto Lewis, Butte des Morts council, 1827, later copied in Washington by Charles Bird King.

Amisquam

Hoowanneka, or Little Elk

HIS WINNEBAGO chief insisted that the artist paint him exactly as he had appeared in the White House in the summer of 1824 before the President, his cabinet, members of Congress, and foreign dignitaries. Colonel McKenney, who was present, recalled the "singular scene, which exhibited the savage orator, painted in fantastic style, and clad in these wild and picturesque habiliments, addressing the grave and dignified head of the American people, in one of the saloons of the White House."

Little Elk had gained a reputation as a war chief during the War of 1812 when he fought for the British. When he and his chiefs discovered Great Britain had made a separate peace, leaving their Indian allies at the mercy of the United States, Hoowanneka denounced the commander of Fort Malden and led his people to seek protection "under the American flag."

Never again, he vowed, would he raise his tomahawk against the United States. Other chiefs had made the same promise, and their influence helped to maintain peace on the frontier. He signed his first treaty with the United States at the big Prairie du Chien council in August 1825 and his last at Fort Armstrong in the fall of 1832.

It would be fascinating to know what opinions the Winnebago chief had of the United States when he walked through the gates of Fort Armstrong. By this time his nation had been forced to yield their land south and east of the Wisconsin River and the Fox River of Green Bay and move to territory west of the Mississippi. Farms and settlements were now edging across their ancestral lands.

Painter: Original by James Otto Lewis, Fond du Lac council, 1826, copied by A. Ford. Charles Bird King also made a copy based on the Lewis original in 1827.

L'Ietan

Hayne Hudjihini, or the Eagle of Delight

 HE WAS young, tall, and finely formed, her face...was the most beautiful we had met with. Her hair was parted across her forehead, and hung down upon her shoulders. A small jacket of blue cloth was fastened round her shoulders and breast, and a mantle of the same was wrapped around her body."

This was the way an Indian commissioner recalled the Eagle of Delight after he had met her in the 1830s. A decade before, she had accompanied her husband Shaumonekusse, an Oto chief, to Washington where she had captivated McKenney, the President, his cabinet, and just about everyone she met. She was poised and charming, but she was not the sole love of her warrior chief.

The Eagle of Delight was only one of five wives and their husband was getting on in years when the commissioner met him. That day the women were all "pounding corn, or chattering over the news of the day." The old chief, while eating, "took the opportunity to disburthen his heart" to the commissioner.

As he moaned, five women were just too much, even the Eagle of Delight. Their "caprices, and the difficulties which he found in maintaining a proper discipline [made it impossible for him] where there were so many mistresses and but one master." Unfortunately, no one ever obtained the Eagle of Delight's version of married life to an old man in a tepee with four other women.

McKenney called her "young, and remarkably handsome...." She died of measles soon after her return to the west.

Painter: Charles Bird King, Washington, 1821.

Hayne Hudjihini

Choncape, or Big Kansas

THE BIG Kaw is a short, thick Indian, rather good natured, but gifted with a large supply of mulish obstinacy, and a temper like gunpowder. Oppose him—flash!—he is in a blaze; the children scamper; the squaws scatter; the rabble vanish. None stay to listen to the outpourings of his wrath, unless it may be one or two old fellows, who are too decrepit to get out of his way, or are blessed with so happy a hardness of hearing as to render it agreeable to them to be conversed with, even though by a man in a passion.

"The family of this chief consists of several wives, and a son, who is one of the most intelligent young men in the village. He, however, is the very counterpart of the old man in disposition; and when the two get fairly excited, the village is in an uproar...."

This is how J. T. Irving, in his *Indian Sketches* published in 1835, described Big Kansas, better known on the frontier of the 1830s as Big Kaw. For all his explosive temper, Irving liked the Oto whom he found courteous to strangers, a good administrator of the tribe, and shrewd war captain.

Together with his son, Big Kaw ruled the tribe firmly but fairly. After a twin explosion of their tempers, "until the silence which reigns within gives notice that the storm has blown over....it is said that those who return generally find the old man looking very foolish and the son very angry. From that it is suspected that the former is held in subjection by his graceless offspring...[who] permits nobody to bully his father but himself."

Painter: Charles Bird King, Washington, 1821.

[298]

Choncape

Nowaykesugga

HIS WARRIOR, a rough translation of whose name is He Who Strikes Two at Once, was a member of the Oto delegation that came to Washington in 1837.

The Oto was part of a triumvirate of Siouan tribes, the other two were the Iowa and Missouri; their language differed but slightly. During Colonel McKenney's time they were a small tribe merged with the Missouri and living on the south side of the Platte under the protection of the Pawnee. Unlike the larger nations, their history was more of a struggle to defend themselves against their powerful neighbors and of their migrations. They lived in earthen lodges similar to the Kansa and Omaha but when they were traveling they used skin tepees. In a series of treaties beginning with Prairie du Chien, 1830, including two signed at Washington, they yielded their land east of the Missouri up to the mouth of the Big Sioux River. They eventually moved to the Indian territory with the Missouri.

Painter: Charles Bird King, Washington, 1837.

Nowaykesugga

Mahaskah, or White Cloud

As THE Iowa chief later told Colonel McKenney, he would never forget his visit to Washington. It was not because of his talk with the Great Father, his awe of the white man's city, or the vivid memories he had of the foundry where the cannons were made, but only because of the trouble he had with his wives. He had several, more than any one man could manage—even an Iowa warrior and leader of a great Indian nation.

It started a hundred miles from the Iowa village. Rather than take all his wives, Mahaskah had decided he would journey alone to St. Louis where he would meet General William Clark and the rest of the Indian delegation. His family affairs had been hectic since Rantchewaime, or Female Flying Pigeon, had become his latest, youngest, and prettiest wife. The other women resented Flying Pigeon, and there had been so many battles between the women that Mahaskah had to take a club to all of them —including Flying Pigeon.

He had killed and skinned a deer near the Des Moines River and made camp. As he later told Colonel McKenney, he was bending over his cook fire when someone hit him with a branch across the back of his neck. He spun about, drawing his knife, expecting to find himself confronted with a Sioux or an Osage warrior but it was only an indignant Flying Pigeon who berated him for leaving her behind. Mahaskah, who knew what would happen if he only took one wife and left the others, made Flying Pigeon prepare his food, then he pulled her up behind him on the horse, and they returned to the village. The next day the chief again set out for Washington, this time with all his wives.

Mahaskah's fears became a reality; the women fought with fists, clubs, and knives on canal boats, stagecoaches, and on horseback. They finally arrived in Washington in the fall of 1824; as Mahaskah wearily told Indian agent Benjamin O'Fallon, he was sick of all women.

The bar of Tennison's Hotel on Pennsylvania Avenue saw a great deal of Mahaskah. One night he finished a jug and went upstairs to his room. A short time later the agent heard screams and the sounds of smashing furniture. He rushed upstairs and broke in the door.

Mahaskah, showing no favoritism, was beating his quarreling wives with the leg of a chair. Rather than be disgraced as a man not able to control his family, he yanked open the window and stepped out as O'Fallon rushed into the room.

There was one thing the Iowa had forgotten; he had lived all his life in a wigwam. He now walked out the second-story window and fell to the courtyard. His broken arm was set and McKenney recalled that "so accustomed had he been to fractures and wounds, that he insisted on riding the next day, over rough roads and pavements, a distance of at least two miles, to see a cannon cast."

The Iowa chief had a satisfying visit with President Monroe and returned home inspired by what he had seen. He built a "double log-house" and cultivated his land. Flying Pigeon became the real love of his life, but the other wives stayed on. She gave him a son, who would be known to frontier history as Mahaskah the Younger.

Then suddenly one day their peaceful, serene life was shattered when Flying Pigeon was killed by a fall from her pony. The stunned chief carried her slender body miles across the prairie to his village, his infant son clinging to his back.

After the burial ceremonies Mahaskah slipped into a deep depression. He fasted for long periods and disappeared for weeks on solitary hunts. Time—and perhaps his other wives—dulled his grief and he returned to the administration of his nation.

In 1834, Mahaskah was killed by a warrior he had turned over to General Clark to stand trial in St. Louis for murder.

Thirty years later when Colonel McKenney was gathering material for his portfolio, he found the great Iowa nation "reduced by wars, the smallpox, and by whisky" to a pitiful handful.

The portrait of Mahaskah was painted shortly after the chief had broken his arm. As McKenney pointed out, "a compression of his eyebrows...was caused by the pain he was enduring whilst the artist was sketching his likeness."

Painter: Charles Bird King, Washington, 1824.

Mahaskah

Rantchewaime, or Flying Pigeon

DECADE after this portrait was painted Colonel McKenney called it "a perfect likeness of the wife of Mahaskah. . . . She has been also called 'The Beautiful Female Eagle that Flies in the Air'. . . . by the chiefs and braves of the nation, on account of her great personal beauty."

General Andrew Hughes, General William Clark's subagent in St. Louis, who knew Flying Pigeon, told McKenney she was completely devoted to her husband and was chaste, kind, and generous. Hughes also claimed she was "mild" in nature, but this appears a cavalier's touch by the agent; from Mahaskah's experiences in Washington, Flying Pigeon had her wifely moments.

After her return from Washington, Flying Pigeon gathered hundreds of women of her nation together to describe her journey to the home of the Great Father. There was one important part of her talk: the "vicious courses which she witnessed during that journey, among the whites," and she warned the women of these practices. It would be fascinating to know what she regarded as these evil practices.

Her portrait many times is confused with that of Hayne Hudjihini, who was painted three years earlier. A copy of this portrait was bequeathed to the Redwood Library, Newport, Rhode Island. It was sold at the celebrated Parke-Bernet auction of the library's collection of North American Indian portraits in May 1970.

Painter: Charles Bird King, Washington, 1824.

Rantchewaime

Mahaskah the Younger

FTER THE murder of his father, the famous Iowa chief, his son refused to accept the hereditary title and name. As he told the council, he was too young and lacked the wisdom to lead his people. It was only after the elders, war captains, and braves elected him "chief without a dissenting voice" did Mahaskah the Younger put on the flowing eagle headdress, the symbol of his office.

He warned his first council that he was no man of war; he would always follow his father's philosophy that to survive they must have peace with the white man:

"I believe the Great Spirit is always angry with men who shed innocent blood. I will live in peace."

He completed his father's cultivation of sixteen acres of pumpkins, beans, squash, and potatoes, which he ordered distributed among the poor of his nation.

After the famous Prairie du Chien treaty was signed in 1825 by the Sioux, Winnebago, Chippewa, Menominee, Potawatomi, Sauk and Fox, and Iowa tribes, young Mahaskah became dissatisfied with the boundaries established by Michigan's Governor Lewis Cass and General William Clark and the sale of lead mines by the Sauk and Fox.

In an interview with Clark in St. Louis he pointed out that while the mines were jointly held by both the Iowa and Sauk and Fox, the United States had failed to make any payment to his people. Clark agreed there was justice in his claim but informed Mahaskah that there was no money to send him to Washington.

The Iowa financed their chief's trip to the capital by selling a winter's catch of furs. In Washington, Colonel McKenney brought Mahaskah to the White House where "he told, in his own simple but eloquent style, the story of his wrongs, and claimed the interposition of the Government."

President Jackson, Secretary of War, and members of congress all listened to the Iowa with sympathy and promised that "his business should be attended to. . . " Then they gave him an Indian peace medal along with a tour of the city for ten days and sent him back to the wilderness—at his own expense. Nothing, of course, was ever done about the boundary question or the payment for the lead mines.

Ten years later in the winter of 1837 Mahaskah was back in Washington, this time with a letter from Clark to President Jackson. McKenney had been ousted from office by Jackson seven years before, but now his famous portfolio was published.

An agent for the book met Mahaskah at the studio of Charles Bird King, who was painting the Iowa's portrait and showed him the stunning plates.

Mahaskah slowly turned the pages, pronouncing the names of the great chiefs "as if the originals had been alive and before him." Suddenly there was the portrait of his father. He stared at it with stoical indifference.

"Are you not glad to see your father's portrait?" he was asked.

"It is enough for me to know that my father was a brave man, and had a big heart, and died an honourable death" was his simple, dignified reply.

Mahaskah accompanied Catlin to London in 1843–1844 when the artist was exhibiting his famous Indian Gallery. The chief and fourteen of his braves performed "ten dances, two songs, and one 'Farewell song and dance'" for the spectators who paid one shilling (children half price) and packed the Music Hall on George Street, Edinburgh.

Catlin claimed that "the Ioway Indians were visited by nearly 3000 persons one evening, in the Town Hall, Birmingham." Mahaskah was described by Catlin as "the head chief" of the Iowa. While in Paris, Catlin was commissioned by the king of France to do several portraits of the Indians, including Mahaskah's. They were presented to Louis Philippe at the Tuileries.

Painter: Charles Bird King, Washington, 1837.

Mahaskah the Younger

Shauhaunapotinia, or the Man Who Killed Three Sioux

THE STORY of this Iowa chief is the Indian Damon and Pythias tale of the frontier of the 1830s.

The friendship of two young Iowa or Sioux boys was traditional. As one early ethnologist wrote: "Scarcely a Dakota [Sioux] young man could be found who had not some special friend or *koda*. This was an arrangement of giving themselves to each other, of the David and Jonathan kind. They exchanged bows, or guns, or blankets... what one asked of the other he gave him; nothing could be denied."

When he was a young boy Shauhaunapotinia found his *koda* in his own village. They hunted together, played games together, and dreamed together of the great days to come when they would go on horse-stealing raids among the Pawnee or fight the Sioux or the savage Osage in the north.

They were in their teens when Shauhaunapotinia's friend was killed and scalped. The grief-stricken young brave blackened his face in mourning and after a long fast slipped out of the village.

He trailed the Sioux raiders for over a hundred miles before he found their village in a deep valley. Shauhaunapotinia painted himself and his pony for war, then, leaning far over the side of his horse's neck, he rode into the village at top speed. The Sioux, who probably thought it was a young boy playing war, ignored him. The Iowa brave slipped off his horse onto the back of a Sioux warrior sitting outside his lodge. Before the alarm was sounded he had taken the Sioux's scalp, and then rode to the outskirts of the village where he killed two more.

Personal bravery above everything else was the ruling passion of every Indian nation, and Shauhaunapotinia's solitary raid made him a warrior of distinction. The council of his people selected him to be a member of the Iowa delegation who visited Washington in the winter of 1836–1837.

Painter: Charles Bird King, Washington, 1836.

Shauhaunapotinia

Moanahonga, or Great Walker

N THE year 1824, Indian agents, interpreters, trappers, and traders who entered the land of the Iowa in the vicinity of the Skunk River where it enters the Mississippi in southeastern Iowa were startled by a chief whose face was painted totally black.

When he was asked the reason for this traditional symbol of mourning, Moanahonga, chief of the Iowa, would always reply:

"I am ashamed to look upon the sun. I have insulted the Great Spirit by selling the bones of my fathers—it is right that I should mourn."

Moanahonga, or Great Walker, known to the frontier of his time as Big Neck, was referring to the council of 1824 held in Washington when he had ceded all the lands of his people within Missouri for an annuity of five hundred dollars and some other paltry considerations.

Big Neck told McKenney that he was stunned when he returned to his country to find it overrun with white settlers. When he demanded that they leave he was told that he had sold his country.

It was the familiar bitter story of the Indian's trust and innocence in contrast to the white man's cupidity, avarice, and lack of humanity.

Big Neck traveled to St. Louis to plead his case before General Clark, but Flaming Hair sadly told him there was nothing he could do—he had signed the treaty and accepted the Judas gift of five hundred dollars in gold.

Tragedy continued to stalk Big Neck and his people.

After a confrontation in 1829 with some squatters a militia force marched on Big Neck's village. Scouts warned him and rather than risk a shooting war he moved his people upriver. The militia commander, believing he had the Indians on the run, followed the easy trail and surrounded the Indian camp.

Big Neck came out of his lodge, his peace pipe held high. The commander gave the order to fire and a fusillade swept the circle of tepees, killing Big Neck's younger brother, his sister, some women, and a small child.

The outraged chief led his warriors in a counterattack, scattering the militia in wild retreat.

The militiamen spread the alarm to the settlements, and for a time it was feared that a border war would erupt. In St. Louis, Clark sent a company of regulars from Fort Leavenworth, and the Missouri governor ordered additional troops sent upriver in a chartered steamboat.

Big Neck skillfully escaped through several traps and the frustrated army returned to St. Louis. Then Clark ordered the Indian agent to find Big Neck and deliver a personal plea to surrender and be judged by the white man's court.

The Indian-wise agent waited until dawn to slip into Big Neck's lodge. As Colonel McKenney pointed out:

"Here he was safe; for, in accordance with the Indian practice, no outrage is ever permitted upon any person, though an enemy, who takes refuge within a lodge; no blood is allowed to stain the ground within its precincts."

Big Neck listened to the agent's arguments and agreed to obey Clark.

"I'll go with you," he was quoted as saying, "a brave man dies but once—cowards are always dying."

Big Neck, another Iowa chief and four warriors were later tried for murder in Randolph County, Missouri, where the battle with the militia had taken place.

In an extraordinary display of frontier justice "the jury, without leaving their box, brought in a verdict of *Not guilty*."

McKenney called Great Walker "a man sound in council and brave in battle.... He has heard the war-whoops and his war club, with its delicately touched point, has not been carried for show."

Painter: Charles Bird King, Washington, 1824.

Moanahonga

Notchimine, or No Heart

NOTHING MATTERED to this Iowa warrior, as he told Colonel McKenney, but waging war, killing one's enemies, stealing their horses, and taking prisoners. His skill and ruthlessness in battle and the contempt with which he viewed life, his own or his enemy's, had gained him his name.

He was fifteen and a veteran of the tribal wars of the plains when he joined a large war party led by his brother White Cloud, an important war captain in the Iowa nation. Notchimine (or Nacheninga, No Heart of Fear) had no horse of his own so he rode double behind his brother.

At dawn they swept into a Sioux village from all sides. When White Cloud leaped from his horse to chase some prisoners, Notchimine took command of the raiders. Before the surprised Sioux could make a stand the Iowa had killed several and driven off their herd of horses.

A later raid on the Osage was not so successful. The weary, disgruntled Iowa were returning home without scalps or prisoners to what they knew would be the taunts and jeers of the women and the elders of their villages, when they came upon the camp of a few Kansa (a Siouan tribe living northwest of the Osage on the Kansas River). White Cloud ordered an attack, and the Kansa braves and their families were killed and scalped.

Notchimine worshiped war. No raiding party was too small, he told McKenney, he joined them all. He soon became a living legend and women sang songs about his greatest raid, a solitary strike at an Osage village. He returned with three scalps and fifty-six ponies.

In his oral autobiography that he gave to Colonel McKenney through an interpreter, the Iowa warrior emphasized the importance of dreams in waging war.

"Previous to going out as leader of a [war] party," McKenney wrote, "he dreamed of taking two prisoners; in the event, one of the enemy was taken, and one killed, which he deemed a sufficient fulfilment." Dreams were so important, Notchimine told McKenney, that war chiefs frequently tried to mold events within the structure of their dreams.

In 1836, when he was thirty-eight, Notchimine grew weary of war and bloodletting and visited the Osage with a peace proposal. He was a hated but respected enemy so the Osage called a council and listened to his proposals. His offer was refused. It was now either a choice of continuing to fight or seeking new ways to promote peace. The Iowa chose the latter.

The following spring with the approval of his people he journeyed to St. Louis to ask General William Clark to arrange a peace between the two tribes. Clark failed but agreed that Notchimine should go to Washington to seek the aid and advice of the Great Father. In 1837, a treaty was finally hammered out between representatives of the Osage and the Iowa and signed in the War Department.

As the Iowa calmly smoked his pipe and the interpreter translated, McKenney took notes of the endless recital of bloody raids, scalping, killing of helpless prisoners, and stealing horses. By now, after all his years of close association with the tribes, the deadly ritual of primitive survival on the plains was all too familiar to McKenney. He wrote:

"His brief history . . . adds another . . . of the sameness of the tenor of an Indian warrior's life. Whatever may have been his vicissitudes, his joys or his sorrows, he tells only of his warlike exploits."

Painter: Charles Bird King, Washington, 1837.

Notchimine

Neomonni

HIS IOWA chief was one of the four leaders of his nation who signed a treaty with the United States on November 23, 1837. Article three of the agreement appeared to have been a singular victory for the Indians; the expenses of negotiating the treaty had to be paid by the United States.

It was the government's rule that expenses for Indian delegations traveling from the western lands to Washington had to be paid by the Indians themselves out of their annuity—unless the government was looking for more land.

Neomonni, or the Cloud out of Which the Rain Comes, was "a warrior of repute" according to Colonel McKenney. In an interview with the Indian superintendent the Iowa chief boasted of his score of war: "three scalps of the Kansas, two of the Omahas, one of the Missouris, one of the Sioux, one of the Sauks and two of the Osages."

His fellow chiefs agreed he had an enviable record for horse thievery, an honorable profession for any Indian tribe of the 1830s. He had either led or joined thirteen horse raids and had brought back sixty-seven war ponies to his village. He had also been the war captain of four "expeditions," and counted among his loot twenty rifles that he distributed among the poorer warriors and old men.

After the interview McKenney, then out of office, showed Neomonni the first edition of his portfolio. The Iowa chief watched impassively as McKenney turned the pages. Suddenly Neomonni pointed to a painting of Shaumonekusse, or L'Ietan. Then he said something to the interpreter who explained to McKenney that Neomonni had recognized the famous Oto chief and recalled how they had explored the River Platte when they were young warriors.

It is believed Neomonni was one of the Iowa chiefs who accompanied Catlin to Europe in 1843.

Painter: Charles Bird King, Washington, 1837.

Neomonni

Tahrohon

I N THE early eighteenth century nothing linked Indian to Indian like the frequent clash of arms. War was a necessity that not only proved manhood but freed the warrior from the drudgery of survival in his primitive society of battling and trying to outguess the weather, the buffalo, his enemies, even his allies.

Like the majority of Indian warriors and chiefs Colonel McKenney interviewed during his sixteen years as Indian superintendent, Tahrohon's story was an endless recital of war parties, horse raids, and the taking of scalps and prisoners. But behind this stoic dark mask McKenney caught a glimpse of humor; here was one Indian who could mock the sacred game of war.

He told one anecdote about when he joined a large war party; Sioux scalps, prisoners, and horses were their targets. Game was unusually scarce on the plains, and they had no food for the two days it took to reach the Sioux village.

They sat like cats in the grass all night; just before the first light Tahrohon was sent in as a scout. The first thing he saw was a buffalo haunch hanging from a pole outside a lodge. He was about to cut down the meat when he caught a glimpse of what appeared in the dim light to be two buckskin sacks filled with meal or corn. With his mouth watering he threw the meat over his shoulder, crawled through the grass and picked up the sacks. They seemed heavy, so quietly but firmly he pulled them toward him, only to discover that instead of sacks of food they were buckskin leggings of an old woman. Tahrohon rolled back into the grass, but the old woman just grunted and started to snore.

On another raid he and some young bucks discovered the trail of a Sioux warrior bringing water to his village. In their eagerness to take a scalp they pursued the warrior to the very edge of the village. Tahrohon had just raised his rifle when his companions shouted a warning. He looked up to see their own war party sweeping over a hill and thundering down on the Sioux village from all directions.

As Tahrohon told McKenney, clouds of dust and smoke from the rifle fire made anyone on foot an enemy. He and his companions spent a good part of the battle dodging arrows and swishing war clubs of both sides before they could reach some horses and join their chief.

Painter: Charles Bird King, Washington, 1837.

Tahrohon

Watchemonne, or the Orator

E WAS more a man of peace than of war, this Iowa boasted to Colonel McKenney.

His proudest moment, he told the Indian superintendent, was what his people called *"the beginning of his making presents."* It took place when a Sauk and Fox war party killed two Iowa warriors. Both nations were prepared to declare war but the Orator insisted that the chiefs of both sides sit and smoke a pipe before the first shots were fired. Acting as an arbitrator he arranged for the Sauk and Fox to compensate the families of the dead men with blankets, horses, and a keg of whiskey. Peace was restored.

Some time later some young Iowa stole four horses from white settlers. For the Indians this was dangerous; the whites could use it as a provocation to start a war, or it could bring the dreaded Dragoons from Jefferson Barracks in St. Louis who would rather kill an Indian than talk to him.

Watchemonne called a council and the warriors were ordered to return the horses. The young warriors defied the chiefs and insisted that they would fight if the white men attempted to recover their property.

Rather than risk a split within his nation, Watchemonne bought the horses and returned them to their owners. McKenney wrote: "This act gained him great credit among the people of the border, who have ever since treated him with confidence and spoken in his praise."

When McKenney tried to trace the history of the Iowa through Watchemonne the chief told him that the memory of the oldest men went back to when "they crossed that lake"—Lake Pepin between Minnesota and Wisconsin.

His father, who had learned the story through eight preceding ancestors, insisted that they had lived on the shores of the lake until they were divided into the Winnebago, Omaha, Missouri, and Iowa tribes because "it was the will of the Great Spirit that they should not be stationary, but travel from place to place, cultivating different ground . . . they will only continue to have good crops and healthy children so long as they obey this law of their nature."

Watchemonne also revealed to McKenney that the heart of the nation was locked inside a sacred medicine bag stored inside a lodge, which had its flaps always fastened and which no woman was allowed to enter.

Ethnologists believe the traditional evidence that the so-called Chiwere tribes, Oto, Iowa, and Missouri, had departed from the Winnebago and drifted westward to the Missouri River country.

At the time Watchemonne was in Washington the Iowa were still mourning the death of White Cloud, four years before. Watchemonne was overjoyed when McKenney gave him a lithograph of the favorite chief's portrait. The Indian superintendent boasted: "He declared [it] to be an excellent likeness."

When the portrait reached the Iowa village the people who had never seen an illustration or a painting were so stunned at the likeness of their chief that "they could not bear to look at it."

Painter: Charles Bird King, Washington, 1838.

Watchemonne

Tishcohan, or He Who Never Blackens Himself

COLONIAL historian tells us that at the time he signed the Walking Purchase this Delaware chief was about fifty years old with a "Roman nose, a large mouth, and several deep wrinkles reaching nearly across his forehead ...of a stout muscular frame...and (what is singular for an Indian) has a bunch of hair growing from his under lip and chin."

When he posed for the Swedish artist Hesselius, who had been commissioned by the Penns to do the portrait, Tishcohan wore a blue blanket wrapped about him with a squirrel-skin pouch hanging about his neck, "in which is stuck a Plaster-of-Paris pipe, proving it to be his tobacco-pouch, and that he was a consumer of 'the weed.' His hair is so long as to be gathered together on the back of his head."

The chief was outraged by the Quaker's method of measuring land. Eight weeks after the walk he told Edward Marshall, one of the swift walkers, that the Delaware "were dissatisfied with the Walk, and that they would go down to Philadelphia the next May, with every one a buckskin, to repay the proprietor for what they had received from him and take their land again."

In Philadelphia, the Quakers told the Delaware to keep the buckskins—the land covered in the Walking Purchase now belonged to the white men.

The disgusted Delaware left Pennsylvania and in the summer of 1758 he was reported living on the Ohio.

The Delaware called themselves *Leni-lenápe*, or "real men," "native, genuine men" but to their conquerors, the Iroquois, they were "women."

After the Walking Purchase, an Onondaga chief denounced the Delaware for selling their land:

"How came you to take upon you to sell Lands at all? We conquered you; we made Women of you: You know you are Women, and can no more sell Land than Women; nor is it fit you should have the Power of selling Lands, since you would abuse it."

The portrait of the Delaware chief measures 24 by 32 inches and was copied for McKenney by permission of the Pennsylvania Historical Society, probably in the 1830s.

Painter: Gustavus Hesselius, Philadelphia, about 1735.

Tishcohan

Lappawinze

ONE OF the more outrageous schemes of white men to defraud Indians of their land was the celebrated Pennsylvania "Walking Purchase." The treaty was signed in Philadelphia on August 1737 in the presence of Thomas Penn, William's son, and witnessed by fourteen whites and twelve Indians. The interpreter at the council had the marvelous name of Barefoot Brinston.

The treaty gave the proprietaries of Pennsylvania all lands "doth extend itself back into the Woods as far as a Man can goe in one day and a half, and bounded on the Westerly Side with the Creek called Neshameny, on the most Westerly branch thereof, so far as the said Branch doth extend, and from thence by line to the utmost extent of the said one day and a half's Journey, and from thence to the aforesaid River Delaware, . . ."

Penn's walkers covered a great deal of ground in that day and a half. Twenty years later one of the walkers claimed that "the walk was performed at such speed...by Edward Marshall, that Solomon Jennings and James Yates, who were selected . . . by the proprietary party, were compelled to succumb before the termination of it, having made, according to the testimony of several of the witnesses present, *the first thirty miles in six hours.*"

Lappawinze and his fellow chiefs were shocked; they had expected the white men to honor the old Indian tradition of pacing out land with great "deliberation, and to rest and smoke by the way..."

Marshall, the swift one, camped the first night of the historic walk near Lappawinze's village. In the morning Marshall asked for some Indians to accompany him. The chief's reply was beautifully comic edged with the tragic and the pathetic:

"They had got all the best of the land, and they might go to the Devil for the bad, and that he would send no Indians with them."

The portrait of Lappawinze was presented to the Historical Society of Pennsylvania by Granville Penn, son of Thomas Penn, during a visit to Philadelphia in 1834. An early historian claimed the "Penn accounts" attributed the portrait to a Swedish artist named Hesselius (McKenney spelled it Cecilius) who had been commissioned by either John or Thomas Penn.

The portrait was painted about two years before the Walking Purchase. Lappawinze was then described as a "stout Indian of about forty years of age. A few black marks are painted on his forehead and cheeks. His hair is long and brought to the back of his head, with a blue blanket thrown around him, and a pouch . . . fastened to his neck."

Many years later a white man who visited the chief reported he had asked him how he felt and the Delaware replied:

"No sit down to smoke, no shoot a squirrel, but *lun, lun, lun,* all day long." The white visitor added: "By this it would appear as if he had been pretty well on in years."

James Logan, secretary to William Penn and the author of numerous scholarly books including a translation of Cicero's *De Senectute* with notes and a preface by Benjamin Franklin, knew the Delaware and called him "an honest old Indian."

Painter: Gustavus Hesselius, Philadelphia, about 1735.

Metea

Wabaunsee

IN GREENVILLE, OHIO, a famous council was held in July 1814, in which the "western" tribes agreed to support the United States against Great Britain. One of the signers was Wabaunsee, an influential Potawatomi war chief who lived on the Kankakee River in Illinois, now Kankakee County, Illinois, about forty miles southwest of Lake Michigan.

Wabaunsee later told Colonel McKenney that he buried the tomahawk forever, in the Indian phrase, on the day he "took the Seventeen Fires by the hand. . . ."

In 1826, he signed the treaty of the Wabash in Indiana, in which he sold the Potawatomi lands to the United States. It was almost a fatal day for Wabaunsee. Whiskey had obviously helped the Indian commissioners persuade the chiefs to sign with the usual disastrous results; Indian turned on Indian and the chief was stabbed. Agent Thomas Tipton, who told McKenney the story, cared for Wabaunsee and he survived.

Ironically, the agent now had a serious problem; the warrior who had stabbed the chief was in hiding, but it was expected that Wabaunsee would seek him out and kill him. Interpreters had warned Tipton that the warrior was popular and his death could bring on a tribal feud.

In the spring when the chief came to the trading post to thank Tipton, the agent begged him to forgive and forget. Wabaunsee grasped Tipton's hand and told him that because he owed him his life, he could "send to him [the warrior] and tell him to come back. A man that will run off like a dog with his tail down for fear of death, is not worth killing. I will not hurt him."

In 1828, Governor Lewis Cass arranged a treaty with Wabaunsee and his chiefs on the shores of Lake Michigan. A few days before the formal signing Cass heard that one of the chiefs intended to denounce the treaty unless he was given a bribe.

When Cass told Wabaunsee the chief was indignant.

"An Indian, who will lie, is not worthy to be called a brave. He is not fit to live. If he refuses to sanction what we agreed to in council, I'll cut his heart out."

As Cass later told McKenney, he and his commissioners had a great deal of difficulty in preventing the chief from "putting his threat into execution."

When Black Hawk began his frontier war, the War Department feared Wabaunsee would lead his warriors to the side of the Sauk and Fox chief; instead Wabaunsee joined the border militia. The following year he told his people that they were now surrounded on all sides by the whites and urged them to accept lands beyond the Mississippi offered to them by the United States. The council agreed, and in 1835 Wabaunsee visited Washington to take "his Great Father by the hand" and sign a treaty by which his nation agreed to be removed from their ancestral lands to a new home near Council Bluffs on the Missouri.

Painter: Charles Bird King, Washington, 1835.

Wabaunsee

Shahaka, or Big White

APTAINS MERIWETHER LEWIS and William Clark first met Shahaka (they usually called him Gros Blanc or Big White in their journals) when they reached the Mandan villages of Metutahanke and Ruptari on opposite sides of the Missouri River about four miles below the mouth of the Knife River in present-day North Dakota.

On October 30, 1804, they hung Thomas Jefferson's medal about his neck after having distributed the Great Father's gifts of medals, flags, cocked hats, and a steel corn mill. The Mandan pulled this apart to use the iron for arrow barbs.

Big White (She-he-ke, coyote) was chief of Metutahanke, or the "lower" Mandan village. The explorers were surprised to find an Indian who could have passed for a suntanned white man. He was not a distinguished warrior nor a skillful diplomat, but rather a jovial fat man with one major fault: he talked too much, "a fault much despised amongest the Indians."

That winter at Fort Mandan, Lewis and Clark saw a great deal of Big White. He accompanied them on buffalo hunting trips, once casually packing a hundred pounds of "very fine meat" on the back of his squaw, Yellow Corn. During the long bitterly cold nights he also helped Clark complete his western map. In August 1806, when Lewis and Clark returned from the Pacific, they persuaded Big White to accompany them to Washington to see President Jefferson. The Mandan chief agreed but only on the condition one of his squaws and his only son, along with René Jessaume the interpreter, his wife, and his two sons, were included in the party.

Lewis's first letter from St. Louis to Jefferson informed the President they were returning "with the principal chief of the Mandans who is now with my worthy friend and colleague, Capt. C, in good health and spirits...."

A few days after Christmas, Lewis brought Big White, his wife, and son to Washington. They saw the White House, walked down Pennsylvania Avenue, "straight as a gun barrel," and attended a glittering dinner held in Lewis's honor. On December 30, 1806, the Mandan chief finally shook Jefferson's hand.

Shahaka and his family spent most of the winter in Washington, but also made side trips to eastern cities where he was exhibited as a typical savage from the wild western lands. In Philadelphia his portrait was painted by Charles Balthasar Julien Fevret de Saint-Mémin, the French artist, who used a device called a physionotrace. The profile shows Big White as a chubby, black-haired man, wearing silver pendants and a fur trimmed robe. Saint-Mémin also did a crayon portrait of Lewis and several Osage.

Shahaka was the most patient of Indians. The jovial chief cheerfully played the role of the wild savage from the West when he was taken on the tours; his only request was the simple question of when would they return home? The white man's answer was usually vague. It wasn't until March when Lewis was appointed governor of upper Louisiana and Clark superintendent of Indian tribes of the West, that plans were finally made to get Big White, his family, and that of the interpreter Jessaume to St. Louis in time to catch the first trading party moving upriver after the Missouri's ice had broken up.

In May, escorted by two noncommissioned officers and eleven privates under Ensign Nathaniel Pryor, a former member of the Lewis and Clark expedition, they started up the Missouri.

The river was busy that summer; also making the trip were three other parties, a delegation of twenty-four Sioux guarded by a special escort and two trading outfits, one under Colonel McKenney's old friend Pierre Chouteau, who was opening trade with the Mandan.

The expedition moved slowly upriver, the spring sun sparkling on the water, the chants of the crews echoing along the wooded shoreline. One can imagine Shahaka, his wife and son sitting on the bales and boxes in the bow, drinking in the crisp clean air so different from the white man's cities, whispering excitedly among themselves as they spotted familiar landmarks.

It was not until September 9 that they reached the Mandan villages only to be attacked by the hostile Arikara. There was only one thing left to do, retreat down the river to St. Louis. Shahaka and his family stayed in the city until the fall of 1808 when the Missouri Fur Company finally delivered the families back upriver at a cost to the government of seven thousand dollars.

Shahaka

Shahaka's cocked hat, his "fine dunghill cock," his medals, knives, trinkets, and ornaments failed to impress his people. They scoffed at his tales of the white man's cities and told their chief he had been bewitched. Shahaka was a great storyteller, but soon he had no audiences. As one chief informed H. M. Brackenridge, author of *Journal of a Voyage up the Missouri Performed in 1811*, Shahaka was "a Bag of Lies."

Shahaka's portrait was not included in McKenney's Indian Gallery. However, he obtained permission from the American Philosophical Society, owners of the painting, to have a copy made.

Painter: Charles Balthasar Julien Fevret de Saint-Mémin, Philadelphia, 1806.

Pushmataha

HE TIME, the early 1800s; the place, the home of Peter P. Pitchlynn, a wealthy Indian trader, friend of Charles Dickens, congressmen, senators, governors, and cabinet members. It was the fourth and last day of a long council with the Choctaw. An elaborate dinner had been given by Pitchlynn in honor of American Independence Day and Pushmataha, the celebrated Choctaw chief, had been invited. A great deal of wine and whiskey was consumed, and when it came time for the guests to leave Pitchlynn discovered Pushmataha had no horse. As a frontier newspaper depicted the scene, the trader ordered a groom to bring one to the front of the big house.

"Pushmataha, my brother," the trader said solemnly, "I give you this horse as a present on the condition you do not sell it for whiskey."

The Choctaw chief, then about sixty, drew himself up and with a great deal of dignity promised he would never part with this fine animal for any part of a whiskey jug.

A few weeks later he arrived at the trading post, but this time he was walking.

The local agent was indignant.

"But did you not promise Mr. Pitchlynn that you would not sell his horse?"

The Choctaw nodded. "I did so, in the presence of yourself and many others."

"Well, then, where is the horse?" the agent demanded.

Pushmataha shrugged. "I did not promise that I would not risk the horse on a game of ball."

His Indian logic was repeated in the War of 1812 when the Choctaw fought under Jackson, who described the chief as the greatest and bravest Indian he had ever known.

A general found Pushmataha hitting a warrior with the flat of his sword. When he asked the Choctaw why he was administering the beating, Pushmataha replied that the warrior had been rude to his wife and he was teaching him better manners.

As Pushmataha said: "But if it had been you, general, instead of a private soldier, I should have used the sharp edge of my sword . . ."

Later, while touring the camp with the general, Pushmataha saw a soldier tied to a wagon wheel. When he asked the reason he was told the soldier had been found intoxicated.

"Is that all?" Pushmataha asked in amazement. "Many good warriors get drunk."

One day at a council the Indian agent asked the Choctaw chief how many wives he had. Pushmataha said two.

"Don't you think this is a bad practice, my brother?" the agent asked.

Pushmataha stared at him in disbelief.

"Brother, I say this," he replied after a long pause, "Is it not right that every woman should be married—and how can that be, when there are more women than men, unless some men marry more than one? When our Great Father the President caused the Indians to be counted last year, it was found that the women were most numerous, and if one man could have but one wife, some women would have no husband."

Pushmataha

In 1824, Pushmataha led a delegation to Washington where he was received by the President, the secretary of war, and members of the cabinet. Lafayette, touring the nation, was in the capital at the time and met Pushmataha. The Choctaw faced the old soldier and made a brief speech, reviewing Lafayette's service to the United States.

"You see everywhere the children of those by whose side you went to battle crowding around you, and shaking your hand as the hand of a father. We have heard these things told in our distant villages, and our hearts longed to see you. We have come, we have taken you by the hand, and are satisfied. This is the first time we have seen you; it will probably be the last. We have no more to say. The earth will part us forever."

Pushmataha's words were prophetic. In a few days he was dead "of the croup" after a one-day illness at Tennison's Hotel on Pennsylvania Avenue.

An account in the *National Journal* of December 28, 1824, has Pushmataha predicting to his weeping braves that he would die "in the land of strangers." He then gave directions about his burial and whispered: "Let the big guns be fired over me." His wish was granted.

The account recalled his great boast that his hand was white. "It has never been stained by the blood of Americans. . . . I am an American. . . . My skin is red, but my heart is white."

Pushmataha was buried in the Congressional Cemetery with full military honors. His eulogy was given in the Senate by John Randolph of Roanoke.

Painter: Charles Bird King, Washington, 1824.

Mohongo

THREE YEARS of incredible adventures took Mohongo, the pretty Osage woman, from the upper Missouri in 1827 to New Orleans across the ocean to France, Holland, and Germany, then back to the United States to be greeted by the President and finally returned upriver to her village.

The villain of her strange odyssey was David Delaunay, described as a French adventurer who had fled his creditors by enlisting in the United States Army. In the 1820s he appeared in the Missouri River country and claimed to be a friend of the famous river trader Manuel Lisa and Indian Superintendent William Clark.

It can be assumed from later events that he was surely an adventurer, but it is doubtful if he was a friend of either Clark or Lisa; they would never have allowed him to take a party of seven Osage down the Mississippi on the steamboat *Commerce* to New Orleans to see the Great Father in Washington.

Even through the mists of time Delaunay appears to have been a fast-talking confidence man. Some legends picture him as dark and handsome with a flashing smile that charmed the ladies of St. Louis.

Somehow he gathered together Kihegashugah, or Little Chief, his wife Mohongo, Little Chief's cousin Grétomih, Washingsabba, or Black Spirit, Marcharthitahtoongah, or the Orator and a warrior called Minkchatahooh and brought them downriver. As Delaunay told the Indians through his interpreter M. Loise, they were first going to New York, then to Washington.

The party sailed from New Orleans and arrived at Le Havre on July 27, 1827. There Delaunay broke the news to the Osage: they were going on a weird roundabout journey to Washington by way of Europe.

Delaunay's purpose was to tour the Continent with a primitive Wild West show, featuring the Indians in their buckskins, knives, headdresses, moccasins, and paint. They were a sensation in Le Havre and later were a hit in Paris, "everywhere being the objects of marked attention and curiosity . . . showered with gifts, [and] entertained by people of prominence . . ." When Charles X heard about these colorful people from the American wilderness he ordered them brought to St. Cloud where they performed their dances before the royal court.

Mohongo

The tour continued through the provinces, later traveling across Holland and Germany. When the Osage patiently asked when they were going home or continuing on their journey to the Great Father, they were told it would be only a short time more.

There are two versions of the disastrous end of the show: one that Delaunay's creditors threw him into jail, the other that he ended the tour after the show had lost its popularity, then ruthlessly abandoned the Indians in Paris. The latter seems more logical.

The plight of the Osage in Paris was incredible. They wandered about the busy city clad in worn and tattered buckskins, unable to speak the language, and too proud to beg for food. Mohongo was also pregnant. Someone brought them to Lafayette who paid their return passage to the United States. But tragedy stalked the Osage: smallpox killed some of the party including Mohongo's husband.

The survivors landed at Norfolk, Virginia, where once again they became penniless wanderers. A kind stranger brought them to a boarding house where the landlady got in touch with the army who notified McKenney.

After three years of traveling about Europe as a curiosity, Mohongo and her child were finally received by the Great Father in 1830.

Painter: Charles Bird King, Washington, 1830.

Le Soldat du Chene, or Soldier of the Oak

THE SOLDIER of the Oak, as he was called on the frontier, was taken on a tour of eastern cities the summer of 1804 after he had visited President Jefferson at the White House and had his portrait painted in Philadelphia.

The Osage chief's portrait was presented to the American Philosophical Society in Philadelphia where McKenney found it and had a copy made for his Indian Gallery.

The Indian superintendent called the Soldier of the Oak "an Osage chief of high reputation," and Zebulon Pike and Major Stephen H. Long mention him in their journals. He signed several treaties between 1815 and 1835.

In the early nineteenth century the Osage claimed all the land in Missouri, Arkansas, Kansas, and the Indian territory. Year after year they were forced to yield vast tracts to the United States until 1870 when their last lands in Kansas were turned over to the government in exchange for a reservation in northeastern Indian territory (Oklahoma).

Interpreters told McKenney that the Osage chief won his name after a desperate battle in which he used a large oak tree as shelter to successfully fight off enemy raiders.

He was undoubtedly a member of the delegation of twelve Osage chiefs and two boys who met President Jefferson in 1804 and later visited New York, Philadelphia, and Baltimore.

Painter: Probably Charles Balthasar Julien Fevret de Saint-Mémin, Philadelphia, 1894.

Le Soldat du Chene

Stumanu

HE FLATHEAD warriors and their horses were inseparable. Riding bareback across the plains on a buffalo hunt they appeared welded together. They were also superb bronc busters who could tame the wildest mustang. In the 1830s a friend of Colonel McKenney, who knew the Flatheads, told him how Incilla, chief of the nation, broke his horses:

The chief threw himself upon the back of a wild horse recently taken, holding in one hand a small flag, and in the other a hoop covered with a skin, after the fashion of a tambourine. On being turned loose, the animal dashed off, rearing and pitching, and using the most violent exertions to disengage himself from his fearless rider, who, clinging with his heels, maintained his seat, in spite of the efforts of the horse to throw him. When he wished to check the speed of the animal, he blinded him by throwing the flag across his face; while he guided him, by striking him with the tambourine, on the one side or the other of the head. This exercise he continued, scouring the plain at full speed, and directing the course of the furious steed at will, until the latter was wearied out and subdued.

During McKenney's administration the Chinook, or Flatheads, inhabited the north side of the Columbia River, Washington. Lewis and Clark met them in 1805, but they had been known previously to fur trappers. They received their name from the custom of flattening the heads of their children by means of tying a board hinged at the top of the cradle against the infant's forehead.

Warriors who lived close to the mountains were excellent horsemen, while those along the rivers and near the Pacific Ocean were known as superb and fearless boatmen, skillful fishermen, and strong swimmers.

McKenney found the Flathead women had greater equality with the men than those in the plains or southern tribes. As expert fishermen and canoe makers "they share all the toils and dangers of the other sex, they naturally become the companions and equals, and in virtue of their superior industry, the *better* halves, of their lords and masters."

McKenney pointed out that because the principal occupations of the plains tribes were hunting and war, "a certain degree of contempt attaches to the weaker sex," but in the north country where both warriors and their women "contribute equally to the support of their families," a different relationship exists.

The Flatheads were usually nomadic, following the buffalo or fleeing from their enemies, the savage Blackfeet.

Stumanu, who lived on the Columbia, was an expert fisherman who, McKenney claimed, "would right his little vessel, when overturned, and pursue his voyage as if nothing had happened."

He was educated in the Indian school of Dr. John M'Loughlin, the "Father of Oregon," and taken on a tour of eastern cities by the Reverend Jason Lee, a noted missionary of the northwest frontier who had crossed the plains in 1834 with Nathan J. Wyeth's second expedition. Lee's hope was to raise money for his Indian mission school. Contributions totaled $42,000, but Stumanu was suddenly taken ill and died in New York City on May 29, 1839.

Painter: This portrait is not listed in the catalogue of government-owned Indian paintings compiled in 1859 by William J. Rhees. The artist is unknown.

Stumanu

Monchonsia, a Kansa Chief

THIS CHIEF may have been one of the sixteen Pawnee, Omaha, Kansa, Oto, and Missouri who visited the Great Father in the winter of 1821–1822, toured the city, and entertained thousands of spectators with a war dance in front of the White House.

In the 1820s the Kansa was a small Siouan tribe living northwest of the Osage on the Kansas River. The earliest recorded notice of the Kansa is by Juan de Onate who made a trip from St. Gabriel, New Mexico, in 1601 until he encountered the "Escansaques" in 1804. Lewis and Clark found them living in large earth lodges on the Kansas River. Raids by their traditional enemies, the Sauk and Fox, and Iowa, had greatly reduced their strength and numbers.

In 1822, Benjamin O'Fallon, McKenney's agent on the Missouri, estimated that the nation numbered about fifteen hundred men, women, and children. Three years later O'Fallon accompanied their chiefs to St. Louis where they signed a treaty with William Clark, relinquishing to the United States all claims they had to lands in north Kansas and southeast Nebraska. They retained a large tract of land on the Kansas River.

Before he left office in 1830 Colonel McKenney claimed that the Kansa totaled about twelve hundred warriors, women, and children, and had been under constant attack by the Pawnee. In 1873, their land was overrun by white settlers and once again they were forced to yield up their homes and move to Indian territory near their old allies, the Osage.

McKenney recalled Monchonsia as "a man respected by his tribe, cautious, fearless and brave."

Painter: Charles Bird King, Washington, 1821.

Monchonsia

Kanapima

HE STRANGE story of this Ottawa chief begins in 1829 in his village at L'Arbre Croche, or Wagankisi, near the lower end of Lake Michigan, when he was sixteen and his brother, the Blackbird, was fourteen.

A Catholic missionary, impressed with the intelligence of the boys, asked for permission to send them to a school in Cincinnati. The chiefs agreed and Kanapima and the Blackbird spent three years at a Catholic seminary.

It was the familiar story of wild Indian boys confined in a staid white man's school. Colonel McKenney recalled years later:

"They both exhibited much restlessness under the confinement of the school, and a decided fondness for the athletic exercises. They loved the open air; when the sun shone they could scarcely be restrained from wandering off to the romantic hills which surround this beautiful city; and when it rained, however hard, they delighted to throw off their upper garments and expose themselves to the falling showers."

The Catholic order, determined to form a group of Indian missionaries, prevailed on the chiefs to let them send the boys across the great sea to another white man's school. Again the chiefs gave their permission and in 1832 Kanapima and the Blackbird entered the Propaganda Fide in Rome. Kanapima was now named Augustin Hamelin, Jr., his brother Maccoda Binnasee.

Two more years passed. Kanapima became a promising scholar, but the Blackbird was terrified of the noisy city and the white people who spoke a strange tongue. He grew pale, listless, and refused to eat. The Order was planning to send the Blackbird back to his people when he died.

Kanapima buried his brother and returned home. Within a year he became chief of his nation "and resumed the costume and habits of his people."

He never completely severed his ties with the old teachers, and legend has him visiting classmates in Cincinnati, a tall, dignified copper-skinned man, dressed in buffalo robes, buckskin leggings, and beaded moccasins.

In the 1830s one of his former Cincinnati teachers, the Reverend Edward Purcell, published a long moving poem, "On the Death of Maccoda Binnasee, at Rome," which gained wide popularity.

On March 28, 1836, Kanapima came to Washington to sign the important treaty between the Ottawa and the United States in which his nation yielded up vast tracts of land. The Indian chief who could still write and speak Latin signed his name Augustin Hamelen, Jr.

Painter: McKenney gives the name of the artist as "Otis," who painted this portrait in Washington, 1835. He may have meant Bass Otis, who has been credited with producing America's first lithograph. McKenney identified Bass as the artist who copied F. Bartoli's portrait of Cornplanter for his portfolio.

Kanapima

Timpoochee Barnard

ENERAL ANDY JACKSON never forgot the bravery of Timpoochee Barnard in the Creek war of 1814 when the Yuchi chief led his band of warriors under heavy fire during the Battle of Callabee Creek (now Macon County, Alabama). Just before dawn the Creek had hurled human waves against the American forces to cut off Captain John Broadnix's post and pushed to within thirty yards of the cannons. Suddenly Timpoochee Barnard led his howling, painted braves in a wild charge against the Creek to enable Broadnix and his riflemen to fight their way out of the trap.

The Yuchi was severely wounded twice, and Broadnix later told how the Indian warrior, his body dripping blood, kept fighting until the Creek retreated, leaving their dead piled high on the shore.

When the Creek nation was reunited, "Major" Barnard was welcomed back to the agency on Flint River, Georgia, where he settled with his wife and six children.

In 1827, Colonel McKenney successfully negotiated a treaty with the Creek. Before he left the chiefs begged him to take two of their sons back to Washington to be educated in the white man's schools. One was William, son of Timpoochee Barnard.

The boys remained with McKenney for three years.

One day he brought them to the White House to meet the President. After they had been formally introduced Jackson stared down at William, the oldest.

"Young man, did I hear your name is William Barnard?"

The Indian boy looked up at him. "Yes sir."

"Are you the son by chance of Major Timpoochee Barnard?"

The boy nodded. "Yes sir."

Jackson placed his hand on the head of the boy, and said, "A braver man than your father never lived."

A few years later Jackson ousted McKenney from office and ordered the War Department to remove the Indian boys from school and return them to their people.

William, who had carried a President's praise back to his father, found it difficult to fit in with the life of the backwoods. He returned to school in the East where he fell in love with an attractive white girl. When her family refused to allow them to marry he committed suicide.

Shortly after his son's death Barnard insisted that his daughter marry a Creek chief who had two wives. As she told her father, the "degradation" of being a member of a backwoods harem was too much and she killed herself.

Painter: Charles Bird King, Washington, 1825.

Timpoochee Barnard

Nahetluchopie

COLONEL MC KENNEY called this chief a Muskogee, which meant he was a member of the Muskogean family, an important linguistic stock composed of the Choctaw, Creek, Chickasaw, Seminole, and other tribes.

The Muskogean tribes were confined to the gulf states east of the Mississippi, at one time occupying all of Mississippi, Alabama, and parts of Tennessee, Georgia, Florida, and South Carolina.

The savage and bloody Creek War of 1813–1814 and the twenty-year-old guerrilla campaign waged by the Seminole ended the struggles of the various tribes to remain in their homelands. By 1840, most of the Muskogean nations had been robbed, cheated, or forced to yield up their ancestral lands and move to the Indian territory.

Nahetluchopie (Little Doctor) told McKenney that the red spots on the costume he wore to Washington marked the bullet holes from an attempt on his life. The paint on his face "is commemorative of the same event, as the blood ran down from his nostrils and from his mouth." The men who tried to kill him, probably from a tribal feud over the Indian removal question which had split many Indian nations, had surprised him in his hut, the Muskogee told the Indian superintendent, shot him several times, and left him for dead.

Painter: Charles Bird King, Washington, 1825.

Nahetluchopie

Ongpatonga, or Big Elk

ONSIDER THE scene: a blazing hot day in July 1815 on the western plains. General William Clark, Indian superintendent from St. Louis, called Flaming Hair by the western nations; the celebrated Indian trader Auguste Chouteau; and two commissioners from Washington, Colonel John Miller and Ninian Edwards, are sitting around the flagpole, the American flag hanging in the stagnant heat like crumpled tin.

Behind them are the chiefs, feathered headdresses flowing to their knees and row after row of their warriors, the carefully combed scalps dangling from their coup sticks. The wailing women are now quiet; in their grief they had slashed their arms and legs with knives and the blood drips to the grass.

Before them on the traditional burial platform is the body of Black Buffalo, ancient chief of the Teton Sioux who had died suddenly at the conclusion of the great council called by the Americans at the Portage des Sioux. His favorite war pony, its throat cut, has been painted, and is now ready to take the dead chief on his last ride. One of his slaughtered dogs lies at his feet, so he can bark a welcome to the messenger of the Great Spirit.

Clark had ordered the small cannon fired in Black Buffalo's honor, and the dirty cloud of smoke still hangs in the shimmering air. Ongpatonga, orator of the Omaha, is about to give his funeral oration.

A tall, impressive man with a nose so prominent it reminded one trader of a mule's, the chief faces the council of silent mourners.

There were men present who would never forget his words. Some repeated them in later years for McKenney, but the English explorer John Bradbury, author of the fascinating *Travels in the Interior of North America in the years 1809, 1810, and 1811* published the Omaha's oration only two years after the council.

Do not grieve. Misfortunes will happen to the wisest and best of men. Death will come, and always comes out of season. It is the command of the Great Spirit and all nations and people must obey. What is past, and cannot be prevented, should not be grieved for. Be not discouraged nor displeased, that in visiting your father here, you have lost your chief. A misfortune of this kind, under such afflicting circumstances, may never again befall you; but this loss would have occurred to you perhaps at your own village. Five times have I visited this land, and never returned with sorrow or pain. Misfortunes do not flourish particularly in one path; they grow everywhere. How unhappy am I that I could not have died this day, instead of the chief that lies before us. The trifling loss my nation would have sustained in my death, would have been doubly repaid by the honours of such a burial. They would have wiped off everything like regret. Instead of being covered with a cloud of sorrow, my warriors would have felt the sunshine of joy in their hearts. To me it would have been a most glorious occurrence. Hereafter, when I die at home, instead of a noble grave, and a grand procession, the rolling music, and the thundering cannon, with a flag waving over my head, I shall be wrapped in a robe, and hoisted on a slender scaffold, exposed to the whistling winds, soon to be blown down to the earth—my flesh to be devoured by the wolves, and my bones trodden on the plain by wild beasts. Chief of the soldiers! (addressing Colonel Miller,) your care has not been bestowed in vain. Your attentions shall not be forgotten. My nation shall know the respect that our white friends pay to the dead. When I return I will echo the sound of your guns.

Ongpatonga came to Washington in 1821 with a delegation of his people to sign a treaty. At that time, McKenney recalled that the chief was "one of the few Indians who can tell his own age with accuracy." He was sixty-six.

Catlin painted Big Elk in 1833, and the chief returned for another visit to Washington four years later. He signed the Prairie du Chien treaty of 1830 and another six years later at Bellevue (Omaha), Nebraska. On each treaty his name was first, indicating his importance.

Painter: Charles Bird King, Washington, 1821.

Ongpatonga

Amiskquew

HE MENOMINEE were People of the Wild Rice, the Oat Eaters, as the early French explorers called them. They were first encountered by the white man in 1634 at the mouth of the Menominee and Fox rivers. Pike described them as "straight and middle sized, their complexions generally fair for savages, their teeth good, their eyes large and rather languishing. They have a mild but independent expression of countenance that charms at first sight."

The Menominee was not a warrior race and lived in peace with the powerful Chippewa and the Sioux; neighboring Algonkian tribes were their only enemies. They subsisted partly on wild rice, which they refused to sow rather than "wound their mother the earth."

McKenney called Amiskquew: "A well disposed man, and one that generally has a good blanket, leggings, etc. Nothing remarkable in his history."

Painter: Original by James Otto Lewis, Butte des Morts council, 1827, later copied in Washington by Charles Bird King.

Encampment of Piekann Indians

Buffalo Hunt

THIS PAINTING is the work of Peter Rindisbacher, a Swiss artist who lived at Lord Selkirk's Red River colony from 1821 to 1826 when he made a series of paintings, watercolors, and sketches of frontier life. About sixty-four of his paintings are known to exist. Some were lithographed during his lifetime and some were published in the *American Turf Register and Sporting Magazine* in the 1830s and *Burton's Gentleman's Magazine* of the 1840s as crude wood engravings.

On the whole, Rindisbacher's works are amateurish—he was only twenty in 1826. However, he was one of the earliest of western painters and his watercolor *Inside of a Skin Tent* dated 1824 may be the first illustration of a plains tepee, but, as Bernard DeVoto pointed out, "it looks like no tipi known to ethnology." Colonel McKenney used Rindisbacher's *Buffalo Hunt* as a frontispiece for one of his portfolios.

In describing early buffalo hunts that he had witnessed, Colonel McKenney told of a favorite trick the Indian hunters used when moving in on a vast buffalo herd.

Sometimes, having killed the prairie wolf, of which the buffalo has no fear, an Indian wraps himself in the skin, keeping the head in its proper position, and drags himself slowly towards the grazing herd, taking care to advance from the leeward, so that the watchful animal shall not scent his approach upon the tainted breeze. When the object is first seen, the buffaloes raise their heads, and eye it suspiciously, but the appearance of the wolf's head, with which they are familiar, re-assures them—nor are they undeceived until their wily foe darts his arrow into one of the fattest of the herd, with an aim so true that it is sure to pierce a vital part. Pitfalls and inclosures are also sometimes contrived. But, although these devices are practised, the number thus taken is inconsiderable; and the only mode of taking this noble prey [is] openly in the field. For this purpose most of the tribes who reside in the vicinity of the great plains resort to them, after having planted their corn in the spring, and spend the whole summer and autumn in the chase. As the buffaloes often change their pastures, and the laws which direct their migrations are but imperfectly known, the wanderings of the natives in search of them are often long and wearisome; hundreds of miles are sometimes traversed, by a way-worn and starving band, before they are gladdened by the sight of their favourite game. Sometimes they are mocked by discovering the footprints of a retreating herd, which they pursue for days with unavailing toil; not infrequently a hostile clan crosses their track, and they are obliged to diverge from their intended course; and sometimes, having reached a suitable hunting-ground, they find it preoccupied by those with whom they cannot safely mingle nor prudently contend.

At last the young men, who scout in advance of the main body, espy the black, slow moving mass wading in the rich pasture, and preparations are made for a grand hunt. An encampment is made at a spot affording fuel and water; the women erect lodges, and all is joy and bustle.... Horses and harness are inspected; weapons are put in order; the medicine men practise incantations; offerings are made to the Great Spirit; the solemnites of the dance are gone through; and the more superstitious of the warriors often impose upon themselves the austerities of fasting, wounding the body, and incessant prayer, during the night, or even a longer period, preceding the hunt. Duly prepared at length, they mount for the chase . . . and approach the herd cautiously from the leeward . . . each selects his prey . . . the hunter drops the bridle rein, fixes his arrow, and guiding his well-trained horse with his heel, and by the motion of his own body, watches his opportunity to let fly the weapon with fatal aim. This he does not do until his steed is abreast of the buffalo, and the vital part, immediately behind the shoulder, fairly presented ... Usually, therefore, the wound is fatal . . .

Buffalo Hunt

The Peabody Collection of the
Henry Inman Portraits

COLONEL THOMAS LORAINE MC KENNEY commissioned Henry Inman, the American artist, probably in the winter of 1832–33, to copy the Indian portraits which hung in his former office in the Bureau of Indian Affairs, Washington, D.C. The paintings were used for the superb lithographic reproductions in McKenney and Hall's famous *History of the Indian Tribes of North America*, published in Philadelphia in 1836.

Inman, who would become one of the nation's eminent portrait artists, was a founder of the National Academy of Design and its vice-president, when he moved from New York to Philadelphia where the former Indian superintendent and his wife were living in a Chestnut Street boardinghouse.[1]

Inman, who was also an excellent engraver, helped to establish the famous lithographic firm of Childs & Inman. Cephas G. Childs, a pioneering lithographer, had opened a small shop soon after Bass Lewis had published his famous landscape, generally recognized as America's first lithograph.

A craze for lithographs swept the country in the 1820s and 1830s until the birth of photography. Millions were produced to decorate the parlor walls of early American homes. Scores of publishing houses and printers worked feverishly to supply the demand but the lithographs produced by Childs & Inman were among the best.[2]

In 1836 to stimulate sales of the McKenney-Hall portfolio, Inman's portraits were placed on exhibition in Masonic Hall, Chestnut Street, a short distance from McKenney's boardinghouse. As McKenney wrote:

"Visitors to the Gallery will see on comparing the likeness of this Specimen No. with the portraits with what fidelity the portraits are lithographed. The portraits are by Inman, from the celebrated collection in the War Department in Washington, most of which were taken from life by [Charles Bird] King of that city."[3]

In addition to copying the portraits, Inman evidently also assisted Childs with engraving the lithographs on stone. In conjunction with Childs he prepared what may have been the first plate, Shingaba W'Ossin, for Volume I.

The portraits finally came into the possession of a Boston firm in partial payment of a debt for paper contracted by McKenney's publishers. In 1882 they were presented to the Peabody Museum of Archaeology and Ethnology, Harvard University, Cambridge, Massachusetts, by the heirs of Edmund P. Tileston and Amos Hollingsworth.[4]

---

[1] A biographical sketch with a catalog of the works of the late Henry Inman, an exhibition for the benefit of his widow, held at the Art-Union Rooms, 322 Broadway, New York City, 1846. The Boston Athenaeum Library, Boston.

[2] See *America on Stone* by Henry Peters, New York, 1931.

[3] Catalogue of One Hundred and Seventeen Indian Portraits, Representing Eighteen Tribes, by Colonel Thomas L. McKenney and James Hall, Philadelphia, 1836. New York Library.

[4] Main overall label of the McKenney-Hall Portrait Collection, Peabody Museum of Archaeology and Ethnology, Harvard University, Cambridge, Massachusetts; Report, Peabody Museum, 1884, Vol. III, pp. 189, 199 (additions to the museum).

Fox Warrior

Kee-me-one

John Stedman

Notes

CHAPTER I: McKENNEY'S GREAT DREAM

1. *Washington Daily Intelligencer*, Nov. 22, 1821; *Perley's Reminiscences* by Benjamin Perley Poore, Philadelphia, 1886, V. 1-42–62; McKenney to the Secretary of War, April 21, 1826, Bureau of Indian Affairs, letters sent hereafter BIA, LS.
2. "Expenses of the Choctaw Delegation while in Washington," 1825, BIA, letters received (hereafter LR), Choctaw Agency. See also *Indians and Pioneers* by Grant Foreman, Norman, Okla., 1930, pp. 158–59.
3. Margaret Bayard Smith, to J. Bayard Smith, Nov. 30, 1828, *The First Forty Years of Washington Society*, N.Y., 1906, p. 245; House Doc. 20 Cong. 2, No. 129, (Serial 286) pp. 4–5.
4. See McKenney's anecdotes in his *Catalogue*, NYPL. Rantche-wai-me, Female Flying Pigeon, was the youngest wife of Mahaskah, who was brought to Washington in 1824 by Governor William Clark.
5. See *Gazette of the United States*, March 24, 1792, v. 3, No: 95, whole no. 303, p. 379, C. 3. For a description of the visit of the Iroquois to Philadelphia, see the *Gazette*, April 4, 1792, v. 3, no. 98, Whole No. 306, p. 389 cols. 1-2.
6. McKenney to Madison, March 20, 1824, Library of Congress.
7. "Portraits, Presents and Peace Medals" by Herman J. Viola, American Scene, Vol. XI, no. 2, 1970.
8. "Charles Bird King, Painter of Indian Visitors to the Nation's Capital" by John C. Ewers, 19th Annual Report, Smithsonian Institution, 1953.
9. Charles Francis Adams (ed.), *Memoirs of John Quincy Adams, Comprising Portions of His Diary* from 1795 to 1848, 12 vols., Phila.
10. William Faux, *Faux's Memorable Days in America, 1819–1829*, reprinted in Reuben Gold Thwaites (ed.), *Early Western Travels* 1748–1846, Vol. XII, p. 51; *Philadelphia Gazette*, Feb. 11, 1822, *National Intelligencer*, March 7, 1822.
11. See the *Redwood Library Collection of Charles Bird King* copies of the McKenney-Hall portraits, sold at auction, May 21, 1970, Parke-Bernet Galleries, Inc.
12. Bernard DeVoto, *Across the Wide Missouri*, Houghton Mifflin, Boston, 1947, p. 399.
13. *Washington Daily National Intelligencer*, Feb. 16, 1822.

CHAPTER II: THE EARLY YEARS

1. See Introduction by Frederick Webb Hodge, 1933 Edition, *The Indian Tribes of North America, with Biographical Sketches and Anecdotes of the Principal Chiefs*. By Thomas Loraine McKenney and James Hall, Vol. 1, Edinburgh, John Grant. Hereafter cited as Hodge; McKenney to Thomas Forward, Nov. 3, 1841, Simon Gratz Collection, Historical Society of Pennsylvania.
2. Thomas L. McKenney, *Memoirs, Official and Personal; with Sketches of Travels Among the Northern and Southern Indians; . . . Embracing a War Excursion*, N.Y., 1846; Appendix I, pp. 311–12. Hereafter cited as *Memoirs*.
3. In his letter to Thomas Forward, McKenney describes his early business ventures. See also the affidavit from Edward C. Hall, (Affidavit "A," Appendix, p. 307) in his *Memoirs* which tells of his relationship with the Halls, Washington businessmen.

CHAPTER III: McKENNEY AND THE WAR OF 1812

1. In addition to the standard works on the War of 1812, I have based this chapter on the material contained in a series of pamphlets published and issued by both McKenney and Kos-

ciusko Armstrong, son of Secretary of War Armstrong. This battle of pamphlets began when McKenney discussed Armstrong's incompetence which led to the burning of Washington, in his *Memoirs*, published in 1846.

Armstrong's son retaliated with a pamphlet of his own, denouncing McKenney, and the publishing war went on for some time. Both authors exchanged massive broadsides of tortured rhetoric but some of the affidavits McKenney collected from his former fellow officers, including his commanding officer, General Walter Smith, reveal McKenney's activities in the Battle of Bladensburg: *Memoirs, Official and Personal; with Sketches of Travels Among the Northern and Southern Indians . . . Embracing a War Excursion . . . Plates*, 2 vols., N.Y., 1846, Vol. 1, pp. 43–48; *Narrative of the Battle of Bladensburg in a Letter to Henry V. Manning, Esq.*, n.p. *Reply to Kosciusko Armstrong's Assault on Colonel McKenney's Narrative of the Causes that led to General Armstrong's Resignation of Office of Secretary of War in 1814*, N.Y., 1847; *Examination of Thomas McKenney's Reply to the Review of his Narrative by Kosciusko Armstrong*, N.Y., 1947; Hodge, Vol. 1, viii.

CHAPTER IV: SUPERINTENDENT OF INDIAN TRIBES

1. *Memoirs*, Vol. 1, p. 3.
2. ibid., vol. 2, Appendix A, pp. 307–8.
3. "Prayer of Thomas Loraine McKenney, Good Friday, April 12, 1816," Huntington Library and Art Gallery, hereafter cited as Huntington.
4. Strouding is a coarse cloth or blanketing used in the early Indian trade.
5. *Memoirs*, vol. 1, p. 24.
6. Circular Letter to All Factories, Dec. 21, 1816, Office of Indian Trade, hereafter cited as OIT, LS. Huntington.
7. McKenney to Jacob Varnum, Factor, Chicago Factory, June 18, 1816, OIT, LS. William Clements Library, University of Michigan, hereafter cited as Clements.
8. ibid.
9. McKenney to Varnum, Jan. 22, 1817, OIT, LS; Circular Letter, Office of Indian Trade, Georgetown, July 22, 1817, OIT, LS, Clements.
10. Recorder of Deeds, Washington, D.C., Liber AP-40, 1817; Report of the Committee on the District of Columbia, Feb. 14, 1818, Sen. Doc., 20 Cong., 1 Sess. No. 103 (Serial 165) pp. 7-11.
11. Astor to Monroe, Jan. 10, 1821; Astor to Monroe, April 5, 1820, both from Paris, Monroe Papers, Manuscript Division, N.Y. Public Library; also Monroe to Madison, March 28, 1828, Madison Papers, Library of Congress, Monroe to Mc-Lean, Aug. 7, 1828, Monroe Papers, Library of Congress. See also *Lewis Cass: Indian Superintendent of the Michigan Territory, 1813–1831*—A Survey by R. W. Unger (dissertation), 1967, Muncie, Indiana, 1967, pp. 87–96.
12. Biography of Major Irwin, *The Fur Trade and Factory System at Green Bay, 1811–1821*, Wisconsin Historical Society, 1908, p. 269, hereafter cited as Irwin.
13. Irwin to McKenney, March 10, 1817, Irwin, p. 270.
14. McKenney to Irwin, May 28, 1817, Irwin, p. 271–72.
15. McKenney to Jacob Varnum, Aug. 3, 1818, Clements.
16. *Furs by Astor*, by John U. Terrell, N.Y., 1963, pp. 250–51. See also *John Jacob Astor: Business Man*, by Kenneth W. Porter, Cambridge, 1931.
17. Irwin to McKenney, Sept. 29, 1817, Irwin, pp. 273–75.
18. Irwin to McKenney, June 18, 1818, Irwin, pp. 275–76.
19. Irwin to McKenney, Aug. 10, 1818, Irwin, p. 276.
20. Irwin to McKenney, n.d., apparently 1819, Irwin, pp. 277–78.
21. Irwin to McKenney, Feb. 15, 1820, Irwin, pp. 278–79.

22. McKenney to Rev. Dr. Philip Milledoler, Aug. 3, 1821, Milledoler Papers, New-York Historical Society, hereafter cited as Milledoler.
23. ibid.
24. *Report to the Secretary of War on Indian Affairs*, by Jedidiah Morse, New Haven, 1822, hereafter cited as Morse.
25. ibid., p. 85.
26. Irwin, pp. 282–88.
27. ibid.
28. McKenney to (?) June 21, 1818, Clements.
29. David Folsom to McKenney, Oct. 1, 1818, Clements.
30. *Memoirs*, p. 191.
31. The affidavits McKenney gathered and later introduced in his defense during the congressional investigation of his administration of the Indian Trade Bureau can be found in his *Memoirs*, pp. 293–315, Appendix B to H. A comparison of McKenney's letters with what appeared in his book reveals he did not depart from the original.

CHAPTER V: THE GREAT QUESTION OF INDIAN REMOVAL

1. *The History of the Events Resulting in Indian Consolidation West of the Mississippi* by Harriet Abel. Annual Report, 1906, American History Association, 1908, Vol. 1, p. 241. Harriet Abel's article and Grant Foreman's books, based on his pioneering work in the National Archives and War Department files, are still the best studies on the complex, tragic question of Indian removal.
2. *Handbook of the American Indian North of Mexico*, by Frederick Webb Hodge, Vol. 2, p. 944; *Recollections of the Last Ten Years in the Valley of the Missouri*, by Timothy Flint, p. 155; *The Cherokee Nation*, by Charles P. Royce, pp. 200–10.
3. *American State Papers; Indian Affairs*, Vol. 1, p. 725.
4. Lovely to Madison, Sept. 1815, OIT, LR; Lovely to Meigs, Aug. 6, 1813, OIT, LR.
5. Governor Joseph J. McMinn, to the War Department, Nov. 11, 1817, OIT, LR; see also U.S. House Executive Doc. No. 136, 18 Cong., 1 Sess.
6. Miller to Calhoun, June 20, 1820, OIT, LR; *Louisiana Herald*, Jan. 6, 1821, *Indians and Pioneers*, By Grant Foreman, Norman, Okla., 1936, p. 77. Hereafter cited as Foreman. Miller was appointed governor of Arkansas Territory which included the present states of Arkansas and Oklahoma.

CHAPTER VI: THE BRAVEST OF THE BRAVE

1. *Life of Washington*, by Washington Irving, V, pp. 93–116.
2. ibid., p. 93.
3. There are any number of books on Brant and Butler's campaign in the Mohawk Valley during the Revolution; the standard work is William L. Stone's *Life of Brant*, 2 vols., hereafter cited as Stone; Francis W. Halsey, *The Old New York Frontier, Its Wars With Indians and Tories, Its Missionaries, Schools, Pioneers and Land Titles, 1614–1800*, N.Y., 1901; two books by J. R. Simms, *History of Schoharie County*, 8 vols., Albany, 1865, and his *Frontiersman*, Albany, 2 vols., Albany, 1873. The best biography of Walter Butler is *War Out of Niagara: Walter Butler and the Tory Rangers*, by Howard Swiggett, N.Y., 1933.
4. Extracts from *The Journal of Elizabeth Drinker*, Henry Biddle (ed.), n.d., p. 184.
5. Gazette of the United States, March 24, 1792.
6. *The Life and Times of Red Jacket*, by William L. Stone, N.Y., 1841, pp. 72–73; *Red Men Calling on the Great White Father*, by Katherine C. Turner, Norman, Okla., 1951, pp. 3–28.
7. *Handbook of the American Indians, Bureau of American Ethnology*, Vol. 2, Wash., 1910, p. 363.
8. *The Writings of George Washington*, (ed.) Jared Sparks, 12 vols. Boston, 1934, 1937, X, pp. 240–41.
9. Stone, Vol. 11, pp. 328–29.
10. *The Original Journals of Lewis and Clark*, (ed.) Milo M. Quaife, Publication of the State Historical Society of Wisconsin, Madison, 1916. Describe Big White's journey downriver and later to Washington. For an account of the visit of the Osage chiefs to Jefferson and their tour of the eastern cities, see *The National Intelligencer and Washington Adver-*

tiser, Oct. 12, 1804; *Baltimore American*, July 31, 1804; *New York Gazette and General Advertiser*, Aug. 16, 1804; The St.-Memim Indian Portrait by Luke Vincent Lockwood, New-York Historical Quarterly, vol. XII, 1928.
11. *The Writings of Thomas Jefferson*, (ed.) A. E. Bergh, 20 vols. Wash., 1903, XVI, pp. 412–17.
12. *Journal of a Voyage up the Missouri, Performed in 1811*, by H. H. Breckenridge, Baltimore, 1815, p. 178.
13. O'Fallon to Calhoun, April 5, 1821, OIT, LR.
14. *Daily National Intelligencer*, Nov. 22, 1821.
15. *Washington Gazette*, Jan. 2, 1822, Hodge, pp. 38–50; *Sketches of The History, Manners, and Customs of the North American Indians*, London, 1824, pp. 38–42.
16. *National Intelligencer*, Jan. 29, 1822.
17. ibid.
18. ibid.
19. *Metropolitan and Georgetown National Messenger*, Feb. 12, 1822.
20. ibid., March 2, 1822; McKenney and Hall, Vol. 1, p. 208.
21. "Charles Bird King, Painter of the Indian Visitors to the Nation's Capital," by John Ewers, Smithsonian Institution Annual Report, 1953, pp. 463–73; "Washington's First Museum, The Indian Office Collection of Thomas L. McKenney," by Herman J. Viola, Smithsonian Journal of History, Fall, 1968, pp. 1–18.

CHAPTER VII: McKENNEY AND THE RICHEST MAN IN AMERICA

1. McKenney to Henry Thompson, April 13, 1820, OIT, LS, Newberry Library, hereafter cited as Newberry.
2. *Memoirs, Official and Personal With Sketches of Travels Among the Northern and Southern Indians, Embracing a War*, by Thomas L. McKenney, 2 vols. in 1, New York, 1846, pp. 26–27, hereafter cited as *Memoirs*.
3. *The American Indian* by Thomas L. McKenney, sent to the American Board of Commissioners for Foreign Missionaries, Oct. 18, 1817, and published in *Portico*. See also the Calhoun Circular distributed Sept. 3, 1818, "Constitution of the Officers for the Protection of the General Welfare of The Indian Tribes in America" of which McKenney was the author. Library of Congress.
4. *American Indian Policy in the Formative Years* by Francis P. Prucha, Cambridge, 1963, p. 92n.
5. See also the series on the factory system published in the *Detroit Gazette*, Dec. 15–20, 1820. They were unsigned but were undoubtedly written by Governor Lewis Cass. Excellent studies on the factory system include *A History of the United States Indian Factory System* by Ora Peake, Denver, 1954, and *Sixty Years of Indian Affairs*, by George Harmon, Chapel Hill, 1941.
6. *Memoirs*, pp. 24–31.
7. *National Intelligencer*, April 22, 1822.
8. McKenney's statements, affidavits, etc., can be found in Appendix A, pp. 285–310, of his *Memoirs*. Also *House Journal*, Feb. 14, 1823, 17 Cong., 2 Sess. (Serial 75); Report of the Committee on Indian Affairs, March 1, 1823, House Doc., 17 Cong., 2 Sess., No. 104 (Serial 82).
9. McKenney to Irwin, July 5, 1821, pp. 280–82, Irwin; McKenney to Varnum, Feb. 22, 1822, Clements.
10. Crooks to Benton, April 1, 1823, Prucha, 92n; see also Thomas H. Benton, *Thirty Years View*, N.Y., 1854.

CHAPTER VIII: THE NEW SUPERINTENDENT

1. McKenney to Varnum, Sept. 13, 1824, OIT, LS, Clements.
2. McKenney to Madison, March 20, 1824, Madison Papers, Library of Congress. Hereafter cited as Madison.
3. Jefferson to McKenney, July 2, 1822, Jefferson Papers, Library of Congress.
4. *American Journalism* by Benjamin Mott, N.Y., 1950, has a brief mention of McKenney's editorship but a good account of the other Washington newspapers; Hodge, p. XI; the file of the *Washington Republican and Congressional Examiner*, New-York Historical Society and Library of Congress.
5. Calhoun to McKenney, March 10, 1824, Office of Secretary of War Unregistered Series, Letters Sent.
6. *Memoirs*, pp. 56–57.

7. William Chamberlain to McKenney, June 20, 1825, BIA, LR.
8. McKenney to Secretary of War Barbour, June 20, 1825, BIA, LS.
9. McKenney to William Clark, March 19, 1827, BIA, LS.
10. McKenney to John McIntosh, March, BIA, LS. McKenney to Duval, April 23, 1825, BIA, LS.
11. McKenney to Clark, Nov. 29, 1825, BIA, LS.
12. McKenney to Barbour, April 21, 1826, BIA, LS.
13. McKenney to Cass, April 9, 1825, BIA, LS.
14. McKenney to Superintendent of Indian Schools, Aug. 9, 1824, BIA, LS; "Washington's First Museum; The Indian Office Collection of Thomas L. McKenney," by Herman J. Viola, *Smithsonian Journal of History*, Feb. 1968, p. 7; McKenney to Albert Gallatin, July 31, 1828, BIA, LS; see Gallatin's *Synopsis of the Indian Tribes Within the United States East of the Rocky Mountains and the British and Russian Possessions in North America*, 1836.
15. C. Van Derventer, Dept. of War, to McKenney, Dec. 2, 1824, BIA, LR; William C. Chamberlain to McKenney, June 10, 1825, BIA, LR; David Arnil, Tuscarora Village; Lewiston, N.Y., to McKenney, Sept. 27, 1824, BIA, LR; McKenney to Arnil, Sept. 28, BIA, LS; *Historical Sketches of the Ten Mile Square Forming the District of Columbia with A Picture of Washington Describing the Objects of Natural Interest or Curiosity at the Metro of the Union by Jonathan Elliott*, Wash. 1830, p. 165.

CHAPTER IX: THE AUGUSTIC TREATIES

1. *Indians and Pioneers*, by Grant Foreman, Norman, Okla., 1930, p. 251.
2. *The Aboriginal Races of North America*, by Samuel Drake, N.Y., 1880, p. 392.
3. Hodge, Vol. 1, p. 782; *American State Papers: Indian Affairs*, 11, pp. 563, 768; *Louisville Public Advertiser*, June 11, 1825.
4. *Indian Removal* by Grant Foreman, Norman, Okla., 1933, p. 51.
5. George B. Catlin's notes on James Otto Lewis, Burton Collection, Detroit Public Library.
6. Cass to Calhoun, Dec. 15, 1824, BIA, LR; McKenney to Cass, Jan. 14, 1825, BIA, LS; McKenney to Duval, Feb. 21, 1825, BIA, LS.
7. *Personal Memoirs*, by Henry Rowe Schoolcraft, Phila., pp. 198–200. Hereafter cited as Schoolcraft.
8. *Lewis Cass: Indian Superintendent of the Michigan Territory, 1813–1831* (dissertation), by R.W. Unger. Hereafter cited as Unger.
9. *The Literary Voyager*, (ed.) Phillip Lesson, East Lansing, 1962, p. 15; Schoolcraft, p. 217.
10. Carter, Clarence (ed.), *The Territorial Papers of the United States* (26 vols.). Washington, 1934—, XI, p. 298. Hereafter cited as Carter.
11. *Detroit Gazette*, Dec. 20, 1825.
12. Carter, p. 298.
13. Unger, p. 133.
14. McKenney's *Sketches of a Tour to the Lakes, of the Character and Customs of the Chippeway Indians, And of Incidents connected with the Treaty of Fond du Lac*, Baltimore, 1827, consists of daily letters and reports he wrote to Secretary of War Barbour. See also Unger, pp. 127–50; *Documents Relating to the Negotiation of Ratified and Unratified Indian Treaties, 1813–30*, Record Group 75, Records of the Bureau of Indian Affairs, National Archives; "The Winnebago War," by Thomas L. McKenney, Wisconsin Historical Collections (ed. by Lyman Draper, Madison, Wisconsin, 1866).
15. *Detroit Gazette*, Sept. 12, 1826.
16. *Indiana Journal*, Nov. 1826, reprinted the *National Journal's* article on McKenney's arrival in Washington.
17. McKenney to Madison, March 20, 1824, Madison Papers, Library of Congress.
18. *Memoirs*, pp. 59–61.
19. *Wau-bun, The Early Days in the Northwest*, by Juliette Kinzie, Phila., 1873. Hereafter cited as Kinzie.
20. ibid.
21. Schoolcraft p. 266; Carter, XI; *National Intelligencer*, reprinted in the *Vincennes Western Sun and General Advertiser*, June 16, 1827; *Detroit Gazette*, Aug. 28, 1827; *Columbus Ohio State Journal*, Oct. 4, 1827; *Outlines of the Life and Character of Lewis Cass*, Albany, 1848, by Henry Rowe Schoolcraft, p. 18.
22. *Detroit Gazette*, Aug. 28, 1827; *Ohio State Journal*, Oct. 4, 1827.
23. Hamilton left West Point to join the staff of Colonel William Rector, surveyor-general of Illinois, Missouri, and Arkansas in 1821. He resigned and settled in Wisconsin, where he made what could be one of the first cattle drives in the Northwest. In 1825 he bought a herd and with the aid of some early cowhands he drove it to Green Bay by way of Chicago where he sold the beef on the hoof to army garrisons. He founded Wiota in Lafayette County and commanded the Rangers in the Black Hawk War. Gold fever gripped him and he joined the '49 rush to the diggings. He may have made a strike because he settled on a large ranch in Red Bluff, Tehama County, California. He died in 1865. Wisconsin settlers recalled him as a "profound thinker," a cold, aloof man who was too much of an aristocrat to be a frontier lawmaker.
24. It is surprising to discover how extensively the council was covered in the frontier newspapers. The *Detroit Gazette* either interviewed McKenney on his return from the Indian country or had letters sent to its editor by Schoolcraft from the wilderness. Smaller publications used the age-old city room method of "exchange," merely reprinting news of the council which had appeared in the big city press. Some selected newspapers were: *The St. Louis Advertiser*, July 11, 1827; *Indianapolis Gazette*, July 31, 1827; *Niles National Register*, July 4, 1827. See also Schoolcraft and Carter and *Memoirs*, p. 93.
25. *Memoirs*, Schoolcraft, Carter, XI; *Vincennes Western Sun and General Advertiser*, Sept. 15 and 22, 1827; *Ohio State Journal*, Sept. 27, 1827.

CHAPTER X: JOURNEY AMONG THE SOUTHERN TRIBES

1. *Memoirs*, pp. 120–22.
2. ibid., pp. 132–33.
3. McKenney to Barbour, Chickasaw, Oct. 10, 1827, BIA, LR.
4. McKenney to Barbour, Mayhew Mission, Choctaw Country, Oct. 10, 1827, BIA, LR; *Memoirs* Appendix E, pp. 318–24; Levi Colbert, Tishomingo and others to McKenney, Oct. 23, 1828, BIA, LR; *Memoirs* p. 187; McKenney to Barbour, Milledgeville, Georgia, Nov. 17, 1827; BIA, LR; *Memoirs*, Appendix H, p. 339–40.
5. *Memoirs*, pp. 188–90; McKenney to Barbour, Oct. 28, 1827, Nov. 2, 1827, March 24, 1828, BIA, LS. For Ridge's comments see *Cherokee Phoenix*, June 25, 1828.
6. *Memoirs*, pp. 191–92. A complete record of McKenney's councils and treaties with the Chickasaw, Choctaw, and Creek can be found in: *Reports and Proceedings of Colonel Thomas L. McKenney on the Subject of his Recent Tour Among the Southern Tribes as Submitted to Congress With the Message of the President*, U.S.A., Washington, 1828. For McKenney's defense against the charges of the federal auditor over his travel expenses, see *To The Public*, a sixteen-page pamphlet published by McKenney in July 1828, in which he outlines his explanation. Included is the congressional Minority Report, a letter from Governor Cass, etc. Also McKenney to Richard Smith Coxe, July 1828, Huntington.

During his government career, Colonel McKenney brought four Indian boys to Washington to be educated: James McDonald a half-breed Choctaw, Dougherty Colbert, a Chickasaw, and the two Creek boys. All were raised at Weston with "humanity." McDonald became an attorney, studying under Judge John McLean, later a Supreme Court Justice. But he committed suicide after a white woman rejected his proposal of marriage. After he had removed McKenney from office in 1830, President Jackson ordered the two Creek boys returned to their people, despite bitter protests of McKenney and the chiefs.
7. McKenney to Barbour, Nov. 29, 1827, BIA, LS.
8. *House Journal*, Dec. 11, 1827, 20 Cong.,1, Sess. (Serial 168), p. 34; *House Journal*, March 26, 1828, 20 Cong., 1 Sess. (Serial 168), p. 318.
9. McKenney to Clark, June 10, 1828, BIA, LS.
10. McKenney to Lewis Colbert, George Colbert, Tish-ho-mingo, and Others, Aug. 14, 1828, McKenney to John Bell, Aug. 14, 1828, BIA, LS.
11. *Cherokee Phoenix*, Aug. 27 and Oct. 15, 1828.
12. There were strict federal laws in McKenney's time forbidding the sale of whiskey to Indians. Congress put teeth in the 1802

statute by allowing government agents to search and seize whiskey discovered among a trader's supplies. McKenney was always sending letters to his agents ordering them to be vigilant and to help him end "this destructive commerce." McKenney to Crowell, April 7, 1824; McKenney to Ward, Nov. 3, 1825, both BIA, LS.

13. *Cherokee Phoenix*, May 21, 1828, Sept. 23, 1829.

CHAPTER XI: THE GREAT FATHER'S RED CHILDREN COME CALLING

1. *The First Forty Years of Washington Society*, (ed.) Gaillard Hunt, N.Y., 1906 (Margaret Bayard Smith to J. Bayard Smith, Nov. 30, 1828), p. 245; House Doc., 20 Cong., 2 Sess., No. 129 (Serial 186), p. 4–5.
2. McKenney to Barbour, Jan. 24, 1828, BIA, LR; McKenney to Porter, Doctor Brereton and Major Robert A. Forsyth, all same date, Nov. 1, 1828, BIA, LS.
3. N.Y. American, Oct. 31, 1828; Niles Register, Vol. XXX, V, Nov. 8, 1828; *Daily National Intelligencer*, Nov. 3, Dec. 3, 6, 11, 1828; McKenney and Hall, *The Indian Tribes of North America*, vol. 1, p. 144.
4. McKenney to John Litz, Georgetown, July 24, 1824, BIA, LS; McKenney to Captain Noyes, Georgetown, BIA, LS.
5. *Wau-bun, The Early Days in the Northwest*, by Juliette Kinzie, pp. 74–75, 85–87.
6. McKenney to Burgess, Aug. 4, 1824, BIA, LS.
7. McKenney to Deringer, July 29, 1824, BIA, LS.
8. McKenney to Surgeon General Lovell, Dec. 1, 1824, BIA, LS; McKenney to Dr. Nathan P. Cousin, June 21, 1825 ("For Treating Cole"), BIA, LS.
9. "Expenses Choctaw Delegation While in Washington," BIA, LR, Choctaw Agency, 1825.
10. ibid. ("Death of a chief in the company of Colonel Folsom").
11. Calhoun to Ross, May 1824, BIA, LS.
12. McKenney to General Jesup, Jan. 26, Feb. 9, April 16, 1830; McKenney to Clark, Jan. 26, 1830, all BIA, LS.
13. *N.Y. American*, June 11, 1833.
14. *I Am A Man—The Indian Black Hawk*, by Cole Cyrenus, Iowa City, 1938, p. 250; *Autobiography of Ma-Ka-Tai-Me-She-Kia-Kiah or Black Hawk*, (ed.) J. B. Patterson, Oquawka, Ill., 1882; *Red Men Calling On The Great White Father*, by Katherine C. Turner, Norman, Okla., 1951, pp. 88–101.
15. *Daily National Intelligencer*, Sept. 18, 1837.
16. McKenney excused the use of whiskey at the Fond du Lac and Buttes des Morts councils, 1826–1827, with the explanation that he and Cass only distributed "an Occasional drink, out of a wine glass and that we would dilute." *Memoirs*, p. 300. McKenney may have had in mind the 116 barrels of whiskey Cass ordered for the 1827 council; Cass to McKenney, Dec. 15, 1826, BIA, LR.
17. "Rifles for Indian Trade," Deringer to McKenney, July 10, 1826, BIA, LR; Deringer to McKenney, Jan. 15, 1829, BIA, LR.
18. *Handbook of American Indians*, (ed.) Frederick Webb Hodge, vol. 1, p. 831.
19. McKenney to Calhoun, May 1825, BIA, LS.
20. Furst to McKenney, June 25, 1825, BIA, LR.
21. *National Intelligencer*, May 21, 1828.

CHAPTER XII: THE PRETTY CHIPPEWA WHO STOLE WASHINGTON

1. The details of how Tshusick appeared at the tinsmith's shop, her activities in Washington, and how McKenney tried to find her are in McKenney's three-column letter to the *National Intelligencer*, May 21, 1828, hereafter cited as *Intelligencer*. He added some details in his *Indian Tribes of North America*, Vol. 1, hereafter cited as McKenney and his Memoirs. See also *Red Men Calling on The Great White Father*, by Katherine C. Turner, Norman, Okla., 1951, pp. 67–72.
2. *Mr. and Mrs. John Quincy Adams*, by Dorothie Bobbé, N.Y., 1930, p. 211.
3. See King's portrait of Tshusick in her costume, *The Indian Tribes of North America*, Vol. 1, p. 355.
4. *Memoirs*, p. 355.
5. ibid., pp. 355–56.
6. McKenney, Vol. 1., p. 360, *Intelligencer*.

7. *Intelligencer*.
8. *Intelligencer*; McKenney, Vol. 1, pp. 362–63.
9. ibid., p. 363.
10. *Intelligencer*.
11. "Address of Thomas T. Moore to his Constituents" of June 27, 1828. The *Louisville Advertiser*, July 29, 1828; also *Portraits, Presents, and Peace Medals, The American Scene*, 1970; "Washington's First Museum: The Indian Collection of Thomas L. McKenney," by Herman J. Viola, *Smithsonian Institution Journal of History*, Fall, 1968, pp. 11–18; "Charles Bird King, Painter of Indian Visitors to the Nation's Capital," by John C. Ewers, *Smithsonian Institution Annual Report*, 1953, Wash. 1954, pp. 463–73.
12. Report to the Committee of Retrenchment, May 15, 1828, House Rep., 20 Cong. 1 Sess. No. 259 (Serial 179).
13. *National Intelligencer*, May 31, 1828; *Alexandria Gazette*, May 22, 1828.
14. Report, Minority Committee on Retrenchment.
15. McKenney to Charles Bird King, April 3, 1830, Miscellaneous Manuscripts, New-York Historical Society.

CHAPTER XIII: McKENNEY AND JACKSON

1. McKenney to Milledoler, Dec. 12, 1821, New-York Historical Society.
2. *Reminiscences*, by Ben Perley Poore, Vol. 1, pp. 45–46, 123–24.
3. *Peggy Eaton: Democracy's Mistress* by Queena Pollack, p. 77; *The First Forty Years of Washington Society*, by Margaret Bayard Smith, p. 234.
4. *John C. Calhoun: American Portrait*, by Margaret L. Coit, Boston, 1950, p. 194.
5. *Memoirs*, Vol. 1, pp. 55–56.
6. ibid. Vol. 1, pp. 204–6.
7. Correspondence between Colonel McKenney and Rev. Philip Milledoler, in the 1820s, Milledoler Papers, New-York Historical Society.
8. McKenney to Baldwin, May 11, 1829, BIA, LS.
9. McKenney to Baldwin, June 27, 1829, BIA, LS.
10. McKenney to John H. Eaton, Secretary of War, July 21, 1829, BIA, LR.
11. McKenney to Eaton, July 22, 1829, BIA, LR.
12. *Documents and Proceedings Relating to the Formation and Progress of a Board In The City of New York, For the Emigration, Preservation, and Improvement of the Aboriginals of America*.
13. "Removal of the Indians" by Lewis Cass, *North American Review*, (Boston), XXX, Jan. 1830, pp. 62–121; *N.Y. Post*, Oct. 25, 1829, Jan. 7, 9, 1830.
14. Baldwin to McKenney, Oct. 19, 1829; BIA, LR; McKenney to Baldwin, Oct. 23, 1829, BIA, LS; Baldwin to McKenney, Oct. 22, 1829, BIA, LR.
15. *Memoirs*, pp. 252–55.

CHAPTER XIV: THE EAGLE AND THE RAVEN

1. Houston to Arbuckle, July 8, 1829, BIA, LR; for John Ridge's account of the raid, (ed.) Carolyn Thomas Foreman, see *Chronicles of Oklahoma*, Vol. IX, p. 233.
2. *Sam Houston*, by Marquis James, N.Y., 1929, pp. 128–29, hereafter cited as *Houston*.
3. *Houston*, p. 33.
4. Details of the so-called "Ration Scandal" can be found in the Congressional Select Committee hearings, in May and July, 1832, Rep. No. 502, House of Representatives, 22 Cong., 1 Sess., pp. 1–75. Hereafter cited as Committee. Colonel McKenney was one of the chief witnesses. His estimate of the cost of the removal of 80,000 Indians in the East to the West can be found in his letter to Secretary of War John Eaton, April 6, 1830, introduced into the hearings. The chapter on the scandal is discussed in his *Memoirs*, pp. 191–223.
5. Committee, p. 8.
6. ibid., p. 9.
7. ibid., p. 12.
8. ibid., p. 24; Houston, p. 133.
9. Committee, p. 25.

10. ibid., p. 47.
11. ibid., p. 7.
12. ibid., p. 36.
13. ibid., p. 38.
14. ibid., p. 12.
15. ibid., p. 44.
16. *Memoirs*, p. 223.
17. ibid., p. 262.

CHAPTER XV: THE LAST ACT: THE GREAT PORTFOLIO

1. *Memoirs*, p. 261–62; McKenney to Sparks, April 20, 1833, The Jared Sparks Papers, The Houghton Library, Harvard University. Hereafter cited as Houghton; John Johnson to McKenney, Nov. 3, 1829, BIA, LR.
2. McKenney to Louis Clephane and John Gardiner, April 26, 1830, BIA, LS; "Washington's First Museum: The Indian Collection of Thomas L. McKenney" by Herman J. Viola, *Smithsonian Journal of History*, Fall, 1968, p. 14.
3. Schoolcraft, *Memoirs*, p. 343.
4. McKenney to Milledoler, Aug. 22, 1831, Milledoler Papers, New-York Historical Society.
5. McKenney to Sparks, Jan. 8, 1831, Houghton.
6. McKenney to Sparks, Jan. 18, 1831, Houghton.
7. House of Rep. Doc., No. 502, 22 Cong., 1 Sess., July 5, 1832.
8. ibid., p. 2–3.
9. McKenney to Sparks, April (?) 1833, Houghton.
10. McKenney to Sparks, April 11, 1833, Houghton.
11. McKenney to Sparks, May 7, 1833, Houghton.
12. Hall to Sparks, Nov. 12, 1835, Houghton.
13. Hall biographical notes.
14. *Aboriginal Port-Folio*, by James Otto Lewis, first and second editions, Library of Congress; biographical notes on Lewis, Burton Historical Collections, Detroit Public Library.
15. Hall to Catlin, Introduction by Frederick Webb Hodge. *Indian Tribes of North America* by Thomas L. McKenney and James Hall, Edinburgh, 1933. For Catlin's rebuff of Hall's offer, see his letter to the editor of the American Turf Register, Spring, 1836.
16. McKenney to Sparks, Nov. 24, 1836.
17. McKenney to Sparks, May 11, 1838.
18. McKenney to William Lewis, June 11, 13, 20, 1839; Oct. 27, 1840; Aug. 28, 1841; Nov. 16, Dec. 13, 1843; all Huntington.
19. The various editions of the McKenney-Hall portfolio can be found in the Library of Congress; Rare Book Room, N.Y. Public Library; and the New-York Historical Society.
20. McKenney to Sparks, May 20, 1843, Houghton.
21. McKenney to Sparks, Oct. 15, 1843, Houghton.
22. McKenney to Sparks, Nov. 16, 1843, Houghton.
23. McKenney to Sparks, Sept. 30, 1844, Houghton.
24. McKenney to Sparks, July 13, 1846, Houghton.
25. See citations in chapter three for pamphlets issued by McKenney and Armstrong's son.
26. McKenney to Sparks, March 9, 1847, Houghton.
27. *N.Y. Times*, Feb. 21, 1859; McKenney's death certificate, Municipal Archives, City of New York, Park Row, N.Y.C.

Bibliography

NATIONAL ARCHIVES AND RECORDS SERVICE

The bulk of the voluminous correspondence of Thomas Loraine McKenney, which I consulted for this book, can be found in the Records of the Bureau of Indian Affairs in the National Archives. The main source is his letters, sent and received, as Superintendent of Indian Trade (1816–1822) and as head of the Bureau of Indian Affairs (1824–1830). There are no overall indexes to this series of records. For the most part letters sent by McKenney as Superintendent of Indian Trade are arranged in chronological order. There are no registers or indexes for the letters received but the letters sent are arranged by addressee.

The letters received are under many jurisdictional and subject headings. To locate individual letters it is necessary to consult registers for the bureau's incoming correspondence.

The collection was in the Library of Congress from 1910 to 1956 when it was placed in the custody of the Archives as "Record Group 75: Records of the Office of Indian Affairs," with subsection, "Records of the Office of Indian Trade, 1795–1822."

Physically, the enormous collection consists of several hundred letters, journals, accounts, transcripts of journals of McKenney's factors stationed at Indian factories at Prairie du Chien, Fort Edwards, St. Louis, Chicago, the Choctaw Trading Post, Arkansas Territory, etc.

There are also extensive microfilms of the records. (See *Records of the Bureau of Indian Affairs*, by Edward E. Hill, Washington, 1965.)

In addition to these records I have consulted other McKenney letters in many historical institutions around the country.

The Ayer Collection, Newberry Library, Chicago: A valuable group of McKenney letters, books, and pamphlets.

The George Boyd Letters, State Historical Society of Wisconsin: Correspondence between Indian Agent George Boyd stationed at Mackinac and McKenney, 1818–1830. Boyd was married to Harriet, sister of Louisa Adams, wife of President John Quincy Adams. The Green Bay and Prairie du Chien Papers also contain a few items from McKenney, Cass, and Boyd.

The Burton Historical Collection, Detroit Public Library: Miscellaneous notes on the life of James Otto Lewis, the frontier artist who painted many of the original portraits, later copied by Charles Bird King for McKenney's Indian Gallery.

William L. Clements Library, The University of Michigan, Ann Arbor: There are 21 McKenney letters, 1818–1824, his correspondence with his Chicago factor, Jacob Varnum, and a fine letter from Cherokee chief David Folsom.

Simon Grantz Collection, Historical Society of Pennsylvania: some excellent McKenney letters. One to the Hon. Walter Forward, Nov. 3, 1841, which describes his family, youth in Maryland, business in Washington, career in the Indian Bureau and his political feuds, is invaluable as a rare autobiographical source.

Huntington Library and Art Gallery, San Marino, California: Some excellent McKenney letters.

John McLean Papers, Manuscript Division, Library of Congress: A few McKenney items. One is a twelve-page letter from McKenney to McLean, Jan. 29, 1831.

New York Public Library Manuscript Division: McKenney's original, handwritten subscription list for his portfolio.

Andrew Jackson Papers, Manuscript Division, Library of Congress: Some interesting letters on Jackson's connection with early Indian affairs. Nothing on McKenney.

Jefferson Papers, Manuscript Division, Library of Congress: Jefferson's wry, delightful letter to McKenney.

Milledoler Papers, New-York Historical Society: Letters from McKenney to the nineteenth-century clergyman written during the period when McKenney was in Washington and Philadelphia. The Miscellaneous Manuscripts also contains a few McKenney letters.

Monroe Papers, Manuscript Division, New York Public Library: John Jacob Astor's letters to Monroe.

Jared Sparks Papers, Houghton Library, Harvard University, Cambridge, Mass.: A superb, revealing collection of letters from McKenney to the eminent historian and written during his tragic, last years. The collection also includes two letters from James Hall and one from Charles Bird King.

MUNICIPAL ARCHIVES

Municipal Archives and Records Center, Park Row, New York City: Death certificate of Thomas L. McKenney.

BOOKS

American Folklore Reader, by John Flynn and Arthur Palmer. Hudson, New York, 1958.

American State Papers, Indian Affairs (2 Vols.), Washington, 1832–1834.

Anderson Auction Company of New York, Records of "Mainly the Collection of Miss Nellie Malcolm, London, England, 1902." New-York Historical Society [McKenney's penciled comments on James Otto Lewis's Aboriginal Port-Folio.]

Annals of Iowa, 3rd Series, Vol. 1, Des Moines, 1895.

Armstrong, Kosciusko. An examination of McKenney's Reply to the Review, etc., New York, 1847.

———. Review of McKenney's Narrative of the Causes which in 1814 led to General Armstrong's Resignation of the War Office, New York, 1846.

Atwater, ??. Tour to Prairie du Chien, History of Ohio, 2nd ed., 1838.

Bancroft, H. J. History of Oregon (2 Vols.). 1886.

Beckwith, Hiram. The Illinois and Indiana Indians. Chicago: Fergus Historical Series, No. 27, 1884.

Benton, Thomas Hart. Thirty Years' View (2 Vols.), New York, 1854.

Bibliography of American Literature, Vol. 3, by Jacob Blanck, New Haven, 1959.

Brant, Joseph. The Gospel According to St. Mark, Translated into the Mohawk Tongue by Capt. Joseph Brant, and Book of Common Prayer. London, 1787.

Buley, R. Carlyle. The Old Northwest (2 Vols.). Bloomington, 1950.

Burton, C. M. City of Detroit, Michigan, Vol. 2, 1880.

Butler, Mann. An Appeal from the Misrepresentation of James Hall, Respecting the History of Kentucky. Frankfort, 1837.

Butterfield, Consul Willshire. History of the Girtys. Cincinnati, 1890.

Campbell, W. W. Annals of Tryon County, N.Y., 1831.

Carter, Clarence E. (ed.). The Territorial Papers of the United States (26 Vols.). Washington, 1934–

Cass, Lewis. Inquiries, Respecting the History, Traditions, Languages, Manners, Customs, Religion, etc., of the Indians Living Within the United States. Detroit, 1823.

Catalogue of the Museum and Gallery of Art of the New-York Historical Society, 1903 (Second Part).

Catalogue of Works by The Late Henry Inman, With a Biographical Sketch: Exhibition for the Benefit of His Widow and Family, at the Art Union Rooms, No. 322 Broadway, New York. 1846. (Library of the Boston Athenaeum)

Catlin, George. *Letters and Notes*. London, 1884.

Catlin, George B., *The Story of Detroit*. Detroit, 1923.

Chittenden, Hiram Martin. *History of the American Fur Trade in the Far West* (2 Vols.). New York, 1902.

Cohen, M. M. *Notices of Florida and the Campaigns*. Charleston, 1836.

Coit, Margaret L. *John C. Calhoun: American Portrait*. Boston, 1950.

——. *Andrew Jackson*, Boston, 1965.

Colden, Cadwalader. *History of the Five Nations* (8 Vols.). New York, 1727.

Comfort, Benjamin. *Lewis Cass and the Indian Treaties*. Detroit, 1923.

Cotterill, R. S. *The Southern Indians*. Oklahoma City, 1949.

Couses, Elliott (ed.). *History of the Expedition Under the Command of Lewis & Clark*, New York, 1893.

——. *The Journal of Alexander Henry Thompson, 1799–1814*. New York, 1891.

Documents and Proceedings Relating to the Formation and Progress of a Board in New York City for the Emigration, Preservation and Improvement of the Aboriginals of North America, New York, 1829.

Donaldson, Thomas. *Report of the National Museum of 1885*. Washington, 1886.

Drake, Benjamin. *Life of Tecumseh and His Brother, The Prophet*. Cincinnati, 1852.

Drake, Samuel. *The Aboriginal Race of North America*. New York, 1880.

Edwin, James. *An Account of an Expedition from Pittsburgh to the Rocky Mountains in the Year 1819 and '20 . . . under the Command of Major Stephen H. Long*. Philadelphia, 1824.

Eggleston, Edward, and Seelye, Lillie E. *Tecumseh and the Shawnee Prophet*. New York, 1878.

Elwood, Mary Cheney. *An Episode of the Sullivan Campaign and Its Sequel*. New York, 1904.

Farmer, Silas. *The History of Detroit and Michigan* (2 Vols.). Detroit, 1884.

Faux, W. *Memorable Days in America*. London, 1823.

Fergus Historical Series, Nos. 22–27, Vol. 3.

Foreman, Grant. *Indian Removal*. Norman, Okla., 1932.

——. *The Last Trek of the Indians*. Chicago, 1946.

The Four Kings from Canada Being a Succinct Account of the Four Indian Princes Lately Arrived from North America. London, 1710.

Gatschet, E. *Migration Legends of the Creek Indians* (2 Vols.). Philadelphia, 1884.

Greve, Charles T. *Centennial History of Cincinnati*. 1904.

Groce, George C., and Wallace, David H. *The New-York Historical Society's Dictionary of Artists in America, 1564–1860*. New Haven, 1957.

Hall, Basil. *Travels in North America in the Years 1827–1828*. Edinburgh, 1829.

Hale, Horatio. *The Iroquois Book of Rites*. Philadelphia, 1883.

Hall, James. *Trial and Defence of First Lieutenant James Hall of the Ordnance Department, United States Army*. Published by himself, Pittsburgh, 1820.

——. *The Western Souvenir, A Christmas and New Year's Gift, for 1829*.

——. *Legends of the West*. Philadelphia, 1832.

——. *The Soldier's Bride; and Other Tales*. Philadelphia, 1833.

——. *The Harpe's Head; A Legend of Kentucky*. Philadelphia, 1833.

——. *Sketches of History, Life and Manners in the West; Containing . . . Descriptions of the Country and Modes of Life in the Western States and Territories of North America*. Cincinnati, 1834.

——. *Tales of the Border*. Philadelphia, 1835.

——. *Memoirs of the Public Services of William Henry Harrison of Ohio*. Philadelphia, 1836.

——. *Notes on the Western States: Containing Descriptive Sketches of their Soil, Climate, Resources and Scenery*. Philadelphia, 1838.

——. *Memoirs of Thomas Posey, Major-General and Governor of Indiana*. (In the *Library of American Biography*, conducted by Jared Sparks, Vol. XIX, Boston, 1846.)

——. *The West: Its Commerce and Navigation*. Cincinnati, 1848.

——. *The West: Its Soil, Surface and Productions*. Cincinnati, 1848.

——. *The Wilderness and the War Path*. New York, 1849.

——. *The Romance of Western History: Or Sketches of History, Its Manners and Life in the West*. Cincinnati, 1857.

——. *Legends of the West: Sketches, Illustrative of the Habits, Occupations, Privations, Adventures and Sports of the Pioneers of the West*. Cincinnati, 1874.

Hodge, Frederick Webb. Introduction, *The Indian Tribes of North America*, by Thomas L. McKenney and James Hall, Edinburgh, 1933.

Irving, J. T. *Indian Sketches*. Philadelphia, 1837.

Isham, Samuel. *History of American Painting*. New York, 1905.

McCarthy, Dwight G. *Territorial Governors of the Old Northwest. Iowa Historical Society*, 1910.

McKenney, Thomas Loraine. *Sketches of a Tour to the Lakes*. Baltimore, 1827.

——. *To the Public*. Washington, 1828.

——. *Reports and Proceedings of Colonel McKenney on the Subject of his Recent Tour Among the Southern Indians as Submitted to Congress with a Message to the President of the U.S.A.* Washington, 1828.

——. *Extract of a Letter to Dr. Samuel Worcester of the American Board of Commissioners for Foreign Missionaries*. Baltimore, n.d.

——. (Aristides, pseudonym). *Essays on the Spirits of Jacksonism, as exemplified in its Deadly Hostility to the Bank of The United States and in its Odious Calumnies employed for its Destruction*. Philadelphia, 1835.

—— and Hall, James. *The Indian Tribes of North America with Biographical Sketches and Anecdotes of the Principal Chiefs*. Folio ed., 2 vols. Philadelphia.

——. *Memoirs, Official and Personal; with Sketches of Travels among the Northern and Southern Indians*. 2 vols. in 1. New York, 1846.

——. *A Narrative of the Battle of Bladensburg in a Letter to Henry Banning, Esq. By an Officer of Gen. Smith's Staff*. n.p., 1814.

——. *An Opening Reply to Kosciusko Armstrong*. Brooklyn, 1846.

——. *A Reply to Kosciusko Armstrong's Assault on Colonel McKenney's Narrative*. New York, 1847.

McLaughlin, Andrew C. *Lewis Cass*. Boston, 1892.

Monroe, James. *Autobiography*. New York, 1859.

Morse, Jedidiah. *Report to the Secretary of War*. Washington, 1822.

James, Marquis. *Sam Houston*. New York, 1929.

Josephy, Alvin M., Jr. *The Patriot Chiefs*. New York, 1961.

——. *The Artist Was a Young Man: The Life of Peter Rindisbacher*. Fort Worth, Texas.

Journals of Alexander Henry and David Thompson, 1799–1814. (ed.) Elliott Coues. New York, 1897.

Journals of the Military Expeditions of Gen. John Sullivan Against The Six Nations of New York in 1779. (ed.) Frederick Cook. Auburn, N.Y., 1887.

Kappler, Charles J. (ed.). *Indian Affairs; Laws and Treaties*, (Vol. III). Washington, 1903.

Keating, William H. *Narrative of an Expedition to the Sources of St. Peter's River . . . In the Year 1823 . . . Under the Command of Stephen H. Long, Major*. Philadelphia, 1824.

Kinzie, Juliette. *Wau-bun, The Early Days in the Northwest*. Philadelphia, 1873.

Lanman, Charles. *Recollections of Curious Characters and Pleasant Places*. Edinburgh, 1881.

Lewis, James Otto. *Aboriginal Port-Folio*. Philadelphia, 1835.

——. *Catalogue of the Indian Gallery*, Painted By J. O. Lewis. New York, 1850.

Linton, Ralph. *The Sacrifice to the Morning Star by the Skidi Pawnee*, Chicago, 1922.

Long, S. H. *An Account of an Expedition from Detroit to the Rocky Mountains*. Philadelphia, 1823.

——. *An Account of an Expedition from Pittsburgh to the Rocky Mountains*. Compiled by Edwin James. Philadelphia, 1823, 2 Vols.

——. *Narrative of a Second Expedition to the Source of St. Peter's River*, (ed.) William Keating. New York, 1824.

Lossing, Benjamin. *The American Revolution*. New York, 1875.

Palmer, Friend. *Early Days in Detroit*. n.d.

Peake, Ora. *A History of the United States Indian Factory System, 1795–1822*. Denver, 1954.

Porter, Kenneth W. *John Jacob Astor: Business Man* (2 Vols.). Cambridge, 1951.

Potter, Woodburn. *The War in Florida*. Baltimore, 1836.
Prucha, Francis P. *American Indian Policy in the Formative Years*. Cambridge, 1962.
———. *Broadax and Bayonet: The Role of the United States Army in the Development of the Northwest*. Madison, 1953.
Quaife, Milo. *Chicago and the Old Northwest*. Chicago: University of Chicago Press, 1913.
Schoolcraft, Henry Rowe. *A Narrative of Travels from Detroit, Northwest through the Great Chain of American Lakes, to its Sources of the Mississippi River in the Year 1820*. Albany, 1821.
———. *Personal Memoirs*. Philadelphia, 1851.
Reid, W. Max. *The Mohawk Valley, Its Leaders and Its History*. New York, 1901.
Rhees, William. *An Account of the Smithsonian Institution, Its Founder, Building, Operation, etc.* Prepared by Prof. Henry for the Regents, and Other Authentic Sources. Washington, 1859.
Simms, J. R. *The Frontiersman* (2 Vols.). New York, 1872.
Six Indians rogues de la tribe des grande Osages, arrivés du Missouri au Havre le 27 Juillet, 1827, sur la navire Americaine, New England, cap. Hunt Troisième Edition (etc.,) Paris, 1827.
Smith, Margaret Bayer. *The First Forty Years of Washington Society, Portrayed by the Family Letters of Mrs. Samuel Harrison Smith from the Collection of her Grandson, J. Henley Smith. Gaillard Hunt* (ed). New York, 1906.
South Dakota Historical Collections (State Historical Society), *History of the Dakota or Sioux Indians*, by Doane Robinson (2 Vols.). South Dakota, 1904.
Stone, William L. *Life of Joseph Brant* (2 Vols.). New York, 1838.
———. *Life of William Johnson* (2 Vols.). New York, 1865.
———. *Red Jacket*. New York, 1866.
Swiggett, Howard. *War Out of Niagara; Walter Butler and the Tory Rangers*. New York, 1933.
Stevens, Frank. *The Black Hawk War*. Chicago, 1903.
Tanner, John. *Captivity of John Tanner*. New York, 1830.
Tipton, John. *The John Tipton Papers*, (ed.) Nellie O. Robertson and Dorothy Ricker (3 vols.). Indianapolis, 1942.
Terrell, John U. *Furs by Astor*. New York, 1943.
Travels In To The Interior of North America, by John Bradbury. Liverpool, 1817.
Treaties Between the United States and Several Indian Tribes, from 1778–1817. Washington, 1873.
Turner, Katherine C. *Red Men Calling on Their Great White Father*. Norman, Okla., 1951.
Wakefield, John Alden. *The Black Hawk War*. Chicago, 1903.
Weddell, Alexander Wilbourne (ed.). *Memorial Volume of Virginia Historical Portraiture, 1585–1830*. Richmond, 1930.
Wheelock, Rev. Eleazar. *Narrative of the Indian Charity School at Lebanon, Conn. 1762–1765*. Boston, n.d.
Williams, Amelia W., and Barker, Eugene C. (eds.). *The Writings of Sam Houston, 1813–1836* (8 vols.). Austin, 1938.
Woodford, Frank. *Lewis Cass: The Last Jeffersonian*. New Brunswick, 1950.

PERIODICALS, ARTICLES, PAMPHLETS, QUARTERLIES

Abel, Annie H. "History of Events Resulting in Indian Consolidation West of the Mississippi," *Annual Report of the American Historical Association for the Year 1906* (1908).
Bryant, W. C. "Joseph Brant." *American Historical Record*, July 1873.
Cass, Lewis. "The Winnebago Outbreak." *Wisconsin Historical Collections* V (1867–1869).
Collections, The American Antiquarian Society. "Synopsis of the Indian Tribes of North America" (Vol. 2). Worcester, Mass., 1836.
Donaldson, Thomas. "The George Catlin Indian Gallery." *Smithsonian Report, 1885* (1886).
Doty, James. "James Doty's Journal of a Trip with Lewis Cass in 1820." *Wisconsin Historical Collections* XLLL (1895).
Dunbar, John B. "The Pawnee Indians," *Magazine of American History*, Vol. IV, April, November, 1880; November, 1882.
Ewers, John C. "Charles Bird King: Painter of the Indian Visitors to the Nation's Capital." *Smithsonian Report*, 1953.
Grinnell, George Bird. "Tenure of Land Among Indians." *American Anthropologist* (1907).

Hale, Horatio. "Obsequies of Red Jacket, Buffalo, Oct. 9, 1884." *Transactions of the Buffalo Historical Society, Vol. III* (1885).
Historical Collections of Ohio (1896). "A Description of Read's Town."
Irwin, Mathew. "The Fur Trade and The Factory System at Green Bay, 1816–1821." *Wisconsin State Historical Society* (1876).
Lockwood, James H. "Early Times and Events in Wisconsin." *Collections of the State Historical Society of Wisconsin* (Vol. 2) (1856).
Magazine of Western History. "Crawford's Campaign" by Colonel W. Crawford, Ohio, 1885.
Mason, O. T. "Cradles of the North American Aborigines." *Report*, National Museum, Washington, 1887.
Midwest Folklore, Fall, 1955.
Minnesota Historical Society Collections, Vol. 1, "A Sketch of Joseph Renville."
Minnesota Historical Society Collections, Vol. 5, "History of the Ojibways" (1885).
Peabody Museum Reports, Vols. 3 and 17, The Henry Inman Collection.
Prucha, Francis Paul. "Early Peace Medals." *Wisconsin Magazine of History*, Dec. 1963.
———. "Indian Removal and the Great American Desert". *Indiana Magazine of History LIX*, Dec. 1963.
———. "Thomas L. McKenney and the New York Indian Board." *Mississippi Historical Review* XLVIII, March, 1962.
Royce, Charles (comp.). "Indian Land Cessions in the United States." *Eighteenth Report of the United States Bureau of Ethnology* (1889). 1899.
Snelling, Josiah L. "Early Days at Prairie du Chien." *Wisconsin Historical Collections* V (1867–1869).
Viola, Herman J. "Washington's First Museum: The Indian Office Collection of Thomas L. McKenney." *The Smithsonian Journal of History* (Fall 1968).
———. "Portraits, Presents and Peace Medals, Thomas L. McKenney and Indian Visitors to Washington." *American Scene* Vol. XI, No. 2 (1970).

GOVERNMENT PUBLICATIONS

Report of the Secretary of War of a System Providing for the Abolition of the Existing Indian Trade Establishments, Dec. 15, 1818, House Doc., 15 Cong., 2 Sess., No. 25 (Serial 17)

Report of the Committee on Indian Affairs, March 1, 1823, House Doc., 2 Sess., No. 104 (Serial 82)

Annual Report of the Bureau of Indian Affairs, Nov. 30, 1825, Senate Doc., 19 Cong., 1 Sess., No. 2 (Serial 125)

Documents submitted by the chairman of Indian Affairs accompanied by a Bill for the Establishment of a General Superintendent of Indian Affairs in the Department of War, March 31, 1826, House Doc., 19 Cong., 1 Sess., No. 146 (Serial 138)

Annual Reports of the Bureau of Indian Affairs; Nov. 1826, Senate Doc., 19 Cong., Sess. No. 1 (Serial 144); Senate Doc., 20 Cong., 1 Sess. No. 1 (Serial 163)

Report of the Committee on Retrenchment, House Report, 20 Cong., 1 Sess., No. 259, No. 103 (Serial 181)

Report of the Committee on the District of Columbia, Feb. 14, 1828, Sen. Doc., 20 Cong., 1 Sess., No. 103 (Serial 165)

Expenses of the Winnebago Deputation, Feb. 25, 1829, House Doc., 20 Cong., 1 Sess., No. 129 (Serial 186)

Columbian College, March 2, 1830, House Doc., 21 Cong., 1 Sess., No. 290 (Serial 200)

Report of the Select Committee of the House of Representatives, Including the Message of the President of the United States of the 5th and 8th of February and March 2, 1827, Washington, 1837. 19 Cong. (No. 98)

NEWSPAPERS (1808–1859)

Boston Evening Transcript
Cherokee Phoenix
Cincinnati Enquirer
Detroit Journal and Michigan Advertiser
Farmers & Mechanics Journal (Vincennes)
Gazette of the United States
Georgetown Columbian Gazette
Georgetown Metropolitan
Harrisburg (Pa.) Intelligencer
Illinois Intelligencer
Indiana Democrat
Indiana Journal
Indiana State Gazette
Louisville Public Advertiser

Michigan Herald
National Journal
New York American
New York Mirror
New York Times
Niles Register
Paulson's American Daily Advertiser
Pennsylvania Enquirer
The Tatler (London)
United States Telegraph
Washington Gazette
Washington Daily National Intelligencer
Washington Republican and Congressional Examiner
Vincennes Gazette
Western Register
Western Sun

Index

TO THE McKENNEY-HALL PORTRAIT GALLERY OF AMERICAN INDIANS